UNFOLDING REVELATION

THE NATURE OF
DOCTRINAL DEVELOPMENT

THEOLOGICAL RESOURCES is a series of books taking its impulse from the striking renewal of interest in theology to-day. That renewal is unique in theological history, because its impetus derives from all the churches and because evidence for it abounds in all countries. The contributors to the series have been chosen, therefore, for their suitability to particular subjects rather than for denominational uniformity. There are two General Editors, John P. Whalen, formerly acting head of the Catholic University of America, and Jaroslav Pelikan, a prominent Lutheran Pastor, at present the Titus Street Professor of Ecclesiastical History at Yale University.

In commenting on the current theological revival, the General Editors write—'this interest, vital though it is, stands in danger of being lost in superficiality and trivialized into a fad. The answer to this danger is greater depth. *THEOLOGICAL RESOURCES* is intended to supply that depth.'

JAN HENDRIK WALGRAVE

UNFOLDING REVELATION

THE NATURE OF
DOCTRINAL DEVELOPMENT

WESTMINSTER OF PHILADELPHIA

HUTCHINSON OF LONDON

THE WESTMINSTER PRESS
Witherspoon Building, Philadelphia, Pa. 19107

Copyright © 1972 Corpus Instrumentorum, Inc.

Library of Congress Catalog Card Number: 76–102204
First printing, 1972
MANUFACTURED IN GREAT BRITAIN

Contents

Part One

INTRODUCTION

v

Part Two

THE IDEA OF DEVELOPMENT IN PATRISTIC AND MEDIEVAL THOUGHT

Part Three

THEORIES OF DEVELOPMENT

Abbreviations

Apologia	J. H. Newman. *Apologia pro vita sua*. London, 1914.
Church Dogmatics	Karl Barth. *Church Dogmatics* 1/1, translated by G. Thomson. Edinburgh, 1936.
Denz	H. Denzinger. *Enchiridion symbolorum*, edited by A. Schonmetzer. 3d ed., Freiburg i. Br., 1963.
Development	J. H. Newman. *An Essay on the Development of Christian Doctrine*. London, 1914.
DTC	*Dictionnaire de théologie catholique*, 15 vols. Paris, 1903–56.
EncDictBibl	*Encyclopedic Dictionary of the Bible*, translated and adapted by L. Hartmann from A. Van den Born's *Bijbels Woordenbook*. New York, 1963.
Forcellini LTL	E. Forcellini. *Lexikon totius latinitatis*, 4 vols. Leipzig and London, 1839.
Grammar	J. H. Newman. *Grammar of Assent*. London, 1898.
Greg	*Gregorianum*. Rome, 1920–.
Harnack	A. von Harnack. *What is Christianity?* translated by T. B. Saunders. London, 1901.
History and Dogma	M. Blondel. *History and Dogma*, translated by A. Dru and I. Trethowan. London, 1964.
Kittel ThW	*Theological Dictionary of the New Testament*, edited by G. Kittel, translated by G. Bromiley. Grand Rapids, Mich., 1964–.

Life of von Hügel	F. von Hügel. 'Letter to A. Thorold,' in M. de la Bedoyère, *The Life of Baron von Hügel.* London, 1951.
Loisy	A. Loisy. *L'Evangile et l'Église.* 2d ed., Paris, 1903; English translation by C. Home, *The Gospel and the Church*, new ed., London, 1909.
RevScPhilTh	*Revue des sciences philosophiques et théologiques* Paris, 1907–.
RevThom	*Revue Thomiste.* Paris, 1893–.
RGG³	*Die Religion in Geschichte und Gegenwart,* 6 vols. 3d ed., Tübingen, 1957–63.
RHE	*Revue d'histoire ecclésiastique.* Louvain, 1900–.
Theokratie	V. Solov'ev. 'Geschichte und Zukunft der Theokratie,' *Werke*, vol. 2, Freiburg, 1957.
Tyrrell	G. Tyrrell. *Christianity at the Crossroads.* London, 1909.
van Buren	Paul van Buren. *The Secular Meaning of the Gospel.* 4th ed., New York and London, 1966.

General Editors' Foreword

If Christian theology is to be taken seriously as an enterprise of 'faith in search of understanding,' it must come to terms with the fact that its doctrines have developed in history. Although there had been intimations of this fact before, it may safely be said that the full scope of the issue did not become visible to theologians, whether Protestant or Roman Catholic, until the nineteenth century. It was above all John Henry Newman's *An Essay on the Development of Christian Doctrine*, first published in 1845, that thrust the development of doctrine into the centre of theological concern, where it still is. As the author of a book on *Newman the Theologian* (whose French title was *Newman, Le Développement du Dogme*), Father Walgrave has special qualifications to undertake this difficult assignment.

From his discussion it is obvious that neither Roman Catholicism nor Protestantism was prepared for the issue of development. Roman Catholics had asserted, in opposition to the theological 'innovations' of the Reformers, that Rome was *semper eadem* and that what Bossuet called 'the variations of Protestantism' were proof of its apostasy from the old ways of orthodox teaching. Protestants, on the other hand, defined *Sola Scriptura* in such a way that subsequent history could not expand nor even unfold what was already so clear and explicit in the Bible; therefore the true doctrine could not have developed, but had only been obscured by later theological change. It was partly as a result of the historical study of dogma and partly in anticipation of such study that the question of development was raised. The author summarizes the 'development of development' in the century and a quarter since Newman's *Essay*, and he outlines the chief options made available by that development.

Student of Newman though he is, Father Walgrave is not content to repristinate, or merely to refine, Newman's idea of development. Maurice Blondel's *History and Dogma* of 1904, long neglected, makes its contribution here to a further clarification of the problem. Other thinkers of the nineteenth and twentieth centuries, too, are exploited for their views. The author is especially sensitive to the positive implications of the idea of development for ecumenical theological thinking, and many readers, both Protestant and Roman Catholic, will find his *Auseinandersetzung* with Karl Barth particularly illuminating. John Courtney Murray declared a decade ago: 'That development has taken place in both communities cannot possibly be denied. The question is, what is legitimate development, what is organic growth in the understanding of the original deposit of faith, what is warranted extension of the primitive discipline of the Church, and what, on the other hand, is accretion, additive increment, adulteration of the deposit, distortion of true Christian discipline?' *Unfolding Revelation* does not answer these questions with any finality; the very notion of development would preclude this. But it does define the questions with precision, and it points to the theological resources available for an answer.

J.P.W.
J.P.

PART ONE

Introduction

CHAPTER ONE

The Problem

The idea of doctrinal development was present from the beginning in Christian self-understanding and was never entirely obscured in the course of its history. Only in recent times, however, has development as such become a puzzling problem and an object of concern and profound reflection. The aim of this study is not to give an account of the historical development itself.

HISTORY AND HISTORICITY

For reasons that will become clear in the course of our exposition, it is no longer possible to separate the historical from the systematic treatment of a theological problem. History is not an account of the vicissitudes that happened to beings who remained unaffected by them. In a very profound sense man is history. His being is historical. On a larger scale humanity, or the social reality of human existence, is historical. The history of mankind is the making of man. This holds true not only for human history as a whole but also for any function or aspect of human life. As thought may be said to be the expression of the self-understanding of man in his relation to the world and the whole of being, it follows that his insights, his beliefs and doctrines are no less historical than his nature. Human existence is a thinking existence. Man makes himself by thinking his life. The development of his personality is the development of his real convictions. The development of a culture is directed by the development of the first principles on which it is based.

These basic insights will be returned to later in this work. Suffice it now to say that a doctrine cannot truly be understood except in its historical as well as in its systematic context. What the doctrine of

3

Incarnation really means can only be grasped in its relational unity with the whole pattern of salvation-history. And in the same way contemporary understanding of the Christological dogma is the outcome of what past generations have thought about it, transmitting their doctrinal views in living continuity and with increasing clarity and penetration. The history of Christian doctrine is the pattern of its genesis and growth in the mind of the Church. One cannot thoroughly understand the present state and convictions of another if one is ignorant about the influences and circumstances of his individual history and the way he reacted to them. In the same way there is no serious chance that the present state of a doctrine shall be understood if one refuses to follow patiently the historical path that leads to it. Of course the aid of specialists is needed to dig up the building blocks of history, but their work would be meaningless without a synthetic view of the building-process that led to the present frame of the edifice. The history of dogma is not merely the object of an independent auxiliary science, useful perhaps for dogmatic theology as a quarry of possible arguments but not necessary to it. It is a living dimension of dogma itself in its present state and, if it is ignored, attempts at systematization will be like imaginary castles floating in the void.

The history of dogma, then, is an inherent part of the systematic treatment of dogma itself. It does not belong, however, to the field of the present inquiry, whose scope is a more limited one, dealing not with the history of dogma but with its historicity. This inquiry seeks answers to such questions as: Why does Christian doctrine have a history? What is its nature? Is it a story of variations or the growth of an idea? Is it characterized by continuity or discontinuity? Or is one to distinguish between an aspect of continuity and an aspect of discontinuity? May one say that it is subject to change, maintaining at the same time that it is *semper eadem*? How are the two aspects related to each other? How to reconcile them? How to account for the facts that history sets before us? In order to answer such questions a theory is needed: an insight into the nature of revelation and its relation to human history, to human thought and language; a coherent pattern of categories to explain satisfactorily the actual facts of the past and the possible evolutions of the future.

It follows, then, that this enterprise, though limited in its scope as a reflection on the historicity of dogma, is nevertheless closely connected with the actual history of doctrines. A theory of development provides a general model by which to explain and justify what the history of the several dogmas reveals. However, a satisfactory theory of development cannot be devised if there is no exact knowledge of the particular facts of dogmatic history. Therefore they cannot be omitted. Some of them will have to be drawn into the argument as typical examples and illustrations.

Since it is the thought of the Church, a human translation of the word of God, guided by the Holy Spirit, an expression of Christian experience and life, Christian doctrine moves as a whole through the stages of history. The development of any living unit, be it social or individual, is organic. All its parts grow together in continual differentiation and mutual adaptation under the guidance of a directive principle that determines its specific life. This study will try to show how in the development of doctrine the life of the whole is present in the process of differentiation and adaptation by which the parts become increasingly distinct and conspicuous.

DEVELOPMENT OF DOCTRINE: A THEOLOGICAL PROBLEM

Development of doctrine has to be dealt with in theological terms. Theological problems have their origin in the acceptance of faith. Of course, to unbelievers the matter under consideration may pose all kinds of questions, even questions akin or related to those of theology. But theology as such has no concern with them except as far as situations of fact involve problems of faith. If one does not accept the divine origin of Christian doctrine, for him there is no special question distinct from the general questions connected with the historical character of human thought. If, for instance, one believes that the word of God or divine revelation is utterly beyond the reach of reflective thought and human language, so that it can only be attained in mystical silence or unspeakable experience, then doctrines may perhaps be valued as helpful in pointing one toward the possibility of faith; but they are no longer essential to faith itself, and the problem of their development is completely altered. For the real question then no longer concerns the development of doctrine as such but the very relevance of any doctrine to faith or religious belief, although a theory about that relevance must entail a certain view of the nature of doctrinal development.

Consequently, the theological question of development can only be stated as a special question, on the acceptance of a number of presuppositions resulting from a certain conception of the nature of revelation and faith. The theologian has to explain how a revelation, if its truth must be expressible in human language, may be objectively closed at a fixed period of history and nevertheless admit of further development not only by way of subjective penetration but also by way of objective understanding.

The first presupposition, then, is that the word of God really comes to man in the form of human language. Revelation, the objective correlative of faith, is understandable truth. It can be dealt with by means of human concepts and expressed in linguistic propositions. This does not mean that the word of God can be adequately expressed in terms of human language. For indeed, as shall be seen, it will be one of the most important tasks of this study to explain how and how far truth may go together with inadequacy.

The presupposition just mentioned is the first and the most important. Newman called it 'the principle of *dogma*, that is, supernatural truths irrevocably committed to human language, imperfect because it is human, but definitive and necessary because given from above' (*Development*, p. 325). For it he fought the battle of his life. Its negation he called liberalism: 'By liberalism I meant the anti-dogmatic principle and its developments' (*Apologia*, p. 120). From the principle of dogma follows the principle of *theology*: 'Faith, being an act of the intellect, opens a way for inquiry, comparison and inference, that is, for science in religion, in subservience to itself' (*Development*, p. 325).

The second presupposition is that objective revelation has been communicated in a definite epoch that closed, as is generally admitted by orthodox Christianity, at the end of the apostolic generation. If one admits that the process of divine revelation is going on till the end of time, then the fact that new dogmas seem to arise in the course of history is no problem at all.

The real problem of development of dogma arises indeed from the fact that these two presuppositions being admitted, it remains true that some points of doctrine apparently not pertaining to the primitive deposit of faith, at least not explicitly, have nevertheless emerged in the course of dogmatic tradition. How to reconcile these facts of history with the principles of faith? No one who accepts both presuppositions can possibly get round the problem. To all those who reject the principle of liberalism, the actual development of doctrine is a real difficulty that asks for a clear and straightforward solution. Not only the Roman Catholic and the Eastern Orthodox Churches have to face it, but Protestants and Anglicans too, if, clinging to the principles of dogma and Scripture—i.e., that objective revelation is wholly contained in Scripture—they neverthless allow that the creed may propose doctrines of faith that, although agreeing with Scripture, are not explicitly stated in it.

The statement that the problem of development of doctrine is a theological one calls for further specification. To what branch of theology does it belong? According to a famous dictum of St. Anselm, quoted and commented on with approval by such men as R. Bultmann and H. Ott, theology is *fides quaerens intellectum* (faith seeking understanding). It seems to mean that theology tries to clarify the objects of faith or the *fides quae creditur* through intellectual contemplation and reflection. There is, however, a later distinction made by William of Auvergne and Thomas Aquinas that should be taken into account. On the one hand one may view revealed truth *in particulari*, that is, considering the content of the several dogmas and their relation to one another within the objective system of divine truth. To clarify such content and connections is the proper task of dogmatic theology. On the other hand it is possible to consider revealed truth *in universali*, that is, not attending to the doctrines themselves but to their common epistemological status of being known by revelation. Such problems as, for instance, the possibility and the actual occurrence of revelation, the criteria for discerning what belongs to it and what not, and the relation between revealed mystery and human language come under that kind of consideration. They constitute the proper domain of fundamental theology.

It is clear that such principles as the principle of dogma, the principle of theology, the principle of Scripture and/or tradition are not particular dogmas, integrated into a system of truth about God and salvation. They are rather presuppositions on which the nature, the use, and the range of Christian doctrine in general are dependent. They are indeed 'principles' rather than 'doctrines' according to a well-known distinction of Newman. They express the general conditions under which the objects of faith are revealed. Although we are sure of them through faith, it is better to say that they are not parts of the object of faith (*objectum fidei*) but rather determine the general conditions of the object (*conditio objecti*).

It is a kind of paradox, of course, that we are sure of something through faith but that it is better said not to belong to its object. The solution, however, is not so difficult. In a certain sense they are objects of faith. In believing a doctrine we believe implicitly or indirectly the necessary conditions under which they are presented. When one believes that there is a tree, one implicitly believes that the testimony of sense-perception is reliable. In the same way, when one accepts a doctrine about God or salvation as an object of faith, one implicitly believes that its truth is warranted by the Holy Spirit who inspired the Scriptures and never ceases to guide the Church in its authentic interpretation of them. Speaking of the distinction between doctrines and principles Newman says: 'The difference between the two sometimes merely exists in our mode of viewing them' (*Development*, p. 179). The principle of dogma states that the dogmas of faith are truths about God that can never be revoked. To be true in that sense is a common condition of all genuine statements of faith. It is not a particular truth about God or His work of salvation, related to other truths and forming with them a corpus of doctrine. It is a general reflexive statement about the nature of truth proper to all the dogmatic statements that together make the one objective doctrine of salvation studied by dogmatic theology.

Development of doctrine, then, is a problem of fundamental theology. It is not a particular point of doctrine about God the Savior, or about a fact or aspect of His plan of salvation. It is an aspect of the general condition of all dogma. If dogma is divine truth in forms of human thought and language, then from the nature of the case it is imperfect or inadequate. If human language is the vessel of divine truth, the question must arise how such a vessel is able to carry its heavenly freight through the flux of history in which it is involved. How is it possible to reconcile the truth of dogma with the historicity of thought and language? This is, as we shall see, the real problem of development of dogma. That there is a development is not only a fact of history, but, prior to the determination of fact, it should be anticipated from a consideration of the very nature of those human media through which divine truth is conveyed to man. If development is to be expected, then from the nature of the case it must be a law or general principle of divine dispensation. In the revised edition of his *Essay on the Development of Christian Doctrine* (1878) Newman added to his enumeration of the principles of Christianity a footnote in which he said: 'Development itself is such a principle also . . . giving a character to the whole course of Christian thought' (*Development*, p. 326). Fundamental theology, then, will have to show that development arises from the nature of the case and that the actual variations that seem to arise in the course of Christian history do not contradict the definiteness and irrevocability of revealed truth.

IMPORTANCE IN CONTEMPORARY THEOLOGY

For Newman the theory of development was intended to solve a personal problem. Starting with the principle of dogma, he had tried to build a dam against the rising tide of liberalism in matters of faith and philosophy. Various historical facts gradually were impressed on his mind and converged to a conclusion that at first he heartily disliked; he began to doubt that the Anglican Church could be the bulwark against the coming floods. Time and again his attention was drawn to the great Catholic body of the continent, organized round the See of Rome. One by one his prejudices against the Church of Rome faded: 'From the end of 1841, I was on my death-bed, as regards my membership with the Anglican Church' (*Apologia*, p. 257). There remained however one lingering difficulty: Could it be denied that the Church of Rome had added corrupting doctrines to the deposit of faith as defined in the great ecumenical councils of the 4th and 6th centuries? As an Anglican he based his case on the Fathers against Romanism. The first thing to do, then, was to take a fresh glance at the facts. History should decide. Going deeply into the historical facts, he discovered that the Council of Nicea was already the outcome of a long process of development. Why then should the process of development come to a stop? Why should the Council of Trent be less acceptable than the Council of Nicea or of Chalcedon? How to decide between Rome and Canterbury? Under what conditions could an earthly institution such as the Church, composed of men, and living in the midst of the dangerous currents of an ever-changing world, be the faithful exponent of unalterable truth? By means of what criteria could true developments be distinguished from corruptions? Such questions led him to the tremendous effort from which the *Essay on the Development of Christian Doctrine* was born.

When Newman wrote the *Nunc Dimittis* at the end of his *Essay*, he hardly suspected that the questions he had tried to answer for

himself should become the focus of the most burning problems of
the coming age. He realized it later when he saw how the attacks of
liberalism were gradually concentrated on dogma and fought with
the weapons of historical criticism. For reasons that will be investigated in their proper place, the problem of development became the
chief bone of contention between the defenders of dogma and their
adversaries.

> From the second part of the century the objections drawn from
> the 'variations of doctrine in the Church of Rome,' supported by
> Protestant treatises on the history of dogma, was urged with
> increasing insistence in the field of apologetics . . . It was a
> considerable difficulty. The grievances accumulated by contro-
> versy against the shortcomings of churchmen paled by its side.
> The essential claim of the Church to dispense among mankind
> a truth divine and therefore absolute was at stake. This was a
> difficulty of principle, a blow struck at the base of the system
> and gradually extending shock waves to all parts of the struc-
> ture.[1]

It is clear to us now that scholastic philosophy was no match for
the new problems. The real process of history cannot be reduced
to an operation of abstract reasoning. By the end of the century
the question could no longer be ignored, and for lack of any pro-
spect of a satisfactory solution the crisis became unavoidable.
Newman, though honored as a great champion of the Church, had
never been really accepted in the camp of Catholic theology. He
did not fit into the system. There seemed to be no common ground
on which Newman and traditional theology could meet and join
forces. The outburst came in the form of Modernism.

In the Catholic Church the rupture between Modernism and
traditional thought was more radical than in the Church of England
and most of the Protestant congregations. The stand taken by
Catholic Modernists especially on the continent was more radical.
Dean Inge, the most prominent of Anglican Modernists, was more
than shocked by the position expounded by Loisy. He would have
nothing to say for it.[2] It was more than a question of temperamental
or cultural differences between the English and the French attitudes
of mind; it was the general intellectual situation that was so different.
The Anglican mind was more akin to Newman's way of dealing
with problems. Unconsciously it had assimilated more deeply the

principle of development. The questions posed by the progress of
science were sooner faced; and the controversies, sharp as they were,
could run their course in a more ordinary way.[3] Roman Catholic
theology, because of the rigidity of its categories, was poorly
equipped for the new intellectual tasks, and as the principle of
authority was more predominant, it was less disposed to be in
sympathy with novelties or to consider them carefully and seriously.

The Church was entirely taken by surprise. The general impression was one of utter bewilderment. The time was not yet ripe for
dialogue. As the spirit of ultramontanism was still in the ascendant,
there was no remedy other than a hasty operation. The incipient
cancer had to be excised and all its metastases traced. A terror of
suspicion began to reign. It became difficult to tell a friend from an
enemy. Not only were great contemporary thinkers such as Blondel
and von Hügel, who tried to cope with the real problems in a spirit
of loyalty to the Church, considered dangerous, but Newman too
was suspected of heresy.

The operation proved to be efficacious, at least for a time. But
condemnations are not solutions. It is dangerous to neglect a real
problem on the ground that Rome has spoken. A condemnation is
not a theological crutch. It is not the end of an affair. It is rather a
point of departure for new intellectual explorations. By their very
nature intellectual problems demand intellectual solutions and not
decisions of authority. Such decisions may be necessary for a while
in order to preclude dangerous roads and blind alleys and to prevent
waste of time. They should never be considered as invitations to
stop thinking but rather as occasions for opening up new avenues
of theological investigation and insight. An ecclesiastical condemnation provides theology with further time to pay an intellectual debt, but it does not remit it.

Today it seems evident that, generally speaking, Catholic theology between the two wars of theological liberalism did not sufficiently understand the signs of the coming age and neglected to
adapt and to refit its intellectual equipment. Great work was done
by individuals in special branches of historical investigation and
criticism, but too often such pioneers were treated with distrust and
suspicion. They would not frankly state their full meaning. Meanwhile theological liberalism, swept from the surface of public
opinion, was slowly growing underground, biding its time.

It is one of the lessons of contemporary history that it is not enough to accept reluctantly new advanced positions in matters of Biblical exegesis and historical criticism. What is needed is a shift in the general outlook, a new spirit, a well-adapted store of intellectual tools and of explanatory ideas and principles, a comprehensive intellectual framework fitted to the facts and able to interpret their meaning and to arrange them in a satisfactory pattern. Nothing less than a comprehensive theory can dispel confusion and prepare men to face confidently fresh developments that lie ahead.

In the course of history the idea of Christianity has abundantly proved its assimilative power. But in order to exercise it in a changing world, it had always to create new organs and to free itself from the shackles of obsolete models and mental habits that had lost all of their functional value. This is not a cry for theological revolution but an advocacy of constructive wisdom. It is unwise to destroy a tradition if one has nothing to put in its place. Patiently and cautiously one must search one's way, listening to the voices of the past as well as to the clamors of the present. It is fashionable at the present time to cry down our theological inheritance without feeling the need to consider it carefully. Applicable to such a theological situation are the wise words of Professor Broad in his appreciation of contemporary linguistic philosophy: 'There certainly are changes of fashion in philosophy. When a new kind is in vogue, many things in the philosophy of an earlier day, which are of permanent value and perhaps highly relevant to contemporary problems, tend to be altogether forgotten or carelessly and ignorantly dismissed, simply because they occur in an out-of-date setting and are clad in an unfashionable dress.'[4] An exact knowledge and profound comprehension of the past is as necessary a condition for constructive and really modern theology as is a delicate feeling for the vague and often unspoken contemporary needs and for the new problems posed by the changing situation of a technological world or that emerge on the surface of history from the mysterious depths of human experience. To be steeped in Thomas Aquinas is a better preparation for a fruitful dealing with contemporary religious problems than to be well-read in a library of scientific and theological pocketbooks. The case here, then, is not against theological tradition but against its being frozen by thoughtless traditionalism. When one turns from Newman's *Essay on Development,* so bursting with life and intellectual energy, to many of the Latin treatises to which generations of priests have been subjected, one cannot shake off the impression of *rigor mortis*. All these books, as devoid of genuine thought as they are full of imaginary problems, verbal lore, and formalistic reasoning, in which the pulsing life of the real is reduced to concepts and finally to words, may rest in peace on their shelves. But Sts. Augustine, Bonaventure, and Thomas Aquinas will forever remain rich sources of quickening inspiration and masters of theological training.

It is said that in the 1960s man entered a new era of theological thought and religious life. Did man really enter, or is he only trying to do so? Vatican Council II is likely to be a turning-point in the history of the Church. The positive attitude with regard to the world, its needs, and its problems is *toto coelo* different from the prevailing intellectual note of the last century under the hegemony of ultramontanism. Indeed, new avenues are opened up for theological thinking. The Council cleared the air, cleaned the ground, and traced new paths. But it did not solve many problems. There is a new will, a fresh spirit, a sincere desire to meet the realities of history. The way lies open, but the work is still to be done. The Council is not the end but the beginning of a new period. There is no finality about it and there cannot be. The Council was not intended to cast the new insights into theological form. It should rather be considered as an invitation to go on thinking in certain directions. The Council, positive as it may have been, is as little a theological crutch as the condemnations of the beginning of the 20th century. Some theologians use the conciliar texts as if they were a new Bible limiting the future efforts of Christian thought to commentaries on its letter. This is as dangerous as the attitude of those who considered the condemnation of Modernism as the final word to which nothing might be added.

Vatican Council II witnessed on almost every point the encounter of two parties radically antagonistic to each other: on one side, a strong and united conservative minority, at odds with the current of modern thought and opposed to every semblance of novelty, but having the benefit of verbal clarity and theological traditionalism; on the other side, a rather loose majority, moved by a new spirit and asking for far-reaching adjustments in all matters of life and doctrine, but suffering from vagueness and lack of clarity. It could not be otherwise. Clarity and distinctness are the fruits of time and of agonizing efforts. Though the protagonists of *aggiorna-*

mento were the winners in the first round, they have not gained a final victory. They just started on their way and it is a long road with no turns. It is not a vain fear that the movement of renewal may, through lack of discipline and clarity, lead to confusion and spiritual anarchy. On that point history is an infallible teacher. Bold sayings, flippant criticisms, exciting theological journalism cannot further the cause of true renewal; this needs hard work, discipline of mind, and keen reflection. No new theology is needed, but rather a new clarity in the movement of theology as conditioned by rapidly changing cultural and technological factors and by the consequent rise of new problems. If a new clarity is not created, a reaction will prove unavoidable.

Among those things that imperiously demand clarity, the cluster of problems of which development of doctrine is a main issue comes foremost. There can be no doubt that the opposition between the two parties of Vatican Council II was rooted in a different view of the nature of dogma and the range of its possible extension and evolution. In the eyes of the traditionalists truth is not so much an unchangeable value viewed in the changing light of human historical existence as it is an immutable, closed system of eternal essences, clear and fixed, to each of which a fitted linguistic symbol is attached. Although extreme forms of traditionalism have been condemned by the Church, theological conservatism is of necessity essentialistic and traditionalistic. A treasure of truths is handed down in traditional propositions, like diamonds in an old and irreplaceable setting of gold. Logical truth or the truth of our thoughts is conceived as an exact mental duplicate of ontological truth or the truth of things.

The advocates of ecclesiastical and theological adjustment, on the other hand, had a keen feeling of the historical nature of the Church as far as it is a part of the world, incarnated in patterns of culture. Incarnation means 'historization.' The invisible reality of the Church, its ontological truth, is translated into human forms of expression. As historicity belongs to the very nature of these forms, the temporal Church is not exempt from the necessary laws of all historical existence. On the level of cultural incarnation no distinction can be made between a part that is suprahistorical and beyond change and another part that is historical and subject to change. The ontological reality of the Church is simply suprahistorical and therefore always the same, but its expression in human forms of life and thought is entirely historical and therefore always moving with the stream of history. There should be no distinction between life and thought because man's thinking activity is a function of human life, the expression of its self-understanding. The dogmas of the Church are not immovable monuments erected on the shore of the ocean but living currents and streams in the flux and reflux of its waters.

All this was keenly felt by the Fathers of the Council, but it cannot be said that they all possessed a clear and distinct view of its principles and implications. Their view was a practical one and their aims were pastoral. They were aware of the fact that the Church and the world had parted company; that the Church was on the way to becoming a glorious monument of the past, a venerable piece of antiquity; that it had gradually ceased to be a living force in the movement of history; that immobilism was a deadly policy; that accommodation was an urgent existential necessity for the Church. They could not believe that the present position of the Church in the world was simply due to the wickedness of man. They saw that they could as well put it down to a kind of ecclesiastical immobilism in most forms of life and thought. The general situation that called for readjustment was the result of a natural development of society, and no one could be blamed for it. If, then, the need for accommodation had its roots in the nature of the present situation, it was practically certain that it somehow did fit in the scheme of divine Providence and that it was a duty of religious obedience to understand its indications and to act according to its requirements.

If this be the case, it is at once clear that the movement of the Church toward renewal and adaptation is badly in need of guiding principles. Such principles, however, should be taken from a clearly argued insight into the nature of history and into the manner and measure in which it affects the Church, especially the expression of that truth from which the Church draws its life. The Church is an organ of salvation in a moving world. It has to keep alive among men a message of divine mercy. That message entails a general view of God, man, and the world. It works as a theory by which the present state of things can be explained. To accept it, however, is more than an intellectual belief. One must acknowledge a Christian pattern of behavior, accept a Christian way of life, submit it to its moral demands. There is nothing in one's thinking existence that it leaves unaffected. It is not simply added to a man's natural way of viewing and doing things. It must penetrate and change his life in the most radical way. It is not a private business, a solitary relation to an invisible world. It tries to recast all man's social relationships. It is related to the world 'like leaven which a woman took and hid in three measures of meal, till it was all leavened' (Mt 13.33). Consequently, the Church cannot be separated from the world. If its vocation is to penetrate the world and to change its face, the Church must itself become world, must translate its life into forms of human culture. The Church cannot transform the world without being conditioned by the historical nature of the world. The Church has to keep pace with that world to which it addresses itself. If the world of man is a world of culture in a continuous development, a world that by creating itself becomes history, then the Church must also become history, not in some of the aspects of its life but in all of them, including the doctrine and the language of the Church.

What does it mean, then, to say that the Church in the state of its earthly incarnation assumes an historical character? To put that question is to ask how far the law of development affects the Church's life, and how the Church succeeds in being true to its divine origin by becoming an historical reality. If one can grasp firmly the true idea of development and its proper application in the fields of Christian doctrine, one would be on the way to solving the most critical questions of contemporary Christianity. It could help perhaps to understand and to acknowledge the anxieties of both the conservative and the progressive wings of the Church and to bridge the cleft that separates them. The basic opposition, the opposition of principle, between theological conservatism and progressivism has to be overcome. There is no danger in a dialectical rivalry between conservative-minded and progressive-minded groups in the Church. Such competition is part of the very structure of history. But if these cease to understand and accept one another, if they are separated by a radical split based on opposing first principles, the consequences may in the long run become disastrous. This study shall try to show that self-conserving development is the only way in which ideas are able to keep themselves alive in the conditions of earthly existence and how this truly applies, within definite limits, to the life of dogma in the Church without affecting its lasting truth and its substantial invariability.

CHAPTER TWO

Basic Notions

It is impossible to start with a real description of the things under consideration in this chapter. Such a description can only be the outcome of a careful analysis of the process itself. However a general notion of the concepts will be useful in distinguishing them from other cognate notions and determining the particular meanings in which the relevant terms will be used.

DEVELOPMENT AND EVOLUTION

The etymology of the term *to develop* is uncertain. It comes perhaps from the Latin *volvo* and then has the same root as *evolution*. As evolution is opposed to involution, so development is opposed to envelopment. Common to the two contraries is the notion of wrapping, which today exists in the Italian word *viluppo* (bundle or wrapping). The notion of wrapping suggests two possible actions: drawing a covering around something or unwinding it. The notion of entwining and unwinding suggests a gradual process of folding or unfolding. Hence, according to the semantic law of analogy the terms in question did receive various meanings. The common idea of development and evolution seems to be a gradual process or action of bringing out something concealed or latent in whatever way from another thing or a previous state of the same thing. A priori there is no apparent reason to distinguish between evolution and development. If different shades of meaning come to be attached to the two terms, there is no other reason than usage. In fact the term *evolution* is preferred in reference to a natural process,

17

while the term *development* is more apt to suggest an action. That usage however is not exclusive, and ordinary language cannot be simply appealed to in order to justify a clear-cut distinction between the corresponding notions.

For the sake of clarity the term *development* is here reserved for a specific human phenomenon, while *evolution* is intended to mean the progressive aspect of unconscious nature. Development is an historical category and evolution a category of natural science. Of course, the distinction between historical development and natural evolution is a problem in itself. For materialists or philosophical naturalists the process of history is only one stage in the general evolution of nature. It may have distinctive features that set it off from the unconscious course of the universe. But man is conceived as being no more than a product of nature. The same principles are at work in the formation of atoms and in the most complicated patterns of social and cultural life. This study, however, starts from different assumptions. The formal principle of evolution as defined above is nature; the formal principle of history or development is human freedom. Freedom is above nature but not without nature. Freedom is a principle of conscious self-possession and self-realization. But as far as its working is known, it can only be realized in and through nature. It has to make use of the resources and implements of nature in order to establish its rule over nature. The powers and processes of nature are taken up in the development of culture. Freedom is culture's formal directive principle. Just as the presence of the soul is invisible to the eye and can only be perceived by mental intuition in and through a certain pattern of bodily behavior, so the proper principle of culture is no part of its description. Freedom's active presence can only be detected in and through the proper characteristics of its making. Reflection may confirm and in a certain measure establish the belief that a principle of freedom is at work in human behavior and in the development of culture. But nature being the material principle of culture, we must admit that the face, the visible side of history, can be described in terms of nature. Only through the interpretation of the meaning of human phenomena is one able to get at the formal principle of culture in contradistinction to that of natural evolution. The concluding part of this study will try to develop and justify the idea of culture as contrasted with that of nature. Let it suffice now to indicate the general meaning of the distinction and to lay bare the reason for the apparent continuity of both. It is true that historical development prolongs the general evolution of nature in a certain direction. If one takes a general view of the whole process, one may rightly describe it with Teilhard de Chardin as a phenomenological unity. One may even be justified in reading it as a continuous story with a perfect plot in which the development of history toward a perfect social organization appears as the fulfillment of what nature from the beginning was aiming at. By reason of their interpenetration one may, according to the law of analogy, speak of 'natural history' and 'social evolution.' The distinction between evolution and development seems in the end to be no more than a scientific terminology of our own making, introduced for the sake of analytical clarity.

Newman in his *Essay on the Development of Christian Doctrine* used the term in three senses, which will be followed here: the process of development, the result of that process, and both process and result, either in a neutral sense including true developments and corruptive ones, or in a qualified sense applying only to true developments.

DEVELOPMENT IN CULTURE AND DOCTRINE

Thus far the discussion of cultural development or historicity in general has not made specific reference to the development of doctrine. In a certain respect the problem of the development of doctrine is distinct from that of cultural development in general. It raises questions of a special kind. In another respect, however, it is only a part or aspect of cultural development. Human existence is a thinking existence. As such, it creates culture. It changes the conditions of existence according to ideas, the products of thought. They may arise spontaneously in one's consciousness or be the result of mental concentration. But whether ideas are spontaneous outgrowths of experience or insights acquired through laborious efforts of concentration, they have to be clarified, to be related to other ideas by reflective operations of analysis and synthesis. They have also to be worked out for practical purposes according to the situation in which they are intended to be realized. There is a kind of analogy between the way ideas are related to cultural creation and the way natural forms are related to the evolution of unconscious life. Both natural evolution and cultural creation seem to invent new forms of life. But in the first case—at least as far as consideration is committed to the immanent view of the universe —they are spontaneous fruits of an unconscious cosmic growth; in the second case they appear to be effects of a process in which natural growth is penetrated and partly guided by human planning and conscious effort. For reasons to be analyzed further on, the development of culture, springing from liberty but always limited by the possibilities of a given situation, is a Janus with a bright face of victorious liberty and a dark face of inescapable fate. At any rate, this study is committed to the view that liberty is the efficient cause of culture while ideas are its formal cause, nature its material cause, and the perfection of 'persons in relation' its final cause. Because matter, as Plato and Plotinus clearly saw, is a reluctant element, it sets limits to human creativity, but at the same time it is full of promise for those who can handle it with intelligence and skill.

Nature, then, brings forth its forms according to rules of spontaneous pullulation; freedom, however, recasts nature into patterns of thought according to devices of intentional operation. Nature sprouts a world of forms and things according to laws of innate wisdom; culture calls forth into nature a world of tools and organizations, according to patterns based on activities of interpretation. The world we live in is not simply a world of brute things but a world of things interpreted by means of ideas and organized by man in accordance with those interpretations. Therefore the development of culture affects not only the world of things but also the world of human meanings. Objective culture or the sum total and organization of the products of free, intelligent action in the world of nature has its counterpart in subjective culture or the sum total and organization of ideas in the mental life of human society. The one mirrors the other. This does not mean that objective culture is the exact replica of subjective culture. For once realized in things that are independent of conscious creative life, objective culture is detached from it and acquires independent existence. Although created by freedom it becomes a part of the situation in which freedom has to make its way. There is a dialectical interaction between a human situation, continually modified by active ideas, and those ideas themselves, continually challenged by their own situational products. Culture lives under the law of incessant effort and vigilance. There are periods of rise and creative progress but periods, too, of fall and passive decay. One's ideas may be ahead of one's practical realizations. They also may remain behind through sloth, false security, or lack of an educational scheme well-fitted to the tasks and duties of the moment. From all this it follows that the development of ideas, worked out in the form of doctrines, has a ruling function in the development of culture. Development of doctrine is a part of the development of culture. It is one of its factors, dialectically related to other factors in the same process but with a nature of its own. The flourishing of culture depends on the soundness and wisdom of men's ideas, on the measure in which they effectively command men's actions. It depends on technical skill to actualize them in the stuff of history.

PHILOSOPHY AND SCIENCE

As implied in the foregoing description, two functions of the mind are involved in the process of cultural creation. The first has to do with ends, the second with means. Both, however, are based on a certain interpretation of the world, although different in character. The first is an interpretation of experience in terms of values and leads to concrete ideals projected by the imagination; the second is an interpretation of experience in terms of functional relations and may be converted into power and skill whereby man can change the material conditions of earthly existence according to his desires. The interpretation of the world in terms of value is the proper object of philosophy and theology; the interpretation of the world in terms of existing functional relations is the proper object of the sciences. This study will not enter into the recent discussions about the nature of philosophy; it takes a practical common-sense view: 'Philosophy is what philosophers do. If, then, we want to decide what philosophy is, we shall naturally begin by considering what kind of activities have been pursued by men whom everyone would regard as philosophers when engaged in what everyone would regard as their characteristically professional work.'[1] This is a sound principle and seems to be evident. Of course it might be argued that the objects pursued by those professional philosophers of the past were unreal phantasms, linguistic confusions, or absurd attempts to say something about experiences that by their very nature are beyond human words. Such a view may be held, although it is improbable that all through history men of outstanding genius and influence have wasted their constant efforts on

B

nonsensical enterprises. If one holds to the view that the sole object of philosophy is analysis of scientific language, then he should be honest enough to proclaim the inanity of all philosophy. It is true that philosophers have always practiced some forms of language analysis, but it was only to deal with problems about reality that by their very nature were beyond the range of exact or experimental investigation. To say, then, that the only task of philosophy is to analyze and to criticize the language of the sciences is itself at least an abuse of language, and those who preach avoidance of misleading expressions might well be urged to begin at home.[2]

Philosophy and science are attempts to clarify two different but equally basic aspects of human experience. Both aspects are undeniable. Man's conscious existence is not only a consciousness of what he is, but also of what he is not but ought to be. Moreover, since his temporal existence is by its very nature a coexistence with other persons, he is aware not only of the actual social patterns of human life but also of an ideal of a socially structured common life. This implies, as far as existence and coexistence are related to the world of nature and dependent upon it, an awareness of an ideal general state of things beyond their present condition. It is a basic trait of man that the movement of his thinking existence produces ideas not only about how things actually are but also about how they are to be. In the reality of his life, his physical milieu, and his social surroundings—in existence these three are one—he not only perceives facts as they happen to be but also possibilities and ideals that appeal to freedom and conscience and to creative imagination and power in order to be realized. Human life is not simply determined by nature; it is open to free self-creation. Life is not so much a structure of data as a pattern of duty. One is not only responsible for the moral quality of each single deed, but also for the contribution of one's life as a whole to the universal state of things: the condition of human society and the transformation of nature in the service of a better world. The goodness of one's deeds in the world consists in their positive and constructive relation to the goodness of common human existence. Life is for action. Although my inner life or the incommunicable relation between 'myself and my creator' (Newman) is the highest of all moral goods and leads beyond this visible world, it cannot be genuine if on the level of social coexistence it does not contribute, in one of a thousand possible ways, to the common good of the world-in-gestation, the

promotion of which is man's privilege and duty. 'In one of a thous-
and possible ways' can refer, for instance, to forms of contemplative life, which in the bustle of this extroverted world are no less
necessary for the *ressourcement* of social coexistence than moments
of recollection are for the inner renewal of personal life.

It will now be possible to define more accurately the domains
of philosophy and science in their relation to human life. Both are
methodical modes of thinking existence, taking place within its
movement and subservient to it. Their real meaning is dependent
on their relation to existence or life in a vague sense including all
that is specifically human. It is clear now that the world one is living
in and of which one's life partakes is not a world of immovable
substances but a world of continuous becoming, a world in the
making. Freedom, since it appeared in nature, is ever casting and
recasting the world, trying to humanize it, to make it a better world
for man. Mankind is making the world or making a human world in
the world of nature. In making its own world, humanity as a collective person is making itself. Earth is a 'vale of soul-making.' It is
no less a 'vale of world-making' in the service of soul-making.

Here then the domain of philosophy lies open before man. If he
is to make the world, the first question is not *how* to do things but
what to make of it. What is the meaning of human life? What is the
sense of man's appearance in the stream of cosmic becoming? Does
it have a value beyond its becoming? Does it have a value beyond
its transitory and ephemeral occurrence? Are there absolute values
not depending on man but on which man depends? Is man's world-
making activity subject to a moral rule independent of his self-will?
Or can he make and organize life and society according to taste or
fancy? Is his being a vocation? Is being man a duty to realize an
ideal of true humanity over which one has no moral power because
it is one's very being? Is conscience the true reality of consciousness and freedom, or is one allowed to dispose of one's own destiny
according to will or wish? And if the secret of consciousness be
conscience, what is its rule and how can it be known? Such are
the questions that great philosophers have always asked and it
cannot be denied that these are the questions that all alert or non-
anesthetized souls keep asking for themselves.

Now, it is clear that such questions entail other questions
about the nature of being, man, and the universe. How man has to
live depends upon what he is. There is no ethics without meta-

physics, meaning by metaphysics the domain of such questions
about reality as cannot be reduced to questions about the regularity
of phenomena that physical science has to deal with. From its very
nature exact science is unable to pass judgment on questions of
ends and values. Science can only state facts and order them. Facts
about human behavior cannot be converted into unconditional rules
of moral conduct. At its best it may yield conditional rules: If one
is willing to attain that goal, one has to behave that way. But why
should one pursue that goal? Does it give a satisfactory and acceptable meaning to one's life? To such questions science gives no
answers, and it cannot possibly give an answer because of its proper
nature and limited scope. And yet man cannot do without an answer
to such questions. If rules of conduct are no more than conventions,
nothing can bind a man to them in his conscience. And if man is
the being he appears to be from his autobiography written across the
face of history, it cannot be doubted that in the long run, life will
seem to him utterly absurd if he finds himself unable to fall back
upon values that are independent of his contingent existence. Man
may go on for a time without such values, carried by the impetus
of traditional ethical conviction and by secret irrational hopes. But
if he once becomes certain that no objective values invite him, that
his contingent liberty is absolute, that he is left entirely to his own
arbitrary will, then the impetus of life cannot but come to a stop
and there is no other honest solution for him than to return his
ticket to nature.

Philosophy then—and theology in its own way—is about questions of man's ultimate concern: moral values or rules of duty
founded on the rock of metaphysical truth. But once one has a
reasonable idea of which ends and ideals one ought to pursue, then
the question arises of how to attain them. Since existence, with its
exercise of creative freedom, is essentially related to a material
world with an objective structure of its own, the question really
devolves into one of technical knowledge and professional skill:
how to realize one's ideas and conceptions in a world governed by
the physical laws of nature? Moreover, personal freedom itself is
no more than a possibility. It has to be actualized and developed
in a psychophysical and a sociophysical medium that prompts one
to act according to the law of inertia and the compulsion of psychological and social habits and complexes. Therefore the main
difficulties along the road toward a better world have to do not so

much with economic problems as with the problem of man himself, the conditions of the biopsychological medium and the social structures in which he is living. The problem of how to make life better is no less a problem of improving man himself than one of improving upon his economic situation. Therefore, when we speak here of technical insight and skill, this does not mean exclusively man's powers of adapting the non-human world according to his needs. It means also those other skills by which the social world is adapted to the requirements of personal life or by which man himself is adapted to the tasks of being man in the actual conditions of existence. Without education in the widest sense of the word all improvement of his economic welfare will be unable to produce a better world or a state of greater happiness.

As ethics goes together with metaphysics, so technical knowledge and skill are based upon an understanding of the laws of physical and human nature. Moral philosophy, grounded in metaphysical insight, shows man which ends are in accordance with his true being and happiness. Technical knowledge smooths the way toward the realization of such conditions of happiness as are within the power of methodical treatment. For the basic condition of all human actualization is the free will of man over which he has no power except by eliminating it. The world is in the making through and for man. Philosophy tries to answer the question, 'What is man to make of it so that he may become truly man and attain to happiness?' Science creates the means to fulfill man's aspirations. From his point of view, sciences and technical power are blind, neutral, ambivalent. They may lead to enslavement and destruction as well as to the liberation and enhancement of life. Moral convictions are the leading powers that ultimately decide the course of history.

IDEAS AND DOCTRINES

It will be possible now to define more accurately what the term *doctrine* means and to determine the place of the development of doctrine in the course of human life or the movement of culture. A doctrine is a statement or a coherent set of statements and arguments about moral ideas. By 'moral ideas' is meant both the moral values or imperatives and the metaphysical intuitions or conceptions that they entail or on which they are based.

This implies a distinction between ideas and doctrines. Ideas are expressed in doctrines. Doctrines are expressions of ideas. Ideas are the mental objects one tries to express in a set of consistent sentences. We say 'mental objects' in order to distinguish ideas from objects of actual sense-perception. Such mental objects as are called ideas are wholes, more particular or more comprehensive according to the case: the idea of man, the idea of society, the idea of being. There is a margin of liberty left for defining the units one may call ideas. On the whole, however, this study is committed to a holistic conception of ideas. It does not admit the theory of Locke that there are simple mental atoms corresponding to simple sense-impressions, and that such mental objects, called simple ideas, are the building blocks of more complex ideas and ultimately of one's mental universe. In man's mental universe to which an extra-mental universe is supposed to correspond—how far this is true is not to the point in the present context—he distinguishes wholes, either ultimate individual wholes (*substances* in scholastic terminology) or different kinds of relational wholes (groups, society). These wholes, as far as they are mental, are ideas. The idea of a thing is the whole, not as it exists in itself—if there be such a thing—but as it is present to a mind or consciousness. It is possible to apprehend vividly ideas to which nothing corresponds in reality; there are imaginary ideas. It is possible, too, to dwell upon ideas for the sake of analysis, description, or investigation without their having any reference to realities. To unbelievers, religious conceptions may be interesting as mere ideas to which no realities correspond. To believers, on the contrary, mental ideas are like windows through which they look at realities. Some philosophers say that ideas are the stuff of reality itself. Such epistemological problems need not be discussed here. Suffice it to say that ideas are mental wholes considered as such. 'The idea which represents an object or supposed object is commensurate with the sum total of the possible aspects' (*Development*, p. 34). *Object* is taken here in the sense of extra-mental thing. This study would rather reserve the term *object* for the correlate of subjective apprehension, be it real or only supposed to be so: therefore, ideas are mental objects in contradistinction to real things. This does not mean that mental objects are unreal but that this study considers them apart from the truth of their relation to existing realities.

The sentence of Newman just quoted sets us on the right track. An idea is a whole present to the mind as a focus from which several lines seem to proceed in various directions of conceptualization. Concepts are aspects of the idea, distinguished from one another through abstraction and analysis. The idea, on the contrary, is always present to the mind as a whole. Concepts are results of analysis. They are combined in sentences intended to say something about what the idea is supposed to stand for. Now it is difficult, if not impossible, to decide whether the analysis of an idea is complete. Therefore, as Newman says, the idea is the sum total of the *possible* aspects of an object. The idea somehow transcends the sum total of the actual aspects obtained by the process of reflection. Therefore it tends to coincide with the mystery of the real itself as far as one apprehends it by a kind of confused or implicit intuition. Or when it is used not to signify existing things but human projects, the term *idea* points to an ideal model or exemplar to which the things to be done ought to conform, without perhaps ever realizing its absolute perfection. Such is the sense of 'the idea of a university' in the title of Newman's famous book.

All this is very much to the point. For a doctrine is a system or sub-system of concepts and statements that express our apprehension of a moral idea. The term *doctrine* does not have the same meaning as the term *theory* although common language does not always distinguish them. A theory is a system of models by means of which one tries to explain a category of facts. Development of doctrine, for instance, is an historical fact; and a systematic attempt to solve the problem arising from these facts is a theory.

Neither is doctrine to be confused with ideology. An ideology in the modern sense of the word is either an interpretation of life withdrawn by its followers from the test of experience or, more specifically, a worldview built as a kind of superstructure upon presuppositions that depend on social and ultimately economic situations. They are said to be held as self-evident by the social class that is defending its interests against the inescapable movement of history.

Would it not be better to speak of a development of ideas instead of doctrines? Both ways of speaking are admissible. For doctrines are to ideas as fruits to trees. One may say 'the tree grows' or 'the tree grows fruits' or 'fruits are growing on trees.' The tree grows in the gradual expansion of its branches and twigs. The hidden nature of the seed from which the tree sprouts becomes manifest in the gradual development of its characteristic form. In a similar way ideas develop into doctrines. The implicit riches hidden in the mental seed of an idea are unfolded in the process of history. One may say then 'the idea develops' or 'the idea develops doctrines' or 'doctrines develop from ideas.' The idea develops through a gradual unfolding in concepts and sentences, principles and conclusions, forming together a more or less coherent and characteristic whole that is called a doctrine. Doctrines, then, are conceptual tenets in which ideas either receive an articulate expression or are worked out in patterns of practical or ethical conduct.

The analogy of the tree suggests another aspect in the structure of a doctrinal system. As a tree branches out in various directions, resulting in branches of different size and form, so the development of an idea produces various ramifications expressing typical aspects of the idea. The term *doctrine* may be used to signify either the whole or one of its characteristic parts. Within the doctrine of Christianity, for instance, we distinguish between different doctrines such as the doctrines of the Trinity, the Incarnation, the atonement, and so on.

DOCTRINES AND PRINCIPLES

The most important distinction in the structure of a doctrinal system, however, is the distinction mentioned above between doctrines and principles. As was remarked on that occasion, the demarcation between them is not always obvious. Whether one will call them principles or doctrines often depends upon one's mode of viewing them. Principles are general presuppositions directing the typical development of a system in a way comparable to the influence of the chromosomes on the evolution of an organism.

Together they make a structural pattern. Thus Newman derives the principles of Christianity from the idea of the Incarnation (*Development*, p. 324). Of course, the Incarnation is a doctrine too, but it is so central in the Christian view of salvation that it may safely be said to be the living focus from which all the rays or principles proceed, refracting its light through the medium of human consciousness into a spectrum of multi-colored doctrine. In that sense the Incarnation is the idea of Christianity and at the same time it is one of its doctrines. At the risk of allegorizing, one may even push the biological analogy so far as to say that as the harmonious growth of an organism supposes the full working of all the normal constituents of a chromosomal structure, so the faithful development of a doctrine supposes the unhampered influence of all the essential principles through which an idea energizes the process of its development. If one of the genes in a chromosome is missing, the whole growth of the organism will be crippled. In a somewhat similar way the absence of one of the essential principles will have its repercussion on the whole of a doctrinal development.

As the chromosomes are the hidden directive forces that command the evolution of a certain pattern of life, so principles are the rather unconscious directives in the development of doctrines. On the level of spontaneous thought principles tend to remain unnoticed: 'You cannot see yourself; and in somewhat the same way the chance is that you are not aware of those principles or ideas which have the chief rule over your mind. They are hidden for the very reason that they are so sovereign and so engrossing.'[8] This holds equally true for collective thought. Men do not think only as individual persons. Individual thought is largely submerged in the collective thought of the cultural generation whose living members we are. Man's thinking activity, then, is governed by various kinds of principles. Some of them almost belong to human nature. They are generally accepted by all minds. They are part, as it were, of the very mechanism of thought. All men make use of them in a spontaneous unconscious way. They are implicit in all exercise of natural reason. Newman analyses some of them under the heading 'Presumption' in his *Grammar of Assent*. Such are, for instance, 'There are things external to ourselves,' 'There is a right and a wrong,' 'a true and a false' 'nothing happens without a cause,' 'Things happen uniformly according to certain circumstances, and not without them and at random.' These are considered as self-evident by all unsophisticated minds. The generality of people never comes to think of them or to formulate them. They are tacit assumptions. Men do not use them consciously as premises of explicit reasoning and do not so much appeal to them as think from them. Men trust them; men do not think them or argue about them. Only a few philosophers are busy with them and sometimes they come to the conclusion that they are beset with insuperable difficulties. In ordinary life, however, the philosophers trust them as much as the man in the street.

Above that basic level of common nature there is a second level of social first principles. They are historic superstructures, pro-

ducts of culture, and proper to a civilization, a generation, or a
special group. They call for a more careful consideration because
they play a prominent part in the development of doctrine. They are
in the limelight of the contemporary philosophy of history.
Gadame, for instance, calls them *Vormeinungen*, or *Vor-urteile*
(antecedent opinions or pre-judgments). One does not criticize them,
nor is one explicitly aware of them. Through them man is given
to himself as part of the larger society. That he is a social being
does not mean only that he cannot live without the aid of his
fellow men, or that his being is a vocation to realize himself by
living for his fellow men. It also means that together with his fellow
men he shares a set of common presuppositions that enter into his
mental constitution insofar as he is an historic being. Man's common presuppositions are the basic features of man's historicity. The
past is spontaneously interpreted according to them. They have an
unconscious and sovereign power over man. Because they spread
through him, they often make him deaf to the voice of the past
speaking through tradition. Their influence is at the origin of the
contemporary problem of hermeneutics. 'Properly speaking
history does not belong to us but we belong to history. Long before
we understand ourselves through introspective reflection, we
already understand ourselves in a matter of course way in the
family, the society, the nation of which we are members. The self-
reflection of the individual is no more than a flickering within the
streaming circle of historic life. Therefore the pre-judgments of an
individual are not so much his own pre-judgments. They are rather
the historic reality of his being.'[4]

In a still more radical way Ortega y Gasset states the same thing
in his *Ideas y creencias* and in other essays. It is indeed one of the
basic principles of his historiology. He is more radical because
according to his view all *creencias* are social in the most comprehensive sense of the word. They are proper to a culture through
many generations. Common presuppositions of particular groups
are not strictly speaking *creencias*. The distinction between *ideas*
and *creencias* is perhaps too clear cut. An *idea* in Ortega's terminology is the object of actual thought. *Creencias* (the meaning of the
term corresponds more or less to the meaning of *credence* in
Newman's *Grammar of Assent*) are not objects of thought but
rather its sources. They are trusted; they are not thought about. One
finds oneself in them. Common self-evidence or 'common validity'

is their essential property: 'They are ideas which we do not have but which we are. Still more, for the very reason of their being *creencias*, they are identical for us with reality itself. They are our world and our being.'[5] Together with the theory of generations, the distinction between *ideas* and *creencias* is for Ortega the historical category *par excellence* that helps man understand the nature of historical crises. From generation to generation changes take place in the general world-view of a given civilization. But as long as those changes affect only the superstructure of men's ideas, there is no historical crisis. From the moment, however, that the living force of its *creencias* is weakening, crisis is within sight.

An historical crisis is a period in which the first principles that underlie a pattern of culture slowly die in the depths of collective consciousness. The relentless criticism of experience gradually reveals their inaptness to cope satisfactorily with the problems of life. The world built on them is at the end of its tether. As their influence is largely unconscious the process of their weakening begins in the unconscious regions of life. They are not destroyed by intellectual criticism but are undermined by a kind of existential doubt. They simply don't work any longer, and men find themselves unwillingly in the rolling movement of doubt. Nobody is to blame. Prophets of a new world may arise and proclaim the end of the old one. In their own times they may be ignored as fools or rebels. Later they will perhaps be honored as forerunners and geniuses. They are not the makers of a new world but rather the first spokesmen for a world in the making. They bring to consciousness something that is secretly at work in the bosom of society. Then the unconscious principles of the past emerge into consciousness and are turned over to devastating intellectual criticism. Mankind slowly awakens to a new and unknown world with mixed feelings of perplexity and liberation.

In a given space of time mankind is floating as it were over an abyss between two worlds: a world already disappearing and a world not yet existing. Chateaubriand, it is said, was 'the man of an epoch of crisis when an old civilization is crumbling and a new one is not yet born.'[6] This is a fair description of man in the crisis. In the meantime the principles of the new world are gradually clarified. They rapidly spread through man's social being. They, in their turn, become self-evident and gradually sink back into the collective mind as the invisible foundation of a new epoch. They accede to

the throne of the secret palace whence the world of thought is
governed.

The general description of the nature of *creencias* or social self-
evident principles worked out by Ortega in order to explain the
phenomenon of cultural crisis is certainly true as far as it goes. This
study is inclined, however, to accept with Newman that social first
principles are not only to be found at the basis of a culture viewed
as a whole but may also be characteristic of a nation or even of
certain groups within a given society. What is called 'fashion' in
philosophy and literature may perhaps be explained as a temporary
domination by some basic assumptions in the mind of certain
groups of thinkers. They do not sink so deep beneath the surface
of consciousness as the first principles on which civilizations are
built, but they are so engrossing that they tend to escape criticism
and to be considered as self-evident by those who hold them in
common. Their reign may last for a time till it becomes clear that
they are unable to yield the expected fruits.

Such is, for instance, the anti-metaphysical principle in recent
logical empiricism. Metaphysics has become almost a term of abuse.
But, as Prof. Price comments, 'It looks as if there were a kind of
rhythm in the history of human thought on metaphysical subjects.
A long period of metaphysical thinking is followed by a shorter
period of criticism and agnosticism, and then speculative thinking
begins again in a different form. At the moment we happen to live
in one of the critical and agnostic periods; and perhaps the widespread complaint that "Clarity is not enough" is itself one of the
symptoms that the period is approaching its end.'[7] And Prof. Broad
in the same volume: 'Time and again some new general principle
is brought forward with a flourish of trumpets. As originally formulated it is vague and ambiguous, but this is not at first apparent . . .
The time for evangelical power is when the ambiguity is still unde-
tected and the principle seems to be at once evidently true and fruitful in its consequences.'[8] Both texts hint at the causes of the rise
and fall of philosophical principles. The human mind cannot remain
inactive. The disappointment that leads to the rejection of certain
principles is the very cause of the rise of new ones. But after a time,
once they are clarified and their consequences worked out, it appears
that they cannot fulfill the demands of life. Life is the supreme
master of thought. Principles or doctrines that cannot answer its
questions are sooner or later abandoned.

This is not to say that the illusions of thought are useless. They are necessary stages in the conquest of truth. If they do not provide us with absolute truth, they at least prove that certain roads of thought may be considered as impracticable. Philosophic illusions are 'carrots which nature dangles before the noses of philosophers, luring them on to do much valuable thinking which would otherwise never have been undertaken.'[9] Wisdom is the fruit of repeated disillusionment. This holds true in the case of human history as well as in that of individual life. It is no excuse for skepticism, which is always weakness. It requires humility and patience, which are the true conditions of intellectual health and strength. The current of history carries truth in its mixed waters as a river contains precious minerals. In the dialectical movement of history, some parts of truth are sifted out as nuggets in the shaking of the gold prospector's sieve. Cultural crises and minor crises in philosophy may be compared to shifts in the viewpoint from which the things are looked at. At every turn new light falls on the objects of experience.

Thought, indeed, is like a searchlight directed on the same object by one who walks around it in successive circles, different in distance and height. One never sees the whole, but the different views have enough in common to assure one that he is looking at the same thing. Those views, succeeding each other, are recorded and conserved in historical consciousness. They correct and complete each other. All kinds of optical illusions are gradually dissipated. Imagination enriched by past experience acquires a certain power to construct for itself a picture of the whole beyond the special aspects that actually come into sight. Of course, the movement is not infallibly for the better. Being the work of succeeding generations, each engrossed by its own way of seeing things, the lessons of the past may be temporarily obliterated. But each new crisis leads to a fresh scrutiny of the past and long forgotten insights come back to the mind in new forms and often in a richer setting of experience. Therefore, however dark the night may be at a given moment, one may be confident that human thought as a whole moves toward the light.

So much for the social first principles and their influence upon the course of historical thought. An idea develops into a doctrine through the directive activity of principles. These principles are different in kind, range, and power. At the base one finds principles so common that they almost belong to the constitution of the mind itself. At a superior level, one meets social principles proper to a culture in a definite phase or stage of its development. Such principles, too, are a part of one's being, but only as far as it is essentially historical. Social principles may be at work at different levels of profundity. The common principles of a culture may be understood by different nations in slightly different ways, and through the influence on them of more particular principles, proper to each country, there may arise within the common world of culture various typical patterns and characters. There are other cross sections, too, not so much national as philosophical. There are, for instance, English, French, and German materialists, positivists, and idealists. Each of these three philosophical groups has some first principles in common, although influenced by different national principles they may result in different patterns with a spirit of their own.

Lastly, then, individual thought, submerged in a world of principles that act as the very roots from which it springs, emerges with its own personal configuration. Most men have no personal thought at all. They think as everybody seems to think and are moved to and fro, without apparent consistency according to the influences of propaganda and fashion. For that reason it is possible, for instance, that institutional democracy may coexist with a lack of real freedom. But there are always minority groups or persons who try to think for themselves, sparing no pains to establish their principles in accordance with experience and their own conscience or insight. Sometimes they exercise a deep though hidden influence on the course of history. Man is personal as far as in thought and action he preserves his irreducible individuality against the more superficial layers of his social being. This does not mean that he tries to be different but that he tries to be critical and to save his conscience, the personal viewpoint from which he judges all things. Although society spreads through him, he strongly resists the caprices of fashion. It is difficult to explain how one may remain a true child of his social world and at the same time preserve his personal originality. Every man has in his own soul the seeds of conscience and personality. It is possible to develop them faithfully although the fruits of such development are molded into the forms of a given social pattern. In a partly conscious, partly unconscious way the social influences are sifted, purified, personally assimilated, and adapted in the process of self-making. Originality is not otherness but selfness. A man may be of one mind with his own time without sharing its moods.

Of course, it is necessary to distinguish between true and spurious personality. To say of somebody that he is original or that he is quite a personality often means that he is rather odd or eccentric. There are men indeed who seem to live according to the principle of otherness. They shut themselves up in a world of imagination or willfully cultivated singularity. They are not in sympathy with their social surroundings. They do not seek any real contact with the ideas of their time. True personality, on the contrary, eagerly communicates with the social world that it recognizes as a part of its own being. The categories of openness and closeness are perhaps most apt to mark the distinction between true personality and mere singularity. There is an infinite distance between, on the one hand, the impoverishing separatedness of the eccentric individual who pursues some particular ends for himself without caring for the world about him and on the other hand the enriching participation of the independent personality in the whole of experience. The deeper one is rooted in his own self, the more he is able to learn from others and to build up his undimmed and unalienated personality with the materials of his social world.

Speaking of personal first principles, Newman concludes: 'They are, in short, the man.'[10] That is true both of individuals and of social units. The pattern of one's principles defines, as it were, one's personality as far as it is a unity of thinking existence. Now, so considered, man is the medium through which ideas develop into doctrines. Doctrines are the ultimate historical elaboration of ideas, and therefore they determine in the concrete the ideals for which humanity is striving. Since they express man's interpretation of human life in terms of value and duty, it is their proper function to direct the whole of existence toward valuable ends. Those ends are not only individual and spiritual. They are social and historic. It is the privilege and the responsibility of mankind to humanize the world, to create a human world out of the brute materials of nature. Therefore metaphysical and ethical doctrines are not enough. Man must penetrate the inmost structure of things as they are given to him, in order to learn to manage them and to use them efficiently for the realization of his ends. Doctrines and techniques are two factors of a single movement. Through the former man tries not to lose sight of valuable ends. The latter should teach him how to accomplish his human ideals in a world that is given to him and governed according to laws he did not make. Technical knowledge and skill are means through which ideals are converted into possibilities. There are and have been civilizations or stages and phases in a given civilization characterized by a firm grasp of noble ideals in spite of their poverty of technical means.

Man is currently living in a period of immense technical power, but his convictions about valuable ends and motivations are rather vague and uncertain. There is a real danger that he will be passively pushed along by the impetus of the forces he has unchained in the world. If he is unable to rule those energies by a clear sight and a firm will for valuable ends, man will blindly be ruled by his own creations; and there are reasons to believe that it will not be for his good. A sound condition of civilization, then, requires a balanced proportion of philosophic insight and scientific knowledge, of moral earnestness and technical skill.

DEVELOPMENT AND TRUTH

The main object in the foregoing section has been to achieve some clarity about the nature of doctrines, the mental mechanism of their development, and the part they play in the general movement of history. There are, however, further points that need elucidation. In the first place, then, doctrine is subjected to a specific norm that man calls truth. Although it is a function of life, human thought is from its very nature in quest of truth. This has to do with the nature of man himself. If to be man is a vocation, if man has to realize himself not according to fancy but according to his own truth, that is, an idea of human perfection that belongs to his being as much as or even more than his biological nature; and on the other hand, if to be man is essentially conditioned by his existence in a world or a universe of things and persons, so that to exist in a cosmic situation is an essential dimension of his being, it follows that the truth of man cannot be separated from the truth of the universe. One cannot know one's own truth save in the context of universal truth. The inquiry into the rule of one's own nature is an inquiry into the mystery of being. Therefore, to say that thought is a function of life is in no way to indulge in pragmatism or utilitarianism. Life itself, as far as it is human, can only be based on the rock of objective truth. For such a being as man real usefulness ultimately coincides with truth. The very concept of utility implies a relation. Something is useful insofar as it aids one to attain certain ends. If then it be true that the self-realization of man, the perfection of which is a state of happiness or blessedness for which all hearts are longing, is based upon the truth of his being and of Being in general, it follows that truth is the highest principle and the ultimate norm of genuine utility. Man has to live according to the claims and the necessities of reality. As far as he is morally bound to its claims, he is a philosopher: as far as he is subjected to its necessities, he becomes a scientist and a technician.

Ultimate truth, then, about the meaning of life and universal existence is the proper value that philosophy and theology are in search of. Its results are doctrines. All men possess a hint or vague idea of truth and value. Such awareness is constitutive of consciousness itself. The seeds of truth are secretly at work in prereflective thought. But the truth that possesses men's minds previous to reflection cannot be applied to life if it is not worked out for the intellect in the form of an articulated doctrine. Life is given to man, but he is called to take it in his own hands. Truth too, in a certain sense, is given to him. It possesses him independently of all efforts of thought. But he is called to express it in human language, to possess it in the very act of being possessed by it, so that he may apply it to life in an orderly and conscious way as becomes free beings that are responsible for their existence.

The same holds true, with due accommodations, in the case of Christian doctrine. Through faith one lives in the reality of divine self-revelation. The truth of the saving God, His self-disclosure, possesses one previous to theological reflection. This is the core of faith. Faith is an existential act or an existential situation in which one finds oneself through the grace of God. But in order to live by faith the consciousness of divine revelation, or its living idea in man, has to become articulated so that men possess in a human way the glorious truth that divinely possesses them. Doctrine is the human way in which ideas are incorporated into historical life.

THEOLOGY, DOGMA, AND TRADITION

In connection with Christian doctrine and its development a few further preliminary questions are to be answered. The first question is about the expression *development of doctrine*. There are two possible senses, closely connected but distinct. On the one hand, doctrine may mean theology. Indeed the proper mental activity by which the object of faith is converted into a coherent and systematic whole of sentences and proofs is theological reflection. It is true that historical influences of all kinds are at work in the living process of Christian thought: heresy, devotion, political circumstances and intrigues, the challenges of philosophy and science. History is a living whole. Development of thought, not unlike organic growth, is a process in which the working of each part influences that of all other parts. But theological reflection is the proper and formal activity by which, under whatever influences, the idea of Christian revelation is worked out in patterns of Christian doctrine. Any theological interpretation of the Christian message, any system of Christian truth may rightly be given the name of Christian doctrine, at least as far as it is recognized as really inspired by Christian revelation and generally faithful to its essential claims.

On the other hand, however, Christian doctrine may be understood in a more restricted sense. Then doctrine means dogma. Dogmas are such propositions about revealed truth as are generally accepted by the consensus of the Church or consecrated by a definition of its highest authority in matters of doctrine. By 'propositions' is meant the content of dogmatic statements. A proposition is what a statement means or the common meaning of equivalent statements. This corresponds to the generally accepted distinction between dogma and dogmatic formulas. A dogma may be stated in various formulas that express its meaning with different degrees of fullness or accuracy. It is important to see this point because it means that the irrevocability of dogma does not entail the immutability of dogmatic formulas. All dogmatic statements are open to correction or adjustment so that they may express more adequately what they mean. And since dogmatic truth, to which dogmatic propositions refer, is a divine mystery that passes all comprehension and remains hidden in the very act of its unveiling itself to faithful understanding, it is difficult to fix definite limits to a possible reconsideration of dogmatic language. This, as shall be seen, is a cardinal point in any theory of the development of dogma.

Christian doctrine, then, in its more restricted sense is limited to the official teaching of the Church. That official teaching is supposed to voice the teaching of the apostolic Church. As such it is *semper eadem* and handed down from generation to generation within the Church. Dogma viewed in its undisturbed historical continuity is a tradition, and development of dogma is a characteristic of living tradition. As it passes through the chain of generations, each with its own spirit, its own controversial situations, intellectual problems, and spiritual needs, the continuous reflection of the faithful is constantly remolding and recasting its understanding of the mystery of Salvation according to the changing human focus from which the object of divine faith is illuminated. This, at least, is the normal case. There may be epochs of stagnation in which the anxiety to conserve the letter prevails over the spirit that enlivens the letter, inviting men to obedient reconsideration of revealed truth and to rejuvenating accommodation of its linguistic vessels. Such epochs were never epochs of intense Christian life. Where the letter prevails, there is a tendency of faith to become entirely objectified and reduced to the acceptance of words without real communion with the truth they are intended to convey. Dogmatic formalism tends to become the grave of the spirit.

Tradition, then, is a process of living continuity. In its course new aspects of the reality in which faith is living come into sight. It is like a stream, always the same from its source to its mouth, but rising and widening through the influx of fresh waters as it runs through different landscapes. The comparison is valid as far as it suggests an accession of ideas from different sources. It breaks down, however, as far as it suggests the idea of a mixture. The image must be corrected by the image of assimilation. Fresh food and other influences from without do not lead to mere accretion. They are assimilated by the organism in order to build up the structures of life according to its own intrinsic pattern.

Is it not better, then, to speak of development of tradition instead of development of dogma or doctrine? Strictly speaking, development of tradition seems to be more adequate. According to a general law of semantics words that signify an action come to be used to signify its object or result. They have a subjective and an objective sense. In theology such terms as *creation, revelation, tradition,* and even *faith* originally signify the acts of creating, revealing, handing down, and believing, but they also may mean that which is created, revealed, handed down, and believed in. Tradition, then, in the objective sense is the same thing as dogma. That which is handed down is the deposit of faith expressed in dogma. The term *tradition,* however, has certain advantages. First, it is more apt to signify the sum total of dogmatic truth. According to ordinary use *objective tradition* more readily means the whole deposit of faith while *dogma* rather implies the idea of a particular truth. Objective tradition is a plurality of dogmas. Karl Barth makes a distinction between *Dogma* and *dogmas,* meaning by the former term the sum total of actual and possible dogmas in which the Word of God comes to man, while the plural form stands for the ecclesiastical propositions in which the believing community expresses its faithful perception of *Dogma.* But the technical distinction is unusual. *Objective tradition,* on the contrary, means in common language the whole deposit of faith as far as it is handed down from generation to generation. It has the advantage of signifying dogmatic truth in its unity and entirety not only including actual dogmas but all possible dogmas that may emerge from the consciousness of faith in the course of historical reflection.

Objective tradition, then, has exactly the same meaning as Dogma has in the terminology of Barth. Moreover, while Dogma suggests the idea of a static proposition, tradition taken in its objective sense connotes the more dynamic idea of handing down, from which it is derived. By reason of this shade of meaning it is more apt to be combined with the idea of development. *Development* aptly qualifies the notion of tradition, suggesting that tradition is a living process and not merely a passing on of inert objects. One may conclude, then, that the vague traditional expression *development of doctrine* may be narrowed down to its true meaning by the expression *development of dogma* and then restored to its full meaning by the expression *development of tradition.*

The relation between the development of doctrine in the more restricted sense of dogma and the development of doctrine in the wider sense of theology is at once clear from what has been said up to now. Theology, according to the dictum of St. Anselm already quoted, is *fides quaerens intellectum*, faith that seeks understanding. As far as he is a theologian, the Christian thinker tries to understand his attitude of faith and the object thereof. Theology is ruled by faith. Divine revelation as expressed for the human mind in the form of a tradition, constantly nourished from within through meditation or reflection and guided from without through ecclesiastical authority, is the proper rule of theological truth. But within the limits of dogmatic tradition, theology is from its very nature the exercise of free thought. It is the proper duty of the theologian to formulate and to face honestly the problems that constantly arise from the encounter of faith and reason, or established dogma and the discoveries of science, or the products of man's restless intelligence. Theology is the living link between Christian tradition ruled by authority and autonomous human thought trying to understand and to order by its own means the continuous stream of new experiences and thoughts. Therefore it partakes of the nature of both: as far as it is an exercise of faith, it is ruled by authority; as far as it seeks understanding, it is characterized by free questioning, investigation, and systematization. In spite of its being bound to tradition trying to know the past by means of the methods of historical research and criticism, theology never ceases to be creative. However much it may depend on the history of the past, its true nature is not historical but systematic. It always tries to fit the expression of faith into the patterns of contemporary thought, and to influence in return the products and movement of the modern mind. Its attitude toward contemporary thought is at once assimilative and critical. It is always in the process of creating, retouching, and correcting a system of thought in which the equilibrium between revelation and the modern mind is maintained and constantly restored through an interchange that is at once a dialogue and a conflict. Theology, then, guides the progressive movement of Christian belief within the Church. It is the instrument by which faith is continuously incarnated and reincarnated in human culture, assuming and purifying its earthly historical body.

It follows, then, that the theologians' study is the intellectual work house in which the development of doctrine is ultimately achieved. It is true that all the factors that determine the course of history may influence the historical development of dogma. But the proper medium of doctrinal growth is the living, creative activity of theological thought. Theology incessantly copes with the new problems, discusses them, clarifies them; and some of its fruits are gradually recognized by the Church as true developments of its divine deposit.

The Idea of Development in Patristic and Medieval Thought

Introduction to Part Two

Preparatory to a critical synthesis of the contemporary views on the present problem, the following pages will give a brief account of its history. The idea that revelation is itself a history, a gradual unveiling of God in His work of salvation, seems to be an essential part of the self-understanding of Christianity. The idea that the understanding of the revealed deposit itself will in its turn take the form of a gradual unfolding of its riches in the mind of the Church seems to be a natural extension of the Christian consciousness of historicity. As will be seen, the fundamental law underlying the two processes of development is the same and the acceptance of progress in the dispensation of the Word of God prepares the mind to expect a similar progress in its understanding of that Word, entrusted to the Church. Such progress is not merely subjective in the sense of a deeper insight or penetration into the mystery of God. From its very nature such a subjective progress is individual. A saint of the 2d century may enjoy a deeper real apprehension of revealed truth than the greatest theologian of our own time. To be sure, 'realizing is the very life of true developments.'[1] 'Developments [arise] out of a keen and vivid realizing of the Divine Depositum of Faith' (*Apologia*, p. 209). But the inner life of faith and devotion, the contemplation of the revealed mysteries, combined with man's natural tendency to express in words what he apprehends in experience, gradually leads to a notional adjustment and expansion of revealed truth in his common understanding. Real apprehension is incommunicable. It is transhistorical. Only notional expressions can be imparted, handed down, and shared by a community. Developments as such, then, take place on the level of notional expression. Their acquisition becomes part of objective culture, and as such they enter into the public scene of history. From the nature of the case, historical development cannot but be objective. It belongs to the domain of objective truth. It is ambiguous, then, to say that objective revelation is closed with the end of the apostolic generation and that since then there is only a progress in subjective understanding. Although nothing new is added to the deposit of faith since the closing of apostolic times, it may be said that the living process of revelation goes on till the end of time. God has completed His self-communication in Christ. But revelation is not only something that proceeds from God. It has to be received in the human mind. The process through which the mind of the Church is penetrated by the Word of God, leading to a progressive under-standing of all its implications, can go on as long as history lasts. This will be explained further on.

The idea of a development of doctrine, prolonging the develop-ment of revelation, may be presumed to be a natural idea that was never absent from Christian consciousness. It is itself a first princ-ciple, as Newman says. It is supposed; it is taken for granted. As is often the case with first principles, they are at work from the begin-ning, leading the progress of thought; but it is only after a time that they emerge into consciousness and become themselves objects of reflection. 'It might be expected that the Catholic principles would be later in development than the Catholic doctrines, inasmuch as they lie deeper in the mind, and are assumptions rather than objective professions' (*Development*, p. 179). It may be expected that all through the history of Christian thought one will find utterances that betray the self-evident assumption that the *semper eadem* does not exclude true development. From the beginning the idea of development was present in the Christian mind. The possibility and the fact of development were generally taken for granted. But as long as there was no difficulty about it, the idea was not carefully examined or analyzed. In recent times, however, the problem arose of how to reconcile the historical facts of development with the claim of substantial immutability. Hence the quest for a theory to explain the facts and to prove the assumption on which the justification of Christian history is based.

The history of the problem will be dealt with in the following order: first, an examination of the nature and the principles of the economy of revelation itself; next, a search for the presence of the idea of doctrinal development in the mind of the Church; and last, a study of the rise of the problem, its causes, and the various theories devised for its solution.

CHAPTER THREE

Development of Revelation

It is part of the self-understanding of the primitive Church that the coming of Christ, His Passion and death, His Resurrection and glorification, His eschatological promises, all happened according to the Scriptures. It is evident from the Gospel that Christ Himself applied to His person and His mission the main ideas of the OT about the Messiah, the suffering Servant, the Son of Man, the kingdom of God. St. Luke's story of the two disciples on the road to Emmaus clearly reflects the conviction of the early Church that everything that happened to Christ, together with its salvific meaning and power, was written about Him 'in the law of Moses and the Prophets and the psalms' (Lk 24.44). The very way in which the relationship of Christ and the nascent Church to the history and the scriptures of Israel was viewed supposed the idea of a development in the economy of revelation. Unlike Mohammed who conceived his message as a simple return to the doctrine of Abraham, to be purified from the corruptions introduced by both Jews and Christians in spite of the warnings of the Prophets and of Jesus Himself, Christ and the Apostles did not see the gospel-message as a return to the purity of the Abrahamic conception of God but as a fulfillment of the promises given by God to Abraham and as the final completion of an ideal relationship between God and man of which the covenant of Sinai had been a beginning and a prefiguration.

CHRISTIAN SELF-UNDERSTANDING

It is only by the end of the 2d century that the idea of a Christian canon of Scripture added to that of the Jews came to be fully recognized. When Clement of Rome or Justin speak of the

49

Scriptures they always mean the books of the OT. The early controversy between Christians and Jews was entirely centered round
the 'Christic' meaning of the holy books of Israel. As Justin writes
in his *Dialogue with Trypho*: 'The Scriptures are much more ours
than yours. For we let ourselves be persuaded by them while you
read them without grasping their true import' (*Dialogue* 29). And
in a fragment of the apocryphal *Preaching of Peter* quoted by
Clement of Alexandria one reads: 'But we, unrolling the books
of the prophets which we possess, who name Jesus Christ, partly
in parables, partly in enigmas, partly expressly and in so many words,
find His coming and death, and cross, and all the rest of the tortures
which the Jews inflicted on Him, and His resurrection and
assumption . . . For we know that God enjoined these things and
we say nothing apart from the scriptures' (Clem. *Strom.* 6.15).

It is clear then that from the beginning the sacred history of
Israel and its literature were considered by the Christians as directed
toward Christ and accomplished by Him. Christ was the final
revelation of God and of His concern with man, prepared in the
history of Israel and the inspired words of the Prophets. Consequently, the greatest scandal in the ancient Church was the teaching
of Marcion and other gnostics who refused to accept the OT as a
Christian book, either wholly as Marcion himself or partially as
in the case of other gnostics. The God of love, who revealed Himself in Christ, could not be the same God whose image was imparted
to man through the cruelties of ancient Hebrew history. The OT
then was a work of the Demiurge, not of the Father in Heaven.
Hence the defense of the continuity of the two testaments became
closely connected with the defense of the unity of God. The great
Christian battle of the 2d century centered around the position
of the OT in the world of Christian belief.

The solution of the Christian writers was not uniform on all
points. Not all of them fully recognized the character of development in the history of revelation. Those, for instance, who like
Barnabas, following the exegetical method of Philo, took the easy
way of conceiving the relation of the OT Scriptures to the
Christian events as merely allegorical, did not care much for history.
The OT *en bloc* was a collection of allegories and had to be understood as such. All allegories are equally good. The only thing that
matters is their interpretation. One can read the deepest truth in
the grossest of allegories. There may be a development and refine-

ment in the spiritual interpretation of allegories, but the succession of the allegorical figures themselves can hardly be conceived as a process of development. It can only be viewed as an enrichment after the manner of material accumulation.

THE CHRISTIAN PHILOSOPHERS

In the school of Alexandria the idea of a development or a history of revelation does not come to the fore. It is not altogether absent, but it has no real importance. All over the world the deepest mysteries of Christianity could be known not only by the Prophets but also by philosophers if they were illuminated by the eternal Word. According to Clement of Alexandria, truth is everywhere, because the same Christ who dwelt and suffered among us was always active as the hidden Word in whom all things had been created and all minds are illuminated. The truth of that diffuse revelation is often obscured and distorted by those who live by the flesh. Christ is the rule according to which all human wisdom is to be judged. Faith is the starting point of *gnosis* or spiritual knowledge in which all the seeds of truth spread through the world are taken up in Christ, harmonized in Him, and integrated. The Son is at the origin of all human knowledge and science. He has spoken in successive revelations of which the Mosaic is the most important before Christ. He descended to earth in order to reveal the meaning of the OT, to unite all human knowledge and all peoples, to give men the possibility of seeing God, and to save them.[1] Christ is not so much the all-illuminating end of a progressive revelation that beginning with Abraham is gradually clarified in the prophetic history of Israel. In the state of His Incarnation He should be conceived rather as a visible focus at which all rays meet after they have invisibly proceeded from Him in all the parts of the world. True, the OT writings have a privileged position: 'Faith in Christ and knowledge [*gnosis*] of the Gospel are the explanation and fulfillment of the law' (Clem. *Strom.* 4.21). The Greek philosophers did attain to a pure though still negative conception of God only by leaning upon the 'barbaric philosophy' of the Bible. Still, the Bible is only a more condensed beam of the true light that enlightens every man.

The thought of Clement is not wholly consistent. As a Christian he cannot ignore Christ as a central historical event that casts its light upon the past and the future. 'And if, too, the end of the wise

man is contemplation, that of those who are still philosophers aims
at it, but never attains it, unless by the process of learning it receives
the prophetic utterance which has been made known, by which it
grasps both the present, the future, and the past—how they are,
were and shall be' (*Strom.* 6.7). But Clement is so intent on the
attainment and the spreading of gnosis which, although starting
with faith and grounded in faith, tends toward a timeless knowledge
of God beyond images and concepts, that his real interest does not
lie with the historical aspect of salvation-economy.

ST. IRENAEUS

Alongside the free hellenizing thought of Justin and Clement
there is another trend that faithfully prolongs the Hebraic way of
thinking, although in open dialogue with Greek philosophy. The
leading representative of that theological movement is Irenaeus, the
first great champion of Orthodoxy and the royal gate of patristic
theology. The idea of a development of revelation is central to his
theological view. This is his organic view of the one economy of
salvation, beginning with creation, gradually going up toward
Christ in whom God's intention is perfectly realized, and then expanding in Him through His body the Church toward a final consummation.

According to the most basic principle of Irenaeus, the divinization of man in Christ is the very object of creation. In Adam or the
creation of mankind Christ, who is the divinization of mankind,
is already at work. History as a whole is a process in which the
divine intention, implicit already in the first stage of creation, is
gradually unfolded and perfected. Absolutely speaking, God could
have created man in a state of final perfection. The idea of divinized
man is the only true idea of man. But such a creation did not suit
man's creaturely condition. By creaturely condition Irenaeus
means something that begins to exist, that does not have existence
by itself. Concretely he has in view man who unites in his being
earth and heaven, being made out of earth but enlivened by the
breath of God.

Irenaeus' doctrine of man is thoroughly Biblical. There is no
trace of Greek dualism in his thought. Man is not a spirit held
captive in the flesh and longing for liberation. He is a being of the
earth, animated by the Spirit of God. It is natural that a being of

this kind grows from infancy to manhood. Irenaeus projects upon mankind as a whole the idea of growth experienced in all earthly life. Moreover, man is free and if he is to be divinized by being united to God Himself in the incarnated Logos, he has previously to be tried and to choose God freely before being confirmed in the possession of eternal life. Before becoming a 'god' in God he has to experience to the full his creaturely condition, his freedom, his weakness, his need of God.

Hence the idea of a divine economy of salvation that is to be conceived at the same time as a *paideia* or corrective education of mankind through different stages and phases. God gives Himself and reveals Himself gradually according to the receptivity of man. The difficulty is not on the part of God but on the part of man: 'For the Uncreated is perfect and is God. But it was morally necessary that man should, in the first place, be created, and having been created should grow, and having grown, should reach man's estate, and having done so should receive strength, and having got strength should be glorified, and having been glorified should see his master. For it is God who is to be seen. Now the vision of God confers immortality, but immortality makes one near to God' (*Adv.haer.* 4.38.3). Therefore the historical economy was a gradual education:

> Thus it was, too, that God formed man at the first, because of His munificence; but chose the patriarchs for the sake of their salvation; and prepared a people beforehand, teaching the headstrong to follow God and raised up prophets upon earth accustoming man to bear His Spirit [within him], and to hold communion with God: He Himself indeed, having need of nothing, but granting communion with Himself to those who stood in need of it, and sketching out, like an architect, the plan of salvation to those that pleased to Him. And He did Himself furnish guidance to those who beheld Him not in Egypt, while to those who became unruly in the desert he promulgated a law very suitable [to their condition]. Then, on the people who entered into the good land He bestowed a noble inheritance. . . . Thus, in a variety of ways, He adjusted the human race to an agreement with salvation. [*Adv. haer.* 4.14.2]

The general setting of Irenaeus' idea of a gradual self-communication of God to man is, as was remarked above, the doctrine of recapitu-

c

lation. It is not easy to explain because of its organic unity and richness. Three aspects may be distinguished, and a right understanding of the doctrine is only possible by viewing these aspects in their unity. The first aspect is that of a summing up or recapitulating. The whole history of salvation together with its end is already present in its starting point, in Adam, but at the same time Adam himself together with the whole of creation and human history is conserved and summarized in Christ the consummation. The whole is present and at work in the initial as well as in the final stage.

The second aspect is that of repetition. God tried first to achieve His plan with Adam. The disobedience of Adam, however, was the cause of its failure. Time and again, in different ages and with different means God renewed His attempt with man. Time and again it came to nothing. At last He realized the Adam-project in the most perfect way by the Incarnation of His eternal Son who is God visible among men, a self-gift of God fully adapted to the condition of man. The divine plan could only be realized through the Incarnation:

> For it was incumbent upon the Mediator between God and men, by his relationship to both, to bring both to friendship and concord, and present man to God, while he revealed God to men. For, in what way could we be partakers of the adoption of sons, unless we had received from Him through the Son that fellowship which refers to Himself, unless His Word, having been made flesh, had entered into communion with us. [*Adv. haer.* 3.18.7]

The proof is given in the history of sinful mankind.

The third aspect is that of addition. It is closely connected with the foregoing. The repetition is no mere repetition. The first attempt was in itself unfinished. The later attempts were corrected. There is a kind of progress, of 'emergent evolution' through the creative and salvific power of God. At long last God produces Christ. Christ is not only a more effective method. He is also a more perfect gift. More is given in Him than was given on former occasions. That which in Him is summarized and repeated is at the same time heightened and transformed in Him.

That salvation and revelation are historic events subject to a gradual process of development has never been stated more forcefully in patristic literature than in the work of Irenaeus. He not only admits the idea; it is the head and front of his Christian view of things. Moreover, he bases his idea on a view of man. From the very nature of man it is to be expected that God will reveal and communicate Himself according to the growing receptivity of man, which is itself a work of divine education. The nature of man and his essential historicity: such too will be the leading principles of Newman's general theory of the development of doctrine.

TERTULLIAN

A contemporary of Irenaeus is the great African theologian Tertullian. Unlike Clement, who stresses the unity and harmony of Greek and Biblical thought, he is rather convinced that they have nothing in common. He too, however, clearly sees revelation as a gradual unveiling of the will and the intention of God. In *Adversus Judaeos* 2 he states that in the primitive law given to Adam and Eve, the law of Moses that would develop from it in due time was already present in embryo. He compares the growth of salvation (justice) in mankind to the natural growth of fruits (*De virginibus velandis* 1).

In the same way he compares the opposition between the Gospel and the Law to the opposition between the seed and its fruit: 'But still we make this concession that there is a separation, by reformation, by amplification, by progress; just as the fruit is separated from the seed, although the fruit comes from the seed. So likewise the gospel is separated from the law whilst it advances from the law' (*Adversus Marcionem* 4.11). The image of natural growth will return in the writings of Möhler, Newman, and others. As the texts already suggest and as will be seen further on, Tertullian applies the same views to post-apostolic development of doctrine, but in a special way connected with his inclination toward Montanism.

ORIGEN

Irenaeus, Tertullian, and Clement are contemporaries. They are the main sources of three different trends in Christian theology, characterized by the Greek philosophical (Clement), the Roman legalistic (Tertullian), and the Hebraic organic (Irenaeus) turns of mind. Those strains of theology will not develop independently but will influence and correct one another, producing various types of patristic theology. Origen is to be situated at the confluence of the Christian gnosis of Clement and the Biblical theology of Irenaeus. 'He has to solve, if possible, the most formidable problem of Christian theology—how to make room for the Jewish philosophy of history by the side of the Platonic philosophy of eternal life.'[2] He unites the points of view of exterior historical development and interior spiritual growth. On the one side, there is a gradual 'dispensation of the glory' (knowledge of God), adapted to the measure of human capacity for receiving it. There are different sources of divine knowledge and different stages. They complete one another. God teaches all men through their inner conscience and through the outer testimony of His works. This knowledge is perfected by His Word who communicates the 'elements' (*stoicheia*) of revelation in human language, first in the law, next in the Gospel. However, because human language is inadequate for transmitting the divine mysteries, both are still imperfect. They have only the value of introductions (*eisagōgē*). The dispensation of the Gospel is itself progressive. The divine pedagogy does not come to an end with the Incarnation: the work of Christ extends itself from a beginning (His first coming) to an end (His second coming). Between His beginning (*archē*) and His end (*telos*) there is a constant development under the guidance of the Spirit: 'Revelation proceeds through successive stages: the natural law is a preparation for revelation; in the course of revelation the Old Law prepares for the New; within the New Law the Gospel, preached by Jesus, is a preparation for the final Gospel, the Gospel of His second advent, which otherwise is already prefigured in and begun with the first.'

To the Biblical idea of different stages in the history of revelation Origen joins the Greek conception of different degrees of understanding in the personal development of the individual mind. Together with an historical pedagogy for mankind, adapted to its capacity, there is an interior pedagogy appropriated to each heart. Historical development, conveyed in words, signs, and events, remains at the level of aids (*ōpheleiai*) to divine knowledge. These aids are always inadequate. But through the seeing of the events, the hearing of the words, the representation of the symbols, the mind penetrates the mysteries of divine reality. This personal and existential growth is beyond history. It introduces the mind into the timeless world. In this respect being in time does not involve a privileged status. At every point of the horizontal development of the perceptible aids, the eager, well-disposed spirit may penetrate through the manifold letter to the one spiritual meaning, if aided interiorly by the Spirit of God. The measure of depth does not depend on the clarity of the surface. The penetration of the spirit does not correspond to the perfection of the aids. However imperfect the point may be from where the spirit starts its flight, it is able to attain to the highest regions of heaven.

The movement from image and language to mystery, from the visible and audible to the invisible and the unspeakable, from appearance to reality, is, as de Lubac rightly pointed out, the true meaning of the spiritual sense of the Scriptures. The spiritual or mystical sense does not consist in the allegorical interpretation of texts or events, although allegorical interpretations may point one toward it, but consists in the mystery of divine reality, unveiling itself to man through the deficient media of the letter and the related facts. All theological or exegetical interpretation remains on the level of mental representation. It may help man to see the way he has to go; however, he cannot go that way by the verbal activity of intellectual understanding but only by the wordless penetration of spiritual understanding. Commenting on a passage in which Origen says that the Prophets themselves, conducted by the Spirit, passed from the typological introduction to the vision of truth, M. Harl remarks: 'The formula is very strong: the typological introduction is not limited to a definite epoch, the epoch before Christ; nor is the vision of truth reserved for the time of Christ. The progressive order of revelation, going from typology to the vision of truth, is repeated in each individual according to the work of the Spirit in him.'[4] The 'saints' of the OT did attain to the same knowledge as the Apostles. Moses, Isaiah, and Ezekiel did explicitly know the mysteries they announced in typological form.

Of course, the position of those who lived before Christ and that of those who were the witnesses of His coming is not altogether the same. Origen, however, is rather vague and hesitant in explaining the difference. His intuition is open to interpretation. The object of faith is not only the eternal and the invisible. This is its ultimate object. Faith is no less essentially about an historical economy of salvation. Origen distinguishes between the purely intellectual comprehension of the future mystery and the vision of its actual accomplishment in Christ. Sometimes he says that the latter is not of a higher quality than the former. On other occasions, however, he explicitly states that the appearance of Christ was a privileged moment bringing with it the revelation of privileged teachings. Christ did give His Spirit who, through Him, is now working in mankind more deeply and more universally. But this is not satisfying. It does not introduce a qualitative difference between the epoch before Christ and the time of His coming.

There is something that points toward a more satisfactory solution. Origen's thought is markedly eschatological. The ultimate revelation of God through Christ is not so much the Incarnation in the form of the Servant. To be sure, in the Christ of history the ultimate revelation is already present, but in a hidden way. By the time of His second advent, on the contrary, His Godhead, the ultimate goal of our spiritual pilgrimage, will shine undimmed through His glorious and spiritual body. Mankind will really see God in Him. The contemplation of the highest mystery will be one with the perception of His visible form. The invisible will be transparent in the visible in a way adapted to the double nature of man. In its final stage, then, the historical plane of bodily representation rejoins the timeless plane of spiritual contemplation, and in the union of both—in the mutual presence of the one in the other—creation will be consummated in perfect knowledge and blessedness. Here Greek duality is overcome by the unitary conception of the Bible. Now, the unity of the final consummation is already anticipated, although imperfectly, in faith that sees God in Christ. The humanity of Christ is the sacrament of the saving God. To the perfect union of the timeless end corresponds the sacramental unity of sign and reality in the economy of salvation through Christ.

What was said just now is not so explicit in Origen. He never could free himself from the general scheme of Platonism, as can clearly be seen from his doctrine of the universal restoration of all things and the infinite succession of world-cycles. His thought has here been extended in a direction suggested by some of his remarks, not easily reconcilable with other utterings of his restless, mercurial genius. It is, however, of paramount importance. Origen's problem of how to reconcile the historic development of revelation with the personal and transhistorical character of true knowledge is at the core of the problem of development. What does the relation between expanding doctrine and realizing faith consist in? The Christians of the 2d century could have as perfect a faith as those of contemporary generations, although the notional fabric of doctrine was not so explicit or articulated. There is a dimension in the life of faith in which there is a possibility of personal progress, independent of changing historical situations. Newman will solve the problem of their interrelation in a more consistent and satisfactory way. There is, however, an undeniable continuity. The endeavors of Origen to bring together the horizontal development of objective faith and its vertical movement towards real knowledge, certainly belong to those portions of his teaching of which Newman says that they 'came like music to my inner ear' (*Apologia*, p. 26). In Newman's doctrine of the relation between notional and real apprehension there are certainly reminiscences of Origen's intellectual struggles.

LATER THEOLOGY

It would be tedious to follow the further history of a doctrine that in its general lines became classical. It can be summarized in a famous dictum of St. Augustine: 'In the Old Testament the New is concealed, in the New, the Old is revealed' (*Quaest. hept.* 2.73), and in the *auctoritas* of Gregory the Great: 'According to the progress of history, the knowledge of the spiritual fathers increased. Moses was better instructed in the knowledge of Almighty God than Abraham, and the prophets knew more than Moses and the Apostles more than the prophets. . . . For the nearer the world approaches to its end, the wider the entrance to eternal knowledge becomes for us' (*Homiliarum in Ezechielem* 2.4). Gregory makes a distinction between the spiritual Fathers and the multitude of the Jewish people. The Fathers somehow knew the mysteries of the Trinity and the Incarnation, but they did not communicate this knowledge because, owing to their rudeness, the many were still incapable of understanding. The knowledge of the Apostles was superior to that of the Prophets because the Apostles saw in the flesh what the Prophets could only see in the spirit. The general influence of Origen is clear enough.

In the Middle Ages the problem was amply considered by Hugh of St. Victor in three chapters of his *De sacramentis* (1.10.6–8). He argues against those who hold that the goodness of God cannot be reconciled with the idea that earlier generations did not enjoy the same knowledge of salvation as the later ones. He draws a distinction between the minimum necessary for salvation, in which minimum all later doctrines are implicitly contained (faith in God, Creator, Lord and Ruler of all things, from whom sinners may expect salvation if they repent of their sins) and the dogmas in which the mystery of God and the economy of salvation are explicitly stated. He concludes:

> Creator in respect of nature and Redeemer in respect of Grace. These two comprehend the whole and the one; that in which the faith of all believers was one from the beginning, although with respect to the same faith some did enjoy a more perfect knowledge than others according to the diversity of the times, just as in one and the same time we find in some people a greater knowledge of faith and in others a lesser one according to their personal capacity. Although, then, faith did increase in such a way that sometimes and in some people it was more extensive, nevertheless it did not change in such a way that it became different. [1.10.8]

In ST 2a2ae, 1.8 Thomas Aquinas comments upon the *auctoritas* of Gregory the Great, as found in Hugh of St. Victor. The first principles of Christian doctrine, he writes, are the articles of faith. But one article may be implicit in another, as for instance, the Incarnation, Passion, and other articles are implicit in the belief that God is the Redeemer of mankind. There is no addition, then, with regard to the substance of the articles because what was believed by the later Fathers was contained implicitly in the faith of the early Fathers. As an object becomes more distinct the nearer one draws to it, so the economy of salvation in Christ becomes more distinct as the time of His advent approaches (ad 1). In the teacher, God, there is no increase of knowledge, but the disciple is gradually instructed by Him up to the measure of his capacity (ad 2). An agent who does something in a given matter gradually proceeds from an imperfect to a more perfect effect. Moreover, the general condition of man is more perfect as he approaches maturity (ad 3 et 4).

St. Bonaventure, too, in three luminous articles, explains how faith has increased in the course of history: (1) by objective multiplication of the articles, so that the new articles are not true additions but rather explications of more indeterminate expressions of faith; (2) by fuller illumination, at least in humanity as a whole, not because of the historical changes as such but because of a clearer manifestation of truth, a wider diffusion of grace, and a fuller instruction, caused by the appearance of Christ and the work of the Holy Spirit among us; (3) by firmer assent and certitude on the part of the receiver, because in later ages there was a clearer knowledge and greater devotion (*In 3 sent*. 25.2. 1, 2, and 3; *Opera* 3).

CHAPTER FOUR

Development of Doctrine
in Patristic Theology

It is important to note from the beginning that the same general principles by which Irenaeus and Origen, Tertullian and Gregory the Great, Hugh of St. Victor and Thomas Aquinas justify a development in revelation may be invoked as well to anticipate that between the first and the second coming of Christ too there may be a development of doctrine. Origen explicitly states that although Christ is the fullness of revelation the real fullness is not found in His humble Incarnation but is awaited in His glorious manifestation. The period between the two advents is the reign of the Spirit, who is the main gift of the glorified Lord to His Church. It is the Spirit, then, who guides the Church toward the final stage of divine revelation.

ANTECEDENT PROBABILITY

The notion of revelation in early Christian writers is, of course, not altogether the same as that of the later schoolmen. In both the Old and the New Testaments the idea of revelation is a living comprehensive view of God's dealing with man insofar as it is a gradual manifestation of His hidden nature and of the mystery of His saving condescension. It is a continuous process, the end of which is eschatological.

According to the OT the majesty of the heavenly Lord is by itself absolutely transcendent. His holiness separates Him from all created beings. He is unknowable except as far as He communicates Himself, revealing to the created intellect the secret of His eternal Being and His will. From the beginning the revelation of Yahweh's personal mystery is the real object of his self-communication. Revelation is divine self-communication in the literal sense of the word: a self-gift of the merciful Lord to His people inviting it to reciprocate with a similar gift of self, uniting both in a covenant of love and a fellowship of life. 'Revelation is not the impartation of supernatural knowledge or the excitement of numinous feelings. Knowledge can certainly come through revelation, and the revelation of God will be accompanied by numinous feelings. But revelation is not to be identified with these. In the proper sense it is the action of Yahweh. It is the removal of His essential concealment, His self-offering for fellowship.'[1] Revelation, then, may involve moments of divine instruction but is essentially an event, an action of divine self-offering for fellowship, and as such it does not begin at a given moment of history nor does it come to a stop in the course of time. Its consummation is the eschatological community in which revelation will attain to its final fullness:

Here we find in Revelation a unity and continuity making use of a multiplicity of means, understanding them as God's free disposing of the powers of the phenomenal world. Creation too is not a special independent realm of revelation. It is taken up in the series of deeds through which the Lord of history establishes His dominion. The witness of creation is not an object of natural science but of history and, being inserted in the process of historical consummation, its nature is eschatological.[2]

Revelation, then, is the whole work of creation, conceived of as one single process of divine self-communication to be consummated in the eschatological future.

In the N.T., too, revelation denotes, not the impartation of knowledge, but the actual unveiling of intrinsically hidden facts . . . It is the turning of the holy and gracious God to men who are lost in sin and death. This is prepared in the salvation history of the O.T. and actualized in the Incarnation, crucifixion and resurrection of Jesus Christ. It now awaits its consummation at the *parousia*. By derivation, however, revelation is also the

message which transmits this content. . . . In brief, revelation
in the N.T. is the self-offering of the Father of Jesus Christ for
fellowship.[3]

In the same sense one reads in the EncDictBibl:

> According to Paul, then, revelation has a predominantly active
> meaning with stress on the agent, rather than a passive meaning
> with stress on the object, the latter being the complex of the
> revealed truths themselves; it is not 'closed' and does not belong
> to the past, but is rather God's eschatological activity; more
> of a creative intervention of God in the work of salvation, than
> a mere communication of knowledge to man's intellect.
> Naturally, in the Pauline concept, revelation also includes an
> imparting and enriching of spiritual knowledge, but with Paul
> the concept of revelation does not have the strongly intellectu-
> alistic connotation which it largely received in scholastic the-
> ology. [EncDictBibl 2041–2042]

It is important to note that according to the Bible revelation is
one single process of divine self-manifestation and self-offering,
beginning with the *fiat lux* of creation and ending in the heavenly
city that has no need of sun or moon 'because the glory of God is
its light, and its lamp is the Lamb' (Rev 21.24). In that process there
are moments of divine teaching. But it does not come to a stop when
God through Christ and apostolic inspiration completes His public
teaching on earth, giving to His Church a deposit of faith, the
objective content of which does not admit of any further additions.
Salvation being an action in history is by its very nature, and consequently by the will of its divine originator, a dynamic reality.
There is no history without novelty. The history of the universal
Church is no less salvation-history than that of the Chosen People.
One may expect, then, that between the coming in the world of
'the true light that enlightens every man' (Jn 1.9) and its full manifestation in the city of heaven there will be a growth of light too,
although it be different from that which took place between
creation when the Word in whom was life began to be 'the light of
men' (Jn 1.4) and the time when the Word came into the world,
shining through the form of the Servant. What is called 'objective
revelation' may come to an end with the apostolic generation, but
the light of Christ in the bosom of the Church leads the bride from

light to light until his final advent. The content of the 'idea' of God, impressed on the mind of the Church through the light of illuminating grace, is not exhausted by the human, culture-bound expression of the evangelical message. Meditation and reflection upon its inner mystery through the medium of its human expression may give to the Church a progressive 'objective understanding' of the deposit, and such a progress may normally be expected. Having thus argued that the same reasons by which the actual development of revelation in the course of its dispensation is justified naturally must lead to the presumption that in the course of its preservation there will be a growth of its objective understanding in the Church, one must verify the presumption by looking at the facts. From the beginning there was in ancient Christianity a vivid consciousness of the development of salvation-economy. Is there any evidence that the Fathers were conscious too of a development in the ecclesiastical understanding of the doctrine of Christ?

First consider the general situation. Christianity presented itself as the true continuation of Israel (the Israel of God), as the fulfillment of the promises given to Abraham and his posterity, as the consummation in Christ of the self-offering of God. Therefore it is easily understood that in the primitive Church consciousness of the evolutive character of the divine dispensation and revelation was particularly vivid. In relation to the past, then, the position of Christianity was clear enough. In relation to the future, however, the situation was altogether different. For the first Christian generation had an intense feeling that the fullness of time in which they lived was the daybreak of the eschatological consummation of history. With Christ, the kingdom of Heaven had come to earth. It was already transforming the world. With the Resurrection, Ascension, and glorification the movement of earth toward heaven was already taking place. The early Christians did not think of a distant future in history. They felt rather that the second advent of Christ was imminent. In such a situation it was improbable that the question of ulterior development should be asked.

Moreover, problems about facts generally do not arise *ante factum*. Development of doctrine could not present itself to the Christian mind as a problem as long as time had not created a sufficient distance from the epoch of the beginnings and nothing had happened that could invite a reflection. It is a reasonable presumption, then, that the idea of a post-apostolic development of doctrine did not emerge into consciousness except after a sufficient lapse of time and under the stress of relevant circumstances. Even if Christians were entirely disposed to accept such an idea once it was pressed upon their minds, they could hardly form the idea as long as it was not brought home to them by facts. The fact, then, that the primitive Church laid the whole stress on the finality of Christian revelation is no argument that it was not disposed to accept a development in the objective understanding of the Gospel. Suppose now that after a time historical facts forced them to face in some shape or form the question of development, could they find in their mind positive reasons to accept the idea? Of course, one must take account of the presence in Christian consciousness of the general idea of historicity and progressiveness in the dispensation of divine mercy and knowledge. As has been argued here already, this was one of the characteristic features of the Christian spirit. If history showed it to continue for centuries, why should all further progress be excluded? This is a powerful motive, but it is rather subjective, general, and hidden in the mind as a first principle. The question, then, is whether Christians, facing an actual course of development, could have recourse to objective reasons to justify it: reasons taken from their sacred Scriptures.

There are indeed some hints in the apostolic writings that could readily suggest to Christian thought the idea of a further progress in the ecclesiastical understanding of revealed truth.

BIBLICAL FOUNDATIONS

To begin with St. Paul, it is evident that the nature and growth of faith were objects of his constant preoccupation and reflection. Faith introduces man to the knowledge of God. In order to give the assent of faith and to obtain the knowledge of God, the hearing of the word is a necessary condition: 'Faith comes from what is heard, and what is heard comes by the preaching of Christ' (Rom 10.17).

But to hear is not enough. In order to attain to the knowledge of God, the Father of glory Himself must give 'a spirit of wisdom and of revelation in the knowledge of him, having the eyes of your hearts enlightened' (Eph 1.17–18). It is God Himself 'who has shone in our hearts to give the light of the knowledge of the glory of God in the face of Christ' (2 Cor 4.6). But the light does not shine in those who are ill disposed. 'Hardness of heart' leads to 'darkness of mind' (Eph 4.18).

The principle of interior illumination is the gift of the Spirit. It is necessary. For 'no one can say "Jesus is Lord" except by the Holy Spirit' (1 Cor 12.3). Through faith one acknowledges the revelation of God, His hidden thought; and 'no one comprehends the the thought of God except the Spirit of God' (1 Cor 2.11). The 'Spirit of God' is opposed to the 'spirit of the world' by which all things are judged according to the flesh and human wisdom. The carnal-minded or unspiritual man 'does not receive the gifts of the Spirit of God, for they are folly to him, and he is not able to understand them' (1 Cor 2.14). According to the measure of the Spirit in man, he attains a deeper understanding of revelation. When St. Paul says that the Corinthians are still unspiritual, he does not mean that they have nothing of the Spirit. For without a gift of the Spirit they could not believe at all. But the activity of the Spirit is still hampered in them because they still act and judge 'as men of the flesh.' Therefore they are 'babes in Christ' (1 Cor 3.1). Consequently there is a growing knowledge of God according to the measure of the Spirit given to man, and he receives more of the Spirit by purifying his heart through the exercise of virtue for the love of God. The love of God is the source, the inspiration, of all Christian virtue and at the same time its consummation and synthesis.

As many as are baptized in Christ 'have put on Christ' (Gal 3.27). This is a gift and at the same time a vocation. We have to 'put on the new nature, created after the likeness of God in true righteousness and holiness' (Eph 4.24); that is to say: 'Put on . . . compassion, kindness, lowliness, meekness, and patience . . . And above all these put on love, which binds everything together in perfect harmony' (Col 3.12–14). Through the purifying exercise of virtue faith grows toward its perfection in the love of God. This perfection is also a deeper knowledge (gnosis). Faith is the beginning of virtuous life, and gnosis is its completion and perfection. Gnosis supposes the love of God 'poured into our hearts through the Holy Spirit who has been given to us' (Rom 5.5). The love of God has to be understood in both the objective and subjective sense: our love of God is God's love in us. Through a virtuous life, then, inspired by love, faith grows toward understanding in perfect love of God. Knowledge and love cannot be separated. It is the same Spirit who brings about in the faithful a higher love of God together with a deeper understanding of his mystery.

It is clear, then, that in his theology of faith, St. Paul has already worked out the Christian idea of a faith growing toward a deepened understanding, not so much through intellectual reflection as through virtuous faithfulness in a spirit of love. But does he suggest somehow that the growth of realizing faith may lead to a development of doctrinal expression? In the second chapter of 1 Corinthians he makes a distinction between two levels in his teaching. The Corinthians, babes in Christ, he feeds with milk, abstaining from lofty words or wisdom for fear that they might deceive themselves, interpreting their faith as a result of plausible words rather than the power of God. They are not spiritual enough to receive a spiritual teaching. 'Yet among the mature we do impart wisdom, although it is not a wisdom of this age . . . but . . . a secret and hidden wisdom of God' (1 Cor 2.6–7).

According to the maturity of his hearers the Apostle imparts a lower or higher teaching. Differences in teaching may therefore correspond to differences of spiritual capacity in the hearer, but in themselves they are differences in the way of expressing the truth that is taught. 'We impart this in words not taught by human wisdom but taught by the Spirit, interpreting spiritual truths to those who possess the Spirit' (1 Cor 2.13). This suggests the idea that to a deeper spiritual penetration into the truth of the gospel corresponds a more ample and adequate expression of it in human language. The Spirit who bears witness in man's spirit to the truth of Christ not only is a source of a deeper wordless 'realizing' of that truth, but he also inspires a more perfect grasp of the intellect, leading to higher modes of expression in linguistic forms. 'If they [the Corinthians] did belong to the perfect, Paul could not teach them new truths but he could unveil to them the connexion of those truths, their harmony, their deeper meaning and practical consequences.'[4] It seems obvious then that from a deeper understanding of the Christian message worked in the Church by the Spirit that enlivens it, there may flow in the course of history a gradual explicitation in human language of the inexhaustible riches that are hidden in the mysteries of faith. Paul does not say this, but it is at least a plausible conclusion that may be drawn from his principles.

In St. John also the possibility of a continual development of doctrine is clearly pointed to, namely in the passages about the holy Spirit and His work in the Church. They all occur in the Lord's instructions at the Last Supper (Jn 14.16–17, 26; 15.26–27; 16.13–15). In these passages Jesus says that after His departure He will send, or the Father will send on His request or in His name, 'another Counselor to be with you for ever' (14.16). The historical and visible presence of Christ among His disciples is coming to an end. He is going back to the Father. But He will not leave them orphans. He will remain with them in an invisible way. For the Spirit who, like Jesus Himself, knows the Father as He knows Jesus, will be with them for ever. The ministry of Jesus was marked by historical transience; the ministry of the Spirit will be marked by permanence.

The object of that ministry of the Spirit is the faithful preservation of revealed truth on earth. He is 'even the Spirit of truth' (14.17; 15.26; 16.12), the spirit of divine Reality. Two things are stressed as to the nature of that ministry. On the one hand, in the dispensation of truth through the Spirit there will be no advance beyond or outside the Lord in His historical manifestation. 'He will teach you all things, and bring to your remembrance all that I have said to you' (14.26). He will bear witness to Jesus (15.26) and 'He will guide you into all the truth; for he will not speak on his own authority, but whatever he hears he will speak and he will declare to you the things that are to come' (16.13).

In the texts just quoted there is, however, a second aspect shining through the first. He will teach all things, all the truth. He will declare the things that are to come. 'He will glorify me, for he will take what is mine and declare it to you. All that the Father has is mine; therefore I said that he will take what is mine and declare it to you' (16.14–15). Jesus is the revelation of the Father. He can reveal the Father because everything that the Father possesses belongs to the Son. The Spirit will introduce the Church into the full knowledge of the Father as He manifests Himself in Jesus. He will take the revelation of the Father that belongs to Jesus and declare it to the disciples. He will declare the things to come that are already given and anticipated in Christ as latent consequences of His historical work and redemptive activity. The result of the activity of the Spirit in the Church will not so much be a bringing to remembrance of the letter of Jesus' teaching; it will rather be a deeper knowledge of His truth, His reality. For according to St. John truth is reality. The point is not that the words of Jesus will materially be remembered; but that the reality that shone through His words and deeds, the reality that appeared in Him and spoke through Him, will gradually be brought to full consciousness. If the Spirit, then, will be with the Church forever, the question arises whether the full meaning of Jesus' words, i.e., the inexhaustible reality that they point to, may not continue to develop in the mind of the Church till the end of the world.

> The idea of progressive revelation could hardly find a clearer expression than it now receives. . . . He tells the disciples that he has many things to say to them—may we add, to their growing enlightenment?—which at present are beyond their grasp. But again, just as the Lord did not speak or teach from Himself ([Jn] 7.16, 8.28, 12.49), so the Spirit of truth will not speak from Himself, but only all things that he 'hears'; and this will include explanation and interpretation of the events now imminent . . . the Spirit of truth will glorify the Son (16.14), by revealing the nature, depth and meaning of the Son's love. The disciples will thus be guided into all the truth. But it is their Master's truth into which they will thus be guided, and since their Master is Himself the truth (14.6) and is one with the Father (10.30), no limit can be set to their advance in knowledge of the truth. On the other hand this advance will only be in the increasing understanding of their Lord's revelation already made in His historic ministry.[5]

Since the same Spirit is at work in the community of the disciples and in the Church after them, and since the truth or reality of Christ is by its very nature of inexhaustible depth, does it not seem reasonable to presume that, just as in the apostolic community so in the later Church too, there will be an advance in the understanding of the Lord's revelation, although that advance be qualitatively different in both cases? The idea of a possible development of doctrine is not far off. It is rather suggested by the principles that are implicit in the statements of St. John.

That the gift of the Spirit, with its proper effects of progressive knowledge and understanding, is not an exclusive privilege of the Apostles but something which the whole Church is presented with, is clearly confirmed by the later 1 John, chapter 2. The general context is the same. As in the last instructions of Jesus the Apostles received the promise of the Spirit who would give them the true knowledge of Christ unlike the unbelieving world, which cannot apprehend it, so now St. John assures his addressees that, in contrast to the Antichrist, i.e., the false teachers who left the Church, they 'have been anointed by the Holy One and consequently know everything' (1 Jn 2.20, 27). This anointing is commonly understood as the gift of the Spirit. Added to the opposition between the believers who have the Spirit and the unbelievers who reject Him, there is the same distinction between the two aspects of the Spirit's working. On the other hand, He teaches nothing that is new: 'Let what you heard from the beginning abide in you' (2.24). It is clear that the hearing in question is not only the internal listening to the Spirit but also the external learning of the message (1.1–5, 3.11). On the other hand, it is equally stressed that the Spirit teaches them all things: 'But the anointing which you received from him abides in you, and you have no need that any one should teach you; as his anointing teaches you about everything, and is true, and is no lie, just as it has taught you, abide in him' (2.27). Such words as 'received' (*elabete*) and 'abide' (*menei*) suggest a permanent gift. So then, the parallelism between the Gospel teaching and the doctrine of the Epistle justifies the conclusion that according to the Apostle Christians in general did receive the gift of the Spirit, which was promised by Jesus to His disciples. Consequently it seems to be plausible that a certain progress in the knowledge of Christ and God is not restricted to the apostolic age but must be extended to the whole of Christian history.

TERTULLIAN

Among the ancient Christian writers, the first who drew the conclusion from the text of St. John analysed above, that a continuing development of doctrine had to be admitted, was Tertullian, the first and—except for St. Augustine—the most important and original of the great African theologians. His case is somewhat complicated through his growing sympathy with Montanism. But the principles from which in his later years he drew conclusions so excessive that they had to be rejected by the Church were already at work in his earlier thought and clearly entailed a view of post-apostolic development of doctrine that fitted in with an orthodox point of view.

The starting point of Tertullian's reflection in this matter is the doctrine of St. John about the work of the Spirit in the Church:

Christ, the first, visible Counselor, who in the flesh instructed His disciples and gave them the rule of faith, sent after His disappearance from among us another, invisible Counselor, the Spirit of God who guides the Church into all truth. The whole view of Tertullian rests upon a basic distinction between the rule of faith (*regula fidei*) that can never be corrupted or added to and the discipline that in the course of time may be expanded and perfected by the indwelling Spirit.

The question of how to interpret the meaning of Tertullian on the development of doctrine resolves itself into the question of how to mark off the field and range of the rule of faith from that of the discipline. The question is not easy to solve, the more so as it became an object of controversy among the interpreters of the great African teacher. Some of them limit the domain of *disciplina* to the moral law and the prescriptions of the ritual and ecclesiastical discipline. The Latin word *disciplina*, however, does not impose such a limitation. To be sure, Tertullian himself often employed the term in that narrow sense. But in other passages it has a wider meaning: 'Sometimes it means the whole of Christian doctrine inclusive of the rule of faith. . . . Sometimes it means Christian religion exclusive of the rule of faith. This use is proper to Tertullian. It occurs undoubtedly in those passages where the writer defends in principle the evolution of the discipline. It includes accordingly those points of doctrine which are not mentioned in the rule of faith.'[6] Among the points explicitly stated by Tertullian as coming under the head of *disciplina* are: the determination of the Canon of Scripture; the Sacraments; the inner structure of the Church; the doctrine of purgatory; the dogmatic truths that are the basis of the moral law, inclusive probably of the doctrine of original sin. With regard to all those points Tertullian already recognizes that a development has taken place in the course of time.

How, then, can one determine the contents of the one and invariable rule of faith? Tertullian's criterion is that in the rule of faith those doctrines alone are included that are immediately connected with an essential point of the message about Christ: Christ is the Son of God; He himself is God and the Creator; He became man in the fullest sense of the word; He was born from the Virgin, suffered, died, and rose from the dead; He ascended into heaven and He will come back in order to judge all men after the universal resurrection; in the meanwhile He sent the Spirit that

He may guide the faithful. These points are absolutely sure 'because from the beginning Christ demonstrated them so clearly in his own person and stated them in terms so unequivocal that all misunderstanding concerning them is excluded. . . . The rule of faith is the foundation of Christianity; it contains those truths of Christian tradition which from the start were incontrovertibly fixed.'[7]

The general idea is very clear now: the rule of faith does not include all the doctrines of faith, but only those that were incontrovertibly revealed by Christ Himself and centered round the meaning of His own person and mission. There is a wide range of doctrinal truth implicit in the fact and teaching of Christ but which He did not clearly state, leaving it to the Spirit to reveal them in due time. The revelations of the Spirit thus are not entirely new or unexpected. Tertullian states the conditions to which developments of doctrine must answer: (1) The Spirit governs and perfects the *disciplina* through a gradual unfolding of that which is hidden in the seed of the *regula*. (2) In accordance with the doctrine of St. John, the Spirit does not speak on His own authority. He only says what He hears from Christ. So doing He glorifies Christ and reminds us of Him. He only confirms and improves that which is given in the *regula fidei*. (3) In connection with the development of *disciplina*, it is said that the Spirit opens the Scriptures to man, giving him a deeper insight into its meaning. (4) The Spirit declares the things that are to come and thus he guides the Church into 'better things' (*meliora*), i.e., He brings to consciousness the more austere moral claims that follow from the acceptance of Christianity and which the first Christians were still unable to bear.[8]

It is evident now that Tertullian's theology of the Holy Spirit and the development He works in the Church is entirely penetrated by a meditation on Christ's farewell discourses in the Gospel of St. John. His doctrine is already well balanced and clearly articulated. In its essence it is orthodox, but in the course of his bitter opposition to the great body of the Church he came to proclaim the Spirit as the sole guide of the Church in matters of doctrine and to deny to the hierarchy the power to interpret authoritatively the content of tradition. He did not clearly see the distinction between the objective increment of revelation itself and the development of objective understanding in the Church.

To conclude with a text of Tertullian himself, he states the rule of faith and continues:

This law of faith being constant, the other succeeding points of discipline and conversation admit the 'novelty' of correction; the grace of God, to wit, operating and advancing even to the end. For what kind of [supposition] is it, that, while the devil is always operating and adding daily to the ingenuities of iniquity, the work of God should either have ceased, or else have desisted from advancing? whereas the reason why the Lord sent the Paraclete was, that, since human mediocrity was unable to take in all things at once, discipline should, little by little, be directed and ordained, and carried on to perfection, by that vicar of the Lord, the Holy Spirit. . . . What then is the Paraclete's administrative office but this: the direction of discipline, the revelation of the Scriptures, the re-formation of the intellect, the advancement towards 'better things'? Nothing is without stages of growth: all things await their season. In short, the preacher says 'A time to everything' (Eccl 3.1). Look how creation itself advances little by little to fructification. First comes the grain, and from the grain arises the shoot, and from the shoot struggles out the shrub: thereafter boughs and leaves gather strength, and the whole that we call a tree expands: then follows the swelling of the germen, and from the germen bursts the flower, and from the flower the fruit opens: that fruit itself, rude for a while, and unshapely, little by little, keeping the straight course of its development, is trained to the mellowness of its flavor. So, too, righteousness—for the God of righteousness and of creation is the same—was first in a rudimentary state, having a natural fear of God: from that stage it advanced, through the Law and the Prophets, to infancy; from that stage it passed, through the Gospel, to the fervour of youth: now through the Paraclete, it is settling into maturity. He will be, after Christ, the only one to be called and revered as Master; for He speaks not from Himself, but what is commanded by Christ. He is the only prelate, because he alone succeeds Christ. [*De virginibus velandis* 1]

The witness of Tertullian is very important. It is not invalidated by the fact that he afterwards became a sectarian and that the most striking texts on the development of doctrine are found in his later writings. For looking at them in the perspective of his constant and basic principles, which undoubtedly were orthodox, one clearly sees that the heterodox doctrines that he adopted in his later life were only exaggerations by a stubborn passionate mind of conclusions that followed from sound premises, gained by a profound theological reflection on the texts of St. John. The case of Tertullian suggests that the principle of development was a 'first principle,' as Newman would call it, unconsciously at work in the mind of the Church, and ready to come to the surface on occasion when circumstances required it. It was unlikely that the reflective consciousness of the fact of development should so soon be recognized in the Church. On such problems reflection only sets in when difficulties arise. The case of Tertullian shows that the idea of development itself was not only not objected to in the Church but implicitly taken for granted.

The influence of Tertullian has been immense. To be sure, 'The man's subsequent error has lessened the authority of his writing,' as St. Hilary of Poitiers observed (*Comm. in Mat.* 5.1). The condemnation of his heresy after his death has been a *damnatio memoriae*. St. Cyprian never mentions his name although at every moment he draws on his work. St. Augustine, too, who severely condemns him, is in great measure indebted to him. St. Jerome, on the contrary, sounded his praise and attributed his fall to the envy and the calumnies of the Roman clergy.[9] It is to be expected, then, that his ideas on the evolutive influence of the Spirit in the mind of the Church did make their way into Christian thought. Moreover, it is a remarkable fact that although his rejection of Church authority was repudiated, the idea of development itself was never used against him.

ST. IRENAEUS

The theological view of St. Irenaeus, as was seen earlier, was based on an organic conception of the Salvation-economy and its growth in the course of time. He did not, however, develop an explicit doctrine of post-apostolic development in the Church. The heresies he fought were not concerned with the future but only with the past. Against those who opposed the New Testament to the Old, he had to defend the organic unity and continuity of revelation. There is, however, a remarkable passage in his *Adversus haereses* that seems to suggest that the idea of a continual development of Christian insight was implicit in his thought: 'But . . . that the preaching of the Church is everywhere consistent, and continues in an even course, and receives testimony from the prophets, the apostles, and all the disciples—as I have proved—through [those in] the beginning, the middle, and the end, and through the entire dispensation of God, and the well-grounded system which tends to man's salvation, namely, our faith; which, having been received from the Church, we do preserve, and which always, by the Spirit of God, renewing its youth as if it were some precious deposit in an excellent vessel, causes the vessel itself containing it to renew its youth also' (*Adv. haer*. 3.24.1).

St. Irenaeus stresses the fact that the preaching of the Church, based on the Prophets, Apostles, and disciples, and which we spiritually assimilate by faith, always remains the same through the successive stages of the economy of salvation. Not only do men keep the faith that is received from the Church, but faith itself through the action of the Spirit always becomes young again and rejuvenates the vessel, i.e., the ecclesiastical tradition that it expresses. To rejuvenate the tradition is to restore to it the strength of youth. The image at least suggests that the object of faith (that which is received from the Church), which is handed down in the process of tradition, is not something inert but a living dynamic thing capable of growth. This is in accordance with the general view of St. Irenaeus set forth earlier, and with his personal bent.

ORIGEN

Dealing in *De Principiis* with the relation between Scripture and tradition on the one hand and theology on the other, Origen makes some important statements that are relevant to the question here. He distinguishes between two kinds of truth preached by the Apostles: necessary truths, clearly and explicitly stated for all men, although their explanation may be hidden and remains to be investigated by those who deserve more excellent gifts of the Spirit and receive from him special graces of speech, wisdom, and science; and secondary truths of which it is stated simply 'that they are, but not how and why they are' in order to give those who love wisdom an opportunity of exercising their ingenuity so that they may bear fruits according to their deserts and capacities (*De Principiis* 1 Introd. 3). This is similar to Tertullian's distinction between the rule of faith and the *disciplina*. Indeed, Origen gives a list of the necessary truths of Christian faith, which it is interesting to compare with those of the African doctor: (1) one God, the Creator, God of the OT; (2) Jesus Christ, Son of God, who was incarnate, born of a Virgin, suffered, died, rose again, and is now glorified; (3) the

Holy Spirit, who inspired the men of the OT and the NT; (4) the future life and the Resurrection of the dead; (5) free will and the struggle against sin; (6) the existence of the devil and his angels; (7) the creatureliness and final destruction of the world; (8) that the Scriptures are inspired by the Holy Spirit and have two meanings, the second intelligible only to those who have wisdom and knowledge from the Holy Spirit; and that there is a spiritual law; (9) the existence of angels.[10]

It is notable that the enumeration of Origen, although more extended, corresponds fairly well to that of Tertullian, except the mention of the existence of devils and angels and of scriptural inspiration. All the points that in Tertullian are brought together under the heading of *disciplina* are absent from Origen's list of necessary truths. In connection with those truths that are manifestly stated in the apostolic tradition, Origen noted a series of questions that are not clearly answered by tradition, and he concludes:

> Every one, therefore, must make use of elements and foundations of this sort, according to the precept, 'Enlighten yourselves with the light of knowledge' (Hos 10.12), if he would desire to form a connected series and body of truths agreeably to the reason of all these things that by clear and necessary statements he may ascertain the truth regarding each individual topic, and form, as we have said, one body of doctrine, by means of illustrations and arguments—either those which he has discovered in holy Scripture, or which he has deduced by closely tracing out the consequences and following a correct method. [*De Principiis* I Introd. 10]

The meaning of the last words is open to question. R. Cadiou reads in the message a distinction between 'basic dogmas' (formally stated in Scripture) and 'secondary dogmas' determined by investigation, ruled by the rule of faith.[11] R. Hanson objects that the doctrines enumerated above are probably Origen's version of the rule of faith itself—this is true—and gives his own translation of the last clause: 'discovered by the investigation of the logical consequences of the Scriptures and adherence to accuracy.'[12] The expression 'adherence to accuracy' is rather obscure. *Recti tenor* naturally means a continuity or progress of that which is right (Forcellini LTL 4:292), so that the meaning could be: 'doctrines

. . . which he has discovered by the investigation of the consequences
and by continuity [or development] of what is right [or true].' Now
it seems obvious that the 'right' that in the context is the norm of
continuity (or development) is that which, according to Hanson
himself, is Origen's rule of faith. One may conclude, then, that
Origen's object in *De Principiis* was to construct a system of doctrine in which the 'rule of faith' (the necessary doctrines, clearly
stated in the apostolic tradition) and the logical consequences or
true developments should harmoniously be blended together.

Here is the same distinction made by later scholasticism between
the articles of faith that are like principles (the rule of faith) and
other insights won by establishment of their connection and the
investigation of the 'why' and the 'how.' The whole leads to fresh
doctrines within the living context of a theological system. This is
a process of development; not only a deeper personal penetration
into truth but also an expansion of truth in the domain of explicit
thought; the latter through the former mediated by intellectual
reflection. For in the mind of Origen there can be no separation
between the mystical and the intellectual elements in religious
thought. Just as for the Neoplatonists of his own time philosophy
was a matter not only of reason but also of moral purification and
faithful conduct, so for Origen 'Christian philosophy' is not a purely
intellectual occupation but a way of life in which better knowledge
is a fruit of moral earnestness and of mystical participation in the
reality of that which the knowledge is about. One may conclude,
then, that according to Origen the growth of Christian truth in the
mind of the believer is at the same time a deepening of personal
penetration and a broadening of conceptual expression.

Two final remarks have to be made. First, Origen does not make
so clear-cut a distinction between dogma and theological truth as is
found in later theology (neither did Newman when he wrote his
Essay on the Development of Christian Doctrine). Therefore one
should not search his works for an exact borderline between the
development of dogma and the development of theology. Second, in
different contexts Origen draws similar distinctions that are not
simply identical. They are rather analogous and subtly related to
one another. Origen's ideas cannot be reduced to a wholly
consistent system. In several places there is a distinction between
exoteric and esoteric doctrines. In *Contra Celsum*, for example,

Origen refutes the accusation that Christians keep their doctrine secret, by replying:

> Almost the whole world has come to know the preaching of Christians better than the opinions of philosophers. Who has not heard of Jesus' birth from a virgin, and of his crucifixion, and of his resurrection in which many have believed, and of the proclamation of the judgment which punishes sinners according to their deserts and pronounces the righteous worthy of reward? . . . In view of this it is quite absurd to say that *the doctrine is secret.* The existence of certain doctrines, which are beyond those which are exoteric and do not reach the multitude, is not a peculiarity of Christian doctrine only, but is shared by the philosophers.[13]

The first member of the distinction seems to be a shorter version of Origen's rule of faith quoted above. It is distinguished, however, not from dogmatic growth but from esoteric tradition. That Origen believed in a tradition of secret doctrine is undeniable. But it is not at all clear that from the beginning those secret traditions go together with the overt teachings, as two sets of explicit statements, the latter to be delivered to the many 'who are uncultured and have made little progress in faith or study,' the former being intended to 'reach only a few and those secretly' (*In Rom.* 6.8). For here and in other passages of his *Commentary on Romans* he says that such esoteric doctrines occur in the writings of St. Paul but are deliberately hidden, so that it would seem that they are only implicit in Scripture and have to be extracted from it through discernment and reflection. If this be true, the distinction drawn in *Contra Celsum* comes very near to that which was studied earlier in *De Principiis*; and Origen means only that the more advanced few who infer them from the sacred text 'are to conceal among themselves the meanings of this sort of thing in the silence of God as a mystery, and not expose it indiscriminately to those who are unqualified and less accomplished' (*In Rom.* 8.12). Those mysteries, which the Apostle perhaps taught to Timothy, Luke, and other disciples whom he knew to be fit to receive them, are said to be 'unspeakable,' 'greater than either human speech can pronounce, or mortal ear listen to,' so that even the Apostles perhaps did not expound them fully: 'I did not say that they are not fully understood but that they are not fully expounded' (*Homilies on Joshua* 23.4). The distinction between 'fully understood' and 'fully expounded' points to the heart of the matter. It means that revelation as expressed in Scripture is beyond all human language. It can be hinted at in a more or less expressive way by means of words, but it can only be fully understood in wordless experience. The human expression is always inadequate and therefore no limit can be put to its perfectibility.

By way of conclusion, there is a remarkable organic unity and consistency in Origen's view on the nature of revelation and its growth in human understanding. The principles on which his interpretation of the growth in revelation itself is based are the same as those that command his insight into the nature of development in post-apostolic tradition.

POST-NICENE GREEK FATHERS

The ante-Nicene Christian writers are of particular importance for the problems under investigation. As Christianity, separating itself from Judaism, rapidly spread over the Hellenistic world, the problems connected with authority became paramount. Such problems were the criteria of common faith and tradition, the canon of the sacred writings, the relation of the New to the Old Testament, the relation of the *canon ecclesiasticus* (the rule of the Church) to the *canon sacrae scripturae* (the rule of the sacred writings), the qualified spokesmen of authority in matters of faith and life and Scripture-interpretation; these and similar problems were from the nature of the case the first that a nascent world religion based on a common belief had to face. The social structures of ecclesiastical life were not yet entirely fixed. Under the influence of historical factors, such as national genius, culture, dominant personalities, among other things, different traditions sprang up from a common inspiration, not only in matters of liturgical usages, rules of moral conduct, and patterns of social relations, but also on the plane of the concrete presentation of the creed. Therefore the preservation of unity through the definition of the rule of faith became a problem of primary importance that had to be settled before all other things. It was necessary, then, to agree on the essential points of the kerygma and to determine what was undoubtedly taught by Christ and the Apostles: the *dominica traditio*, the *divina traditio*, the *evangelica atque apostolica traditio* as St. Cyprian calls it (*Ep.* 63.1; *Ep.* 74.10), and to separate it from controvertible opinions and merely human traditions. Moreover, the gospel had to be preached in a highly cultured pagan world. Accommodation and assimilation were necessary and unavoidable, but such operations are by their very nature beset by all kinds of dangers and difficulties. Various forms of syncretism and compromise arose. As in the struggle for life in a common cultural milieu Christianity spontaneously tended to assimilate the spiritual and intellectual treasures of Greek religion and philosophy, so pagan culture in its turn attempted to interpret and assimilate into its own systems the powerful elements of Christian belief and moral principles. It was often difficult—as it is still—to tell Christian-colored heathenism from genuine Christian thought clothed with Hellenistic wisdom.

In the light of that general situation one understands the concern of both Tertullian and Origen not to mix up the creed—the *regula fidei*, that which undoubtedly came from the Lord and the Apostles and was to be preached to the many as necessary for salvation—with the *disciplina* (Tertullian) of the Church or the mystical-theological wisdom (Origen) of the few, the development of which they both advocated.

As to the second concern, that of adaptation and assimilation, the former represented the most extreme attitude of defense, although Tertullian's own way of thinking was as little Hebraic as that of Origen, while the latter and Clement of Alexandria stood for an open reconciliatory attitude toward the riches of Hellenistic tradition. Both attitudes were necessary. For even Origen, the greatest thinker of the patristic age in the Greek world, could not keep himself entirely free from all forms of dangerous Hellenization.

After Constantine, however, the situation was entirely altered. Christianity had won the battle against paganism and could triumphantly carry along the spoils of Greek civilization. It became the new religion of an old culture. The controversy against paganism continued, but Christians had no longer to defend themselves against a ruling enemy. They could easily destroy its retreating remnants, as can be seen clearly from the apologetic works of Eusebius, Athanasius, or Theodoret of Cyr. The real enemies now rose from within Christianity itself. The golden age of patristic theology was characterized by struggles against heresies or heretical tendencies, leading to the great councils of the 4th and the 5th centuries in which the Trinitarian and Christological dogmas were clarified and defined. The Fathers were as scrupulously Biblical as one could be. Athanasius, for instance, did but reluctantly accept the term *homoousios* in order to settle the case against Arianism. The term hardly occurs in his own works. He continued to prefer the Biblical term *homoios*. The new terms and distinctions of philosophical coinage were pressed upon the Church in order to clearly express the orthodox intuitions in contrast to the subtleties of the heretics. But from the nature of the case, new terms always carry with them new ideas, at least in a certain sense. Truth, as expressed in terms of a definite culture and epoch, is by its very nature not a closed static thing, but an open dynamic power of meaning, inviting to further reflection and new discoveries. Truth lives in the living thought of successive generations. New insights may express the very truth of an old truth. In such a case they are not added to it from without, but they clarify it, unfold it, and purify it from within as it lives in the human mind. For truth, formally speaking, is not in texts or formulas but in the mind that thinks them and tries to penetrate their true and full meaning.

The doctrine of the Trinity, for instance, as it emerged from the first Council of Constantinople, although in strict accordance with scriptural truth, was as an object of mental apprehension a new idea, not opposed to what Scripture said or added to it but clarifying it from within and expressing more perfectly its very truth. As such it was a true development. For true development means precisely a newness arising from the very heart of an initial truth. Newman clearly saw, as is now generally accepted, that the dogmas of Nicea and Chalcedon were the outcome of a real and true development.

The Fathers of the 4th and 5th centuries, then, lived through the most important stage in the process of the development of Christian doctrine. It may be expected that they were not entirely unconscious of the dimension of newness in their dogmatic definitions and that they took for granted that a certain kind of development was not inconsistent with strict faithfulness to the past. If they did not state the problem, if they did not discuss it, one may suppose that there was no difficulty about it. Their consciousness of development remained, so to say, marginal. It generally did not come into focus. They were intent on the truth of the realities in which they believed as Christians and which they had to safeguard against corruptions. According to the measure in which our attention is engrossed and absorbed by the effort of thinking about objective reality, it is diverted from the process of thinking itself. Questions about thought and its psychological or logical implications only arise when specific difficulties present themselves to the mind. Therefore, if the Fathers did not discuss the problems of development, it does not follow that they were unaware of the fact of development. Their existential awareness of it, involved in their partaking in its preformation, may have been more lively than that of a contemporary scholar who has objectified it as a problem to solve.

If in the mind of the Fathers the general idea of development of doctrine did not create any difficulty and, consequently, was not brought under discussion, it may be expected nevertheless that occasionally, in given circumstances, it was directly or indirectly betokened. This indeed is the case. Some utterings of the Fathers betray the active presence in their mind of the idea of development. Speaking of the growth of Christian doctrine in his own mind, St. Basil gives a fair description of the general fact of dogmatic development: 'For just as the seed, in developing, becomes larger instead of small, but is the same in itself, not changing in kind but being perfected in development, so I consider that also in me the same doctrine has been developed through progress, and what now is mine has not taken the place of what existed in the beginning' (*Ep.* 223).

The most convincing argument, however, may be collected from the attitude of the Cappadocian Fathers between the Councils of Nicea and Chalcedon when the controversy about the Holy Spirit had come to a head. About 375 St. Basil wrote his work *On the Holy Spirit* and about the same time he sent a letter to the priests of Neocaesarea in which he defends himself against the accusation in admitting into the Church persons suspected of sympathy with Arianism. It is a general rule of the Church, he says, confirmed by our Fathers, to receive into the Church those who come over from Arianism if they confess the faith of Nicea. While he was writing he had in hand a letter of St. Athanasius in which he recommends that use, and it was now a general policy with all the bishops of Macedonia and Achaia (*Ep.* 204.6). Athanasius himself had defended the substantiality and divinity of the Holy Spirit in his *Letters to Serapion* (about 360). But it is curious fact that he did not affirm directly or explicitly that the Holy Spirit was God like the

Father and the Son: 'The rule, followed by him, to evade the use of the name *Theos* in speaking of the Holy Spirit, is connected for him, as for other Fathers of his time, with the condition of the doctrine at this time and with his anxiety not to create a priori obstacles to the conversion of the heretics.'[14] This explains at the same time the attitude of St. Basil. Let us imagine for a moment that Athanasius and Basil thought that their doctrine of the Holy Spirit did belong to the rule of faith or the clear and explicit teaching of the Church from the beginning; could they speak and act that way?

The matter is clinched, however, by the intervention of St. Gregory of Nazianzus. In one of his *Orations*, preached at Constantinople in 381, he invited those who still hesitated to call the Spirit *Theos* to a fraternal compromise: 'Let us meet one another in a spiritual manner; let us be full rather of brotherly than of self love. Grant us the Power of the Godhead, and we will give up to you the use of the name. . . . Confess, my friends, the Trinity to be of One Godhead; or if you will, of One Nature; and we will pray the Spirit to give you this word God . . . Yet more clearly and concisely, let me say, do not call us to account for our loftier word, and we will not find fault with what you have been able to attain, until by another road you are brought up to the same resting place. . . . This we concede to you in whom we do find something of vital truth, who are sound as to the Son' (*Oration on Pentecost* 7–8).

Further, in his *Five Theological Orations* (380) on the Trinity, for which he has merited the distinctive title 'The Theologian,' he clearly states and explains, in connection with the new dogma of the Holy Spirit, the principle of the development of doctrine. He first argues that it is not enough to accept what is explicitly stated in the letter of the sacred books. That which may be understood and collected from the Scriptures ought also to be accepted, even if it is not clearly stated in them: 'If, then, there is so much difference in terms and things, why are you such a slave to the letter and a partisan of the Jewish wisdom, and a follower of syllables at the expense of facts? . . . if, when you spoke of a rational and mortal animal (I concluded from your words) that you meant Man, should you think me to be talking nonsense? . . . As, then, in this case, I should have been looking, not so much at the terms used, as at the thoughts they were meant to convey; so neither, if I found something else either not at all or not clearly expressed in the Words of Scripture to be included in the meaning, should I avoid giving it utterance, out of fear of your sophistical trick about terms?' (*5th Theological Question* 24). Further on he develops a view of the 'economy of revelation' which might sound temerarious even to modern ears. He contrasts the case of St. Paul's evolution, which implied a change by subtraction, the loss of the Jewish law, with the development of the doctrine of the Trinity, which took place by additions. Then he proceeds:

> The Old Testament proclaimed the Father openly, and the Son more obscurely. The New manifested the Son and suggested the Deity of the Spirit. Now the Spirit Himself dwells among us, and supplies us with a clearer demonstration of Himself. For it was not safe, when the Godhead of the Father was not yet acknowledged, plainly to proclaim the Son; nor when that of the Son was not yet received, to burden us further (if I may use so bold an expression) with the Holy Ghost; lest perhaps people might, like men loaded with food beyond their strength, and presenting eyes as yet too weak to bear it to the sun's light, risk the loss even of that which was within the reach of their powers; but that by gradual additions, and, as David says, Goings up, and advances and progress from glory to glory, the Light of the Trinity might shine upon the more illuminated. [*5th Theological Oration* 26]

Therefore, he adds, Christ Himself only gradually came to dwell in the disciples, measuring Himself out to them according to their capacity to receive Him and afterward promising and sending them the Spirit of Truth to declare His Words little by little. All this reminds one of Tertullian.

When one considers as a whole the words and the ecclesiastical policy of the three most outstanding personalities among the Greek Fathers of the 4th century, it at once becomes evident that however much they were the defenders of tradition and orthodoxy, they nevertheless fully accepted the principle of the development of doctrine and saw no difficulty in it.

THE LATIN FATHERS

For the Latin Fathers of the golden age of patristic theology, as for their Greek contemporaries, the conviction of the substantial unchangeableness of the deposit of faith little excludes the idea of a

D

development of doctrine. Commenting on the parable of the mustard seed (Mt 13.31–32), St. Jerome clearly expresses the general idea of dogmatic growth. The seed is the preaching of the Gospel sowed in the heart of the faithful or in the whole world. In due time, however, it becomes a tree, and the birds of the air come and make nests in its branches. The branches of the evangelical tree are the 'different dogmas' that grew from it and the birds are the souls of the faithful or the powers that serve God, coming to rest in the branches (*Comm. in Matt.* 2.13). It is the same image that was met in the text of St. Basil noted above; but Basil gives a more suggestive description of the nature of growth, whereas St. Jerome more clearly states that it takes place not only in the individual soul but also in the world as a whole and that the ramifications of the Gospel truth are the different dogmas that grow from it.

St. Augustine, whose mind is as conservative as his imagination is fertile, writes against the Donatists who invoked the authority of St. Cyprian to defend their conservative doctrine of Baptism:

> Who does not know that the holy canonical Scriptures of both the Old and the New Testaments are fixed within their definite limits? that they so surpass all the later writings of the bishops in such a way that there can be no discussion about it being true or right, whatever may be found to be written in it? that, on the contrary, such books as were or are now written after the fixation of the Canon, may be reprehended by the wiser words of one who is perhaps more competent in the matter or by the greater authority and the more grounded judgment of other bishops, or by the councils, if there is something in them that may be deviating from truth? that the regional and provincial councils are entirely subjected to the more plenary councils in which the whole christian world comes together? that often the earlier plenary councils are corrected by later ones; when, to wit, in virtue of a certain experience of things, gates are opened that before were shut and hidden things come to be known? [*Bapt.* 2.3]

VINCENT OF LÉRINS

This investigation of patristic theology concludes with a more detailed treatment of the *Commonitorium* of Vincent of Lérins, which exercised on the later ages a preponderant influence. A passage on the growth of doctrine but '. . . in the same doctrine, in

the same meaning, and in the same purport' was inserted in the
Constitutio de fide catholica of Vatican Council I (Denz 3020).

Vincent took up a position with the Semi-Pelagians against the
doctrine of St. Augustine and Prosper of Aquitaine on predestination. In view of the dominant authority of St. Augustine, however,
he had to be very cautious. He never names him and he writes
under the pseudonym 'Peregrinus'. How to attack a giant? He
opposes other giants against his adversary: Origen and Tertullian.
His eulogy on Tertullian recalls the praises of Jerome: 'Who was
more scholarly than this man, and who better trained in divine and
human matters? . . . Almost each word of his is a thought, and each
sentence a victory.' He confounded all heresies, but nevertheless in
his later years he fell into the gravest errors (*Comm.* 18). The suggestion is clear. Is it not possible that the other African champion
of the Church who confounded all the heresies of his time also
committed a serious mistake?

The way in which Vincent establishes his case is of utmost
importance. The final ground of Christian truth is holy Scripture.
But Vincent, like the patristic Church in general, is well aware of
the fact that Scripture texts are open to various interpretations and
endless discussions. How to settle controversies in matters of faith?
One of the most important criteria in the Church was the *lex orandi,
lex credendi*. Tertullian already had used the Lord's Prayer as an
all-inclusive compendium of the gospel law. St. Cyprian follows
him and St. Augustine in his final work on predestination and grace,
De dono perseverantiae, concludes his argument with a passionate
appeal to the liturgical prayers of the Church. 'He has recognized
that the faithful handing down of the deposit of faith takes place in
no small degree in worship, that the liturgy is an important vessel
of tradition without separating it on that account from the succession of the bishops.'[15] All this Vincent does not deny but he stresses
the principle that no interpretation of Scripture or ecclesiastical
prayer has any authority if it is not backed by a universal consensus of the ancient Church. Hence the famous canon: *quod
ubique, quod semper, quod ab omnibus creditum est* (*Comm.* 2).
Together with the *le orandi*, and correcting it, there is the con-
firming authority of the Church. Vincent does not speak of a special
Church authority, of the Roman see. The authority of the Church
is the consensus of the whole Church. Universality, antiquity, and
consensus are the touchstones of truth. 'The newness of false

doctrines or, to say it positively, the antiquity of the true doctrine and the evidence for it are simply the kernel round which in the *Commonitorium* all Vincent's thoughts are gathered.'[16] The evidence required for proof is narrowly conceived: positive and explicit witnesses alone speak for a doctrine. The silence of the Fathers is sufficient for reproof.

The canon of Vincent is something of his own, invented by himself for controversial purposes. He is the champion of extreme conservatism. If he nevertheless admits the possibility of development, it must be because the idea of development belongs to the very spirit of the Church. He cannot contradict it. Therefore he gives an extensive description of the process of development, making use of the image of natural growth that was noted in Tertullian, Irenaeus, Basil, and Jerome. But his main concern is to preclude all possible misuse by ever recurring cautions. With all this Vincent gives a fine description of the process of true development:

> Teach precisely what you have learned; do not say new things even if you say them in a new manner.
>
> At this point the question may be asked: If this is right, then is no progress of religion possible within the Church of Christ? To be sure, there has to be a progress, even exceedingly great progress. . . . But it must be a progress in the proper sense of the word, and not a change in faith. Progress means that each thing grows within itself, whereas change implies that one thing is transformed into another. Hence it must be that understanding, knowledge, and wisdom grow and advance . . . in a single person as well as in the Church as a whole, and this gradually according to age and history. But they must grow within their own limits, that is, in accordance with the same kind of dogma, frame of mind, and intellectual approach.
>
> The growth of religion in the soul should be like the growth of the body, which in the course of years develops and unfolds, yet remains the same as it was. . . . There remains one and the same nature and one and the same person . . . The joints of adult man are as many as those of young children; though some are developed only in maturity, they already existed virtually in the embryo. Hence nothing new is later produced in old men that has not previously been latent in children. Therefore, without any doubt, this is the legitimate and correct rule of progress and the established and most impressive order of growth: The course of the years always completes in adults the parts and

forms with which the wisdom of the Creator had previously imbued infants. . . . In the same way, the dogma of the Christian religion ought to follow these laws of progress, so that it may be consolidated in the course of years, developed in the sequence of time, and sublimated by age—yet remain incorrupt and unimpaired, complete and perfect in all the proportions of its parts and in all its essentials (let us call them members and senses), so that it does not allow of any change, or any loss of its specific character, or any variation of its inherent form. [*Comm.* 22–23]

Vincent does not like the idea of development. It gives a chance to his adversary, Augustine. But in view of its universal admission by the Church he cannot give it up. If one takes account of his own rigorism in interpreting his canon, one cannot avoid the conclusion that the principle of development does not fit in with it. There is a contradiction between the canon as he understands it and the idea of development. This latent contradiction will work itself out in later history. The *Commonitorium* will meet with a great and lasting approval and will be the refuge of both conservatives and progressives. 'Therefore two of the great Catholic apologists, Bossuet and Newman, could defend the Church with arguments that seem contradictory. Bossuet says to Protestantism: "You change; therefore you are not in the truth." And Newman to Anglicanism: "You don't develop; therefore there is no life in you." '[17] The contradiction is not merely apparent, as will become clear in the course of further discussion.

CONCLUSION

To summarize by way of conclusion, the preceding inquiry about the idea of development in ancient Christianity has made the following points:

1. In the New Testament was found not only a clear idea of the evolutive nature of revelation itself but also unmistakable indications of a further development of divine truth to be expected in the history of the Church. A deep feeling of the inadequacy of human language to express the mysterious realities in which men live by faith, and an acute consciousness of the active presence of the Holy Spirit guiding the Church to a full comprehension of

what God has given to man in Christ, open the way to the idea of a post-apostolic development of doctrine.

2. From the witness of the Fathers and ancient Christian writers, it can clearly be seen that according to their mind the unchangeableness of the apostolic rule of faith did not exclude an historic progress of objective understanding of the deposit of faith. The principle of development, although it did not become a subject of discussion or an abstract problem considered in itself, was from the beginning clearly at work in the mind of the Church. The Fathers did not so much appeal to it as act from it. It remained largely unconscious because it was taken for granted. Occasionally, however, it came to light. Sometimes the Fathers did speak and act in such a way that the principle of development was clearly expressed or seemed to be tacitly supposed.

3. Because the development of doctrine was not an actual problem, the Fathers were not concerned about an accurate expression of it. They spoke in a loose way. They did not try to mark its limitation, nor did they ask the question of how it could be reconciled with the principle of doctrinal immutability. Not only Tertullian, whose extreme positions were clearly rejected as heretical, but such men, too, as St. Gregory of Nazianzus and St. Augustine spoke of it in such a way that in the 20th century their words can only be accepted under correction.

4. The images employed to indicate the process of development were mostly those of the seed developing into a plant or of man passing from infancy to maturity.

5. With Vincent of Lérins a reaction sets in. Although he admits in so many words the principle of development, his polemic against St. Augustine leads him to formulate the practical rule of Christian truth in a way so rigid (universality, antiquity, consensus) that it hardly leaves room for true development.

6. The idea that it lies with an infallible authority to pronounce a definitive and irrevocable judgment in matters of faith and dogma is still beyond the horizon of patristic thought. It will be worked out in later theology.

CHAPTER FIVE

Development of Doctrine
in Medieval Thought

It is impossible to understand the position of medieval scholastic theology with respect to the problem of doctrinal development if one does not understand something of its origin, nature, and general spirit. The decline and division of the Roman Empire, the invasion of barbaric peoples into old civilized countries, the rise of new empires under the hegemony of uncultured tribes, the destruction of flourishing centers of learning, the general disordered state, could not but cause a general cessation of creative intellectual activity. By the end of the 6th century, patristic theology was on its death bed. Byzantium in the East, and Rome, leaning on the power of the rising Merovingian and Carolingian empires of the North, parted company. From the 5th century on, East and West no longer understood each other's language. A process of gradual estrangement set in, soon to result in tragic misunderstandings that, favored by political and ecclesiastical ambitions, led in the 10th century to a definitive rupture between the Eastern and Western Churches. Since the struggle between the Monophysites of Syria and Egypt and the Dyophysites of Byzantium came to a dead end in the 6th century, the East was dangerously divided against itself. The three monophysite Churches—the Copts and Abyssinians in Egypt, the Jacobites in Syria, and the Armenians to the North in Western Asia—geographically circumscribed as they were, gradually turned against the Byzantine Empire and strove toward political independence. In those circumstances Islam arose in

91

Arabia in the beginning of the 7th century. Its armies were welcomed in Antioch and Alexandria, which suffered under the military and political pressure of the Greeks. Syria and North Africa were before long lost for Christianity. Spain was invaded and largely occupied in the beginning of the 8th century. Constantinople was constantly menaced.

GROWTH AND NATURE OF SCHOLASTIC THEOLOGY

For some centuries after these troubles faith was reduced to its essentials, living on traditional formulas, and no longer enlivened by creative thought. From the end of the 5th century the few great figures in the domain of philosophy and theology preserved and handed down to the Middle Ages a part of antiquity, but generally even the best of them such as St. Gregory the Great or St. Bede were not conspicuous for their originality. Boethius preserved for the Latin schools a few logical works of Aristotle; Cassiodorus provided them with a precious manual of Christian liberal education, together with an outline of ecclesiastical history, and he established in his monasteries a tradition of scholarship that preserved something of the classical culture for the coming ages; St. Isidore of Seville wrote an encyclopedia of information on all possible topics. These were the main sources from which scholastic theology would spring.

The first stage is known by the name of 'Carolingian Renaissance' and was greatly inspired by Alcuin, the adviser of Charlemagne in religious and educational matters. The general characteristics of scholastic theology are already reflected in the works of contemporary theologians. They do not see the past as a history but as a storehouse of materials for their own compilations and for the solution of the problems in which they are interested. Their work is very important for it lays the foundations of the scholastic tradition. Just as individual education must begin with the learning of language and grammar, so the theologians of the epoch of medieval childhood began with linguistic preoccupations. They had on the one hand the holy Scriptures and on the other hand, often in the form of *florilegia* or compilations, an impressive amount of *auctoritates* from the Fathers, the Councils, the liturgical prayers, and the decretals: all texts separated from their context. The very situation reveals the impossibility of any historical perspective. In order to solve their questions they inclined toward one rational instrument—the science of language—whereby to determine the meaning of words and the correctness of grammatical constructions. It is symptomatic that the stirring controversies of the 9th century were nearly all about words and expressions. The eucharistic controversy, for instance, which opposed Paschasius Radbertus to Ratramnus had its roots in the *Caroline Books*, written perhaps by Alcuin, in which one reads that the mystery of the Lord's body and blood takes place *in veritate . . . non in figura*, and it was occasioned by a question put by the emperor Charles II The Bald to the theologians: 'Whether that which in the Church is taken by the mouth of the faithful takes place *in mysterio* or *in veritate?*' (Ratramnus, *De Corpore et Sanguine Domini* 5). The whole controversy largely rests on the interpretation of those expressions. The works of Gottschalk, who intervened in nearly all the theological controversies of his time, are saturated with grammar. An outstanding example is the *una et trina deitas*, defended by Gottschalk and rejected by Hincmar of Rheims. The argument of Gottschalk is based upon the question whether and under which conditions abstract nouns may be substituted for concrete ones. He concludes: 'Consequently, just as God, naturally one, is personally trine, so undoubtedly deity, naturally one, is personally trine.'[1]

After the great depression of the 10th century scholastic theology gradually resumed and carried on its work. St. Anselm of Canterbury coined the formula in which scholastic theology will recognize its program: *fides quaerens intellectum*, faith seeking understanding. Faith is presupposed not only as an assent to propositions but as a living act of communion with the mystery of God. The intellect does not try to rationalize faith from curiosity but from devotion. It is subservient to the mystical movement of faith towards more clarity in its intercourse with God. The *Proslogion* is written in the form of a prayer, and other works of St. Anselm are not seldom composed in a style of meditation. Therefore the movement of Anselm's thought is very simple. He does not distinguish between truths of natural theology and mysteries that are beyond natural reason. The object of faith is one, and reflection is no more than a work of clarification within the progress of faith toward its good. Neither does he distinguish between truths of faith and theological conclusions. On the plane of intellectual clarification truth is of one and the same nature in all its statements, whether they are articles or conclusions. In that sense one must understand his defense of the *Filioque*. He argues that the procession of the Holy Spirit from the Son is a necessary consequence of the common faith in which East and West are united. That from which a doctrine follows and the doctrinal consequence are both taught by the same God. One cannot object that divine authority never said it. It suffices that he neither denies it nor asserts principles from which negation could follow: *satis illam affirmat, cum illa asserit quibus probatur* (*De processione Spiritus Sancti contra Graecos* 26). The most general view that the intellectual expression of faith may develop through a process of reasoning is here already developing.

In the meanwhile new schools arose on the continent, not only connected with monasteries but also with the Chapters of the rising towns. Among the most famous were the schools of Chartres and Paris. In those schools a new intellectual tool was added to Grammar: the *dialectica*, based on some logical treatises of Aristotle and Porphyry, preserved by Boethius. Dialectic became a means of reconciling with one another such 'authorities' as seemed to contradict each other. It was a difficult enterprise. In the school of Chartres some masters, such as William of Conches, did make use of dialectic in order to establish the truth of the 'authorities.' These naive attempts, frankly rationalistic in their tendency, were before long condemned by the Church. For example, Berengarius was a pupil of Fulbert of Chartres. Therefore dialectic soon became an object of suspicion on the part of the traditional theologians, inspired by St. Augustine.

Such was the situation in which Abelard made his appearance. He is the real creator of the epistemological statute of scholastic theology. His point of departure is that of his time. In his *Sic et non* he draws up a list of conflicting 'authorities,' and he too assigns to theology the task of reconciling them by the means of dialectic. He was not devoid of all historical sense, for he states that the 'authorities' must be subjected to historical criticism. The correctness of the text and its historical authenticity must be investigated. In interpreting them one has to take account of the purpose of the author and the circumstances in which a work was written. Abelard was not aware, however, of the problem of development and could hardly be. Against dialectical rationalism, on the one side, he had to maintain that reason had only a subservient function to the understanding of the 'authorities' and that these alone were the supreme criteria of theological truth. With the theologians of his time, Abelard still did not know the idea of a living *magisterium* that could act as a supreme authority in matters of faith and theology. Against the antidialectical mystics, on the other hand, he defended the use of dialectical methods. There is but one adequate way of dealing with the misuse of dialectic: to state the rules of its right use and to conform to them. Therefore Abelard had to define the object of rational theology.

After the simple and powerful proclamation of St. Anselm, a man was needed with a gift for clear distinctions. It is possible to follow in the works of Abelard the evolution of the scholastic idea of theology. In his early writings intellectual reflection is still swayed by the mystical movement of the soul toward God. Later, however, theology is emancipated from mysticism and becomes an independent intellectual enterprise with a scope and character of its own. In both cases, however, the proper study of theology is conceived of in the same manner. Theology has nothing to do with revealed truth itself but only with its clothing in human concepts and language. These must be analyzed and ordered according to the requirements of accuracy and logical consistency. The relation to truth and reality is taken for granted. It is only in his last works that he asks the question about the relation between rational theology and the mysteries of divine revelation. A new dimension of theology comes to the front: that of trying to think, however inadequately, about the object of faith by means of analogies taken from common experience and to confirm them by arguments, not apodictic arguments as in St. Anselm, but persuasive probabilities.

In his own time Abelard found no favour in the eyes of the great *anti-dialectici* of his time: St. Bernard and William of St. Thierry. The quarrel was not so much about the use of reason in theology as about the emancipation of theology from the flight of the soul toward God. The idea of a neutral, purely objective application of reason to the mysteries of faith sounded like blasphemy to the ears of the Augustinian mystics. Human thought is either the self-expression of a righteous mind that loves God—and then it is on its way to truth—or it is exercised by a sinful mind—and then it must needs fall into error. *Ubi amor, ibi oculus*, Richard of St. Victor states, and he explains: 'From love follows manifestation, from manifestation, contemplation, and from contemplation, knowledge' (*De statu interioris hominis* 1.20). It is Abelard's concept of theology, however, that gradually will prevail in the schools. In his spirit Peter Lombard composed the *Four Books of the Sentences*, which became the theological textbook of the Middle Ages.

In the 12th century the whole organon of Aristotelian logic became known. The concept of science made its entry into the universities and was soon included, in spite of a vigorous opposition, in the definition of theology. The translation of Aristotle's physical, metaphysical, psychological, and ethical treatises followed in the course of the 13th century. The situation of the Christian thinker was profoundly affected by it. He had no longer to do with conflicting 'authorities of faith' alone, but also with apparent contradictions between the authority of the Scriptures and that of the Philosopher. In the University of Paris it led to serious troubles. The Averroists of the Faculty of Arts, although submitting to the higher truth of faith, came to think that as a philosopher one might hold opinions contrary to sacred doctrine.

So the time had come for the giants of scholastic theology: St. Albert the Great, St. Bonaventure, and St. Thomas Aquinas. But the method of theology remained substantially the same. To the *sic et non* of ecclesiastical theology a new *sic et non* was added: the seeming conflict between the authority of faith and the authority of the Philosopher. The theologian had now to reconcile the new philosophy with traditional theology. The method, however, was not deeply altered. Just as formerly the 'authorities' were to be interpreted and adapted in order to fit with one another within the framework of a growing system, so now the statements and opinions of the Philosopher were to be interpreted in such a way as to fit in with the statements of the creed within the framework of an all embracing system in which philosophy was admitted as 'the handmaid of theology.' Philosophy provided the analogical models with which to think about the mysteries of faith. This was the fully elaborated actualization of an idea of theology heralded by Abelard. The masterpiece that resulted from it was the *Summa theologica* of St. Thomas Aquinas.

There is an evident unity and continuity in the development of medieval theology. Its nature had been determined by its initial situation. Later changes in the situation did not modify its basic pattern. It was not so much a creative theology in which the life of the Church as a whole was forced to create an orthodox creed in order to preserve the unity of the Church against the destructive menaces of heresies that gnawed at the very heart of faith. It was rather a preservative and continuative theology. It aimed at putting in order the treasures of the past. Generally speaking, the Church was in uncontested possession of its essential doctrines. The further elaboration of theological synthesis could be left to the schools. The great theologians were not, in the main, bishops and popes but schoolmen. The schools enjoyed a large amount of freedom. Occasional deviations from orthodoxy had no real chance in the Church. Authority could cut them short without difficulty. Christian thought was not swayed by a living existential impetus of doctrinal development moved by the compelling force of heresy. The only dogma that made some progress in the course of the Middle Ages was that of the Holy Eucharist. The protagonist of heresy, Berengarius, was promptly silenced. The technical distinction between *substantia* and *species*, as used by the defenders of orthodoxy, was taken in the sense of common language and did not really add a new idea to the realistic expressions of the Greek Fathers. Even the highly sophisticated term *transsubstantiatio* (supernatural change in the order of substance without a corresponding change in the object of sense perception), if rightly understood in its strict dogmatic import, did not really add any new idea to what had been explicitly stated by the Fathers. The Church simply declared repeatedly that what it believed concerning the mystery of Christ's presence in the sacrificial gifts—namely, that before the consecration these gifts looked like bread and wine (species) and really were that (substance), whereas after the consecration they continued to look like bread and wine (species) but really were no longer bread and wine but the body and blood of the Lord (substance)—was aptly rendered by the term *transubstantiation*. What the Church authoritatively declared was free of any philosophical implication.

The purpose of this digression about the nature of medieval theology is to make clear that from that very nature it was not to be expected that development of doctrine should create any problem in the mind of its representatives. They were like specialized artisans who had in their workshop a rich collection of stones of different size, form, and color, which were to be shaped in order to fit into a splendid mosaic. The comparison does not imply any depreciation. Although different from that of the Fathers, theirs was a very great work and produced the most perfect and complete master-pieces of Christian synthesis. They built their systems as their contemporaries built cathedrals, to the glory of God.

ST. THOMAS AQUINAS

Now that the nature of medieval theology is understood, the question of its specific contribution to the history of the problem of development can be answered. The scholastic theologians did not explicitly state the question. How could they? Even Thomas Aquinas is unaware of any problem relating to this matter. But in their theology of faith he and his great contemporaries worked out a view in which the basic principles for its solution were clearly expounded. Just as in some geological strata one contemplates the flux of things in a petrified form, so in Thomas Aquinas one finds a theology of faith, the static structure of which reveals the movement of dogma. Speaking of the possibility of constructing from the elements of Thomism a theory of doctrinal development, H. D. Simonin aptly writes: 'In any case, the thing will only be possible if we take care to project in the order of historical succession what the master teaches us about the requirements and conditions of faith at a given moment of its existence. Indeed, if historical development of faith is possible . . . such a progress should be postulated by the very nature of faith, written in the law of its existence, like the possibility of growth in a living thing.'[2]

According to Aquinas, the object of faith is 'Primary Truth' (*Veritas Prima*). In this context the expression still has something of the Johannine concept of truth as reality. Faith is essentially an assent. But there is no assent without apprehension. The way in which faith apprehends primary truth is twofold: immediate and mediate. The immediate apprehension, worked by the grace of faith and possessed in the 'light of faith' (*lumen fidei*) is the supernatural core and origin of the act of faith. It is a kind of immediate impression (*sigillatio*) of the Primary Truth upon the mind and as such it cannot err (*In Boeth. de Trin.* 3.1.4). In faith there is a kind of real apprehension of God because there is an immediate contact between the mind and divine reality. The nature of that contact, however, is not such that it produces a kind of intellectual vision or intuition. For if so, dogmas would no longer have any meaning: and faith, contemplating its unveiled object, would no longer be a veil. St. Thomas was very concerned with the right expression of the supernatural reality of faith in the faithful. It is a light or perfection of the mind that moves the mind not in an intellectual way (i.e., giving it a direct intellectual intuition) but rather by the way of will (*In Boeth, de Trin.* 3.1.4). Its proper effect is thus that it moves the will to adhere to Primary Truth in an act of assenting to the propositions of the creed. The assent to Primary Truth cannot be reduced to an intellectual acceptance of dogmatic propositions. In assenting to Primary Truth or reality the mind does not rest in the propositions (ST 2a2ae, 1.2 ad 2). It goes beyond them toward divine reality because it arises from the immediate interior touch of that reality. The imprint of Primary Truth comes through illuminating grace as a kind of 'transcendental' knowledge in the preconscious springs of thought. And therefore it tends to its own full explication in the 'categorical' expressions of human thought. Those concepts of modern philosophy 'transcendental' and 'categorical' reproduce very well the real mind of Aquinas. So it must be understood that dogmatic propositions are not so much the objects of faith as 'that through which faith tends in its object' (*De ver.* 14.8 ad 5 and ad 11). There is, of course, a radical difference between the relation of Primary Truth, touching man in the light of faith, to the propositions in which man explicitly attains it and the relation between the transcendental and the categorical in modern philosophy. The Primary Truth that antecedently to the exercise of thought and assent in the believer acts as its source and the ground of its possibility is a pure gift of grace, not a formative element of human nature. And just as man does not possess of himself the supernatural source in himself, so he cannot form by himself, as explications of the interior gift, the propositions of faith to which he assents. They come from without, from the teaching of the Bible and the Church.

Faith then is to cogitate in the act of assenting (*cum assensione cogitare*) according to the authorities of St. Augustine (ST 2a2ae, 2.1). It is an absolute assent because Primary Truth itself, shining in the source of mental life, is the root from which faith springs and the object toward which it strives. But on the plane of explicit knowledge, present to objective consciousness, it cannot rest in the inadequate translations of divine truth in human language, and therefore it keeps tending toward a fuller possession in the movement of thought. Albert the Great had already expressed the same idea in his incisive way. Faith, he says, has two aspects: on the one hand, it is *e auditu* and as such it has a medium (exterior preaching, outward signs, and inner representations) and leads to thought; on the other hand, it is a charisma of the Holy Spirit and as such is without any medium, it is a simple light that convinces the mind and causes an absolute assent, placid and joyful (*In 3 Sent.* 23.8, 17).

It is easy to show that in the Thomistic doctrine of faith the possibility of a development of doctrine is written in the law of its existence following from its very nature. Tending toward Primary Truth, of which one already has a real knowledge of sympathy through grace, man also tends through thought to a fuller expression of it in human terms. The pathos of faith, impelling man toward its real object, carries with it a restless movement of thought, trying to dilate to the utmost the human vessels in which that object presents itself to man's consciousness. Although St. Thomas—and, one may add, St. Bonaventure—did not have to face the problem of development and were unaware of it, their theology of faith unmistakably provides the principles of its true solution.

There are other elements in St. Thomas' doctrine of faith in which the solution of the problem is prepared. H. D. Simonin has pointed them out in the article quoted above. They are connected with the question of the degree of explicit knowledge required for true and saving faith. In ST 2a2ae, 2.6 St. Thomas establishes that the *maiores,* the more cultured people, ought to have a more explicit knowledge of the doctrines of faith than the *minores,* the uneducated folk. For the latter a knowledge of the essential truths —think of the *rule of faith* in Tertullian and Origen—is sufficient. Human society is a stratified whole in virtue of which the faith of the *minores* is implicit in that of the *maiores.* Because of the organic unity of the body of believers, those who by reason of their dullness or lack of education know only an essential part of the creed, implicitly believe what the more educated explicitly recognize. But how is this possible? Is not every man obliged to believe the whole of divine revelation? Yes, but since the object of faith is both simple and complex—simple in itself and complex in its human articulations (ST 2a2ae, 1.2)—it is possible to attain to the simple through an elementary knowledge of the complex. No more is required for an uneducated mind because, from the nature of the case and the will of God, the knowledge of truth has to be accommodated to the conditions and possibilities of the subject. Furthermore, the objective structure of doctrine is like that of an organic whole. The term *article*, used to indicate the various points of the rule of faith, comes from a Greek word that signifies 'a certain coalescence of distinct parts; therefore the parts of the body coalescing in mutual adaptation are called articulated members. . . . In a similar way the points to be believed by Christian faith are said to be distinct articles as far as they are divided in different parts that coalesce with each other' (ST 2a2ae, 1.6).

The doctrine of faith, then, is an articulated whole, a system of truth, so that those who only partially know it and accept it implicitly assent to the whole. Add to this that St. Thomas emphatically distinguishes two kinds of articles: those that belong directly or chiefly or *secundum se* to the object of faith, and others whose connection with faith is only indirect or *in ordine ad alia* (2a2ae, 1.6 ad 1 and 1a, 32.4). The former cannot be denied without falling into heresy. The negation of the latter, however, does not necessarily involve heresy as long as their connection with the former is not clearly perceived and established by ecclesiastical definition (1a, 32.4). On this occasion Thomas clearly implies the possibility of a development of doctrine: some doctrines that in earlier times could be safely denied without heresy may afterwards become such that he who denies them should be qualified as a heretic.

To summarize: according to St. Thomas Aquinas, first, faith is an assent to Primary Truth, embodied and expressed in an assent to dogmatic propositions. The assent of faith then strives beyond the propositions to truth or reality itself. By its immediate imprint the Primary Truth inspires in the human mind a supernatural movement of sympathy in which the believer enjoys a real, although inarticulate, apprehension of the things in which he believes.

Second, the knowledge of the creed must be adapted to the condition of the hearer. In its imperfect knowledge the uneducated mind implicitly attains to the fullness that the educated expressly acknowledges.

Third, to this corresponds, on the objective side, the organic unity of the whole of dogma. It is an articulated body of doctrine, so that in believing a part without knowing or denying the rest, one implicitly accepts the other parts that are united to it in one living system.

Fourth, in the propositional object of faith one must distinguish between essential and secondary components. The former can never be denied without falling into heresy, while the latter sometimes may be.

When we combine these views and translate them in terms of history we at once see the justification of a true development of dogma: 'Since the explication of faith, which may be less or more perfect, depends at every moment upon the subjective conditions of the faithful, it will vary too, in the course of history, according to the different levels of civilization and the psychological, intellectual, and social capacities of humanity.'[3]

ST. BONAVENTURE

In St. Bonaventure's thought Augustinian theology reaches its perfect culmination. St. Thomas Aquinas molded the theological tradition in a new synthesis, the structure of which was marked by his Aristotelianism. St. Bonaventure assimilated Aristotelian elements in a systematic scheme, which remained frankly Augustinian. For St. Augustine, indeed, there is one continuous movement in man's knowledge of God, springing from the seed of an unconscious knowing (*nosse*) and ending in the fruit of contemplative fruition. The initial knowledge and love of God is a 'transcendental,' a formative element of human nature. Therefore it is indestructible. In the states of infancy, sleep, and even damnation, it is necessarily at work in the hidden springs of life. From that first unconscious knowledge of God the mind goes out in search of a full and fully conscious knowledge of Him. It is the restless movement of thought and desire which can only come to rest in the unveiled contemplation of God. On the plane of cogitative knowledge man may err, and in the state of original sin his pride fatally makes him fall into error. Then he turns from God and from himself. For, being estranged from God, he is also alienated from his own true being. Therefore God has to set him right in a way accommodated to his carnal and haughty state of existence. This is accomplished by the Incarnation in which God descends to the condition of man's sinful flesh and by purifying faith in the Incarnation, which humiliates man's pride because it withholds from him the evidence that the mind naturally asks for. Cogitation, then, corrected and conditioned by faith, strives by meditative thought toward that full knowledge for which man is made but which he never can perfectly reach here below.

The systematic thought of St. Bonaventure follows the same ascending line. The transcendental or formative element in the constitution of the human mind is the immediate illuminating presence of God, which rules and moves the life of thought. By its very nature God's first illuminating presence is hidden from man. He thinks from it: he does not think it. On the plane of conscious life, however, it gives rise to philosophical thought. There is a philosophic knowledge of God: a certainty of truth as far as it is the object of inquiry (*veritatis ut scrutabilis notitia certa*).

Faith has its origin in a special illumination that completes the initial light of reason. Although different and caused by grace, its relation to the inborn light is one of continuity: 'That which especially moves us to believe is the illumination itself that begins with the inborn light and is completed in the infused light' (*De mysterio Trinitatis* 1.2 conclusion). Unlike the inborn light that as a formative element of man's being remains unconscious, the work of the infused light is in a certain manner and measure open to consciousness, as is evident 'from experience, if one consults the secret of his heart' (*ibid.*). Faith, although flowing from an infused light (*gratia interius inspirans*), which causes an inner hearing (*auditus interior*), supposes an outer hearing of the message that works as an *instructio exterius manuducens* (*In 3 Sent.* 25.2.2). On the plane of reflection, faith, which perfects the inborn light explicated in philosophy, gives rise to theological thinking, which perfects philosophy. Theology is 'a devout knowledge of the truth as proposed to faith' (*veritatis ut credibilis notitia pia*). Theology, however, exegetic or dogmatic, does not rest in itself. It is only a stage in the movement of faith, which continuing the striving of the inborn light, ascends toward its ultimate perfection: mystical union in which the Beatific Vision is not reached but imperfectly anticipated.

It is against the background of this dynamic conception of religious thought, in which theology is no more than a moment, that one should read the various statements of Bonaventure about the different kinds of religious propositions. Some of them belong to the doctrine of faith antecedently (philosophical truths). Others, which have the value of principles, are such that the light of faith directly leads to them; they are called articles. Others still, which are connected with it as consequences, are 'such as may be elicited from those articles and follow from them. (*In 3 Sent.* 25.1.1). Further on he states that faith grew as to the number of the *credibilia* (objects of thought) 'not by addition of new articles but by a certain process of explication' (*ibid.* 25.1.1). In the following question he admits that faith grew as to the fullness of light, at least in humanity as a whole, not because of historical changes but because of the greater manifestation of the truth by grace and instruction bestowed upon man by Christ and His Spirit. Such propositions or truths as are not necessary for salvation because they are not found in the Creed or Scripture, annexed as they are as explications of the Creed or interpretations of the Scriptures, may be the object of conflicting opinions before they are conclusively settled, but not after. As is evident from the context, Bonaventure means a decisive judgment of the Church, as for instance a conciliar judgment (*In 1 Sent.* 27.1.4).

Let it be noted, first, that in speaking of a process of explication, St. Bonaventure has in mind not only such truths as are mere consequences of articles but also some articles as far as they are explications of a general belief. For example, the seven articles that in the actual creed describe the divine economy of Redemption are explications from the general belief in a future Redeemer. That process, however, came to an end with the Gospel (*In 3 Sent.* 25.1.1). One may gather from his sayings that the same process goes on after the preaching of the Gospel and the mission of the Holy Spirit but its results, although pertaining to faith (*credibilia*), are not articles.

Second, from this it follows that the process of explication in the course of the history of the Church is not guided by formal reasoning alone but by other kinds of inference too, the logical status of which is not further analyzed.

Third, when one tries to place the statements of Bonaventure about the theological explication of faith in the context of his unitary conception of the ascension of the soul toward God, one cannot but conclude that the process under consideration is not a matter of theology alone, separated from spirituality. The growth of an intellectual knowledge of faith has its origin not in reason alone but in love too. It is part of the *Itinerarium mentis in Deum* that, arising from the unconscious light of God's immediate subjective presence in the mind, ascends toward the fully conscious light of an immediate objective presence of God to the mind in the blessed union and vision of peace.

LATER SCHOLASTICS

In the first generations following Albert, Thomas, and Bonaventure theology maintained itself on a very high level. It would be tedious, however, to examine individually the various texts that are relevant to the present question. It will suffice to make some general or more particular remarks in order to understand the direction in which theology was flowing and to read in that context a few hints about the development of doctrine.

First, then, it very soon becomes clear that theology is on the way to succumbing to the dangers inherent in the method of scholastic theology: logical formalism and subtlety, and a certain tendency, too, to turn away from what theology is about (Scripture and the realities of salvation) and to shut itself up in a purely ideal world of self-made questions and controversies. The later decline of scholastic theology will be marked by a lack of scriptural sense and by endless discussions about theological opinions that are examined and appreciated according to their probability. A theology of probable opinions will take the place of a scriptural theology. Theology will become an intellectual occupation of dons. Its formal reasonings will hang loose at both the point from which it should start (Scripture) and the points at which it should arrive (spiritual life and preaching).

In the first generations after St. Thomas the decline was not yet apparent, but its seeds were already at work. Thomas and Bonaventure were still so absorbed by the realities of which the sacred text spoke that methodological questions about the nature and method of theology were clearly but briefly treated without subtleties. Their successors, on the contrary, consecrated to those reflective epistemological problems the most ample and intricate considerations and discussions. Thomas reasoned freely, arranging his ideas within a comprehensive view of reality, and using various models from experience as analogies of heavenly things without any scruple about their strict logical relation to the primary analogies. Those after him became more intent on the strict application of formal logic and lost themselves in technical distinctions and subdistinctions. So the way lay open to skepticism.

As to the problem of development, in Thomas and Bonaventure the proper locus where one should look for occasional remarks on the development of doctrine is the treatise on faith, whereas in

their successors such remarks are more generally found in the context of discussions about the nature and method of theology.

The man who started the problem of theology is the *Doctor
Solemnis*, Henry Goethals of Ghent. It may perhaps be said that
he somehow reintroduced into theology the ancient problem of
gnosis as a special state of knowledge halfway between faith and
the Beatific Vision. Like Clement or Origen he held that theology
supposed a holy life. Between faith, *credere*, and the Beatific Vision,
videre, there is an intermediate knowledge, *intelligere*, which is
proper to theology. It goes beyond simple faith and attains to wisdom, which consists in a certain understanding of the mysteries.
Such understanding is rational. There are three ways of knowing:
'one of faith alone . . . another in which the objects of faith become
evident . . . *in patria* (heaven), a third intermediate, in which the
objects of faith are known . . . as evident to reason' (*Summa
questionum ordinatarum* 13.6).

The source of theological knowledge is a special illumination
added to that of faith. It makes reason work in a supernatural way,
so that going beyond faith it may reach a certain understanding of
supernatural realities, which, although objects of faith, are in themselves most intelligible. As a supernatural gift of intelligence it may
strictly speaking exist without sanctifying grace. Then, however, it
only works as a *gratia gratis data* in order to help the faithful and
to confound adversaries. But united to sanctifying grace (*gratia
gratum faciens*) it causes in the theologian himself a loving assent
and a certain interior taste for supernatural things, resulting from
connaturality with the object. In the best theologians the knowledge of divine things leads to a state of growing contemplation, the
evidence of which approaches to that Beatific Vision without ever
attaining it in this life.

This singular doctrine was already anticipated by Matthew of
Aquasparta who wrote in his *Quaestiones de fide*: 'When once the
intellect is purified by faith, a gift of understanding is added whereby
the mind becomes more elevated and illuminated, so that the things
which it believes and to the understanding of which it cannot attain
by itself, are perceived by most certain reason [*certissima ratione*]'
(*Quaest. 5 de Fide*).[4] By knowledge through a special gift of understanding he certainly means theology. It is Henry, however, who
stated the new gnostic conception of theology in a way so radical
and powerful that it unchained the theological passions.

Henry was severely attacked by theologians of the most different schools: by Thomists such as Hervaeus Natalis and John of Naples, by Aristotelian eclectics such as Gerald of Bologna and Godfrey of Fontaines, and by the Franciscans Duns Scotus and Petrus Aureolus. Hervaeus Natalis states the opinion of Henry as follows: 'There is a certain supernatural light, distinct from the light of faith, and infused by God in some perfect men. Through this light all the articles of faith become evident as far as evidence is required for true knowledge, although it does not give so great an evidence as that which is granted by the vision of the Blessed' (*Defensa doctrina D. Thomae* Pars 1.9.8). A special *lumen theologiae* added to the *lumen fidei*, he answers, is incompatible with the nature of faith as far as it is an assent on authority. It is incompatible, too, with the nature of the *lumen fidei*, which is necessarily supplanted, not perfected by it, and with the merit of faith that supposes the obscurity of its objects. According to Duns Scotus it is self-contradictory to say that in order to understand the Scriptures the light of faith is sufficient while in order to draw conclusions from them— a thing which the unbeliever can do as well as the believer—a different superior light should be required (*In 3 Sent.* 24.9). Godfrey of Fontaines argues that the cooperation of the light of faith with that of natural reason is sufficient to explain theology as we know it. A *lumen theologiae* is consequently superfluous (*Quodl.* 8, 7.77–79).

The controversy about the nature of theology is not devoid of importance for the question of the development of dogma. The reaction against Henry of Ghent will lead to a stricter conception of theology as a merely human science that draws logical conclusions from the articles of the Creed or the Scriptures. This cannot be without consequence for the question of development of dogma, which indeed is the outcome of a process of reasoning (in the largest sense of the term), starting from the Scriptures and the articles of the Creed. If theology is conceived of as a concern of natural reason alone, a twofold danger is not far off. On the one hand, the notional understanding of the deposit of faith, as far as it is the object of theology, will tend to be considered as a natural critical understanding for which faith and the light of faith are no longer required. The light or grace of faith will still be necessary to elicit a supernatural assent, but not to determine the meaning of the articles or Scripture texts as far as theology has anything to do with them. On the other hand, the method of reasoning proper to theology will be simply reduced to an application of the strict logical rules of formal inference. So theology is gradually 'secularized,' and the development of dogma devolves into the question whether theological conclusions may become points of faith.

The Scholastics dealt with here do not go that far. For them theology still proceeds from revealed truths that are apprehended and assented to by the mind under the illumination of a divine light. They all, with the exception of Scotus, still adhere to the doctrine that the light of faith imparts a supernatural certainty, not only to the *objectum quod creditur* (the dogmas) but also of the *objectum quo creditur* (the fact of divine revelation), so that strictly speaking faith is self-sufficient and does not depend upon rational proofs of credibility, however much such probable arguments may be desirable and useful.

As to the question of the nature of theological reasoning, it cannot be denied that there is already a tendency toward logical rigorism. When St. Thomas calls theology a science he uses the term *science* in a loose analogical way, as Hervaeus Natalis, the best of his disciples and defenders, points out (*Defensa doctrina D. Thomae* 1.7). He never intended to conclude from the scientific character of theology that its way of reasoning was subjected to the strict rules of the deductive syllogism, as is evident from his response to the question whether sacred doctrine proceeds by argumentation (ST la, 1.8). The example he gives is that of St. Paul's proving the universal resurrection from the Resurrection of Christ. No one will assert that he was thinking here of an Aristotelian syllogism. The theologians of the following generations, however, reflecting on the nature and method of theology, will stress more and more the strict logical character of theological thinking. Godfrey of Fontaines, for instance, who had a well-balanced mind, was very well aware of the danger of formalism although he too insisted upon the strict scientific nature of theology. In practice he does not urge such requirements, and he opines that the condemnations of 1277 by the bishop of Paris were justified because the authors of the condemned propositions let themselves go too far without keeping reason in check: *sine freno rationis seipsis nimium effundebant* (*Quodl.* 12, 5.104).[5]

In the dynamic context of human existence, theology in spite of its increasing independence was still viewed as a movement of the mind that starting from faith strives toward the Beatific Vision. On that point the influence of St. Augustine, continued by both St. Thomas and St. Bonaventure, was too powerful to be successfully counteracted. Moreover, the general spirit of medieval man, who conceived himself as a 'being toward God,' could not admit of a theology that had no place for the movement of the soul toward the only perfection in which his being could achieve its ideal Self. Even Godfrey of Fontaines who decidedly rejects Henry's conception of a special theological light, which by its dynamic progression mediates between the light of faith and the light of vision, does not reject the Augustinian Scheme. God, he says, calls man to beatific contemplation and will gradually guide him from sheer ignorance to vision. The starting point is faith, but faith by its very nature is obscure. Its object is veiled, and the veil is never lifted here below. Consequently the gradual perfection of divine knowledge in man's present condition cannot be a progress of faith itself. It can only consist in a growing knowledge that is not faith, but is rooted in it. Such knowledge is theology.[6]

On his part, Scotus is the first to reject the Thomistic doctrine according to which the light of faith gives a sure knowledge of the divine origin of its object, professing as he does that reason alone makes us sure of the fact of revelation. He escapes the rationalistic reduction of faith to reason by stressing the point that faith gives man a certain affective knowledge of the objects of faith. Although the fact of revelation can only be known by rational proof, supernatural faith does not assent to the articles because they are thus revealed. That which one assents to is, in the first place, God Himself and consequently the articles about Him, because by virtue or the *habit of faith* one has a supernatural inclination toward the object of faith. 'God infuses in us the virtue of faith (*habitus fidei*) which inclines our intellect to assent to the articles, so that the object of faith is God Himself about whom those articles are formed which we assent to as to secondary objects in virtue of the same inclination. . . . Although the articles are not present for us as objects unless they are revealed, still, the intellect does not tend toward them because it first believes their being revealed. Therefore the formal object of faith is not the *revelari* (the fact of their being revealed) but the articles themselves. They remain obscure, however, because although the virtue firmly inclines us to assent to them it does not

make them present for us through the evidence of the real itself'
(*In 3 Sent*. 23.10–11).

Such, then, is the dynamic setting of the development of doctrine, elaborated by theological analysis and inference. As to the
idea that development takes place, the witnesses abound. Although
they do not introduce anything substantially new—the same types
of distinction obtain throughout the voluminous commentaries on
the same texts and 'authorities'—they are none the less significant
and on some points put us a step ahead.

To begin with Hervaeus Natalis. He rejects the interpretation
according to which faith and theology are distinct from one another
in that the objects of the former are the simple statements of the
Canon (rule of faith) while the objects of the latter are conclusions
derived from these statements. He notices, referring to St. Thomas,
that Scripture itself already draws conclusions. Theology, then,
differs from faith in the strict sense as far as it is about conclusions
that are not explicitly stated in the Canon. Theological conclusions
belong to faith in a wider sense. For theology is nothing else than a
habit of believing by inference. It makes me believe those things
which are virtually and implicitly contained in the articles of faith
because of the credibility of the initial objects of faith, which are
the articles. In this it differs from both faith and science (*Defensa
doctrina D. Thomae*). Hervaeus is more technical than his master.
The terms 'virtually and implicitly contained' already appear but
they do not yet have a different meaning. The new statements at
which theology arrives by inferential processes are, in a sense not
yet accurately defined, objects of faith.

Henry of Ghent, commenting upon the words of Christ in Jn
16.12, 'I have yet many things to say to you,' asks whether all truth
is not contained in Scripture. Like all the medieval scholastics he
answers the question in the affirmative. He even stresses the point
to the utmost: 'Holy Scripture not only is perfect in itself but it is
written in the most perfect way so that nothing remains to be written' (*Summa quaestionum ordinatarum*, 8.6). If Scripture is thus
perfect in itself, a development of divine truth can only consist in a
more perfect understanding by the human mind. All truth is formally but not materially contained in the Bible. The Holy Spirit, then,
without adding anything leads the Church into a more explicit knowledge of the undeveloped material riches hidden in the Bible. In their
letters the Apostles themselves have but unveiled what was formally

although implicitly contained in the Gospel. The relation between the whole of Canonical doctrine and the doctrine of the Fathers is of the same nature. The latter must explain (*exponere*) and complete (*supplere*) what was left unfinished by the Apostles. But there is no question of adding something to the Gospel (*Summa quaestionum ordinatarum*, 8.6, ad 2).[7]

The comparison between apostolic and post-apostolic development is very illuminating. There seems to be no essential difference between them as to the relation of explicit to implicit that connects the apostolic letters to the Gospel as well as the doctrine of the Fathers to that of the Apostles. This suggests the idea of a growth starting from one single idea. Peter Olivi, indeed, suggests that in the objects of faith there is one main object to which all others are subordinated.[8]

Duns Scotus gives the clearest expression to another important aspect of the problem. Dealing with the question of the necessity of rebaptizing heretics or schismatics—a necessity admitted by St. Cyprian but rejected by St. Augustine—he explains:

> Some points belong so plainly to the substance of faith that all men, the uneducated too, must believe them explicitly after they have reached the age of discretion. Such are the articles concerning the Incarnation: that Christ is born and died . . . which all people can apprehend because they are about the manhood of Christ. Other points are to be explicitly believed by the educated (*maiores*) only, as belonging to the substance of faith, for example, that God is one and trine, and generally all such points as pertain to the world of the intellect and imagination. Others are not necessary objects of explicit faith, neither for the former nor for the latter, because their truth is not yet declared by the Church. Such are the numerous conclusions that are necessarily included in the articles of belief; but before they are declared and explained by the Church no one is in duty bound to believe them. [*In 4 Sent.* 5.1, ad 5]

And further on: 'Nothing is to be held as part of the substance of faith except that which is explicitly stated by Scripture or explicitly declared by the Church or evidently following from something plainly contained in Scripture or declared by the Church' (*In 4 Sent.* 11.3).

It clearly results from these quotations that in the view of Scotus all necessary conclusions following from the doctrines of faith may be taken up in the substance of faith. Still, one is not bound in duty to assent to them before a decisive intervention of ecclesiastical authority. But for him who clearly sees the necessary consequence, they pertain to the substance of faith. Therefore Scotus can say in his refutation of Henry of Ghent that the difference between himself and the Jew with regard to their attitude toward a conclusion from St. Paul consists in the fact that for him such a conclusion is a belief whereas for the Jew it is no more than an opinion (*In 3 Sent.* 24.1a.7).

It would be possible to multiply the quotations from medieval scholastics in order to prove that in discussing the nature, method, and range of theology they fully admit the possibility of attaining by means of reasoning conclusions that are not explicitly stated in the Creed or the Scriptures and that, given certain circumstances, may be included in the object of faith. It would lead too far if this study tried to treat them exhaustively; therefore it will be confined to a few considerations.

1. The way in which the conclusions are included in the principles (articles of faith) is mostly indicated by the technical term *implicit*. The conclusions of theology are implicit in the articles of faith. In the 15th century G. Biel already speaks of a *fides implicita*, that is, 'an actual or habitual assent to a general proposition which includes a good many particular propositions.' The particular propositions become explicit through immediate or mediate inference (*Collectorium in 4 libros Sententiarum* 3.25.1a.n.2). The term *virtually* is used too, but its meaning is not different from that of *implicitly*. They sometimes occur together as synonyms. It is also said that theological conclusions are contained in revealed doctrine immediately (Juan de Torquemada) or indirectly (Denis the Carthusian).

2. The distinction between faith and theology, considered as acts, is generally admitted, although the question of their being distinct perfections of the mind (*habitus*) is controverted. By faith one believes without reasoning and by theological thought one comes to believe (or to assent to) propositions as far as they are known by inference. Such conclusions may, after declaration by the Church, become objects of faith. Faith and theology are nonetheless closely connected. Therefore, on the one hand, one may say that theological conclusions pertain to faith in a wider sense (Hervaeus Natalis). On

the other hand, the *habitus* of faith may be called theological (Durandus of Saint-Pourain) or the holy Scriptures may be said to be already a *scientific theology* (Pierre d'Ailly) because the articles of faith are the first principles of theological reasoning.

3. Theological conclusions are generally said to be accepted on faith. William of Ockham, however, the *Venerabilis Inceptor* of the *via moderna*, introduces an important distinction. By applying to theology the Aristotelian notion of science in the strictest sense, he concludes that theology is no science at all because science gives a knowledge of what is stated in the conclusion and therefore supposes a true knowledge of what is stated in the premises. Such a knowledge of principles, however, requires an immediate experience of the thing itself from which the principles are taken. General notions cannot lead to true knowledge. Inferences from general notions are from their very nature abstract and conditional: if that which is stated in the premises is true, then the conclusion too must be true. Notional inferences make one see the *consequentia,* the fact that the conclusion follows from the premises, but not the *consequens*: the truth of that conclusion itself. Therefore theological reasoning as such can only confirm the logical consequence. It cannot lead to an assent. If one assents to them it is not in virtue of theological reasoning but in virtue of faith. Theology explains; it does not judge.[9]

Here an important modern view is clearly anticipated. Cardinal Newman will work it out in the second part of his *Grammar of Assent*: all inferences from mere notions are conditional. Inferences and assent therefore are wholly distinct and irreducible acts.

The significance of Ockham's intervention is that theology is now entirely separated from the life of faith. Theology is inference, faith is assent. Theology does not suppose faith but only a correct statement of what faith is about; and this is within the power of any normal intellect. Moreover, theology as such results only in probabilities, at least if one of the premises is a statement of natural reason, because all statements about the real are only probable except when they are expressions of an intuitive apprehension of real things. Ockham's philosophical skepticism rebounds upon his concept of theological certainty. Theology is thus disconnected from the existential context of faith in quest of its consummation in the Beatific Vision. Newman will bring it back to its religious context by his doctrine of real apprehension from which man, in the exercise of thought, moves as a whole toward a more explicit apprehension of the reality from which he starts: *realizing is the life of true development*.

4. The later scholastics who, as already noted, were mainly concerned with the logical status of theology already draw a clear distinction between two kinds of theological conclusions: those that result from two revealed principles and others that follow from a revealed premise and a rational one. Still, they do not ask the question whether theological conclusions pertain to revealed truth or not. The problem of the definability of theological conclusions is not yet on the horizon. Neither is the distinction between divine faith and ecclesiastical faith. As far as it goes, what follows from the sayings of the theologians of that epoch is that theological conclusions may be integrated into the substance of faith.

CONCLUSION

The points made in this chapter may be summed up thus:

First, the problem of the development of doctrine or the problem of how to reconcile actual development with the claim of immutability inherent in the rule of faith did not arise in the mind of medieval theologians. Owing to the circumstances of its origin, nature, and scope, scholastic theology could hardly be expected to raise the question. The 'authorities' of antiquity were not viewed in their historical setting and succession, but only as building blocks for their dialectical constructions or doctrinal systems.

Second, the idea of development, however, is clearly stated and becomes more distinct in the course of medieval history. The contexts in which it comes to the fore are various: occasional conflicts between early and more recent authorities, as, for example, the contradiction between the attitude of St. Cyprian and that of St. Augustine in the question of rebaptizing heretics and schismatics; the question about possible additions to the creed; the classification of different kinds of religious propositions; and especially in later times, the discussions about the nature and method of theology.

Third, in the course of the evolution of scholastic theology the nature of doctrinal development is more distinctly viewed, but at the same time it narrows down to one rigid type of mental operation: logical inference. In later scholasticism such concepts as science and reasoning are increasingly conceived in a strict Aristotelian sense. In the end the status of science is simply denied to theology, and its work is viewed as an operation of formal inference that, taken by itself, is from its very nature conditional only and leads to nothing more than probabilities.

Fourth, there is another aspect to the evolution just described. In the self-understanding of medieval man, to be a man is to exist for God or toward God. The true movement of existence is vertically directed heavenward and not horizontally, toward a future the accomplishment of which may be the proper task of man in the condition of his existence here below. Therefore, all the valuable efforts of human culture are moved by the sway of heavenly passion. They have meaning only as far as they are integrated into that movement. For a true medieval mind the various operations of theology, i.e., *fides quaerens intellectum*, are essentially stages in the journey of *fides quaerens visionem*. Even when it becomes a distinct and independent science—as it more and more does—it must somehow be reintegrated into the movement of the soul toward God. Only with Ockham who, although a traditional theologian himself, greatly contributed to the spiritual revolution of the Renaissance is theology entirely separated from faith.

Fifth, the most important contribution of medieval theology to a satisfying theory of development of doctrine is to be found in its theology of faith. Linguistic statements, such as dogmas, are conceived of as human expressions of a living existential contact with God Himself, given in the light of faith and utterly beyond human words. The idea is at hand that Christian thought, in its human endeavors toward clarification, is not governed by the rules of logic alone, but also and perhaps mainly by a dim sense of the divine, an inclination of sympathy resulting from the grace of faith and working in the Church through the Holy Spirit.

Sixth, the process of developmental reasoning is viewed as a clarification of what is contained in Scripture or dogmatically summarized in the Creed. Nothing pertains to faith that is not in the Scriptures. The idea of an oral tradition carrying truths that are not in the Bible did not enter the minds of the medieval theologians. The idea however that it is a divine privilege and duty of ecclesiastical authority to pronounce a final judgment upon truth and falsity in matters of doctrinal development is more clearly expounded and more forcibly stressed as the evolution of scholastic theology proceeds.

Seventh, although no theory of development of doctrine was worked out, all the building blocks and all the concepts and distinctions that will be used in what will here be called 'logical theories of development' have already been created.

PART THREE

Theories of Development

CHAPTER SIX

A New Age

In the preceding part of this investigation it was established that from the beginning the idea of development was congenial to the Christian spirit; that in patristic times it was taken for granted that the immutability of the Christian rule of faith did not exclude a real progress in the objective understanding of its content; that its presence in the mind of the Fathers clearly betrayed itself in occasional ways of speaking and acting; that all through the Middle Ages it was generally accepted and gradually clarified in the discussions about the material object of faith and the nature of theological reasoning.

What the idea of development finally looked like may be stated thus: Starting from the articles of faith, in which the essential doctrines of the Bible are condensed, inferences of some kind or other may be drawn that somehow enter into the object of faith but are not to be held as such as long as the Church does not declare them to be so. In this general statement some aspects are left undetermined: What kind of inferences are meant? In what sense do conclusions from the articles belong to the object of faith? What kind of ecclesiastical declaration or intervention is required in order to translate a conclusion from the condition of controvertible opinion to that of a certainty of faith? All these questions will be raised by modern theology.

By 'modern theology' is meant the theology of the epoch that is generally spoken of by historians as 'modern times.' The sentimental overtones to that qualification, setting off modern times as an epoch of enlightenment from the darkness of the Middle Ages, are of no interest for this subject. That there is a difference, and a very deep one, between the Middle Ages and the age that was born

119

from the Renaissance is undoubtedly true as will be shown presently. In opposition to modern theology, the term *contemporary theology* is used in a specific sense. Just as the Renaissance was a period of transition separating the Middle Ages from the modern age, so man is now in the midst of a new epoch of transition separating the modern age from a new age in which, although it is still in the making, he already finds himself. *The New Renaissance of the Spirit,* as V. A. McCrossen called it in an optimistic mood, is pregnant with a new world—one that is taking shape but is not yet completed. The fact is certain. The whole question is one of how to describe and to judge it. Again, this will be dealt with presently. Let it suffice now to state in a general way what such expressions as 'modern age' and 'contemporary age' mean here.

The idea of development of doctrine lived in the mind of the Church from the beginning. This should be clear by now. But the historical phenomenon of development did not give rise to the problem of how the actual developments could be reconciled with the requirement of immutability so strongly stressed all through Christian history. That immutability could go together with development was generally admitted. But how it remained unaffected by the facts of history did not become problematic. This study has attempted to understand why it did not. From its very nature scholastic theology viewed the doctrines of faith as timeless truths. The Fathers and scholastic theologians were not unaware of the fact of history. They knew very well that some doctrines had come to the fore in later times. But they did not look at the facts as historians, and they had no inkling of what historicity might mean.

In the modern age historical circumstances led to the study of the history of Christian doctrine. It was connected with the general awakening of the sense of history. But there were particular reasons, too, that brought about an intensive scrutiny of the history of Christian doctrine. Finally, having for centuries considered the facts, their succession in time, and the various relations of influence that give the succession of facts a certain 'historical' intelligibility, the human mind gradually acquired a new philosophical insight. The idea of historicity began to shine through the facts and dawned upon the understanding. History is an essential dimension of the human phenomenon. Man is history. By its very nature 'existence' makes history. Nothing can enter into the orbit of human life and thought without being affected by its essential historicity. But the entry of this idea, which explodes, as it were, from within the current conception of history itself, removes man from the modern age and places him upon the living stage of the present time. Therefore it will be dealt with not in the historical part of this study but in the systematic treatment that will crown this inquiry.

Let us concentrate now upon the birth of the modern age and its proper characteristics. The Middle Ages are separated from the modern age by the crisis of the Renaissance. Speaking of doctrines and first principles in Chapter One, the concept of historical crisis was already touched. We refer to that part for the general notions. Most historians will admit that the Renaissance was an epoch of transition and cultural crisis. Within the tradition of this civilization it marked a break in the historical continuity of the West. There is still continuity, of course, but the general orientation of the mind was deeply changed. It is not easy to explain. When a stream makes a mighty turn, the waters are the same but the direction in which they flow, determined by territorial conditions, is modified. The bed may become deeper or shallower, broader or narrower; the current may become more rapid and turbulent or slow down to a tranquil glide. The landscape on its banks may take different shapes and colors etc. This is a metaphor, not an allegory. It is intended only to illustrate the idea of a discontinuity in the general form of a process, accompanying a high degree of continuity of content. To say for instance—as this study intends to do—that in the Renaissance the old Christian civilization went through a radical crisis, does not mean that Christianity had passed away or was moribund. It only means that in order to go on living it had to adapt itself to a wholly different historical situation, created by a new world with a climate and spirit of its own, no longer determined by faith in and by hope for heavenly things. Faith and hope persisted but were no longer the leading ideas of culture as a whole.

It is not easy to express in precise dates when a crisis sets in and when it comes to an end. A crisis in individual existence may take several years. A cultural crisis takes more time. Between the moment in which its symptoms clearly appear and the moment in which the principles of a new epoch are established, centuries may go by. It may be argued, for example, that in the 14th century William of Ockham was in philosophy what Petrarch was in literature, a forerunner of an age that did not take definite shape before the 17th century.

What, then, did the spiritual revolution of the Renaissance consist in? The problem has been discussed widely among historians. They have often put the question in terms of historical characteristics that can be established by the techniques of historical science. Some answers still to be found in textbooks of history are often a priori and superficial. A new age, as it arises victoriously from the crisis, has to tear itself away from the grip of a traditional spirit that does not give way without struggle and grim self-defense. Therefore, it has a natural tendency to look upon the age that is passing away as an age of inferior quality and to exalt the distant past, which was once in its turn overcome by its contemporary opponent. The enthusiastic exponents of the new spirit refuse to take the immediate past seriously. They no longer care for it. They cease to study it. Thus gradually a certain set of judgments about one's ancestors degenerates into fixed social prejudices that are taken for granted as first principles. For a time they are not subjected to the test of historical fact. In such a way was the myth of the dark Middle Ages framed. Great historians such as G. Voigt, W. Rüegg, and even J. Burckhardt, who wrote voluminous, learned, and interesting books on the Renaissance, were conspicuous for their naive ignorance of medieval thought. One is now dumbfounded that it did not occur to them that a correct historical understanding and appreciation of the Renaissance was simply impossible without a deep knowledge of the period from which it was born.

In some semi-intellectual circles the myth of the dark Middle Ages is still alive. But it may be added that, since the reaction of romanticism, history has confirmed the view that the Middle Ages, culminating in the 13th century, constituted in their own way a high point of civilization. The new interest in the Middle Ages is not unrelated to the crisis in which the directive principles of the modern age are now questioned and of which the romantic movement has been the first unmistakable symptom. History is a strange thing. Its function of interpretation largely depends upon preconceptions and biases that arise not so much from a consideration of objective facts as from subjective presuppositions, determined by the spirit or the philosophy of the day.

History, then, has a tendency to correct itself when fresh generations arise who are sensitive to the defects of their own age and find themselves more free from the pressure of current social prejudice. Some historians today go so far as to deny that there was any real discontinuity between the Renaissance and the Middle Ages. A more widely accepted view, however, holds to the idea that there is a profound difference of which the following points, stated with due corrections, may be considered as unmistakable tokens.

First, regarding the Greek and Roman classics, the difference is not that the medieval thinkers ignored the classics or were not interested in them so that the humanists of the Renaissance had, as it were, to rediscover them. It is rather a change of attitude and use. The medieval thinker was more interested in the content of classical thought and used its ideas as building blocks for his own theological constructions. The humanists, on the contrary, were mainly engrossed in their formal beauty and studied them for their own sakes as expressions of a refined natural humanity.

Second, medieval man did not consider the humanity of the classics as an ideal to imitate; whereas most humanists, despite the admonitions of the greatest among them, such as Erasmus, looked at it as an ideal model, not only in the domain of literature and style but also in matters of ethical conduct and political organization. Theirs was a spirit of restoring antiquity.

Third, while medieval thought was scholastic, tending toward rational objectivity and systematization, the humanists were rather averse to such things. They exalted individual subjectivity and irrational feeling. Man was no longer considered as a part of an all-embracing coherent system in which he had his fixed place but as the subject of a strictly individual freedom, the greatness of which consisted in the possibility of his remaking his own image according to his own choice.

Fourth, as was already noticed, medieval man had no eye for the historical aspect of the ideas with which he was working. They were materials to be fitted into an objective system, the construction of which was his ultimate goal. The humanist had no such concern. For him antiquity was antiquity, something he valued for its historical distance. He gave his mind to classical literature for its own sake. He wanted to revive it, he hunted for new manuscripts and was delighted whenever he dug from old libraries forgotten works of the venerable past. He then tried to penetrate the spirit of antiquity, to read its utterings with the very eyes of the old writers. He played at being a Greek or a Roman himself. He was not concerned with the truth of their sayings but with their meanings. This is the origin of history as a science working with appropriate methods of philological analysis and historical interpretation. To bring to life again a past world and to understand the witnesses of its spirit exactly as those witnesses themselves understood it: this becomes the supreme goal of the new science, which in the course of time will develop all the refinements of philological and historical investigation. Today the value of that kind of history, which led to such marvellous discoveries and reconstructions, is questioned at least as far as it pretends to be an independent science that simply tries to revive the past for its own sake. In his monumental work *Wahrheit und Methode* Gadamer calls it 'the romantic conception of history.' For him the end of history is not an attempt to revive the past—this is only a condition—but to seek the same truth the men of the past were seeking, and that is our concern as well as theirs. A repeated rediscovery of the past is necessary in order to translate and integrate all insights into a body of truth, which has to be maintained, nourished, corrected, and enlarged by unceasing efforts of thought. Of course, that new conception of the history of thought is closely connected with the discovery of historicity. Just as the past of Western culture is a dimension of its present state, so the thought of the ancient philosophers and poets is an essential dimension of what men are now thinking and feeling. Such insights, however, again go beyond the borderline that separates the modern world from the new world that is dawning on man.

It should be possible to go deeper into the nature of the crisis from which arose the world that this study is now about to interrogate, but first a brief sketch will be given. In the thought of the Fathers and medieval theologians the very being of man is a 'being for': a being for God. It is adequately expressed in the famous dictum of St. Augustine: 'You have made us for yourself and our hearts are restless till they rest in you' (*Conf.* 1.1). The desire for communion with God is not added to our natural being. That being itself is *ad Deum*. Therefore, man cannot be satisfied; his true being cannot be realized except in eternal communion with God. Nevertheless, he has no power in himself—not as a consequence of sin but as a consequence of his creaturely being—to attain to his ultimate selfrealization. The personal communion of the creature with the eternal God cannot but be a gift of God. It is a personal relation and cannot come about except through the freedom of the participants. The initiative must needs be with the Creator: 'In this is love, not that we loved God but that he loved us' (1 Jn 4.10). Divine love by an act of infinite mercy must give men the capacity to acknowledge His love and to answer it. Man is thus that strange paradoxical being that cannot attain to the true perfection of his nature except by a self-gift of God, freely bestowed upon him.

This view expressed the spirit of the ancient Christian world in which the Fathers and the medieval doctors lived and thought. The doctrine of man's natural receptivity for the Beatific Vision and his natural desire to see God as He is was a common belief. It is a strange fact that even in later scholasticism, so inclined to call everything into question, no objections appear against this self-understanding of the Christian. It is an indication that it was in the spiritual air they were breathing. The doctrines of natural receptivity and natural desire appear to be thematizations of a deeper first principle that was not questioned because it was simply taken for granted. In an interesting monograph *Lo natural y lo sobrenatural* (Madrid, 1952), Juan Alfaro has established, to his own astonishment, that the doctrine of the *pondus naturae* is common to all schools of theology after Thomas Aquinas and that no problem was raised with respect to it before the Renaissance.

The same spirit that led the ancient Christian world to see man as a 'being for God' entails some further points. If the only possible perfection and happiness of man consists in an eternal union in which God freely gives Himself to man, then, here below, Christian life through grace must be a real beginning of what eventually will be men's eternal joy. It begins with faith; it strives toward its perfection in the movement of hope; and it lives in divine love, which is a love of friendship. Faith, the beginning of that communion, can by no means have its origin in man himself. It begins in him as a gift of God alone who shines in him through the light of faith. Therefore, faith is self-sufficient. It does not need any foundation in proofs of natural reason. Such proofs, constructed by reflection and starting from data of experience, may be very helpful for God's dispensation of faith through the Church. They may attract the attention of unbelievers. They may help the *pachuteroi*, the thick-skinned (St. John Chrysostom), or the *grossiores*, the rude (St. Thomas), to subject themselves to the Church of God. But faith itself is not in need of them. They may cause a certain 'enjoyment' in faith (St. Albert the Great), but they are not necessary to sustain our belief.

Such, then, are the first principles of ancient and medieval

Christianity. It is not difficult to see that they form a coherent pattern and could not but color and penetrate the whole conscious life of the Christian world and culture. The crisis of the Renaissance was the crisis of that unitary religious self-understanding of man. The revolution is already complete in the beginning of the 16th century. The new conception of man is naturalistic insofar as man understands himself as a being of nature in the same way as all other beings here below. Every nature is related to a natural perfection that corresponds to its active powers. The proper perfection of a thing is the full realization of what that thing is able to achieve by its own inborn powers and means. Hence the proper end or perfection of man does not lie beyond this world but within the limits of the created universe and its natural processes. In this world man, as man, can attain his perfection and, consequently, complete happiness, by himself. Of course, it is not absolute happiness or blessedness, but it is that happiness that he is made for by God, the author of nature. Man should not desire a happiness that is beyond his innate powers. If he finds within himself a desire for union with God, it is a supernatural desire, inspired in the soul by God as the author of grace. Between nature and grace 'a great chasm has been fixed' (Lk 16.26). In man as such there is no inner openness toward communion with God, manifesting itself in a natural desire. There is only the remote possibility of an elevation that is beyond the proper human sphere but that the Omnipotent may realize in man if it pleases His inscrutable good will and mercy. It may be said, then, that medieval man understood himself as a being for God to be realized by God, whereas modern man understands himself in the first place as a being for himself to be realized by himself, at least in the limited sphere of his own nature. For it is evident that man, as do all created things, ultimately exists for God and the manifestation of His glory.

Just as the self-understanding of man in ancient Christianity entailed other views, as pointed out above, so the new self-understanding, too, entails some remarkable shifts in man's way of viewing life and religion. They will gradually be brought to light by the merciless logic of history. First, then, the separation between, on the one hand, man's natural life with its own order of ends and means, complete in itself, and on the other hand, the order of supernatural life, added to the first from without, leads to the conception that in this world righteousness is in the first place a righteousness

of natural morality. Eternal blessedness is something for the here-
after that will befall man according to the moral righteousness of
his earthly conduct. The grace of faith is no longer experienced
as an *arrabōn,* a first imperfect gift of those things that shall be
fully enjoyed only when the whole inheritance shall be given.
Faith loses its essentially mystical character and is reduced to mere
obedience.

From this it follows that faith, deprived of its mystical core,
is practically reduced to a rational act. If the proper perfection
of man is something that is within his own power to achieve, then
the nature of that perfection too and the means that lead to it must
be knowable by natural reason. Man is shut up in the realm of nature
where reason is the only legitimate king. Nothing can enter the city
of man without permission of the king. When rationalism, which
is the natural outcome of naturalism, comes to the conclusion that
it is unworthy of man to accept something as true which cannot be
justified by common reason, the theologians, Protestant as well as
Catholic, readily submit themselves to its claims. The mysteries of
faith, so they say, cannot in themselves be proved by reason but the
fact of their being revealed by the infallible Lord of Heaven can be
convincingly established by arguments taken from common experience. That faith is reasonable comes to mean that, strictly speaking,
a rational conviction of its divine origin is a necessary condition of
faith. Christian thought that, in the patristic and medieval age, was
spendidly theological now exhausts itself in impossible attempts at
apologetic demonstration.

As in the case of the medieval spirit, so now in modern culture
the first principles set forth above together form a consistent pattern. The radical opposition between the two sets of principles marks
the cleft that separates the two stages of this civilization. That
naturalism and rationalism, as explained above, did govern modern
thought in the way of first principles is evident from the fact that,
although they contradicted the principles of ancient Christianity,
they were soon generally accepted as beyond discussion. The texts
of the past, so clear in themselves, were no longer understood, or
they were tacitly circumvented or dialectically interpreted in an
opposite sense. When under the influence of the awakening spirit
of contemporary thought theologians rediscovered and revalued
the true sense of the old texts, they at first met with a fierce and

almost general opposition that is now giving way to a growing agreement in theological quarters.

A true insight into the guiding principles of the modern age is indispensable for a right understanding of what the history of modern times reveals about the theological attempt to solve the problem of development of doctrine. Just as the conception of the nature and requirements of apologetics is closely connected with the way the nature of revelation and faith is conceived, so too is the way of conceiving the nature and requirements of an explanatory theory of dogmatic growth. If, as we shall see, development is conceived of as a process of formal reasoning from one or two revealed premises, the soundness of which is to be judged solely by the laws of logic, the reason is that the starting point is a shallow and incomplete conception of the nature of revelation and faith.

The spirit of the modern age, as set forth in the preceding pages, makes clear two things in connection with the problem under investigation. First, it is understood that because of a certain 'theological rationalism' that fits in with the basic principles of the modern age, there will be a tendency to solve the present problem by theories of logical inference. Next, because of the birth of the historical outlook, it may be expected that the discovery of the facts in their historical setting and perspective will bring about the problem of how to reconcile them with the claim of doctrinal immutability. Both the way of posing the question and the nature of its solution are connected with the spirit of the modern age. There is, however, another fact that will confront the Church with the problem of development. The 16th century witnesses the rise of Protestantism and the tragic separation between what in general terms may be called the North and the South of Western Christianity. In the course of the bitter controversies between the old and the new confessions, both parties appeal to antiquity. Protestantism stands by the Bible and the Bible alone against the claims of the Catholic Church, which in its turn has recourse to an oral tradition, distinct from the Bible but joined to it. As was seen earlier, the idea of tradition considered as a source of revealed truth apart from the Bible and parallel to it was practically unknown to the Fathers and medieval theologians. They knew only a preservative and explanatory tradition, rooted in Holy Scripture. The idea of a separate tradition, however, became an easy expedient for Catholic controversialists. The Council of Trent, which in its doctrinal part was entirely consecrated to the method of dealing with Protestantism and to the defense of Catholic doctrine, resisted the temptation to define a clear-cut distinction between Scripture and tradition, considered as two different treasuries of the one deposit of faith. The question was hotly debated. Time and again Fathers of the Council contested the separation of Scripture and Tradition. All truths necessary for salvation are contained in the Scriptures. There are not two channels through which comes the revelation of the NT but only one, which starting from the Scriptures is continued by tradition not by addition but by authoritative interpretation. This position was successfully defended by A. Bonuccio, one of the ablest theologians of the Council, against the text proposed by the commission and according to which revelation came to us partly (*partim*) through Scripture, partly through oral traditions that the Apostles had received from the mouth of Christ or from the inspiration of the Holy Spirit. After many a heated debate, a compromise was reached. The idea of two distinct streams of revelation was abandoned. Concrete determination of the content of the 'traditions' was omitted. But the idea of a certain distinction between Scripture and oral traditions in matters of faith and morals entrusted to the continuous succession of the hierarchy was maintained, and the opponents had to grant that both Scripture and tradition were to be treated with equal respect (Denz 1501).[1] Further interpretations were left to the theologians. It was a fine specimen of prudent compromise. The contested points were deliberately left aside, just as in the case of the distinction between proto-canonical and deutero-canonical books. Here too the same policy was applied: there certainly is a distinction, but in practice both have equal authority. The Council abstained from passing judgment upon the theoretical position. The possibility of further discussion was left open.

The declaration of Trent concerning the distinction and relation between Scripture and tradition could then be interpreted either in the sense proposed by Bonuccio or in the sense of the two sources theory. Of course, for the time being the second interpretation proved to be more suited to the needs of the Catholic controversy against Protestantism. The reason is clear enough: for lack of a satisfying theory of development of doctrine, the supposition of two treasuries in which the deposit of faith was preserved presented itself as the only possible solution, if one had to argue that the whole of dogmatic teaching as actually proposed by the Church was contained in the primitive deposit.

Easy as it was, it was nonetheless very dangerous. The tendency to consign the doctrines that could not successfully be proved from Scripture to an apostolic tradition, distinct from the NT writings, actually entailed a theory of dogmatic immobilism. For a long time, indeed, it allowed the Catholic controversialists to go on without a hypothesis of dogmatic development.

In the light of that situation it is easy to understand that in the first stages of post-tridentine controversy the canon of Vincent of Lérins was urged on both sides: *quod semper, quod ubique, quod ab omnibus.* Protestants, who stood by 'the Bible alone,' willingly accepted the rule because it made it easy for them to reject as untenable all those doctrines that could not be proved from the Bible. Catholics, in their turn, starting from the principle that apart from Scripture tradition was a distinct source of revealed knowledge, equal to Scripture in authority and dignity, could use it to defend their positions without having recourse to a still non-existent theory of dynamic or evolutive tradition. The rule of Vincent thus proved to be a two-edged sword. It could efficaciously be manipulated by both opponents. The whole question depended upon the first principles from which one started.

This may be illustrated by the controversies of 17th century France that culminated with the intervention of Bossuet and his opposition to Jurieu and Leibniz. The champion of Catholic dogma was most explicit and emphatic in asserting the rule of Vincent in its most unmitigated strictness.[2] The way had been prepared by *les messieurs de Port-Royal*, who in their own time were the most skilled representatives of Catholic theology. They were particularly fitted for anti-Protestant controversy because of their profound learning in the Bible and in patristic theology, especially St. Augustine, and because of the love of clarity initiated by Descartes who influenced them. The theologians of Port-Royal were conservative in the extreme. In the famous Jansenist controversy they took the side of St. Augustine against what they called the Semi-Pelagian novelties of the Jesuits. The same spirit determined their attitude in their quarrel with the Reformation. They applied the Vincentian canon in a strict sense: 'All the dogmas of faith are as old as the Church: they were all explicitly (*distinctement*) believed by the Apostles and have been preserved by an uninterrupted succession of tradition in the consciousness of at least a part of the shepherds and the faithful.'³ Bossuet applauded, and when he entered the arena to fight Jurieu, whose writings were secretly distributed and eagerly read among the Protestants of France, he took his stand on the same principles.

It is rather important to go deeper into the respective positions of Bossuet and Jurieu. Bossuet clearly states the principle that because the works of God are perfect, His revelation too must be perfect from the beginning: 'Catholic doctrine, coming from God, has its perfection from the beginning.'⁴ From the same principle he concludes that divine Providence will preserve the doctrine of the Church from all variations. It is interesting to note that Newman, like Bossuet, starting from an a priori consideration of the nature of God's works, came to the opposite principle: because all the works of God are characterized by evolution, one may conclude by analogy that revelation too and its understanding in the Church will be subject to development. Therefore divine Providence may be expected to guide the process of development and to preserve it from corruptions.

From his a priori principle, Bossuet concludes that all the doctrines of the Church were explicitly known and taught from the beginning, and further, that all variations in doctrine are a clinching proof of the merely human character of a doctrinal system. It apparently never enters his head that the expression of revelation may be perhaps as human as its content is divine, and that the human side of revelation is an essential aspect of it; so that if all human things develop and change, revelation too, in its human expression, will be subject to the law of growth and progress. Bossuet allows only a purely verbal novelty. Referring to Vincent of Lérins, he states that the Councils only 'express by new terms, more proper and precise, a doctrine that never was new.'⁵ So doing, 'it is more carefully defended but not better understood as to its substance.'⁶ For the same reason he categorically denies that heresies gave rise to new insights into revealed truth. All truths were clearly and explicitly believed before the rise of heresy. When Leibniz objects that several doctrines, especially about the canonical character of the sacred books, could not be clearly held from the beginning, Bossuet replies that from the beginning the Church was in tranquil possession of all its sacred books, that the question was only discussed when heretics rejected some of them, and that the Fathers allowed for the sake of peace a certain distinction between *proto*-canonical and *deutero*-canonical books. There are theologians who still try to solve that difficult question in the same way. Bossuet himself applied this 'theory of the three stages in the maturation of the dogmas' to all the cases in which historical facts seemed to present the same kind of difficulties.

To summarize the position of Bossuet in his own words:

> In the course of succession, doctrine is always the same. There-fore, in the style of Scripture, a false doctrine is called another doctrine. . . . So then, if at any time someone says that the faith includes something that yesterday was not said to be of the faith, it is always *heterodoxy*, i.e., *another doctrine* which one opposes to *orthodoxy*; and all false doctrine will betray itself at once, beyond doubt and discussion, whenever it appears, by its novelty, inasmuch as it always will be something not per-petually known.[7]

Bossuet is the very exemplar of the classical systematic mind, clear, logical, massive, absolutely confident in the truth of his posi-tion and impermeable to ideas or facts that do not fit into his all-embracing view of an eternal order. His opponent is a far more subtle and realistic mind. Jurieu is more sensitive to the facts of history and has a better knowledge of the theological tradition. He does not deny the principle of perpetuity; but he accuses Bossuet of rigidity in understanding and applying it, a rigidity that logically should lead to absurd and destructive consequences.

The principle from which the Protestant minister starts is quite traditional: a distinction has to be made between basic articles and others. In order to be basic it is required, first, that the article be revealed; next, that it have an unmistakable importance for the religious life that the faithful can easily establish because God has given them an interior discriminative sense; lastly, that it should clearly be connected with the ends of religion.

In this criteriology there is a new, apparently Protestant note: the appeal to a subjective, psychological rule of discretion, opposed to the objective rule of Catholic tradition, to wit, the actual and common teaching of the Church, led by the vigilance of an infallible institutional authority. If one rejects the latter, the former neces-sarily is imposed, because the Bible by itself, separated from the living exercise of thought, is a dead letter that allows of divergent interpretations. There must be a rule of interpretation. If it is not the objective rule of a living authority, it can only be a subjective rule of private judgment, which must be supposed to be a formative element of the believing mind. This is indeed the meaning of Jurieu: 'God does not make salvation dependent upon truths except such as naturally correspond to the needs and desires of the soul. By this rule I am able to distinguish in revealed truth between those doctrines which must necessarily be accepted for salvation and others which are not necessary.'[8] He takes his stand on human nature as made by God, whereas Bossuet takes no account of human nature but only of the nature of God. Therefore Jurieu argues that since the basic truths of faith correspond to the natural tendencies of man, they somehow participate in the immutability of human nature and consequently in that of God, its creator.

Starting, then, from those criteria, Jurieu comes to the practical conclusion that only the articles of faith included in the Creed are basic truths, which one must believe distinctly in order to be saved. Some of them are essential to all religions while others are proper to Christian faith. The list of basic truths given by Jurieu strikingly reminds us of the *rule of faith* as presented by Tertullian and Origen, although the way he stresses the corruption of sin and the necessity of satisfaction is rather typically Protestant.

The basic articles of faith are contradistinguished from other truths that do not belong to the essence of faith but contribute to its purity. The latter are threefold: first, conclusions from the principles (articles) of Christianity; next, elucidations of the principles themselves; last, religious truths that are neither necessary consequences from nor elucidations of the basic principles. The second category is interesting. They are theological speculations. They may be false, questionable, temerarious, or true, but at any rate, they are not necessary for salvation. In this manner Jurieu explains and justifies the differences in the successive confessions of the Reformation. They are not differences in essential matters but only in matters of theological deduction or explanation. It may be regrettable but it cannot be used as an argument against the Reformation. Moreover, the faith of the Romanists shows similar differences. It could not be otherwise because such differences arise from the nature of man as he appears in history.

Jurieu clearly accepts the perpetuity of objective faith but it should not be interpreted absolutely:

What the question resolves itself into is to know, first, whether in connection with the basic dogmas, there is no possibility of considerable change as to the way of expressing them without this being a mark of error and inconsistency of doctrine; next, whether, with regard to the dogmas that are not essential or necessary as means, there is no possibility of a complete change, not only in the way of expressing them, but also in our conviction concerning them, without it being a mark of false religion.[9]

In the creeds of the Reformed Churches no corrupting doctrines are added to the essentials of faith collected from Scripture. In the Catholic Church, on the contrary, corrupting doctrines are introduced into salvific faith, with an appeal to an undefinable and uncontrollable oral apostolic tradition unknown in the theology of former times.

Jurieu made a very good case against Bossuet. The distinction between essential and non-essential doctrines is as old as Christian theology. What he says about development by way of consequence or elucidation is generally in accordance with medieval scholastic theology. The only difference between Jurieu and the later medieval scholastics is that according to Jurieu such consequences and explanations never become part of saving faith, whereas in the mind of Scotus, for example, they might become objects of faith for the individual who clearly sees the truth and for the whole community after due declaration by the Church. The essential difference between the old Catholic tradition and Protestantism does not consist in the acceptance or rejection of an oral apostolic tradition distinct from faith—this is a false opposition—but in the acceptance or rejection of ecclesiastical authority in questions of faith. The *sola fides* of Luther is not so much opposed to the acceptance of traditions other than Scripture as to the acceptance of a divinely warranted social organ of authority, given to the Church by God in order to settle the problems of faith.

Jurieu no more than Bossuet admits a real development of dogma. The dogmas or essentials are fixed from the beginning. The conclusions and elucidations, however true, are not dogmas at all. The positions of both great champions is weakened by the absence of insight into the true nature and value of doctrinal development.

CHAPTER SEVEN

Origin and Development
of Logical Theories

THE DEFINABILITY OF THEOLOGICAL CONCLUSIONS

The question of the definability of theological conclusions was not raised as a *quaestio disputata* before the intervention of Luis de Molina in the 2d half of the 16th century. It staggered the theological world by its novelty and audacity.

This does not mean, however, that before Molina there was no theory about the matter. Medieval theology accepted as self-evident that conclusions drawn from the articles of faith could themselves become objects of faith for the whole Church through a declaratory act of authority, while before such an act one might deny them without being guilty of heresy. The definability of theological conclusions was taken for granted, at least in a general, unproblematic way. To state it carefully, it was self-evident to the medieval mind that the object of faith was a system, a coherent pattern of divine truth in which all parts were held together by logical relations of some kind. Within the system every part was somehow logically implicit in every other, so that, for example, in the case of simple folk, to accept some parts while ignoring the others without contradicting them came to the same thing as acceptance of the whole of truth; and to deny one of them pertinaciously came to the same thing as to reject the whole. Similarly all elements of truth contained in the articles as possible consequences, but not yet perceived, were considered as potentially pertaining to the content of faith. When

135

they were clearly perceived, they became articulated parts of the one truth that was bestowed on the Church through revelation. But how to be certain that they necessarily followed from the original deposit of faith? To medieval man it was evident that the deposit was entrusted by God to the social body of the Church. To believe was to believe with the Church and within the Church. Therefore a declaration by the religious authority that ruled Christian society was the normal way by which conclusions reached the official status of objective faith, to be held by the whole Church as part of the deposit. This is the point on which the Catholic Church and the Reformation later parted company. Since, however, a conclusion became a dogma not by declaration of the Church itself but by the fact that the conclusions were part of the objective system of faith, it was entirely logical to infer, as Scotus did, that for a theologian who clearly saw the logical inclusion, the conclusion became *ipso facto* a point of faith. St. Thomas did not say it expressly, but neither did he deny it. It is illusory, then, to imagine with Marín-Sola that from the beginning Thomism and Scotism were divided on that point.

The so-called Thomistic position, according to which no theologian is bound to give an assent of faith to theological conclusions as long as they are not declared and defined by the Church, seems to begin with Bañez. Cajetan who, on the occasion of a project of Pope Leo X to examine the definability of the doctrine of the Immaculate Conception, touched the question of the definability of theological conclusions, simply stated:

It does not matter . . . whether something be explicitly revealed (as the creation of the world or the Incarnation of the Word of God) or implicitly only, as is the case with all those statements the opposite of which does not agree with the truth of Holy Scripture or of other things which we hold with the absolute certainty of faith. The only difference is that mental capacity and effort, reason and intellect, are needed in order to make manifest that those things which are said to be implicit are indeed necessarily connected with those in which they are said to be implicit.[1]

It is important to note that Cajetan, who delights in contradicting Scotus on any occasion, does not contest this point. Important, too, is the distinction between what seems to be Scripture and oral tradition. There are four categories of statements which can be defined by the Church: revelation as found in the Bible; revelation as found in apostolic tradition; and inferences from either. Cajetan is already thinking in the categories of anti-Protestant controversy. In the beginning of the 15th century John Capreolus, the *princeps thomistarum*, does not seem to know more than two sorts of Christian truths: the principles of the Bible and the theological conclusions drawn from those principles. 'All, however, are implicitly contained in the Bible.'[2]

After Cajetan, Dominic Soto, a great Thomist, is of one mind with Scotus. 'A theological assent follows from the articles of faith before the consequence is evident; for, if they follow by evident inference, the assent is an assent of faith. Theological assents cannot be said to be assents of faith. Faith, indeed, is either an immediate assent to authority alone or an assent to evident deductions from it, as, for example, that Christ is man and consequently that he has the faculty of laughing.'[3] The way in which Andrew de Vega, Luis de Leon, and Cardinal Toledo set forth their opinion cannot be easily interpreted in a different sense.

Melchior Cano, undoubtedly one of the greatest minds of his time, had been a younger colleague of Soto at the university of Salamanca. He clearly has in mind the position of Soto when he writes that 'it is absurd to call faith something which does not immediately rest on authority but on reason and syllogism. The argument which they afford, namely, that if the connection were certain and clear, the conclusions should no longer pertain to theology but to faith is not in the least acute but rather silly.'[4]

But the position of Cano himself is not so widely different from that of his colleague. His point against Soto seems to be that the difference between the principles of theology (that which is explicitly taught by Scripture and tradition) and the theological conclusions (that which necessarily follows from the principles) is irreducible. There is no difference in the status of the latter before and after the definition. Both principles and conclusions, however, are part of the object of faith before the definition no less than afterward—this is repeatedly stressed by Cano—but not in the same way. The first belong immediately to the object of faith, the second mediately. Through definition a theological conclusion is not elevated to the status of an article of faith, but it becomes objectively certain for the whole Church that it belongs to the object of faith in its own way, i.e., as a conclusion. He who denies it after the definition is a heretic not because he denies the conclusion but because he implicitly denies the principle; and if he does it *bona fide*, he is not so much a heretic as an ass.[5] The difference between principles of faith and theological conclusions according to Cano seems to be more like that between the 'rule of faith' and the *disciplina* according to Tertullian.

D. Bañez explicitly refers to Soto:

> The very learned *Magister,* frater Dominicus de Soto . . . says that if a conclusion follows from the principle of faith by the way of evident inference, the conclusion itself is also a certainty of faith. . . . But that opinion is false. . . . If someone professed that Christ is a perfect man, denying at the same time that he had the faculty of laughing, because he opines that a faculty of that sort does not belong to the perfection of man, he should be a bad philosopher—but not a heretic. For up to now it has not been defined by the Church that Christ has that faculty. But if it were defined by the Church that the faculty of laughing pertains to the perfection of man, then he who denies it should be a heretic.[6]

According to Bañez, therefore, a conclusion from premises one of which is not revealed pertains to the domain of theology, not to that of faith, as long as it is not defined by the Church.

It was Luis de Molina, however, who started the controversy. According to Molina, theological conclusions, even after definition by the Church, do not pertain to the articles of faith, and the assent given to them remains merely theological. He expresses his opinion in a commentary on the same locus in the *Summa* of St. Thomas that provided Bañez with the occasion to refute Soto: 'In this doctrine [theology] principles are all those statements that are immediately and in themselves revealed by God. Such, however, are only those that are contained in the canonical books and also the traditions that, though not contained in Holy Scripture, are preserved by the Church as undoubtedly revealed by God. Some people have stated that among the principles of theology those definitions too are to be reckoned in which the Church stated some propositions because it saw that they evidently followed from revealed truth, as, for instance, that in Christ our Lord two wills have to be admitted, a human, to wit, and a divine. Such doctrines, although not expressed in Holy Writ, are none the less evidently inferred from it.' The principle on which that position is based, he goes on, is that the Holy Spirit assists the Church in the same way that he assisted the authors of the canonical books. 'But I am not at all happy about a statement like this, and it was also rejected by Cano [*De locis theologicis* 12.2]. For the *concursus* by which the Holy Spirit assists the Catholic Church and its head is intended not that something be made to belong to faith that formerly did not, but only that it should not err in declaring that which immediately or mediately belongs to faith. You will ask, then, in virtue of what perfection [*habitus*] the faithful assent to conclusions defined by the Church as following from revelation, if they do not assent to it in virtue of the perfection of faith? I answer that, if they are themselves able to infer them from revealed truth in the same way the Church does, they assent to them in a twofold manner in virtue of the perfection [*habitus*] of theology.'[7]

The appeal to Cano is certainly not justified, for Cano only asserts that if conclusions pertain to faith it is not for the reason that they necessarily follow from directly revealed truths. He does not imply that after an ecclesiastical definition, assent to them is still a merely theological one and not a kind of acceptance on faith.

The difficulty in the theory of Molina, which makes it almost self-contradictory, stares us in the face. For on the one hand, he states that the conclusions defined by the Church belong to objective faith, at least mediately, and that the Spirit works in the Church that it might not err in declaring matters of faith; on the other hand, he tells us that an assent to those propositions that mediately pertain to faith is not an assent of faith, either before or after ecclesiastical definition. If the assent is not an act of faith, neither can the object of the act pertain objectively to faith.

Molina founded a school; he was followed with some modifications by such theologians as Granados, Ripalda, Kilber, and also by great Thomists such as *Salmanticenses* (the Carmelite theologians of Salamanca) and later by Billuart. The theologians of Salamanca are the last great representatives of the neo-Thomistic movement of the 16th and 17th centuries. They recapitulate, as it were, in their vast and ample discussions all the opinions and developments of their predecessors, exposing and criticizing them with all the technical implements of scholastic disputation; and therefore they merit a hearing. In their *Disputationes de fide*, they pose the question: 'What kind of revelation of the Primary Truth constitutes the rule according to which faith attains its proper (formal) object?' They distinguish between private revelations given to individuals and the common revelation given to the Church. They define their terms as follows: 'Revelation is subdivided in formal or explicit and virtual or implicit revelation. It is called formal when it reveals explicitly and immediately a truth in itself, as for instance that Christ is truly man; virtual, when it does not reveal the proposition itself but the principles in which it is included. Thus the revelation of the manhood of Christ just spoken of, includes that He has the faculty of laughing. There are three ways, however, in which one truth may be virtually included in another: as an effect in its cause, as a universal in particulars, as particulars in universals. Therefore, according to these three ways there may be said to be a virtual revelation.'[8] It is stated that the proper reason why a truth is an object of faith consists in its being revealed by God in a formal and explicit way. Then the question is raised about the three kinds of truth that are only virtually revealed. It is answered with a *distinguo*: 'Particular propositions included in a universal proposition which is formally revealed pertain to faith. The proof is that a virtual revelation, which is equivalent to formal revelation or coincides with it, constitutes a revealed truth. Now then, the virtual revelation of a particular proposition, included in a universal proposition that is expressly revealed, comes to the same thing as an explicit and formal revelation of that particular proposition. Therefore it can be defined by the Church.'[9] The formal and explicit revelation by God and man's distinct understanding of its meaning are two different things. It is possible that one does not grasp the adequate meaning of something that is explicitly stated in the Scriptures. When the Church defines something that is part of that adequate meaning, then one is able to see it without hesitation. In so doing the Church does not reveal new propositions but only explains propositions already known. To the difficulty that there is a kind of reasoning in the process of explanation, the Salmanticenses answer with the distinction between processes of thought that are properly discursive and others that are not. In the latter case: 'The consequence is not said to be illative or probative but only explicative. And rightly so, because, from its very nature it is not such that it generates a knowledge specifically different from the knowledge of the premises—

and this seems to be the property of *discursus*—but only perfects and illustrates. Although there seems to be a *discursus* as to the form, there is no real inference or proof of a conclusion.'[10] Explicative reasoning, then, only brings into focus something that is 'formally' revealed but in a 'confused and implicit' way only.[11]

But what about those virtually revealed propositions that are related to the formally revealed propositions as effects to causes, adequate or inadequate? Such truths cannot be held by an assent of faith because they can only be inferred by true syllogisms, which generate new truths. Just as the intellectual perfection that makes one assent to the first principles of natural reason (*habitus primorum principiorum*) cannot be the perfection in virtue of which one assents to scientific conclusions (*habitus scientiae*), so too faith, the perfection in man that makes him assent to the first principles of revelation, cannot be the perfection in virtue of which one accepts conclusions drawn from those principles. The perfection that makes one assent to them is the *habitus theologiae*, and their object is and remains a theological conclusion.[12] Therefore they cannot be defined by the Church as articles of faith. The objection of Suarez that the Church did in fact define true inferences from articles of faith is simply disposed of by a frank negation of the fact: 'The Church never defines as dogma a proposition which before the definition was not already formally revealed in the Holy Scriptures, at least *confuse et implicite*.'[13]

All this seems to be very clear, but it is not as clear as it appears. The difficulty lies in the distinction between genuine and non-genuine inferences, or inferences that lead to new knowledge and others that have the inferential form only but do not enrich us with new knowledge. Where is the demarcation line between processes of reasoning that only bring to light aspects of truth that are formally but confusedly and implicitly contained in the premises, and others that produce a knowledge of effects, distinct from the knowledge of the cause from which they are inferred?

The logical difficulty is very serious and perhaps insoluble. That it is a real difficulty appears from the actual appreciation of facts. According to Molina the doctrine that Christ has two wills is a deduction from His having two natures. Therefore, it is a theological conclusion; and Molina is forced to admit that, even after its definition by the Third Council of Constantinople, it did not become an object of faith, but remained the object of a theological assent. For the *Salimanticenses*, however, it is evident that the Christological dogma of the two wills only makes explicit what is formally, although confusedly, stated in the Christological dogma of the two natures. According to Molina, then, some truths defined by the Church could remain merely theological, even after the definition. This is difficult to reconcile with the principle that dogmatic propositions, defined by the Church, pertain to the domain of faith. This principle is safeguarded by the *Salmanticenses*, who state that the Church never defines truths that are not formally included in the articles of faith. But the price is too high. For, to start with, is nature, in a less real sense, the cause of the will rather than of the faculty of laughter? The connection of both with human nature is equally necessary. Both *voluntas* and *risibilitas*, at least according to scholastic logic, are properties and do not belong to the definition or to one of the elements assumed in the definition. It seems arbitrary when the inference of the first is said not to be a genuine inference, whereas the inference of the second is said to be a genuine one. Moreover, the principle of the *Salmanticenses* will be falsified by subsequent definitions of the Immaculate Conception and the Assumption.

The facts, then, do not fit the system of logical principles. The distinction between explicative and inferential syllogisms is too questionable. All syllogisms either produce or do not produce new knowledge. According to modern logic a deductive syllogism never produces any new knowledge.

The opposite doctrine, championed by Soto, Vega, and others, was logically more consistent. Its main advocate in the controversies, following upon the intervention of Molina, was G. Vázquez. He denies the logical difference between explicative and inferential syllogisms, but he introduces a new distinction. One may assent to a conclusion, he says, as far as it follows from two premises or one premise of faith, and then the assent is theological. Upon that assent, however, follows another assent that does not consider the conclusion as inferred from but as included in the premise of faith. Then it is assented to in virtue of the same light that makes one assent to the premise: the light of faith. There is always a natural assent previous to the assent of faith. Even in the case of formally revealed truth, Christians first believe on human authority that it is defined by the Church or contained in the Scriptures, and then only do they assent to it by faith moved by the infused light. So too the theological assent of those who see the consequence is to the faith of the theologian as the human belief in the fact of an ecclesiastical definition is to the common belief of the faithful: 'Cano and Vega teach that once the evident consequence from articles of faith or from an article of faith and a natural principle is given as a previous condition, the assent of faith follows. For indeed, between a theological demonstration and the theologian who infers it, the same relation obtains as between the Council, when it defines a truth of faith, and the universal Church. The only difference consists in this: that the Council proposes the defined truth to the faith of all men, whereas theological reason only proposes something to those to whom the consequence from the articles is evident.'[14] As a result of what was explained above, the appeal to Cano is probably not justified. It is deduced from a number of texts that are rather general, but it does not take account of the more particular utterings, one of which was quoted in its proper place.

Vázquez made a very good point in distinguishing between an assent to a proposition as inferred from its premises and an assent to a proposition absolutely or considered in itself. It is similar to Ockham's distinction explained at the end of the second part of this study. It is not evident, however, that the second assent must follow upon the first. One may assent to a conclusion as conclusion without giving an absolute assent to the proposition in itself. If there is no other motive than the logical consequence, it is natural that the assent to the conclusion should remain theological only, even if there is a premise of faith. Therefore the theologian may give the conclusion an assent that does not regard it as a conclusion but as an absolute proposition. But is he obliged to do so? Is not ecclesiastical definition required in order to convert a possibility into a duty?

Between the two extremes, one of which simply denies the definability of true theological conclusions—bracketing the question of what is really meant by 'true theological conclusions'—while the other simply admits their definability, there are several intermediate positions.

The clearest of these is the position of D. Bañez already alluded to. His position may be summed up, with Marín-Sola,[15] in four points: (1) A true theological conclusion does not pertain to faith before its definition by the Church; this is against Soto as explained above. (2) After the definition it is *de fide*. (3) The Church may define genuine theological conclusions that are generally accepted by the schools. Thus he states in connection with the theological doctrine that Christ did enjoy the Beatific Vision from the first moment of His Incarnation: 'This is neither expressly stated in the Sacred Scriptures, nor defined by the Church as to be held by faith: but the theologians gather it by sound inference from other Scripture texts and basic truths of faith, and it is a doctrine so common that nobody could deny it without incurring the note of error and the Church could define it as being part of faith.'[16] It is curious to note that Bañez seems to suppose as a condition for the definability of a theological conclusion its common acceptance by the theological schools. (4) Such definitions do not introduce new doctrines of faith. They are only new and more ample explanations of a primitive teaching. They cannot, however, surpass the knowledge of the Apostles: 'It is an error in faith to maintain that after the times of the Apostles the doctors of the Church or the Church herself believes more things as pertaining to faith or that they believed them in a more explicit way than the Apostles did. . . . Up to now the Church never proposed or defined anything to the faithful that was not contained before in the Sacred Scriptures or the Apostolic traditions, either expressly or virtually, so that it may be deduced from it by the way of evident consequence.'[17] Just as the moral philosopher, in resolving the doubts proposed to him, is not the author of truth, but only explains what is latent in the principles, so the pope, in defining a point of faith, 'acts as one who explains a latent truth and not as the author of truth.'[18]

The position of Bañez, which will become more common in the Thomistic school, differs from that of Vázquez only in that according to it theological conclusions of whatever sort are not *de fide* before definition by the Church, even for the theologians who see the consequence, but are simply *de fide* for all Christians after the definition.

The most subtle and intricate theory and one that will exercise a powerful influence on later theology is that of Suarez. He makes a distinction between such truths as are formally revealed (*revelatum formale* or *immediate* or *secundum se* or *in se*) and others that are virtually revealed (*revelatum virtuale* or *virtute* or *mediate* or *in alio*). As to the former he concedes to Vázquez that for those who perceive that they are revealed or contained in revelation, they are *de fide*, even before any intervention of the Church. Concerning the latter, however, he agrees with Bañez that they are not *de fide* before, but only after, the definition. The difficulty results from the new interpretation he gives to the terms in question and the new distinctions he introduces. Suarez still does not make a technical distinction between implicit and virtual. He introduces, however, a new distinction between formally revealed truths that are explicitly stated and others that are only confusedly stated in the word of God.

Suarez always illustrates his meaning by the same examples: the inclusion of a particular proposition in a universal distributive proposition (all sacraments confer grace: therefore this sacrament confers grace) or the inclusion of a definition or one of its formative elements in the concept of what is defined (Christ is truly man: therefore He is a rational animal: His is a true rationality and a true animality).

On the contrary, that which is virtually revealed is a proposition the predicate of which does not pertain to the conceptual nucleus of what God communicates: the two concepts can be separated. The conceptual content of the *revelatum virtuale* is not entailed in that of the *revelatum formale*, although there is a necessary connection between them: not a metaphysical one as obtains from the essence expressed by the definition, and the properties contained in it; but a physical one as, for instance, that Christ being man has a heart or the faculty of laughter. Suarez only employs the second example. It is an ambiguous one because, as remarked above, the faculty of laughter is a metaphysical property in the same sense as the faculty of willing although not so important or necessarily exercised. Therefore Ripalda, a true disciple of Suarez, has to distinguish between risibility as a metaphysical property and risibility as a physical property. 'Therefore, that Christ is radically and remotely risible is part of our faith that Christ is a man; but not that he is formally and proximately risible: which is supposed to be separable and distinct from nature; although in both cases the conclusion is inferred from the revealed truth of his manhood and at the same time from the evident knowledge that manhood is radically and proximately risible.'[19]

The distinction of Ripalda is verbally clear but conceptually muddled. Formal and proximate risibility is neither the fact that Christ has laughed nor that He was inclined to laugh, as it may mean in good English; for the conceptual content of both statements is not only separable from the concept of the nature of man but has not even a necessary connection with it. So then it must mean risibility that is neither a fact nor inclination nor an essential property although it necessarily follows from the nature of man. I have no hint of what the conceptual content of that intermediate 'physical faculty' may be. If one says that in order to exercise the metaphysical faculty of laughing, some physical and muscular conditions are required that accidentally may be wanting in a particular case, I answer that consequently those bodily conditions, although normally fulfilled, are not necessarily connected with having a human nature.

It is important to note that the threefold distinction (*formaliter, confuse, virtualiter*) concerns the relation of a proposition to the conceptual content of divine revelation, not the relation of concepts to reality. Of course the conceptual order may correspond to that of reality, but properly speaking Suarez does not mean a distinction in the things with which the word of God is concerned. The distinction, then, is a distinction between modes in which a statement is contained in God's testimony. It is a difference in the way in which revealed truth is related to subjective understanding: not the understanding of God—for God sees distinctly and explicitly the whole content of His word—but human understanding; for it may be that men do not apprehend clearly and distinctly what is confusedly or virtually contained in objective revelation. The real point in Suarez is that the distinctions made by him are distinctions as to the way in which the integral content of God's meaning is related to human understanding. The point is not that in a given case there is a reasoning process and in others there is not. There is always a reasoning process of some kind. Neither does the difference between the confusedly and the virtually revealed propositions consist in differences in the mental act of reasoning. Suarez does not make a distinction between explanatory and illative syllogisms. Although he admits the distinction, it is not the ground of the differentiation between confusedly and virtually revealed truth.

To revelation and the different ways in which it presents itself to man, there corresponds on the part of the subject an act of assent. With respect to confused revelation, clarified through reasoning, two attitudes of mind are possible, and consequently, two different acts of assent. One may hold the conclusion either because one sees the evidence of the illation or because one acknowledges the authority of God who revealed it. In the first case it is a natural assent, in the second it is an assent of faith, even before any definition by the Church. For it is a truth attested by God independently of ecclesiastical intervention.

The question of an assent given to a virtually revealed truth known by inference is more intricate and problematic. Before the definition by authority two ways of assenting are possible. If one assents because the consequence is evident, then the assent is purely natural and not even theological. But it may also be considered as *suo modo* contained in divine revelation, and then the assent is supernatural although theological only. Before its being defined it can never become an object of faith. 'The reason is that it is of the essence of faith to be immediately founded in the authority of God as in the sole reason of assenting; therefore no true act of faith is possible except about something which is immediately said by God. . . . For if it is not immediately attested by God it is impossible that the authority of God should be the sole reason of assenting.'[20] The definitive reason, then, is that before definition the virtually revealed is not yet attested by God Himself. Certainly, it necessarily follows from something immediately attested by God, but it is not part of its conceptual content nor is the necessary connection attested by God Himself.

This already points to the situation after the definition of authority. In virtue of the definition, that which before was not immediately attested by God now becomes God's immediate word, not only in relation to one's subjective understanding, but objectively in itself: 'A theological conclusion, which before was only virtually contained in revealed truths, is, after definition by the Church, formally and most properly *de fide*, not only mediately but immediately; because such a truth is no longer virtually and mediately revealed, but formally and in itself. . . . The reason is that whatever is defined by the Church is attested by God through the Church. Now then, the Church defines such a truth in itself and formally; therefore God now attests it in itself and formally; consequently, by that very fact it is sufficiently placed under the formal object of faith'[21]

The position of Suarez clearly entails a definite concept of the infallibility of the Church and its relation to the infallibility of God. God alone is infallible. The infallible truth of a proposition depends entirely upon its being spoken by Him. Human media are infallible only insofar as they are in a strict sense instruments of God. For only then are their sayings attested and warranted by God. What my pencil writes is written by me because the pencil is no more than my instrument. In the same way the writings of the Biblical authors are infallibly true because in writing them they were only instruments of the divine author. Suarez applies the same principle to the case of ecclesiastical definition. What the Church pronounces in defining a theological conclusion, it pronounces as the instrument of the Holy Spirit. Therefore by virtue of the definition a statement that before was only natural or theological becomes a word formally attested by God Himself. Suarez emphatically equates the two cases.

The Suarezian solution is beset with insurmountable difficulties, and it is an astounding fact that its originator did not see it. For indeed, if revelation is strictly identical with what is formally and immediately said by God, then the virtually revealed is not part of the originally revealed deposit. If, then, the declaration of the Church is the instrumental cause through which the virtually revealed assumes the nature of an immediate and formal attestation of God, it follows that the proper effect of the definition is that it makes revealed something that before was not revealed. The definition is an instrumental act by which God adds new revelations to the deposit of faith. It is of no use to reply that before the definition the conclusion was already germinally given in the formally revealed principles. For although there be a necessary connection, it is not from this kind of connection that there is divine attestation for a statement. And this, according to Suarez, is the only rule by which the distinction between revealed and non-revealed truth, between an object of faith and no object of faith, can be established.

Of course Suarez, who is a most conservative theologian, does not admit new divine revelations through the instrumentality of a declaration of the Church. He repeatedly and categorically asserts that the truths defined by the Church are not new dogmas but primitive and apostolic truths. Therefore it would be unjust to ascribe to him the theory of new revelations. But on the basis of his principles there is no logical escape. J. Alfaro, the best interpreter of Suarez on this point, overtly concludes: 'We feel obliged to grant that, according to our meaning, it is impossible in this theory to evade the logical conclusion that the definition of the Church concerning the virtually revealed is really a new revelation.'[22]

It is very interesting to compare the position of Suarez with that of Cardinal de Lugo. Lugo works with the same basic concepts and distinctions. But he peremptorily rejects the idea of new revelations that he reads in Suarez. His own solution, curious and subtle as it is, does not meet the case in a more satisfying way. Virtual revelation, he concedes, is not true revelation. Therefore by itself it can never become an object of faith. But it is part of revelation that the Holy Spirit infallibly assists the Church in all its definitions. As a universal distributive proposition this formally applies to each particular case. After the definition, then, a conclusion that formerly followed from a revealed and a natural premise is now inferred from two revealed propositions. The Holy Spirit assists the Church in all its definitions. Therefore He assists it in this particular definition. Particular propositions do not add a new truth to the universal distributive propositions in which they are contained. Hence if the general assistance of the Spirit is an object of faith, then the particular proposition, as defined under that assistance, is an object of faith too.

This is, of course, a most ingenious sophism. If it were true, the problem of dogmatic development would simply not exist. For indeed, as St. Thomas says, the economy of salvation in which God reveals the secret of His being and will is a coherent system, an organic whole. The dogmas that come to light in the course of post-apostolic history are fitted and integrated into the general system, just as the developments of pre-apostolic revelation were gradually unfolded from the same basic principles. In the primitive pattern of the Mosaic revelation, the whole of revealed truth was somehow already contained. This is a common doctrine of patristic and medieval theology. The Holy Spirit unfolded the content of an all-containing primitive revelation by bringing to light some aspects of the salvation-economy that although formerly not attested by God—to speak with Suarez and Lugo—were nonetheless closely and intelligibly connected with the idea that was the object of the first act of divine self-communication. The virtually revealed is to the apostolic revelation as the apostolic revelation is to the Mosaic revelation. If, then, through the medium of ecclesiastical definition, the Holy Spirit continues to do the same thing that he did through the utterings of the Prophets, it makes no sense to say that objective

F

revelation was closed at the death of the last Apostle. The position of Lugo, indeed, entails that after the closing of revelation God puts into operation a new organ of the Holy Spirit, namely the infallible authority of the Church, in order to do what before was done through the Prophets and sacred writers. This is a contradiction in terms.

It is interesting to note that a similar kind of sophistical reasoning was adopted by Lugo in his discussion of the *analysis fidei*, a typical problem of the epoch of nascent rationalism and a much debated one. How can faith be subjectively certain on rational grounds and at the same time remain supernatural? Suarez distinguished between a rational reasoning, insufficient by itself for absolute certitude, and a complementary motion of grace by which the believer confusedly attained the truth of the conclusion (the fact of divine revelation) in itself, raising the unsteady certainty of reason to an absolute supernatural certainty. Lugo rightly rejected the idea of a supernatural reinforcement of a natural inference with regard to subjective certitude because from its very nature such a certitude must be psychological and consequently lie open to interior experience. The believer, however, has no experience of that kind. The inferential act by which the fact of revelation is established can in no way be psychologically different from any other act of natural reasoning. The solution proposed by Lugo himself was ingenious enough. Faith is the conclusion of an argument. That argument is psychologically of the same nature as any ratiocinative act. But the premises and the conclusion are at the same time immediately grasped *per modum unius*, with an absolute supernatural certitude founded in the grace of faith. The one act is psychologically a natural mediate assent to the conclusion of a natural inference and at the same time a supernatural immediate assent based on an apprehension that takes in at a glance the whole pattern of arguments and conclusion. Lugo was a very fine psychologist. He clearly saw that after the process of inferential discourse the mind rests in the possession of its mental acquisition, seeing the process and its upshot *per modum unius*. This is a general psychological fact, which holds true in any case of reasoning. To the experience of the believer, then, faith was a simple acquisition of reason. But while the movement toward truth was an act of rational reason, the moment of rest in the truth was supernatural, unconsciously enhanced by the light of faith.

The theory, so thoroughly elaborated by Lugo, suffers from grave philosophical difficulties, as for instance the identification of seeing a conclusion and assenting to it. It will much later be the weak point in Rousselot's remarkable analysis of faith, which was greatly influenced by Lugo. Newman, the greatest descriptive analyst of mental life, disproved it in the chapters on assent and inference that are among the most original achievements of his *Grammar of Assent*. However, the theological difficulties are no less serious. Faith is practically reduced to an act of reason. According to Lugo there is no difference in experience between the acceptance of faith and the acceptance of a rational conclusion. This runs counter to the whole Biblical, patristic, and ancient scholastic tradition according to which faith, as man's answer to God's self-gift under illuminating grace, is *sui generis,* irreducible to any natural act, and perfectly credible of itself. Rational arguments may confirm its credibility and 'humanize' the life of faith by integrating it into the whole of man's intellectual and spiritual life, but faith as such is in no need of rational support.

The position of Suarez and Lugo is very significant. It points to the radical revolution in the basic first principles of Western civilization already pointed out in Chapter Six. In the theology of Suarez and Lugo we are present, as it were, at the very transition to a new theology of faith, unconsciously inspired by the rationalistic principles of the nascent age. The genius of Suarez, so deeply attached to tradition, tried to save the mystical element of faith from the wreck of the old Christian civilization. But his eclectic positions, intended to reconcile past and present, did not succeed in creating a consistent synthesis.

Add to this that the problem of the development of doctrine and that of the nature and scope of a rational justification of faith are closely connected. To Suarez and Lugo it is already self-evident that the truth, revealed by God and assented to by faith, is no more than a system of propositions. They are part of revelation as far as they are immediately attested by God and warranted by His infallible authority. If this be true, then of course the development of doctrine can only proceed by comparison of propositions and logical inference. This is the propositional solution, to be considered presently. For the same reason, one cannot reasonably assent to revealed truth if one cannot prove by means of reason that those propositions are indeed attested by God. 'Logicalism' in conceiving the development of doctrine and rationalism in evaluating the part and requirements of rational argument in the analysis of faith are two offshoots of the same propositional conception of the nature of revelation.

To sum up the results of this critical inquiry, first, the distinction between Scripture and tradition in the sense of two different channels through which revealed truth comes to man seems to be common currency in post-tridentine theology. It was practically unknown in patristic and medieval theology. The Council of Trent discussed the question and left to the theologians the task of determining their nature and mutual relation. The fact that the discussions of the Council were unknown to later theologians, while the acts of the Council could easily be interpreted in the sense of a double treasury of the one deposit of faith, seems to have been the main reason why the new theory was soon taken for granted. Moreoever, it suited the needs of an easy although ineffective polemic against Protestantism.

Second, in the 17th century discussions about the definability of theological conclusions, the different theories that neo-Scholastic theologians opposed to Modernism in the 20th century are already worked out. But the terminology is still unsteady, varying from author to author, and therefore often misleading. The two opposites of the basic distinction are generally termed: 'immediate' (Thomistic), 'formal' (Suarezian), or 'explicit' versus 'mediate' (Thomistic), 'virtual,' or 'implicit' revelation. The way in which the theological conclusion is contained in the revealed premise is generally said to be virtual (Bañez, Suarez, Lugo, Salmanticenses). The terms *virtual* and *implicit* are mostly still equivalent as they were in the later Middle Ages, although now the term *virtual* is generally preferred.

The main difficulty, however, concerns the subdivisions: what, then, is to be classified under formal and what under virtual revelation? Suarez subdivides the formally revealed truth into explicitly, and implicitly or confusedly, revealed propositions. To the *Salmanticenses,* however, the formally revealed it limited to the explicitly revealed, while confused or implicit revelation is one of the three kinds of virtual revelation. To both of them the confusedly revealed is part of what is immediately attested by God. But the virtually revealed (Suarez) or the revealed *in causa* (subspecies of the virtually revealed according to *Salmanticenses*) is by itself not part of the original word of God, and therefore either it can never be defined by the Church (Molina) and never had been (*Salmanticenses*) or it can be defined and has been (Suarez, Lugo). But then it either becomes formally and immediately revealed in virtue of a divine attestation through the instrumental function of the Church (Suarez), or it is raised to the status of a conclusion drawn by an explicative syllogism from two immediately revealed premises: the revealed truth in which its content is virtually revealed and the truth of the infallible assistance of the Holy Spirit, guaranteed to the Church by divine revelation (Lugo).

Third, the situation created by these historical positions is rather awkward. The solution proposed by the *Salmanticenses* is historically untenable; that of Molina is theologically unacceptable; that of Suarez and Lugo is either logically wrong or leads to theological nonsense, the introduction of new revelations in post-apostolic tradition; that of Vázquez in its unmitigated form is most unsatisfactory, the frontier between the divine objectivity of revelation and the human relativity of theology being too blurred, if the theologian has to give an assent of faith to all conclusions whose consequence is evident to him. The way lies open to subjectivism. There is no objective criterion. For reason is *in concreto* too subtle and personal to function as a rule of faith. Its 'evident conclusions' will vary according to first principles and unconscious prejudices of all kinds. The most plausible position, then, is that of Dominic Bañez. It is simple and straightforward: let theology have its free course. The Church, in accordance with the *consensus theologorum*, will decide which of its fruits is a true unfolding of the mystery that the Holy Spirit keeps alive. Thus stated in general terms it points toward the true solution. To be sure, Bañez, too, keeps the range of possible dogmatic definition within the limits of logical deduction from revealed propositions. The question that a better knowledge and a deeper sense of history will raise is the question whether the real process of development can be aptly described in terms of Aristotelian logic.

THE NINETEENTH CENTURY

The tragedy of modern Catholic theology, which was but an aspect of the tragedy of the post-tridentine Church, consisted in its isolation from the great movement from which the contemporary age was to spring. Modern thought that shaped the world went its own way and was practically ignored by the theologians of the Catholic schools. They continued to move within the orbit of a 'perennial theology,' based on a 'perennial philosophy,' discussing the same questions in the same way, making their choice from a traditional set of conflicting opinions, and adding on occasion a new question, the terms of which had first to be fitted in with the intellectual structures of the system.

The proper excellence that a good intellectual training should impart to the mind is a keen and subtle power of openness, flexibility, comprehension. To be able to enter into a different pattern of thought, to understand its point of view, to distinguish its principles, to see its consequences, to judge its lack of consistency within the perspective of its own view, to criticize it from within, to identify with its spirit and method without losing the sense of objective distance that is the fruit of an independent personal judgment, to see and appreciate it as a whole, to compare wholes with wholes, to get at that kind of understanding that is the basis of a real dialogue. It is a question of education and training, not of native sagacity, intelligence quotient, or acuteness of mind. One may be a genius without ceasing to be a barbarian for neglect of that superior capacity to understand all that is human, which is the prime condition of intellectual culture.

There is, however, a kind of deformation that is characteristic of the man of one book or one system. A mind educated in one single system has a strength of its own. On his own ground, playing according to the rules he is accustomed to, he is undefeatable. But beyond his own ground he feels distressed and forlorn. He simply does not understand what it is all about. As he identifies thought with the requirements of his own system—there is but one truth, one true method, one true philosophy—it seems to him that those who do not think within the same frame of concepts, principles, and methods, are obscure, muddled, or somehow perverted. He is not disposed to take them seriously. He scorns them from the heights of eternal truth. They are but adversaries and villains whose opinions can be set forth in a few lines of the introduction and briefly confuted in a *scholion*. All along there is no real interplay, no dialogue, no advance toward mutual understanding. Nothing is gained, nothing learned from the enemy. There is thus a kind of onesided training in one systematic pattern that closes the mind and makes it insensitive to the outer intellectual world instead of opening it and increasing its sensibility and receptivity, its power to learn from others. It works as a kind of armor that shuts off the mind and protects it against experience instead of opening all its pores to the impression of reality and the lessons of intellectual intercourse. When an abstract system proper to a social group entirely dominates the educational method of that group, its narrowing influence continues from generation to generation by a kind of in-breeding that in the long run must needs lead to spiritual impoverishment, mental starvation, and intellectual sclerosis.

It may seem cruel and unjust to present this characterization as a description of what happened in the history of modern Catholic thought. But generally speaking it is demonstrably true. One who is familiar with the history of modern philosophy or Protestant theology is simply baffled when he reads Catholic textbooks on the history of philosophy that quite recently were still in use in Catholic schools, or Catholic interpretations of the thought of such men as Luther and Calvin. It is evident that the works of these philosophers and religious thinkers were not read at all or not read seriously by the Catholic schoolmen. One can follow from textbook to textbook the tradition of the same abstract schemes and simplifications that often have nothing to do with the real thought of the authors to whom they are ascribed. From generation to generation the same stencilled patterns were handed down without fresh contact with the original texts.

From the beginning the process of isolation set in: Catholic theology, Protestant theology, and the new philosophy parted company and gradually grew away from each other till the separation was almost complete. To be sure, all the wrong was not on one side. Great representatives of modern philosophy were often no less ignorant and disdainful of what was going on in the theological camp. Protestant theology, in its turn, although more open to the successive trends of modern philosophy, was generally unaware of the existence of a Catholic theology. It is enough to read through the five volumes of such an excellent work as *Die Geschichte der neuern evangelischen Theologie* of E. Hirsch[23] to see how Protestant theology developed in a closed world. The learned author himself displays an almost complete ignorance of Catholic thought; and when occasionally he comes to speak of it, it is in a tone of contempt.

Catholic theology, however, was particularly absent in the movement of modern history. Protestant theology, which consciously responded to the influence of contemporary philosophy, was dismissed as being the subject of an *histoire des variations*. Those among the Catholic thinkers who, especially in Germany, tried to keep in touch with modern thought and to bridge the gulf between faith and world were generally considered dangerous. They were distrusted and condemned, if not simply ignored. In the midst of the flowing river the Catholic mind considered itself as a rock of immutability against which the floods of the world could not prevail. This was true in a certain sense. The Catholic Church was a bulwark and stronghold of faith. But most theologians confused unchangeableness of faith with theological rigidity. According to their mind, the safety of faith was dependent upon a radical conservatism in matters of philosophy and theology. If there were movements of renewal, they remained *extra campum theologiae*.

When, after his conversion, Newman visited Rome and entered the mental world of his new coreligionists, he was thunder-struck by the absence of real, vigorous thought. He did not find a living system but a lifeless eclecticism: the scattered remains of what once had been a vigorous body of thought. Thomas Aquinas, whom he admired, was neither studied nor esteemed. The Fathers who had nourished his theological insight and led him to the Church of Rome were hardly known. G. Perrone, the leading theologian of the time, could not understand the *Essay on Development* when Newman submitted it to his judgment. He favored him with his friendship, but all he could do on the question was to put down in a parallel column a number of theological platitudes that did not respond to the ideas Newman had so painfully expounded in a Latin text. The line that separated the two texts of the *Newman-Perrone Paper* was indeed an iron curtain that would not rise on a second act until the recent past. Newman soon understood that he could not expect any real understanding. He had to appeal to history, placing his hope on the future. In the meantime he spent his life in the Catholic Church on problems of intellectual education in order to fortify the walls of what he considered to be the only bulwark that could hold against the coming floods of philosophical and theological liberalism.

In saying that Catholic theology went its own way, separated from and opposed to the general movement of Western thought, we do not mean that it was not influenced by it. It certainly was, but as an unconscious infection of its spirit, not as a free conscious dialogue and assimilation of its ideas. It is a general rule that one is always influenced by one's adversaries. In a certain sense that influence is all the more profound for being unconscious. One can resist an enemy that one can see, but one is powerless against him if he secretly infiltrates the city, corrupting it from within. Hence that high and dry, short-sighted rationalism that gives the impression that theology is a training-school for exercises in formal logic, devoid of any larger, organic view. There is not an idea in it, Newman said. The formal structures of the system subsist, but its parts are loosely held together, hiding the intellectual compromises imposed by endless controversies. One lives in the illusion of continuing a great tradition, but the organic idea, the quickening breath of the Spirit, has vanished.

Newman somewhere says that the notes of the Church may be obscured for a time. He might have said the same of at least one of the seven notes by which he recognized a true development: assimilative power. A healthy organism has a natural power to integrate into its life all sorts of extraneous elements. Its living identity is not weakened but rather strengthened by the well-assimilated elements from without. In the same way a sound idea has a natural capacity for integrating into its living pattern other ideas, correcting and recasting them, pervading them with the vital force of its all-embracing principles. It is the mark of real life that it reconciles into one spirit two attitudes that may seem opposed to each other: a generous open-mindedness, ready to learn from all quarters, and an imperial independence by which it protects itself against corruptive influences and builds up its spiritual empire with elements and forces of the most different kind and origin. Such was the spirit of Thomas Aquinas, and such has not been the spirit of theology in the modern age. Its narrow-minded, one-sided spirit of defense, distrust, and suspicion, always anxious not to be mixed up with modern thought, was as clear a symptom of spiritual and intellectual weakness as the refusal to take food is a token of illness in a living organism.

Account must be taken of all this in order to understand the history of the logical theories of development in the 19th and the first half of the 20th centuries. A few years after his exchange of views with Newman, the occasion presented itself to Perrone for a renewed reflection on the problem of development: the definition of the dogma of the Immaculate Conception. He was not altogether uninfluenced by Newman, whose general idea of development, although not deeply understood, greatly promoted the cause of the definition. There was a glimpse of understanding of the new idea among the theologians who prepared the definition. Passaglia came very near to Newman, as will be seen further on. But the secular habit of scholasticism generally prevented a deep understanding of his originality.

In his paper on the definability of the new dogma, Perrone stated the well-known distinctions between explicit revelation and other truths 'either hidden in it implicitly and half-dark and covered as it were by some veils . . . or included in other explicitly revealed things as conclusions in principles; or otherwise so closely and necessarily connected with other truths of faith, that that they may be deduced from it by easy reasoning and evident inference.'[24] Here again are the age-old distinctions between different kinds of logical inclusion, but expressed in a way as muddled and vague in content as it is elegant in form. Most theologians follow the beaten path of the foregoing centuries. The terminological differentiation between *implicit* and *virtual* becomes more general. There are theologians who opine that the virtually revealed cannot become an object of dogmatic definition, but then they interpret the 'implicitly, confusedly and less clearly revealed' (Franzelin) in so broad and loose a way that it may almost comprehend any possible conclusion. In the presence of the recent dogma it was impossible to become very clear without becoming dangerous.

There seems to be fluctuation and uneasiness in the utterings of the 19th-century theologians. J. M. A. Vacant, M. Scheeben, H. Hurter, W. Wilmers, and others rightly put forward that when a person says something, he not only says what he expressly states but also what he tacitly supposes or implies or connotes or intends to say. Facing a question of definability one must ask oneself if it was God's intention to communicate it to man. But no clear criteria are worked out by which to discriminate between what God intended or did not intend to declare. The intention is elucidated by the fact of the definition, says C. von Schaetzler, because the Holy Spirit infallibly assists the Church in declaring God's meaning. There is a logical inference of some kind. Not the inference itself, however, but the infallible definition clinches the question about what God intended to impart to man. This is a most valuable point and it anticipates one aspect of the contemporary theological theory. But the question remains: how does the Church determine the cases in which something somehow connected with the principles of faith is included in what God intended to say? Are there no objective criteria of some sort? Has one to do with a subjective, uncontrollable charism, occasionally bestowed upon the representatives of the magisterial function of the Church? This is now on the verge of the new insight which should provide the missing link: the non-propositional side of the knowledge of faith, living in the Church as a whole, growing and ripening in its experience, grasped in the light of illuminating grace and authoritatively declared by the magisterium with the infallible assistance of the Holy Spirit. The two aspects of the theological solution—the supernatural discriminating contact with self-revealing Reality, living in the Church as a whole, and the charism of infallibility bestowed on the magisterium in the exercise of its proper power—cannot be separated.

To sum up: in the course of the 19th century, Catholic theological reflection on the connection between dogma and primitive revelation is centered round the problem of the definability of the Immaculate Conception and the infallibility of the pope. The basic presupposition is still a propositional concept of revelation and the way in which the objects of later definitions are contained in and derived from primitive faith is generally thought of in terms of logical inclusion. Hence a certain hesitance and uneasiness and a search for new avenues, which, however, did not prove very successful.

IN THE LISTS WITH MODERNISM

Then the floods came. The study of history and the development of historical criticism, combined with general ideas about history as an evolutive process, gradually drew to a momentous crisis in Christian thought. Newman, with his penetrating historical insight, had anticipated and presaged its coming, but to traditional Catholic theology it came as the crash of thunder in a blue sky. Within the familiar household of Catholic life, Modernism arose as an unfamiliar ghost, a strange apparition. It gave a shock. Minds were unsettled. The perturbation was general. The ghost was exorcized by swift condemnation, and as a natural reaction in the face of the unknown, suspicion began to reign.

What did the theologians oppose against the Modernist conception of dogma and its development? There is a far greater variety of ideas than before, and classification is not easy. Limiting consideration here to the first decade of the 20th century two groups may be distinguished: a majority that still clings to a merely propositional concept of revelation; a serious minority that tries to introduce into the idea of revelation a non-propositional aspect without succeeding, however, in reconciling satisfactorily the old and the new concepts into one consistent pattern.

Among the first is a group of theologians who try a solution of a new type that was called by R. Draguet the 'historical proof.' Their starting point was the supposition that the Apostles, the foundations on which the Church was built, possessed, through a special privilege, an explicit knowledge of all the possible dogmas of the Church. This was indeed a traditional idea, but it was never closely examined or seriously questioned. In the present epoch, however, it is very much to the fore and put forward as the basis of a theory of development. It most naturally combines with the idea of a non-scriptural oral tradition: the Apostles had bequeathed to the Church a number of truths that were not put down in the sacred books. How, then, did it happen that those truths were obliterated in later history? In the first centuries the teachers of the Church did not commit to paper some august truths for reasons of reverence and pedagogical adaptation (see above on Origen, pp. 55 ff.). There was an esoteric tradition secretly handed down to the perfect, but not openly exposed to the sacrilegious criticism of the pagan philosophers and the incomprehension of the crowd. This explains the lack of documentation in the early centuries.

To be logically consistent the protagonists of the historical theory had to suppose that the knowledge of all dogmas possessed by the Apostles was an explicit one and that they were all transmitted by exoteric or esoteric tradition. For if it was only implicit, the defenders of the theory had to ask the traditional questions of how dogmas that later became explicit were contained in those that were explicit from the first, and by what kind of discursive process were they made explicit. Then the path of history, whose proper task is to propound hypotheses in order to ascertain and explain facts, is abandoned and the theory had to fall back upon logical devices. If the Apostles did receive this all-comprehensive knowledge of all dogmas by a *gratia gratis data* because they were the founders of the *traditio constitutiva*, then they had to transmit that all-comprehensive knowledge to the Church that was founded on them. What they received, not for themselves but for the Church, they had to pass on to the Church. But if so, an insoluble question arises. Development had to be conceived as a change-over from esoteric to exoteric tradition. How, then, does one explain that after the persecution the esoteric truth did not appear in the writings of the great theologians and doctors of the Church so that further development might become unnecessary? Or that 'the variations continue beyond the time when it is conceivable that the discipline (*disciplina arcani*) was in force' (*Development*, p. 29)? Or that great theologians not only ignored them but contradicted them or spoke in such a way that they seemed to suppose the contrary?

To answer that some truths were obscured in the consciousness of the Church has no point. For if it be so, and if there were no old documents extant in which they had been explicitly stated, by what means could the Church rediscover them? Not by way of history, for if they had become obscure and somehow implicit, they could not be rescued from oblivion except by reasoning. The historical method, then, opens no way to a possible solution of our problem. Moreover, the hypothesis that the Apostles possessed an explicit knowledge of all possible dogmas is not only historically and psychologically highly improbable, it is also unnecessary to save the values that it was intended to preserve: the fullness of faith in apostolic times. For in the domain of faith as distinguished from that of theology, the perfection does not consist in the range of distinct and notional apprehension but in the depth and vividness of real apprehension. In comparison with the Apostles contemporary man, as believer, has no privileged position simply because his explicit notional knowledge of the deposit of faith may have a wider extension. The idea that the Apostles, in order to possess the fullness of revelation, had to know explicitly all dogmas is obviously connected with a merely propositional concept of revelation. In that supposition, indeed, full knowledge of revelation comes down to a knowledge of all the propositions. So, then, we are justified in dismissing once for all the historical hypothesis, although even in recent times it was advocated by a theologian like H. Lennerz in order to explain and to justify the definition of the Assumption.

A second important group of theologians holds that the development of doctrine is a transition of formally known truths from a condition of confusion, obscurity, or implicitness to a condition of clarity, distinctness, or explicitness. That a true theological conclusion should ever become a defined dogma is emphatically excluded. But there is a remarkable difference in explaining the process. J. V. de Groot and L. Billot abide by the classical distinction between truths that are formally but implicitly, and others that are virtually, revealed. The latter cannot rise to the condition of dogma. The difficulty resulting from the ambiguity of the distinction is: how to explain clearly the logical difference between implicit and virtual? If it is a question of logic, it must be possible to state it with absolute clarity. But, as with the theologians of the 17th century, some statements classed by one author in the category of the implicit are relegated by others to the category of the virtual. In practice the distinction does not work very well. Therefore some theologians try to describe the process of development without having recourse to the distinction between implicit and virtual. Christian Pesch, for instance, hardly mentions the logical categories of implication and inference. Development merely consists in disposing of doubts, difficulties, and obscurities, or in working out some practical consequences: 'Jesus Christ and the apostles have expressed divine revelation in a set of propositions which all in one constitute the body of christian doctrine. . . .' Development can neither add to it nor change it. 'There remains only that it consists in a clearer proposition of old truths. Such greater clarity, however, may be as manifold as the obscurities which are removed by it.'[25]

R. Garrigou-Lagrange is more original. He agrees with E. Le Roy that a dogma is not stated in the language of philosophy but in that of common sense. Against Le Roy, however, he argues that the language of common sense is not only pragmatic but also and essentially metaphysical. Common-sense speech spontaneously proceeds from the same metaphysical principles that philosophical reflection tries to formulate, distinguishing them from one another and reducing them to the notion of 'being' and the judgment in which that notion necessarily presents itself to the mind: the principle of identity or non-contradiction. The way in which human knowledge proceeds from an actually exercised but confused awareness to an actually contemplated and clear perception of its first principles and notions is the true analogy for a right understanding of the development of doctrine. The basic dogmas are actually although confusedly known by all believers and from the beginning. The process of development only translates them from the condition of unreflected and confused awareness to that of reflected and distinct perception, or from the condition of 'implicit actual' to that of 'explicit actual.' The transition from virtual to explicit knowledge belongs to the domain of theology, not of dogma. The idea is most interesting and may shed some light on the development of such basic dogmas as those of the Trinity or the Incarnation. But does it enable one to understand the development of, for example, the doctrine of the Immaculate Conception? By its very nature its explanatory power is limited to the domain of the principles, i.e., the basic and essential articles of faith, and does not go beyond it. Here, then, the well-known difficulty presents itself again: by what criteria can one distinguish between implicit actual knowledge and virtual implication?

In his extensive article 'Dogme' in DTC E. Dublanchy also avoids the use of strictly logical implements. He rightly underlines that the conditions, occasions, and factors entering into the process of development form an altogether historic whole in which human freedom and contingent happenings have their part, so that it is impossible to explain it entirely by necessary laws. According to his opinion the contingencies of history are no more than occasions to perfect and explain by means of a simple and easy analysis the formulas of primitive revelation. The development may be either implicit in those ancient formulas or partly explicit or half-dark until a given circumstance brings them to full light. It is impossible to determine a priori the conditions required to decide whether the inclusion is entirely implicit or partly explicit. The new idea of a partly explicit revelation is a sound one but in practice its historical verification will in most cases be impossible.

The works of Pesch, Dublanchy, and Garrigou-Lagrange mark a turning-point in the manner of considering the problem of development. The categories by means of which the process is described are no longer logical categories of implication and deduction but psychological or epistemological categories such as prereflective versus reflective consciousness, global awareness versus analysis, partly explicit versus fully explicit statement, obscure and confused versus clear and distinct. In a way that rather calls to mind the method of Descartes, the process of thought that leads from initial to perfect knowledge is conceived not according to the model of inference by which one truth is derived from another but according to the model of analysis by which a bud of insight, either innate or spontaneously acquired or divinely infused, unfolds before the mind's eye its preexisting distinctive pattern of leaves from and round its heart.

Two concluding remarks are to be made. There is a controversy about the images of natural growth used by the Fathers, especially by Vincent of Lérins, and also by Newman. German authors, influenced by the organic pattern of romantic thought, are often fond of them. But the scholastic authors generally distrust and often severely criticize and reject them as inadequate and too near to the vitalistic interpretations of Modernism. This is symptomatic, on the one hand, of a new way of feeling about the question, and on the other hand, of a persisting spirit of rationalism. Most authors do not seem to understand what an image is or the logic of its use.

Lastly, it is important to register the fact that some writers, e.g., J. G. Arintero and A. Gardeil, clearly state that the development of doctrine, beyond being a subjective growth of understanding, is also an increase of objective manifestation. With a dogmatic definition, a new star may become visible in the objective constellation of what the Church believes in.

TYPES OF LOGICAL THEORIES

Starting from this situation, contemporary theology develops in two directions: on the one hand, a theological theory (considered in Chapter Nine), and on the other hand, a more perfect elaboration of the logical theory. One word about the expression *logical theory*. H. Hammans, in an excellent work, gives preference to the expression *intellectualistic* theories, because 'the logical element, as we see it, must be present in every development of dogma and hence in every explanation of that development.'[26] This seems fairly plausible, but the equivocalness of the term *intellect* and its derivatives is a disadvantage. Sometimes it means the general power of knowing or a special capacity for knowledge including the capacity of reasoning. Sometimes it is opposed to reason as a faculty of intellectual apprehension of first principles. *Intellectualism* too is ambiguous. It may be used in a pejorative or in a eulogistic sense; one may speak of the sound intellectualism of Thomas Aquinas or or Newman. For these reasons I am not very happy about the term. The qualification *logical* added to a theory clearly marks off that theory from a theological one. A theory of development is called 'logical' because according to it the process of development is simply described in terms of logical inference and the criterion of its truth is the logical test, whereas the qualification *theological* means that the process is conceived of as partaking of the character of mystery that is proper to the object of theology, and that the criterion of its truth does not properly consist in a logical verification but in a charismatic decision accepted by faith.

The most complete and clear elaboration of the logical theory of development in its different versions can be found in the works of R. Schultes, M. Tuyaerts, and M. Marín-Sola. This chapter concludes with a brief exposition and discussion of their respective positions.

Schultes leaves no doubt about his conception of revelation. Revelation is a manifestation of something that is hidden. The thing itself is not revealed, but rather the knowledge that the revealing subject possesses about the thing. This is only possible after the manner of our human understanding, i.e., in the form of propositions. A truth is revealed as far as it is communicated in concepts and sentences. Thus the exclusively propositional starting point is most emphatically stated.

A proposition is either formally or virtually revealed: formally when it expresses what the revealer actually says; virtually when the revealer only communicates either the principles from which human efforts must deduce it or the real cause from which it proceeds as a necessary effect.

The formally or immediately revealed is itself either explicitly or implicitly given: explicitly when the terms of the revealed proposition signify the content of the proposition in virtue of their proper meaning; implicitly when the terms signify the content in equivalent concepts only. Consequently, the implicitly revealed is objectively identical with the explicitly revealed.

There are many ways in which a proposition may be explicitly, implicitly, or virtually revealed. Explicit revelation may express the truth properly or metaphorically, clearly or obscurely, directly or indirectly. Implicitly revealed are the definition in the defined, the parts in the whole, the one correlative in the other, the conclusion in two revealed premises. Conclusions starting from one revealed premise are virtually revealed in different ways according to the different ways in which a conclusion may be contained in its principles.

The transition from explicit to implicit and from formal to virtual entails or may entail in each case an act of inference. In the former case the syllogism is merely explicative, expressing the explicit statement in equivalent terms. In the latter the syllogism is illative, leading to a new truth formally distinct from the truth expressed in the explicitly revealed proposition.

A dogma is a revealed truth, spoken by God and recognized as such by the magisterial authority of the Church. Therefore it must be a statement the content of which is spoken by God Himself in proper (explicit) or in equivalent (implicit) terms. Consequently, the virtually revealed can never attain to the condition of dogma. It is in itself (*quoad se*) a theological conclusion expressing a new truth, whereas the implicitly revealed is only so with respect to man's way of knowing (*quoad nos*), adding no new concept to the explicitly revealed. The conclusion of a true illative syllogism starting from one revealed premise is not properly but improperly or analogically revealed. It is not adhered to on God's authority alone but also in virtue of an insight of human reason. From its very nature it cannot be an object of faith. In the case of implicit revelation, however, as it does not produce a new truth the Church does not propose—and man does not assent to—the truth of the conclusion on the ground of human insight but only because it is part of what God says to us.

At the first blush this seems to be a perfectly articulated and consistent doctrine. But it is a well-known danger with such perfect theories that they easily part company with the reality they intend to explain. With the best will in the world it seems impossible to fit the facts into the theory except by frankly Procrustean proceedings. Moreover—and this is a difficulty inherent to all forms of the logical theory—the distinctions do not stand the test of practical application. Schultes himself admits that it is often difficult to decide whether a development is no more than a statement in equivalent terms or a theological conclusion. A strictly logical distinction that does not work in practice is probably a merely verbal one, invented for the sake of the case. Finally, the assertion that a statement in equivalent terms is identical with the meaning of the speaker himself is no less questionable, for how can one be sure that the expression in new terms is equivalent to the original statement? Not on the authority of the speaker, of course, but on that of human judgment. The new expression may be equivalent to the original one, but this is not guaranteed by the speaker himself.

The theory of Tuyaerts is diametrically opposed to that of his brother-in-religion. In respect of verbal logic it is no less perfectly articulated and consistent. Tuyaerts starts from two principles: first, the range of dogma and that of ecclesiastical infallibility are coextensive (consequently an 'ecclesiastical faith' beyond divine faith is nonsense); second,

Whosoever admits and affirms the truth of an assertion, admits and affirms by that very fact, under penalty of failing entirely in logic, . . . 1. all the assertions whose truth is required as a necessary postulate to preserve the truth of the assertion in question; 2. all the conclusions that necessarily follow from the given assertion. In other words: any affirmation which can be made of a given assertion logically extends to everything that the assertion necessarily presupposes as principle and to everything it necessarily entails as consequence.[27]

On the basis of that principle the distinction between explicative and illative syllogisms is rejected as pointless. The range of possible development of doctrine is coextensive with the whole range of possible inference. Development is objective insofar as in the object of assent all truths are logically connected; it is subjective insofar as the mind has to grasp individually the consequences and assent to the conclusions. Subjective development is logical too as far as the logical nexus is the reason why one assents to the conclusion. The whole process is logical. God uses human reason according to its own rules in order to lead man's knowledge of His word to perfection. Even the way in which God acts upon the mind is logical. His revelation is acknowledged according to the natural rules of apprehension and judgment. Against H. Pinard, Tuyaerts opposes the impossibility of a divine truth exclusively included in a praxis. For a sound praxis is necessarily preceded by a careful consideration of its grounds.

Whatever, then, is necessarily connected with a revealed truth is itself revealed and definable by infallible authority. To the objection that in the cause of an illative syllogism the conclusion partly follows from a natural premise, so that the certainty of the conclusion cannot go beyond that of the rational proposition, Tuyaerts answers that the conclusion is not partly included in both premises but entirely in each of them. The conclusion that John is a rational animal is entirely included in the statement that all men are rational (major premise) and alike in the statement that John is a man (minor premise). The process of development is thus completely rationalized. It is emphatically stated that any comparison with natural growth is wrong and muddled. The development of natural ideas according to the laws of logic is the only valuable model and it is not even an analogous model but the two cases of development are logically of the same nature.

Here we are dealing with a wonderful construction of Euclidean thought. If the axioms are accepted, the rest follows in a geometric fashion. But the epistemological presupposition is all wrong. Human thought about reality does not conform to a geometric pattern in which each proposition logically includes all other propositions, which fit into the same pattern, so that starting with one truth it must be possible to discover all other truths by backward or forward ratiocination. The basic conception is altogether unreal and leads to the absurd consequences that the first principles of human thought, which are involved in any assertion, and the whole of philosophy that follows from them are objects of faith and may be infallibly defined by the Church. Tuyaerts candidly accepts the consequence.

Consideration of the masterpiece of scholastic theology on the question of doctrinal development concludes this chapter: *L'Evolution homogène du dogme catholique* by F. Marín-Sola.[28] It is the most comprehensive work on the subject, not only presenting an amply elaborated and perfectly articulated theory but also embracing in its view the whole history of the question, widely discussing all the opinions of contemporary authors. Marín-Sola is a speculative genius, and his erudition is prodigious; but strictly speaking he is no historian. He does not look at the data of history in a strict historical perspective, and he too often accommodates them to fit into his own system. He systematizes history. In itself this is not a bad thing, but it is a most dangerous enterprise.

To begin with the terminology of his construction, he accepts with Tuyaerts that the domain of ecclesiastical definition and the range of doctrinal development are coextensive with divine faith. There is no *fides ecclesiastica*. The entire question, then, devolves into one of distinguishing the different ways in which a truth or a proposition may be related to revelation or the objective correlate of faith. For Marín-Sola the question concerns not so much the kind of reasoning by which a proposition is derived from the deposit of faith as the way in which it is contained in or related to the deposit. This is the primary question. The logical status of syllogisms is only a secondary question.

A development is homogeneous when the transition does not entail in the *terminus ad quem* a concept different from or contrary to the concepts included in the *terminus a quo*. Concepts are different if they cannot be deduced from one another. If deduction is possible, then the concepts included in the development are said to be 'explicative' of or 'conformable' to those included in the point of departure. A transition that entails different or contrary concepts is not homogeneous but transformistic or heterogeneous. Propositions that are verbally contained in the original deposit are said to be formally and explicitly revealed. All others are implicitly revealed. The modes of implication however are manifold.

1. The difference between the original and the later proposition may be only a difference in terms. Then the implication is *formal* and *implicit*. The way in which it is explicated is not a true syllogism.

2. Also, the relation between them may imply a difference in explicative concepts. Then the implication is *virtually implicit* and is explicated by a true but merely conceptual syllogism.

3. If the difference implies a real distinction but in such a way that the concepts are still explicative only, then the implication is *simply virtual* and the syllogism by which it is explicated is true and real. According to scholastic philosophy, for instance, the concepts of reason and will are connected in such a way that the one can be deduced from the other (explicative concepts), but in the reasonable being there is a real distinction between the faculty of reasoning and that of willing.

A further distinction is to be made between virtual-inclusive and virtual-connective. This is a subdivision of both the virtually implicit and the simply virtual. For Marín-Sola the distinction is of utmost importance because the line that separates what may become defined dogma from what may not runs between the virtual-inclusive and the virtual-connective.

It is necessary, however, to know something of scholastic philosophy in order to understand his meaning. There are three kinds of knowledge each with its own type of certainty: the metaphysical, the physical, and the moral. Metaphysical knowledge starts from the apprehension of an essence of whatever kind and deduces from that essence its radical properties. All judgments of that kind are analytical: the predicate is contained in the notion of the subject and is derived from it by mere analysis. Radical properties are, for example, the basic mental faculties of man. If Christ is man, He has the faculty of willing or laughing. This does not imply that He exercised those faculties. The certainty of metaphysical knowledge is absolute.

Physical knowledge, gained from general experience, is synthetic. The predicate is not included in the abstract essence. Its link with the nature of the thing rests on constant and common experience. The greenness of a tree cannot be deduced from its essence; but if there is a tree, one may safely say, on the ground of common and constant experience, that it must be green. In the same way, if Christ is a man, one may safely say that He ate. The contrary is not absolutely impossible but would have been a miracle. Physical certainty that rests on physical law is not absolutely certain, but has the certainty proper to physical deduction.

Moral certainty rests on regularities in human conduct established by general experience. One may foresee how men will act in given circumstances. Exceptional conduct, however, is not a miracle but an anomaly. If Christ, for instance, is a man it is morally certain that He laughed on certain occasions. If He did not, He was indeed a strange human being.

But is it certain that Christ had two lungs? This cannot be deduced from the essence of man. But if you start with the premise that His manhood was integral, then it is metaphysically certain that He had two lungs. The predicate 'having two lungs' is contained in the subject 'integral man' and can be derived from it by mere analysis.

Did Christ laugh in a sarcastic way? The answer to this question is not necessarily connected with the notion of manhood or integral manhood. But supposing that sarcasm betrays a moral imperfection, it necessarily follows from Christ's being a perfect man that He did not laugh sarcastically. Again, the certainty is metaphysical and the explication is analytical. Consequently the essence of a thing may be considered in three ways: as pure essence, as integrally realized essence, or as perfectly realized essence. From the essence considered in either of these ways one may deduce something with metaphysical certainty, but from the pure essence it is impossible to infer physical or moral fact. The last is the domain of the virtual-connective.

Reasoning not only proceeds from essence to property but also from cause to effect. There are, however, two kinds of causes: metaphysical causes that do not exist antecedently to their effects but contain them in themselves, as for instance the soul in relation to its mental faculties; and real or physical causes that exist before their effects and have by themselves no more than the power to produce them. Inferences from metaphysical causes are virtually included in those causes; inferences from physical causes are virtually connected with them.

There are, then, only two kinds of implication that are virtual-connective; deductions of facts from pure essences and deductions of effects from real physical causes. Truths derived after that manner from explicitly revealed propositions cannot become part of defined dogma. It is interesting to note that according to Marín-Sola dogmatic infallibility extends to what are called 'dogmatic facts,' as for instance the fact that a condemned error has been really held by the authors whose error is condemned. It also extends to the canonization of a particular saint. Both, indeed, are included in the dogma of ecclesiastical infallibility, either as a part in a whole or as a particular in a universal.

Marín-Sola himself thinks that the strict limitation of the explicitly revealed to what is verbally contained in the sources and the clear distinction between the virtual-inclusive and the virtual-connective are the most important pieces of his terminological analysis. Unanimous tradition, he says, admits that theological conclusions may be converted into dogmas. Suarez drew the line between the formally and the virtually revealed in a wrong way. On the one hand, he included in the formally revealed a 'confusedly revealed' that extends to both the formally implicit and the virtually implicit, with the absurd consequence that these, too, must or could be held by divine faith, even before any definition by the Church. On the other hand, he included the virtual-connective in the virtually revealed, which could become an object of faith in virtue of a definition; and this must logically lead to another absurd conclusion: the necessity of new revelations of some kind after the definitive constitution of the deposit of faith.

According to Marín-Sola, then, all propositions that can be inferred with metaphysical certainty from formally, i.e., verbally, revealed propositions are apt to be defined as dogma. Before the definition they are objects of theological knowledge. After the definition they become objects of faith. How does he explain and justify this qualitative change?

A conclusion can be considered in two ways: formally, i.e., as deriving from the premises, and materially, i.e., in itself. Considering it formally, the conclusion is seen in relation to the means through which it is known. As long as logical inference is the only means by which the implicit is known, a proposition inferred from explicit revelation cannot be the object of an assent of faith. But a proposition materially one and the same may formally be known through different means. That Christ ate may be deduced from His being a man. At the same time, however, the Gospel directly reports that He did eat. In the first case it is known by reason, in the second case by 'simple apprehension' of the meaning of a text.

In the same way a conclusion, materially the same, may be known by different dialectical means. It may be known by theological inference but also by ecclesiastical inference. The two inferences are not logically different in kind. The thought of the Church by which a definition is prepared implies all the human efforts of inferential clarification. But a theological inference is merely individual and fallible, whereas ecclesiastical inference, leading to a definition of faith, is infallibly assisted by the Spirit. The first is merely natural, the second supernatural *quoad modum*. Because of their being metaphysically included in the object of faith, the formal-implicit, the virtual-implicit, and the virtual-inclusive are, materially considered, identical with the object of faith. But while the formal means by which theology comes to know the inclusion is merely human, the formal means by which ecclesiastical thought established it is infallibly guaranteed by God. The material object of faith, that to which one assents, is the word of God; and its formal object, the reason why one assents, is His authority alone. But in the present dispensation the proposition by the Church, although not entering into the formal object of faith, is a necessary condition of its working for man. The virtual-connective is not contained in the word of revelation, neither in itself nor for man. Therefore, it can never become immediate for man. The virtual-inclusive, on the contrary, is in itself, though not for man, contained in the word of God. Through definition by the Church, what is in itself immediately spoken by God becomes, in virtue of His infallible assistance, immediately spoken for man; and consequently it acquires the necessary condition required to be presented to man under the formal object of faith. Before the definition it was already formally attested by God but lacked the condition to become such for man. After the definition that condition is fulfilled. Through the authority of the Church God does not give new revelations, but He unfolds His revelation in the Church.

There is a last point of essential importance concerning the way or the process by which the Church attains to its final judgments about the inclusion of a proposition in the deposit of faith. Here Marín-Sola comes near to Newman on the ground of his deep understanding of what Thomas Aquinas teaches on the nature of faith. There are two ways in which human judgment proceeds to its object: the intellectual way either by deliberate and explicit or by spontaneous reasoning, and the affective or mystical way by inner connaturality. The light of faith, which shines in the heart, causes in the mind a certain knowledge of its object by way of sympathy and connaturality. Every virtue, acquired or infused, attunes the mind to its proper object. So the infused light or habit of faith gives us an inner discretion with respect to the self-communication of the revealing God. This way of apprehending the riches included in revelation is more perfect because it proceeds from a higher principle. To be sure the relation between the explicitly revealed and its inclusions is in itself logical. Marín-Sola does not go beyond a propositional understanding of revelation—but the way of knowledge by sympathy is not inferential but direct. Theology may and must afterwards scrutinize, analyze, and justify the intuitions of the heart, but it is possible that the heart is ahead of reason and that reason does not succeed in verifying apodictically that which the believing mind has reached by the *via affectiva* of divine sympathy.

There is no book on the question of development that met with more response among Catholic schoolmen than that of Marín-Sola. Its success and influence have been considerable. Even A. Gardeil, the most original and powerful innovator in the domain of neo-Thomistic fundamental theology, abandoned his own somewhat forced theory and adopted with enthusiasm the views of the great Spanish theologian. But, as was to be expected, all possible objections were urged against him, and the history of the controversy could fill a book. But within the general frame of scholastic thought most difficulties could be either easily solved or rejected as having no point.

Some theologians objected with Schultes that one who says something cannot be charged with all the consequences that his utterance entails for human reason, even with metaphysical necessity. But Marín-Sola could answer that this is true of man, who is not actually conscious of all the entailments of his utterings, but not of God, who perfectly knows the full meaning and extension of His word. Nor does it follow from the theory of Marín-Sola that if the virtual-inclusive be said by God, even the metaphysical principles by which the inclusion is known are, as Tuyaerts admitted, part of revelation and possible objects of infallible definition. For the object of divine revelation is man's salvation, and propositions that do not say something about salvation are not part of revelation. Divine truth is given to man in forms of human thought and language. It would be absurd, however, to contend that God, in expressing Himself in human language, implicitly revealed the principles and rules to which human thought is by its nature necessarily subjected.

Another objection raised by Schultes and his followers is that on the one hand something that in reality is identical with another thing, and thus ontologically included in it, may not be so for man, so that the revelation of the second must be distinct from the revelation of the first; while on the other hand, the existence of something that in reality is distinct and different from another thing may be virtually included in and deduced from it with metaphysical necessity, although it is not contained in it either as a radical property in an essence or as a necessary effect in a metaphysical cause. The alleged examples are odd, in the sense of unique in their kind. The first is that of the unity and trinity that are identical in divine reality, but not for man. The second is that of the existence of contingent being that metaphysically entails the existence of necessary being. Is the Trinity virtually revealed if the existence of the one God be expressly revealed? Would the existence of God be necessarily revealed if the existence of contingent being were revealed?

It could be answered that odd or unique cases do not tell against a general theory designed to explain a certain category of facts to which, because of their oddness, these cases do not and cannot pertain. Moreover, the basic principle of Marín-Sola unites two things that have to be taken together *in sensu composito*: the virtual-inclusive, really identical or not with that in which it is included, is only so insofar as it is apt to be known to man by metaphysical deduction. That which is virtually included is only such if it is included not only in the order of reality but also in the order of possible human knowledge. Marín-Sola's distinction between included *quoad se* and *quoad nos* only means that one truth may be included in another either in such a way that we do not see but possibly could see the consequence (*quoad se*) or in such a way that we actually perceive it (*quoad nos*). If so, the case of divine unity and trinity is not relevant, because the trinity, however identical with the unity of God in the order of reality, cannot possibly be deduced from it.

The second case is, too, unreal. If the contingency of the world were revealed by God and recognized as such by man, His existence should be directly included for man not in the object of that revelation but in the act of God's revealing it.

Nor do I think that the objection of Hammans is really to the point. He contends that the falsity of Marín-Sola's theory is shown by his statement that the Apostles explicitly knew all the possible dogmas of faith. Marín-Sola indeed held and stressed that traditional opinion. However, it does not play so essential a part that the theory stands or falls with it. Indeed, the position of Marín-Sola may be summed up in three points. (1) He who says something actually says all that is implied in the statement and can be deduced from it by mere analysis. Within the general system of scholastic philosophy this is a sound principle. To speak is to say something to somebody. Within the world of common-sense language, to say that this man is physically integral and unmutilated is actually to say that he has two legs, two lungs, etc. Similarly, within the game-world of scholastic thought, if I say that there is a man, I have said that he has the radical potentiality of intellectual knowledge and will. (2) That which is thus implied in a sentence is in one sense immediately said (in itself) and in another sense mediately said (for man: as grasped by the hearer). This is a very subtle distinction. (3) That which is thus immediate in itself but mediate for man becomes immediate for man when the speaker, God, makes it immediate through infallible interpreters appointed by Him. Strictly speaking, nothing is added to objective revelation, but subjectively the revealing activity prolongs itself in its infallible medium, not in order to present new truths but so that old truths begin to function for man in a new way.

It seems clear that the theory stands on its own feet without the supposition of a perfect explicit and immediate knowledge of all possible dogmas by the Apostles. On the one hand the result of ecclesiastical reasoning, assisted by the Spirit, is not that the Apostles explicitly knew that which for us is now a conclusion but that it is infallibly true. On the other hand if the Apostles explicitly knew it, then the supposition that objective revelation is closed with their deaths is not endangered by later oblivion, and the Spirit could remind the Church of what the Apostles knew by any means whatsoever, even by a new illumination; and then the intricate logical scaffolding of Marín-Sola no longer has any use.

Within the logical range of Marín-Sola's presuppositions there are two major difficulties. To start with, the distinction between what is immediate in itself and what is mediate for man is useless. Such notions as immediate and mediate are, from their very nature, relative notions. Something is immediate or mediate in relation to another thing. The present case has to do with a relation of a truth to man's understanding. I see no meaning in the assertion that a truth is immediate in itself but not to man. In particular, to reveal is to unveil something to somebody. That revealed truth could be immediate in itself but not to man does not make any sense. And to say that it becomes immediate as coming from God through a new medium that is not God's revealing act seems to imply a contradiction. The only possible meaning would be that it is immediate as coming from the speaker and consequently as addressed to man, but not immediate as terminated in the hearer; so that the Church by defining it makes us know with certainty that it is immediately addressed to man. If this is the real meaning of Marín-Sola—but I must confess that it would be a benign interpretation —then it could be accepted, or at least it would be free from self-contradiction.

A related question concerns the ecclesiastical definition. It seems to be fairly evident that the definition is either an act that really makes a truth become an object of faith or an act that only guarantees to the whole Church that something really pertains to the object of faith. There is no intermediate position. In the first case the conclusion cannot be avoided that the ecclesiastical definition implies a new act of revelation, and as in the case of Suarez, to deny it seems to be a verbal trick. In the second case, one does not see why a theologian who grasps with certainty—if such a thing is possible—that a dogma is included in a basic article of faith could not be obliged in conscience to assent to it as to an object of faith. And then, of course, Suarez is left behind for Vàzquez.

The second difficulty concerns the way in which Marín-Sola appeals to the doctrine of Thomas Aquinas regarding the affective connaturality established by the light of faith between the believing mind and its object. According to Marín-Sola a conclusion may be reached either by the intellect, through syllogistic reasoning, or by affection, through connatural feeling. Within the general framework of his epistemology, however, the conclusion must at least in principle be knowable by syllogistic reasoning. If so, I do not see why in some cases a conclusion grasped through divine sympathy should remain, after being known, beyond the range of syllogistic deduction. If the link between two truths is in itself a strictly logical one, then it must be possible to show clearly the logical connection. For a strictly logical connection is a connection between propositions, and entirely pertains to the domain of propositional reasoning. It seems contradictory to state that a strictly logical connection between two propositions actually remains beyond the range of strict propositional inference.

This criticism is very important, for Marín-Sola is materially right. Starting from a given apprehension of truth, the mind is able to get at some implications by ways that cannot be traced afterward by processes of strict syllogistic reasoning. But that assertion cannot be justified within the propositional epistemology of Marín-Sola. Another epistemological background is needed. What one's duty consists in here and now can be apprehended with practical certainty by *phronesis*, which is a judgment after the manner of connaturality, as Aquinas says. But *phronesis* goes beyond the range of syllogistic deduction from ethical principles, and its way cannot afterward be traced by abstract reasoning. In a similar way the sense of faith is able to see that certain truths are included in the

revealed Word that is its object. But though the theologian is able
to give them an intelligible position in the general system of
Christian doctrine, he is not able on that account to reduce that
connection to a syllogism. A theory of knowledge is needed in which
there is a place for a faculty of passing from one truth to another
after a manner similar to that of *phronesis*. Newman will call it the
illative sense.

After all, the theory of Marín-Sola about the effective path of
knowledge, though rightly taken from St. Thomas, is not consistent
with his general theory of knowledge because of his rigid conception of reasoning as syllogistic reasoning and, connected with
this, his strict propositional concept of revelation. His theory is
eclectic. The theory of affective knowledge as used here does not
fit into the general theory of neo-Scholastic intellectualism. The
same criticism applies to other sincere attempts to introduce a bit of
Newman into the scholastic scheme of doctrinal development.

With all this, our criticism of Marín-Sola ends in a general criticism of all logical theories of development. Faced with the problems
created by Modernism, many theologians felt that the results of
Newman's thought on the matter must somehow be true if definitions like that of the Immaculate Conception were to be justified.
But they were unable to make them fit with their general theory of
knowledge and revelation. G. Tyrrell, who was trained in scholastic
theology, saw it and drew the conclusion that there was no intermediate position between a propositional conception of revelation
and a non-propositional one. He propounded the dilemma: either
propositional—and then you are bound to explain the development
of doctrine in terms of syllogistic deduction—or not propositional
at all—and then you are bound to a transformistic theory of dogmatic evolution. He failed to see the course between Scylla and
Charybdis.

CHAPTER EIGHT

Origin and Development of the Transformistic Theory

The Reformers in their own way preserved a very important point of the old conception of faith that had been obscured in post-Scotistic theology. The decline of medieval scholasticism was characterized by a growing gulf between God and man. God vanished in the heaven of heavens and His spoken word alone remained on earth claiming an unconditional surrender of the intellect. Faith was reduced to an acceptance of revealed propositions, justified or not by reason. The immediate relation of the believing mind to the First Truth, brought about in the individual mind by 'the instinct of the inviting God' (St. Thomas) and leading to an assent that was a total surrender of the heart to the merciful Lord, was obscured in theology, if not in the living Church. In the history of human thought a one-sided attitude of mind easily generates its contrary. Thus, the one-sided intellectualism of the theology of faith gave rise to a life of devotion that, tender and ardent though it was, became separated from theology and lacked the speculative tendencies of Ruysbroeck or Eckhart. Theology and spirituality grew apart, and the whole history of modern Christianity will be characterized by a perpetual opposition between theology and piety: a theology without piety for the intellect and a piety without much intellect for the heart.

THE PROTESTANT BACKGROUND

The practical school of devotion or *Devotio Moderna* arose in the Low Countries and inspired the movement of the Brethren of the

Common Life. Its promoter was Gerard Grote, but Thomas à Kempis would write the immortal masterpiece of the new devotion, *De imitatione Christi*. 'During the closing years of the fourteenth century compunction took the place of metaphysics in the spiritual life of the Low Countries.'[1]

The influence of the *Devotio Moderna* on the Reformation is generally admitted. But what was no more than a practical bracketing and not a denial among the Brethren of Common Life became with Luther a passionate opposition. He rejected all metaphysical theology and considered the Bible as the only source of Christian thought and devotion. His *sola Scriptura* is not only the negation of the necessary mediation of ecclesiastical authority in establishing truth for the Christian believer, but it also includes a rejection of the theology of scholastic tradition. Up to a certain point he was right, for a theology of intellectual constructions that are of no use or value for the life of faith is not a genuine theology. It is a dead thing, a body without a soul, and could better be buried. Theology is faith in search of understanding. If the function of understanding is separated or alienated from its vital act, it no longer has any right to call itself theology. Moreover, as all forms of mere intellectual occupation, it involves the danger of diverting the mind from what religion is really about.

This was felt by Luther. Although he did not reject the Creed or the principle of dogma, for him the object of faith was the word of God, speaking to man through the Bible; and although not opposed to catechizing—he wrote one of the most influential catechisms—the immediate rule of faith was not something exterior but the inner enlightenment and inspiration of the Holy Spirit who opens the Scriptures to the individual mind. Through the Spirit man not only gets a right understanding of God's word, but the written word of the past becomes a word addressed to the individual and ready to change his sinful heart if he is willing to surrender his whole self to divine mercy in a spirit of unconditional faith or trust. This is, in its essentials, nearer to Thomas Aquinas than that kind of intellectualism that reduces the object of faith to a set of ecclesiastical propositions, and the act of faith to a notional assent that must be justified by reason and in which the necessity of grace, though fully admitted, is not satisfactorily accounted for. To Aquinas, indeed, the object of the act of faith is specified by the *Prima Veritas*, the primary truth manifested to man in the articles of the Creed. Its material object is God (*credere Deum*) and its formal object His authority (*credere Deo*). As for its exercise, the act of faith is elicited under the impulse of the Spirit or the divine instinct, and as such it goes beyond all propositions and is a voluntary surrender to God Himself (*credere in Deum*). A surrender of that kind manifestly cannot be a mere intellectual or notional acceptance of propositions. It is a real assent to God who reveals Himself and His Son to the *cor* or inner man.

The main difference, then, between Luther and the ancient Christian tradition lies in his denial that the living Church and the dogmatic authority of its magisterium are the immediate rule of how the content of faith is to be understood. In the painful controversial situation that set him in opposition to an ecclesiastical structure that in many respects was sadly corrupt, his impetuous spirit came to shake off the oppressing burden of authority. It was an ominous decision, involving the danger of subjectivism that in due time would lead to almost intolerable tensions, deviations, and divisions. By the dawn of the 19th century, Protestantism all over the world had been seriously crippled and debilitated by sectarian dissensions and had failed to prove its vitality in united action and conquering power.

From the beginning of the 19th century, however, it gradually recovered and revealed its inner life-force, spreading over most of the globe and largely overcoming, in the ecumenical movement, the handicap of inner division. The inherent danger of the Protestant position is fully recognized by the best Protestant scholars of ecclesiastical history: 'Here was a grave danger. With its dynamism, individualism, and weakness of institutionalized control, Protestantism, and especially Protestantism of the Puritan-Pietist-Evangelical traditions, was a source of some movements which so denied or distorted the Gospel or so mixed it with elements contrary to the Gospel that they became a threat to Christianity and a secularizing menace not only to Christianity but also to all religion.'[2]

Starting with Luther, then, and proceeding from his initial position, two currents will constantly confront one another in movements of thesis and antithesis: a doctrinal orthodoxy, rooted in Luther's own concern with creed and dogma, and a practical pietism that without denying the part of dogma is not very insistent on it and tends to make light of its acceptance as necessary for salvation. It is significant that, generally speaking, Protestant

G

theology has not occupied itself intensively with the problem of development of doctrine. Two facts may help in understanding this. There is the denial even among orthodox believers of an ecclesiastical organ of irrevocable decision in matters of faith. Between the Bible and present belief there are no doctrinal determinations of unquestionable value. The possibility of appealing to the Bible is absolute and universal. According to Protestants the Church tends toward unity and uniformity in the instruction of its members; but the Church may err at times, even in doctrines that in a given epoch are commonly admitted. There is always room for personal efforts or particular movements to reconsider the patterns of ecclesiastical teaching in the light of Scripture. Therefore, although according to orthodox theology there is a core of dogmatic tradition that will in fact forever survive the test of criticism because it so clearly agrees with the teaching of Scripture, no doctrine is in principle absolutely beyond criticism. Second, there is the Pietist tendency of dogmatic relativism, which stresses the *sola fide* in such a way that the inner decision or experience of faith and conversion become the only thing that really matters. Because of the common rule of *sola Scriptura*, Orthodoxy and Pietism are more akin to each other than either of them to Roman Catholicism. They are really children of one and the same father. Their opposition reflects within Protestantism the original cleavage in the mind of its originators.

Liberal theology actually sprang from the Pietist stem of Protestant religion. Pietism is the background of its great representatives. But Orthodoxy could not make a firm stand against it, because it refused to recognize an objective norm that could raise a dogma above devastating criticism. From its unsystematic and occasional nature, its Hebraic imagery and style, the characteristic differences between its inspired writers, the Bible lies open to divergent interpretations, and in meditating on it with however much devotion, it is difficult to distinguish between the inspiration of the divine Spirit and the hidden influence of one's personal or social make-up. Although by tradition and mental habit orthodox Protestants are as confident as Catholics in defending the scriptural origin of the Trinitarian and Christological dogmas, it is possible to challenge these dogmas in a plausible way on the ground of any interpretation that has no extra-Biblical guarantee of its rightness.

Therefore Newman, when he outlined the *via media* of his ideal

Anglican Church, most strongly opposed current Protestantism because it seemed to him that the very principle of dogma was endangered by its basic assumptions. He foretold the dissolution of Protestantism in liberal religiosity. Actually, and fortunately, his prophecy has not come true. The main Protestant Churches have proved capable of resisting victoriously the assaults of liberalism. The Holy Spirit did not desert His children, who were so deeply devoted to His Word and to their Savior. But there was something very acute in Newman's view; he clearly saw the weak point of the basic position of Protestantism: its tendency to interpret the Bible not according to an objective rule, patiently established by centuries of Christian thought and experience, but according to private judgment, with all the posible deviations following from the partiality of the different points of view represented by individuals, particular groups, or generations. Indeed, let the idea—a very sound idea—of historicity take possession of the mind, pressing upon it the necessity of a continuous translation of the Gospel in terms of contemporary thought, and it at once becomes evident that if there is no living authority to challenge them the moods of contemporary thought will easily dispose of the original truth by way of time-serving interpretation. This is what happened in different measure to the various transformistic theories of dogma.

GERMAN PIETISM

The greatest representative of pietistic theology is Philip Spener (1635–1705), who made a case against Lutheran Orthodoxy. The personal position of Luther was something new and unprecedented in the history of Christianity. It had to make its way in a social world whose intellectual climate was still determined by scholastic habits of thought. After a time the patterns of the old school theology prevailed over the new inspiration and gave rise to the odd phenomenon of Orthodoxy. In spite of Luther's refusal, Aristotelian metaphysics resumed its ruling position in theological thought and systematization. The first principle of Orthodox theology was frankly intellectualistic. Theology is a science that starts with Holy Scripture and in accordance with the confessions of the Reformation establishes the content of faith by means of theoretical reason. The idea that theology is a use of the intellect within the view of living faith and normed by it, is absent. Theology is practical only insofar as it works out the rule to which thought and will have to conform. Moreover, it has no direct concern in its own practical usage; it is only interested in theological accuracy. The attitude is typically objectivistic and intellectualistic. The intellect is separated from life and set above life as an abstract norm. It is self-sufficient. It does not take account of its own vital roots and does not itself descend into the basement of daily life. In most cases the theologian will be a believer, but his personal belief is unrelated to his theological excellence. Belief itself, as a notional apprehension of and assent to the articles of faith, comes before the saving compunction and the personal turning towards God. If faith, then, is essentially an acceptance of propositions about God, the knowledge and acceptance of the true creed is necessary for salvation. That true creed is the creed of the Reformation. The Lutheran idea of an invisible Church that may have members in different confessions is practically abandoned for the doctrine that salvation is only possible within the fold of the Lutheran Church. On all these points, Orthodoxy had swerved far from Luther himself.

Spener takes his stand with what may be called 'the existentialist Luther.' He refuses to call 'theologians' those whose thought is not inspired and directed by living faith. Their thought is only a kind of philosophy concerning holy things. Living faith, then, although ruled by the Bible and articles of faith, does not exist if God does not work through it, making it a word in the personal religious experience of each devout subject. Spener recognizes the fact that most members of the Church do not accept the truth of faith by personal conviction but rather by social influence and habit. Such a faith is of no value and is the main cause of atheism. Atheism, then, cannot be overcome by philosophical controversy but exclusively by the action of living faith.

Faith is an experience of the saving God and a complete surrender to His mercy, caused in man by the inner light of grace or the inner testimony that the Holy Spirit gives in men's hearts. It is an act of the whole person. To be sure, it is conditioned by an eager and devout reading of the Bible and listening to the proclamation of God's word. There is a way to God along the path of obedience and faithfulness of conscience, leading to a fervid application of the mind to the study of the Bible and meditation on heavenly things. But faith itself does not consist in this. It can only be given by an illuminating grace that attracts by a presentiment of its bliss, bringing about a conversion and spiritual regeneration, setting man free and changing the inclination of his own heart.

That inner freedom is a freedom from selfishness. There is no true faith without love. Light is also warmth. Doing our duties towards God and men with a view to individual fulfillment is not a token that men are freed from the bonds of original sin. Love excludes every kind of selfishness and is the perfection of all virtue. It is an answer to the love of God who attracts men by His heart-changing grace.

Just as faith does not exist without love, so it cannot be genuine if it does not exhibit in daily life its own practical consequences. There is no genuine faith without practice of devotion, penance, and moral conduct. Spener goes so far as to say that without praxis one has no true apprehension of what is written in the Bible.

The position of Spener, in contradistinction to Orthodoxy, is thus characterized by a strong and consistent affirmation of the inseparable connection in the reality of faith between the part of the intellect and that of religious experience and life. This stressing of the living unity of heart and reason goes together with a certain depreciation of the latter. Spener is a kind of radical personalist. Everyone has to detect for himself according to his own gifts and vocation the truth of the Bible. A purely notional or intellectual apprehension of what the articles of faith mean is different in kind from the apprehension proper to saving knowledge. A true apprehension of the truth of the articles of the Creed supposes and causes love and moral seriousness. With all this the doctrine in which men believe is still conceived of as something that is simply and objectively given and that the believer has to realize for himself: 'Any reflection on the fact that, in the elaboration of the mentally apprehended content of faith, religious experience has itself an essential part fails in him.'[3]

Such a conception evidently entails a particular evaluation of dogma. Like Thomas Aquinas, Spener underlines that in the various articles one and the same truth, living in the exercise of faith, becomes present to the mind and heart. From this he draws the conclusion that the reunion of the various Christian denominations into one Church is not so much a matter of doctrinal uniformity as a matter of unity in the living relation to one and the same truth, inadequately expressed in the articles of the Creed. It is a curious fact that Spener, who comes so near to the great tradition of medieval theology, excludes the Catholic Church from the possible fold of the one Christian community because he abhors what seems to him an enslavement of conscience under a human authority that intervenes between the person and God's word. That one cannot be saved without the acceptance of the whole of a rigid system of propositions maintained by authority is not something accidental in Romanism as it is in Protestant Orthodoxy. It is the head and front of it, and hence it is irreformable as long as it lasts in its proper form.

Spener, then, in conceiving a possible union in the same truth despite variations in the objective system of the articles, rejoins his contemporary, Jurieu, who opposed Bossuet. Like Jurieu he makes a distinction between basic and non-basic articles. The distinction is recognized in the experience of faith. Those articles that are able to illuminate man's personal experience of the saving God and that from their own nature call forth a life of devotion and moral earnestness are the only basic ones. An objective error that does not destroy the surrender of the heart to God in Jesus Christ cannot be a cause of damnation. It is even possible that a man should be saved who denies a basic article, as long as his denial is only intellectual and does not translate itself into forms of conduct that run counter to the practical exigencies of faith. Thus a genuine *fides quae credit* can go together with a false *fides quae creditur*. As long as faith abides by the doctrine of justification by grace alone, ignorance and error are forgiven by God in the same way as other kinds of human weakness. Faith may be erroneous in its objective expression but genuine in its subjective reality. Likewise it may be objectively true and fail to be subjectively real. Therefore the conscience of those who adhere to objective error must be respected as long as their inclinations and praxis are in accordance with the attitude of true faith. On this ground Spener opposes to Orthodoxy, which made the acceptance of the integral Lutheran Creed a condition of salvation, his own thesis that in all denominations God has His true children, known to Him, even among the members of the Catholic Church. The invisible kingdom of the heart under the scepter of genuine subjective faith, and not a visible congregation bound to the rule of a definite Creed, becomes at once the true reality of the Church.

A few remarks to conclude. First, there is a striking resemblance between the Lutheran position of Spener and the Calvinist position of Jurieu. To be sure, Spener goes beyond Jurieu in the practical conclusions, but the basic principle seems to be the same.

Next, the doctrine of Spener is very important in the history of Protestant theology. Spener is not a liberal. He fully appraises the essential importance of dogma in the structure of living faith. There is a core of scriptural doctrine that must be accepted in order to be saved. The genuineness of the *fides quae credit* normally depends on the correctness of the *fides quae creditur* and this has the character of an immutable dogmatic truth although in order to be true in a real sense it has to illuminate the experience and faith of the individual. In this Spener rediscovered and continued the authentic inspiration of Luther. His theology means the victory of the true Luther over the deviations of Orthodoxy. But the trait of subjectivism, the tendency to accord to the acceptance of a definite Creed a secondary place in comparison with the disposition of heart and will, carries with it the germs of a certain liberal theology. Indeed, Spener's subjectivism, extended by the later insight that all dogmatic expression is historical and therefore, in a certain sense, subject to development and correction, is perhaps not so far from Bultmann. It is an instructive fact following from the nature of historical life that a stressing of different aspects in the same complex of doctrine may in the long run lead to opposite conceptions. Sooner or later, on the ground of a slight dualism in its point of departure, Protestant theology must find itself at crossroads, leading either to Barth or to Bultmann. The theology of Spener, although not at all liberal, is a first step in the direction of the latter.

Finally, it is interesting to compare Spener's view of faith with that of Thomas Aquinas and medieval theology. Starting from the idea that the articles of faith are articulated parts of one truth, which being a reflection of the one reality of the saving God lives as a whole in the human mind, Thomas concluded that ignorance or material error in doctrine do not destroy the infused grace of saving faith as long as a few essential points were explicitly known and assented to and on the condition that the ignorance or error was not caused by willful neglect or stubborn pride. But he also held, on the same ground, that a conscious and voluntary rejection of one point of Biblical truth as proposed by the Church was equivalent to a rejection of the whole and a defection from the kingdom of salvation. In comparing Spener and Thomas, two things become evident. First, there is a similarity in their idea of faith. One would be justified in concluding from the principles of Thomas that material differences in Creed, which a Catholic may judge to be errors in good faith, due to historical circumstances and fixed by centuries of social separation, do not necessarily destroy a true unity in faith that could provide a sound basis for a comprehensive kind of reunion and active collaboration. In itself such a partial union, although rooted in the deepest levels of Christian life, is not the ideal. But it is the best man can do. The divisions that, as Jurieu said, are the consequences of man's common sinfulness, in which all parties have their share, should not be an obstacle to the closest forms of union that are actually within reach. If we sincerely recognize our faults, true repentance should rather drive us to realize the maximum of reconciliation in Christ.

Second, there is between the Protestant Churches and the Catholic Church a profound difference that, as Spener saw but entirely misjudged, makes the question of their union particularly difficult. As social phenomena, they are two different worlds because of their different conceptions of the ultimate practical rule of objective faith. According to Protestants that rule is the Bible; according to Catholics it is the living consensus of the present Church, authoritatively expressed by the hierarchical magisterium. 'A rule defining where authority is to be found in a religious society may leave plenty of scope for theologians to disagree.' This holds true within the Catholic Church as well as within the world of Protestant religion, in which there is an agreement about the scriptural rule. But there is certainly a good deal of truth in the statement that 'Every religion . . . is defined by reference to what it accepts as an authoritative criterion in religious matters. The acceptance or rejection of a religion is thus the acceptance or rejection of such an authority.'[4]

Once more, the cleft between Protestantism and Catholicism does not seem to be caused by the *sola fide* or the *sola gratia* of the Reformers—on these points both could come to agree after due explanations—but by their *sola scriptura*. That the living authority of the Church that interprets the Scriptures is somehow the ultimate practical rule of faith was certainly the position of patristic and medieval theology. In interpreting the Scriptures the Church as a social body is never deprived of the help of the Spirit who inspired them and gave them to the body of which He is the heart and the soul. But it is no less sure that both patristic and medieval theology recognized that the whole of saving truth is to be found in the Bible and that the Church is bound to its rule. In the act of ruling man's faith by its authority, the Church has to be entirely ruled by the Bible. The Church has no power whatever of establishing new dogmas beyond the range of Biblical teaching. For Catholics as for Protestants, then, the ultimate rule of faith is Scripture.

The difference lies in the way the authority of the Bible functions. According to Protestants the Bible rules as understood and interpreted by the individual believer, at least in principle, because actually, man being man, tradition exercises a momentous ruling power over the individual. According to the Catholic conviction the Bible rules as understood and interpreted by the Church, a living social body. In relation to the object of common faith the Church cannot move as a whole except by the voice of an authority that in virtue of its institution is as independent from the will of the believing society as the rule of Scripture. The Church is not simply ruled by the magisterium but by its own growing spiritual insight, founded in Scripture, living in tradition, and objectively voiced by its divinely instituted authority. As long as man is man, the Catholic rule will involve the danger of oppression and abuse of authority, but the Protestant rule will always involve the danger of dissolution and arbitrary private judgment. This should be recognised by both parties, and mutual understanding on that point should be a basic condition of a real communion in the same living faith.

LATITUDINARIANISM

No less important for understanding the development of liberal theology, although of a very different nature, is the current of latitudinarianism within the Church of England. Erasmus, who exercised a deep influence on the intellectual development of the nation, may be called its remote ancestor. He personally was a sincere Catholic and devoted to the Church. But it is understandable that, in the midst of the calamitous controversies that opposed the Catholic Church to the Reformation and led to destructive conflicts and wars, a refined humanistic mind sought for possible means of appeasement. Deeply influenced by the *devotio moderna*, he stressed the moral side of Christianity, and although convinced of the necessity and the immutability of dogma, he rather shrank from too great a stress on doctrinal wholeness, disapproved of the multiplication of essentials in the rule of faith, and preached a spirit of toleration.

In its origins, latitudinarianism is connected with Dutch Arminianism. The two movements indeed appear in history as spiritual twins and, as R. L. Colie has pointed out, the historical relations between them were very close.[5] The background of both movements is Calvinism, whose extremist parties, the Puritans in England, defended the thesis of an unconditional eternal predestination and did not hesitate to put into practice Calvin's theocratic idea of intolerance. Arminius (1560–1609) objected to the idea of unconditional antecedent predestination. He was influenced by the pietism of one of the first great writers of pre-classical Dutch literature, D. V. Coornhert. He gained the sympathy of great ecclesiastical, political, and literary figures, such as Uytenbogaert, chaplain to Louise de Coligny, widow of the Stadholder William the First; Oldenbarneveldt, Pensionary of Holland; and Hugo Grotius, the chief political thinker of that time. In 1610, his followers presented the clergy with a Remonstrance (hence the name 'Remonstrants') in which they rejected both forms of absolute antecedent predestination (supralapsarianism and infralapsarianism) and also the doctrines of Christ's dying for the elect alone, irresistible grace, and the infallible final perseverance of the saints. The conflict came to a head leading to the Synod of Dort (1618–19), the reassertion of the five disputed points, the repression of the Arminian clergy, the beheading of Oldenbarneveldt, and the condemnation of Grotius to perpetual imprisonment. It was through Vossius and other refugees that the views of Arminius were diffused in England where the High Church tendency was soon dubbed *Arminian*, meaning by the term 'sacramentalist, ceremonial, vestiarian, ritualist—and with little doctrinal accusation.'[6]

English latitudinarianism, however, cannot be explained by Arminian influences alone. England at that time was hopelessly divided into uncompromising factions or sects, each of which claimed to be the only saving religion and to have the right, when in power, to persecute its adversaries. This situation led W. Chillingworth (1602–1644), fellow of Trinity and one of the most capable men of his generation, to become a Roman Catholic, because it seemed to him that a living religious authority was the only possible means of settling the endless religious quarrels. He soon left the Catholic Church and after a time of hesitation renewed his adherence to the Church of England. He became the most resolute opponent of Roman Catholicism. The religious changes of Chillingworth were not moods but stages in the development of a logical mind. The first principle from which he started was that there must be a religious rule. This was a practical standpoint—and a very English one—by which to decide in matters of salvation and conduct. According to his experiences the Bible could not afford such a rule. Therefore he left the Anglican Church. But a brief stay on the continent taught him that the way of institutional authority did not leave enough room for individual freedom and conscience. Therefore he returned to England and concentrated on the question of the conditions under which the Bible could function as an efficient means of establishing a state of concordance.

He concluded that a combination of reason or common sense and Scripture could provide the instrument of peace. By following reason and personal conscience in studying the Bible every man could attain for himself as much truth as was needed for his salvation and moral life. Common sense being a common property of the human race, its application to the Bible would lead to common agreement as to the essentials. This is sufficient. For the rest the individual conscience ought to be respected, and differences in the doctrinal interpretation of the Bible should simply be tolerated. Chillingworth went very far in his conclusions. If reason is the rule by which to establish the truth of the Bible, it follows that as the Bible cannot give that kind of certainty proper to sense or science, faith is not 'a most certain and infallible knowledge' and rests on probabilities. Moreover, how could reason establish the authority of the Bible itself? And what does a man do if he does not know the Bible or could not honestly accept its authority? Every man is under the obligation to follow his own conscience; and if he sincerely does so, he will be saved, even if he does not know or cannot accept the Bible: 'Every man is to judge and choose; and the rule whereby he has to guide his choice, if he be a natural man, is reason, if he be already a Christian, is Scripture. which, we say, is the rule to judge controversies by.'[7] As to Christians: 'It is sufficient for any man's salvation to believe that the Scripture is true, and contains all things necessary to salvation; and to do his best endeavour to find and believe the true sense of it.' But 'Men might be saved without believing the Scriptures to be the word of God; much more without believing it to be a rule, and a perfect rule of faith.' For the Bible is only a vehicle for the divine revelation, not the revelation itself; 'so that the books of Scripture are not so much the objects of our faith, as the instruments of conveying it to our understanding.'[8]

Chillingworth's position already displays all the characteristic traits of latitudinarianism: the pragmatic principle of comprehensiveness; the stressing of the inviolability of personal conscience and each man's obligation to judge for himself; the idea that the Bible alone is the rule of faith, but the Bible as interpreted by reason or common sense; the optimistic Cartesian presumption that it should spontaneously lead to a sufficient state of agreement; the principle of toleration; the ethical approach to the essence of Christianity) and the view that honest endeavour was all that was required for salvation. But suppose that what is called 'common sense' is not a uniform and immutable gift of nature but a common way of viewing and judging things, rooted in social first principles that may vary according to differences of culture and age: it at once becomes evident that the rule of reason in interpreting the Bible will lead to variations in doctrine according to the intellectual moods of time and place, and there is no escape from dogmatic relativisim.

Starting from Chillingworth, latitudinarianism developed in two directions: that of the Broad Church and that of Deism. The most typical representatives of the first are known as the Cambridge Platonists, almost contemporaries of Chillingworth. To them, too, reason was the arbiter of natural religion and Biblical interpretation. But in a Platonic twist 'God-given right reason,' at work not only in philosophical reflection but also in common sense, was conceived of as the indwelling of God or the candle of the Lord (B. Whichcote) in the human mind, the true illumination, the spark of God with which man is naturally endowed (R. Cudworth). Its basic activity is conscience, which is subject to God alone; and 'Every Man's Conscience tells him his own Religion is the best.'[9] Hence a 'Right in every Nation and Person to examine their Religion, to hear the Religion of Strangers, and to change their own, if they become convinced.'[10] Hence, too, that the religion of conscience 'is the Queen of all those inward Endowments of the Soul, and all Natural knowledge, all virgin and undeflowered Arts and Sciences are her Handmaids, that rise up and call her blessed. I need not tell you, how much the skill of Tongues and Languages, besides the excellent use of all Philology in general, conduceth to the right understanding of the Letter of Sacred Writings on which the spritual Notion must be built.'[11]

Such lofty optimism about the relation between grace and nature, right reason and faith, was the very opposite of the current Calvinistic pessimism. To contemporary ears, too, it sounds somewhat unreal and naive. But in more or less mitigated form, it will continue to hold sway over the Christian outlook of the British people. Whichcote, the most radical representative of the school, enunciates 'six mistakes about religion.' The first is 'to think that religion lies in a system of propositions.'[12] Further on he states that we ought not to hold another to our form of words or phrases. Different verbal forms are of no real consequence and certainly not an excuse for persecution. To live according to faith is the important thing, not to think about religion. 'The state of religion lies in short in this: a good mind and a good life. All else is about religion and hath but the place of a means or instrument. . . . Better nature alone, though debased, abused and neglected, the very refuse of God's creation, than a religion which is false and insecure. . . . Certainly were I to take an estimate of Christianity, either from popery, or any of the gross superstitions of the world, and the affected modes of persons, I would return to philosophy again, and let Christianity alone'[13] This is an extreme manner of putting it, but Cudworth would have subscribed to its substance. According to him the heathen can live well, and salvation entirely depends upon man's inner dispositions: good-will, honesty, and moral earnestness: 'the gospel, though it be a sovereign and medicinal thing in itself, yet the mere knowing and believing of the inner history of it will do us no good. . . . Salvation itself cannot save us as long as it is only without us.'[4]

It is fairly clear that the Cambridge Platonists, although sincere Christians inasmuch as there was no doubt for them that the Bible, vehicle of divine revelation, was the source of religious truth, are already frankly liberal and on the way to Deism. In trying to determine their first principles one cannot avoid the impression that according to them reason, the spark or candle of divine light in all men, is the source that at least in principle may guide men into all truth, and that consequently exterior revelation, coming to man through the Bible, is only an accidental help, necessary in practice but not required by the nature of man's relation to God. Take away the accidental while preserving the substance, and Deism is in store for human thought.

There is something vague about the Platonists. John Locke (1632–1704), the father of English empiricism in philosophy, reacting against Platonic idealism as later logical empiricism would challenge the idealism of Bradley—idealism and empiricism are the two poles between which British philosophy is always oscillating—takes a quite different view. Starting from the basic principles of his philosophy, he distinguishes between 'above, contrary, and according to reason.' Propositions whose truth one can discover by examining the ideas one has from sensation and reflection or by natural deduction from them are according to reason. Propositions that are inconsistent with them are contrary to reason. Propositions that cannot be derived from them, without, however, contradicting them, are above reason.[15] Faith is above reason, but its truth can be empirically established with sufficient probability by verifiable facts such as the fulfillment of the prophecies about the Messiah and the performance of miracles. In themselves the truths of faith are mysteries to reason. Locke is anxious to preserve the mysterious character of revealed truths. They are reasonable as far as they rest on empirical facts; they are mysterious because they cannot be proved by reason. If I. T. Ramsey is right, there is also a more subtle form of the combination of reasonableness and mystery: 'Reasonableness arises because it appeals to no ontological peculiarity of which we have no echoes elsewhere; mystery and distinctiveness arise because the power of the gospel, like all active power we know, is only in part tractable, in terms of idea particulars.'[16]

Although idealism did prepare the way to Deism, it is Locke who is the father of later Deism. The proofs from prophecies and miracles were subjected to devastating criticism by A. Collins and T. Woolston, and the road ended in a religious philosophy whose nature is clearly expressed in the titles of such books as J. Toland's *Christianity not Mysterious* (1696) and M. Tindal's *Christianity as Old as the Creation, a Republication of the Religion of Nature* (1730). T. Chubb, however, who in *The True Gospel of Jesus Christ Asserted* (1738) came to a similar conclusion, was greatly dependent upon the Cambridge Platonists: 'To these far more than to the deists, Chubb owed an intellectual debt.'[17]

It is instructive to notice that both idealist and empiricist rationalism led to a refusal of all positive religion and that there is no via media for Christianity between the rule of the Bible apart from reason and the rule of authority. Once reason in whatever form is accepted as the only principle of theological hermeneutics, the way lies open to the negation of Christianity, and theology itself is emptied. This will be confirmed abundantly by later history.

J. S. SEMLER

In the history of German Lutheran theology, the first two generations of theologians who, beginning about 1740, were consciously influenced by the philosophy of the Enlightenment go under the name of 'Neology.' They were influenced by both the evolution of Pietist theology and the writings of the deistic controversy in England. The philosophy of Enlightenment that spread all over Europe in the 18th century gave rise to different forms of religious thought. In the Catholic countries, especially in France, the philosophy of natural religion fiercely opposed any form of positive religion. The English Deists regarded Christianity rather as a 'republication of the religion of nature,' and natural theology presented itself as the true interpretation of Christian tradition. In German Lutheranism the course of development was smoother and more anxious not to break with the past. The Neologists sincerely wished to serve the Church and to advance its cause in a changing world. It was their conscious intention not to abolish but to continue and to adapt the theological tradition in which they stood and were rooted. They had a strong sense of history and generally acknowledged and accepted that their attempts were but a link in a process of development that would go beyond them as they themselves were going beyond their predecessors.

The Neologists were also greatly indebted to the philosophy of their own country, and especially the Leibniz-Wolffian system. Leibniz introduced into Western philosophy the idea of a gradual all-embracing evolution, proceeding from the lowest monads through the animal monads up to the highest monad, man, in whom creation attains to the kingdom of the Spirit and ultimately, in the Beatific Vision, to communion with the Creator. Wolff attempted to systematize the philosophical thought of Leibniz and gave a place to Christianity within his system. The movement of creation toward God was met by a movement of God toward the highest step of His creation: this is revelation and grace and its entrance into the world could be recognized by the upward striving reason of man, through the visible signs that accompany it. The background of Wolff was pietistic, and he was a professor at Halle, the main stronghold of later Pietism. Neology, then, developed in an intellectual world dominated by a vision in which the perfect harmony and the evolutive character of the universe were the leading ideas.

J. S. Semler was beyond doubt the central figure of the movement. His religious background is Pietism. Two years before the death of Wolff he became a professor of divinity at Halle. He deeply experienced the intellectual and spiritual tendencies of his time, collected and clarified them, and worked out their principles. In the Latin titles of two of his books, *Institutio brevior ad liberalem eruditionem theologicam* (2 vols, 1765, 1766) and *Apparatus ad liberalem Novi Testamenti interpretationem* (1767), the term *liberal* appears for the first time as a qualification of a theological tendency. But if he is bold in the statement of theological principles, he is rather averse to building a new theological system upon them and circumspect in applying them in the field of religious instruction. His attitude was due on the one hand to historical circumstances, on the other hand, to the first of his basic principles. He had to face, indeed, two antagonists bitterly opposed to each other: a conservative orthodoxy and a movement of radical criticism of Christianity, inspired by French and English Deism. But beyond this the first original insight, conceived when still a student, was 'the distinction between the theology and the religion of Christians.'[18]

Theology is a scientific professional work, which as such is neither necessary nor useful to Christian religion and life. Hegel will say something similar in his philosophy of religion. This distinction between theology and revelation entails a new conception of the nature of revelation and Scripture. The relation of the person to revelation is a moral one, not a physical or magical one. It is not a divine intervention from without, perceptible in outward signs, but an inner experience worked by the grace of God and inviting one to an inner life of devotion and an outer life of moral conduct. Scripture as an objective linguistic composition is not itself revelation or the word of God. It is no more than an occasion that may call forth in the individual soul the enlightening occurrence of revelation. Hence it is impossible to convert the sayings of the

Bible into immutable dogmas, the acceptance of which should be essential to genuine faith or necessary to salvation. Here, in a more radical and subjective style, is a distinction already made by Chillingworth.

But revelation has to become conscious and consequently must be expressed in concepts and forms of language taken from the world of natural reason. It cannot but associate itself with the historical movement of human thought, inspiring it, purifying it, prolonging it, ever prompting it to higher perfection. The Bible does no more than furnish man with an expression of revelation, depending upon a definite situation of the mind in time and space.

If there is an inner continuity, there must be an inner consistency and coherence linking revelation with the acquisitions of natural knowledge and founding the truth of the former in the insights of the latter. This implies, further, that natural reason cannot be amoral or a-religious. Conscience and reason must be able to provide a definite system of moral and religious truth. From the nature of the case a special revelation supposes natural revelation. Revealed truth must agree with the truth of reason so as to form with it one articulated system of knowledge.

Such a view leads to a hermeneutical principle. If it be true that on the one hand revelation has to be inserted in the life of reason and expressed in terms of human thought, while on the other hand human thought is by its very nature evolutive, it clearly follows that the content of revelation, as it is apprehended by the human mind, is subject to the same law of evolution. Successive interpretations in the course of history are unavoidable if revelation is to keep pace with the evolution of scientific knowledge and philosophical insight. However true the written word of the Bible may be, it cannot remain true if it is handed down by mere repetition. A method of interpretation may very well purify the substance of the message from its original historical accidentals and impurities.

Along with the distinctions between theology and revelation, between essential truth and historical accidentals, comes a third distinction, no less important and far reaching: that between interior and exterior religion. It determines the specific character of Semler's liberal theology and will become the axis of Harnack's theory. Inner religion is grounded in conscience, consequent on an apprehension of the pure truth that dawns upon the mind in reading the Bible. The promises of God are promises of inner bliss, victory over death, eternal spiritual life. The contact with Christ transforms us into new and good men. Exterior religion, on the contrary, needs a law imposed from without, bodily practices, binding Creeds, and the authority of a visible Church. To the extent that it is imposed from without and not assimilated by interior faith, it falls under the verdict that Christ and St. Paul pronounced against both Judaism and paganism.

Interior and exterior religion are both necessary. Interior religion is the substance of Christian life, but exterior religion is a condition necessary to its diffusion in a social, historical world. Hence the movement of Christian history is swayed by a continuous dialectical interplay between interior and exterior religion. Interior religion tends toward freedom; it grows from within, spreading through the whole person and freely commanding the entire pattern of his conduct. Exterior religion, on the contrary, supposes a visible Church resting upon a definite Creed or common doctrine, issued, maintained, and controlled by exterior authority in order to secure unity in religious teaching and uniformity in common religious activity.

The distinction between private or interior and public or exterior religion is the key to the history of dogma. Public religion suffers from three inherent imperfections. First is the necessity to create by efforts of human thought a system of dogmatic propositions that are not divinely guaranteed. This necessarily leads to different patterns of doctrine and to conflicts between various confessions. Next, inner religion is very exacting, but the majority of men are rather inclined toward superstitions and easy, external practices; hence impurities and compromises, leading to a constant state of conflict between the great mass of people and the religious élite. Last, human history displays a constant development of spiritual powers. Man's worldview, with the insights on which it is based and the representations whereby it is expressed, is contantly moving and changing. After a while the traditional forms and the real convictions become separate, which leads to repeated conflicts between traditionalism and progressivism. The history of Christian thought, then, springs from the inner tension between two basic forces: the Gospel, which is beyond all ecclesiastical structures and can never be fixed in a definite pattern of thought and conduct; and the forms of social expression and incarnation, which are indispensable to the diffusion and working of the Gospel in the world.

Such a conception produces a new way of looking at history. It allows of understanding the past as past, of seeing and interpreting it as a result of social and historical circumstances that no longer exist and will never come back. One must have the courage to interpret the succession in time as a process of development with an immanent goal: the ethical and religious perfection of man. In spite of hindrances, man is moving toward better insights in moral and religious truth and toward higher patterns of feeling and conduct.

Semler is aware of two properties in the process of development: its gradualness and its infinity. The present state of religion grew from the past and is but a moment in the unfolding of the inexhaustible riches of an idea that from the beginning was at work in the mind, pressing onward in a boundless space, and present to thought although always transcending it.

Because he realizes how much man owes to his past and how slowly the current of history flows, the attitude of Semler toward tradition is rarely subversive. Even on those points on which as a theologian he has outdistanced the actual patterns of doctrine and Church order, he has too much historical sense not to respect tradition for what it is. He can still appreciate its pedagogical value. He advocates a gradual adaptation on the ground of his distinction between theology and religion. The theologian has no right to press his views upon the religious community. As a man of the Church and a preacher he has to speak in such a way that the community is not offended but gradually educated and led on to adapt its religious consciousness to the present state of scientific knowledge and insight. There is more than one way of teaching (*tropos paideias*). The method should differ according to the nature of the case and the particular circumstances. There are indeed some fundamental articles in which the essentials of inner Christian religion are laid down: the one God, Father of all men; the full power of Christ to teach and save us, speaking and acting in the name of the Father; the active presence of the Holy Spirit who preserves and governs what once began with Christ, guiding humanity into the fullness of insight and life. These articles, which loosely correspond to the baptismal formula, are common to all Christian denominations. They are the rule of inner religion but, as such, they are beyond theology. As to their substance they are unchangeable, but the doctrines by which we try to objectify them are always subject to correction and reinterpretation. Besides those common articles there are other articles professed only by the members of particular denominations. These belong to public religion and are simply changeable.

One has to speak, then, in a different way according to the subjects on which one is preaching and according to the situation with regard to those to whom one addresses oneself. When the theologian writes or speaks as a theologian within the common enterprise of scientific thought, he is free to say things as he personally sees them in the light of advancing reason. But when he is addressing himself to a congregation of his Church, he has to abide by its accepted doctrine, using it to point his hearers to the exigencies of inner religion.

With Semler, the general historicity of thought, and consequently of Christian thought, which is the originating power of doctrine, is for the first time fully recognized. The Apostles and Christ Himself could only express the new truth of the Gospel in such a way that their hearers were guided to it from religious representations that were valid in their milieu and depended upon a worldview proper to the culture in which they were living. The NT gives but an initial, imperfect expression of the truth it conveyed. Later generations were to go beyond it, cleansing its true meaning of Judaic representations and setting it free from linguistic forms that were outstripped by the evolution of the human mind.

Semler was the pioneer of German liberal theology. He worked out most of its basic principles, but he failed to unite them in a vigorous synthesis and to draw from them the ultimate consequences. He did not construct a coherent system of doctrine. There is something vague and hesitant about the not-altogether-satisfying way in which he works out his distinction between theology and religion. In particular the relation between them is not very clear. It is as if his mind were vacillating between liberalism and orthodoxy, trying to give their due to each of them. It betrays an inner discord in his mind. He is divided against himself, and the division of his allegiance between reason and faith became conspicuous at the end of his career when he disowned and rejected his life's work, turning toward theosophy and mysticism and trying to reenter the camp of orthodoxy. He is a type of humanity in the crisis. Just as Boccaccio after the daring exploit of the *Decameron*, by which he revealed to his contemporaries the secret of their spiritual change, timidly withdrew to destroy a part of his writings and to take orders in the service of the Church, so Semler, after marching a lifetime ahead of the liberal troops, retraced his steps and abandoned his evolutive view of history for a mystical vision of timeless truth. He ended in spiritual isolation accepted by neither the left nor the right of Lutheran theology. That kind of hesitation will not be found in his successor and disciple, the great leader of liberal theology, F. Schleiermacher.

LIBERALISM AND IDEALISM: FROM LESSING TO SCHLEIERMACHER

To give a provisional definition of liberal theology: a theology is liberal in the strict sense when it rests upon a distinction in Christianity between its essence and its historical accidentals, the latter including the whole of dogmatic doctrine. Semler, although lacking in self-assurance, was already a liberal theologian. To be sure, he still held a number of basic articles, but he was very vague about them and careful to stress that these articles could not be reduced to propositions. Rather they indicated a divine power of truth and goodness welling forth from individual souls and leading humanity on toward a spiritual goal of infinite perfectibility.

The liberal theology of the golden age of German culture was influenced not only by theology but also by a more radical philosophical humanism of which G. E. Lessing (1729–1781) can be called the greatest representative and the most able spokesman. He radically rejects the special authority of the Bible. Starting from the rationalism of the Enlightenment, he holds that moral life must be founded on necessary truths, proved to be such by reason. 'The accidental truths of history can never become the proof of necessary truths of reason.'[19]

To go very deeply into the thought of Lessing would lead beyond the field of theology. Some remarks may suffice. Lessing does not reject Christianity. It has been and is still an important factor in the making of humanity. As such it is to be appreciated positively. But he refuses Christianity a privileged and lasting position in history. History is man in the making. All great positive religions have their part in the process and are all equally valuable and respectable. As long as people have not outgrown them, they are useful and good and are to be tolerated equally. Unlike Voltaire and the French deists, he is opposed to open controversy against the Christian religion. It is all a matter of education. Let all people share according to their capacity in the enlightenment of the present day, and they will by silent growth go beyond Christianity or any positive religion toward the religion of pure reason.

The philosophical background of such assertions is not difficult to guess. Lessing was the first who, in the most uncompromising way, conceived of history as humanity in the making, proceeding from a mere possibility toward its full actualization. All beliefs and practices of primitive or magical religion were good so far as they naturally belonged to more imperfect stages in the process of human development. The humanism of Lessing denied all special intervention of God in the course of nature or history. Nonetheless his conception is thoroughly religious as far as he conceives the whole immanent process of history as secretly governed by Providence. The work of God's creation and governance completely coincides with man's autonomous endeavor to self-realization.

Lessing is undoubtedly the forerunner of the great philosophical systems of classical German idealism. The general idea of an all-comprehensive process of evolution, carrying humanity from a condition of possibility to a condition of full realization, is a definitive acquisition of German classicism. The danger of Lessing's position is that God is considered as an invisible director of the process that is reflected in human consciousness. He is outside, so that the acceptance or negation of His existence makes no difference for human experience and life. His idea of God is still taken from the philosophy of the *Aufklärung*. The God of idealism will be quite different from the detached author of a wholly immanent process of nature and history. Although not identical with God, the process will be a part of His life, and the ultimate perfection toward which it is striving will be conceived of as implying an inner relation to Him. Moreover, there will be no question of going beyond Christianity. According to Hegel and Schleiermacher Christianity is the last and highest form of religion, and the perfection of humanity is identical with the perfection of Christianity. Christianity is not an intermediate stage in the development of the life of reason, but the last stage the perfection of which is identical with the perfection of man. We should never forget that it was the conscious aim of Hegel and Schleiermacher to save the Christian religion from the deadly influence of the *Aufklärung*, not by opposing Christianity to reason but by going beyond the shallow philosophy of *Verstand* to a deeper philosophy of *Vernunft*.

It follows from the very nature of the transformistic theory of doctrinal development that it is itself subject to the law of transformation. To be sure, the basic idea is always the same: A distinction between the essence of Christianity and its changeable accidentals, the latter including all objectifying propositions. The relation between the essence and the accidents can, however, be thought of in different ways. There are also different ways of explaining and justifying the theory. These differences depend upon the various philosophies that determine the intellectual and spiritual climate in which its protagonists are thinking. Various types of liberal theology may be distinguished, each with its own version of the development of doctrine.

1. The rationalistic type, determined by the philosophy of the *Aufklärung* (Semler).
2. The idealistic type, depending upon German idealism (Schleiermacher).
3. The positivistic type, influenced by post-idealistic positivism (Harnack).
4. The existentialist type, connected with the philosophy of Heidegger (Bultmann).
5. The modern empiricist type, inspired by the contemporary philosophy of linguistic analysis (Van Buren).

Let it be clear from the beginning that the relation between a given type of transformistic theology and its corresponding philosophy can be different in kind. Bultmann is not bound to existentialism in the same way that Schleiermacher depends on idealism. The difference is so great that it may be questioned whether Bultmann is a liberal theologian at all.

In order to understand the thought of Schleiermacher it will be useful to trace briefly his philosophical lineage. The romantic form of idealism began with Fichte. In his *Critique of Pure Reason* Kant had tried to establish that all knowledge, mediated by sense-perception, can be no more than a knowledge of phenomena. Consequently, even if one exhausts all the implications of and conclusions from that kind of knowledge, one can never get beyond the phenomena. From the objective knowledge of nature, there is no way to God. On the other hand, it was Kant's intention to destroy all objectivistic metaphysics in order to reconstruct metaphysical beliefs on new and better foundations: the necessary presuppositions of moral conscience. Man's moral conscience is

irreducible to the world of phenomena. Although beyond representation it is no less evident to self-conscious life than the sensible
world. It is a consciousness of living under a 'categorical imperative' or an unconditional sense of duty. Its very idea implies freedom, for 'imperative' and 'duty' have no meaning except for a free
subject. In man's conscious life the passions arise from the impact
of the sensible phenomena on his bodily senses, which are themselves phenomena. The causal relation between the objects of perception and the passions in man belongs to the phenomenal order.
But freedom is not phenomenal. It cannot be apprehended as an
object. One is aware of it in the act of conscience that orders him
not to follow the tendencies of his spontaneous inclinations but to
obey the absolute rule of the Good. Conscience and freedom, then,
are of a different nature from that of the world of phenomena. In
conscience man somehow attains 'reality in itself.'

Hence two contradictory explanations of the universe present
themselves. If the whole is interpreted in terms derived from sense-
perception, it must be conceived as a closed system of causal
relations in which there is no place for conscience and freedom.
A system of mechanical determinism becomes the ideal pattern by
which to represent the universe. If, on the contrary, one starts
with conscience and freedom, the world presents itself as the result
of a free activity governing all things in view of the realization of a
supreme good. The ideal pattern is one of free action directing all
things toward a moral end. The mechanistic and finalistic views are
forever irreconcilable, at least for human understanding. But the
finalistic view, founded as it is on the rock of being, has precedence;
and one must conclude that the very thing that appears to objective
intelligence as a system of determinism is in reality the work of a
moral will that one must partake in by free obedience.

The method by which one concentrates upon consciousness,
withdrawing attention from the objects to which it is related in
order to get at the conditions that, previous to all exercise of
thought, are the foundations of its possibility, is called by Kant
'transcendental' and the ideas arrived at by that method are
'transcendentals': such are, for instance, the categories by which
the mind in the act of perception organizes the sense-data into
definite patterns (space, time, substance, cause, relation, etc.). Such,
too, is freedom that founds the possibility of moral action.

Fichte's point of departure is the resolute rejection of Kantian dualism. It is possible, indeed, to construct a philosophical system starting either from objective sense-perception or from conscience. But one cannot do the two things at once! 'The kind of philosophy a man will choose, depends upon the kind of man he is: for philosophy is not a lifeless furniture which can be dropped or taken at pleasure, but it is animated by the soul of the man who possesses it.'[20] Fichte did not hesitate: 'From conscience alone all truth derives.'[21] Conscience alone is the principle by which the whole of being becomes intelligible. All other attempts are false. The act of conscience is faith (*Glaube*) or feeling (*Gefühl*): 'All my convictions are faith and have their origin in a free disposition, not in the intellect.'[22] 'Faith' does not mean an irrational or uncertain acceptance but an acceptance founded on direct inner intuition and not derived from one's experience of the outer world. In its first originating act, conscience is but a vague sense of vocation to moral liberty, and a blind impulsion to realize it. It is unreflecting. By action combined with thought, one's moral self-consciousness and its implications become clearer, and one's vocation is gradually actualized. That inner clarification has nothing to do with reasoning. It is a growing light of inner self-intuition mediated by the moral struggle to overcome the resistance of an amoral nature and to bring together all things under the domination of the will.

If moral will is the only source of truth, then in a certain sense it must be at the origin of nature. The moral subject sets nature over against itself as a resistance to be overcome. By gaining the victory over its opponent, integrating it into the domain of moral life, the 'I' realizes itself and comes to itself. Every victory leads to further forms of resistance, and so it continues dialectically, aiming at a complete spiritualization and moralization of nature. The final goal is a perfect unity of conscience and nature, the latter being completely comprehended and dominated by the former. These two things, true clarity and true morality, cannot be separated. Perfect consciousness is perfect conscience.

This does not mean that my empirical 'I' creates the things of nature as its representations. They exist independent of human consciousness. Therefore a man's moral victory is real and earnest. But nothing exists except as far as it becomes meaningful to man; and it is only as meaningful, as related to man's moral action, that nature opposes itself to conscience. The things outside have no true reality of meaning except insofar as they are called to be illuminated by consciousness and to be brought together into a pattern of moral existence.

It is clear, however, that the 'I' that posits nature is not my empirical 'I' or the psychological subject, apprehended by direct introspection. It is the 'I' of conscience and of freedom. I am my conscience. My true 'I' cannot be apprehended by direct introspection. It lies beyond my empirical 'I.' In overcoming the resistances of nature I become myself, and I come to myself in a way that can never be objectified. That hidden 'I,' the proper act of which is conscience and free will, is intuitively felt in the exercise of its act. It remains in the margin or the shade of consciousness. It never presents itself to us with the striking evidence of an object of perception or distinct apprehension.

But if conscience, in positing nature, only calls forth in the object its moral meaning, is duality really overcome? If conscience and nature are one in their full, conscious realization, are they not one at the source? Is the incurably implicit and always preconscious 'I' not the original unconscious unity of 'I' and nature—a unity which, in the unfolding of moral existence, splits into the opposition between subject and object? This is indeed the view of Fichte: 'Who am I? subject and object at once, omnipresent consciousness and that of which I am conscious, perceiving and perceived, thinking and thought all in one.'[23]

That 'I' which is the original unity of subject and object is not God, because it implies becoming and therefore imperfection. God is the absolute I, beyond the deepest 'I' felt in our conscience as 'behind' and 'in' at one and the same time. He is the creative source of every 'I' and of all nature. The moral relation between both is also founded in Him. It is impossible, then, to objectify the distinction between God and 'I.' I am God and I am not God. I am God as absolutely depending upon Him and as a free instrument working for the fulfillment of His purpose. Freedom is divine life in me. If I think of my freedom as the life of God in me, I reduce myself to a mere form devoid of substantiality and content.

Fichte is the real originator of the general scheme of idealistic philosophy. Schleiermacher will apply it and work it out in his own way, but between Fichte and Schleiermacher there is F. W. J. Schelling, the child prodigy of romantic philosophy. Schelling is not at all happy with Fichte's one-sided solution of the Kantian antinomy. He starts again with the original opposition of object to subject, of nature to 'I' or intelligence. The subjective and the objective order somehow meet to make a unity. I cannot give a privileged position to one of them. But in order to explain that unity in diversity, I must take one of two possible ways: from object to subject or from subject to object. The former comes naturally before the latter because in spontaneous unreflected thought consciousness of nature comes before consciousness of self.

The first philosophical works of Schelling are consecrated to the construction of a philosophy of nature. Natural science, he says, is the attempt of the intellect to understand nature. Its very enterprise entails the idea that nature, although irreducible to intellect, is nonetheless intelligible. The aim of natural science is to reduce nature to a system of mechanical relations that are entirely intellectual and in which phenomena as sensible data have vanished. The intelligibility of nature implies a relation of nature to intellect. The possibility of reducing nature to a purely intellectual system shows that nature and intelligence are originally one. What is called dead or unconscious nature is only a series of attempts in which nature fails to come to itself or to reflect itself. Unconscious nature, being a ladder of immature intelligence, betrays its true character in the intelligibility that the human intelligence finds in it. Human intelligence is mature intelligence. In it the whole of nature, which is originally one with the intellect, comes to itself or to perfect self-reflection.

The second way leads from the subject to the object or from intelligence to nature. As nature and intelligence are correlatives and consequently imply one another, the end-result of the second way must be the same as that of the first. That second way, by which one comes to see how the objective originates from the subjective, is the way of 'transcendental philosophy.' Its starting point is subjectivity considered as an absolute. Consequently it has to begin with universal doubt about the reality of the objective. This means the exclusion of all prejudgments, not only the social ones but also the basic one of realism, which belongs to nature and can be neither proved nor disproved.

The attitude of thought in transcendental philosophy is the exact opposite of that of common man in the exercise of common sense. Common sense rests on the basic prejudgment concerning exterior reality. It is absorbed in nature and does not turn to itself, i.e., the act and the 'I.' Transcendental philosophy, on the contrary, entirely prescinds from man's basic natural prejudgment, and by an artificial act of reflection concentrates exclusively on pure subjectivity. Unlike the common man, the philosopher recognizes as such the character of prejudgment proper to natural acceptance of an outer world. The proposition 'I am' and the proposition 'things are,' which coincide in natural consciousness, are separated now from one another, and 'I am' becomes the only point of departure, guiding us by itself into nature and proving that 'I' and nature are not only correlatives but strictly identical. The attitude of transcendental philosophy, then, simply consists in the *tour de force* whereby 'that, too, which in all other forms of thought, knowledge, or action shrinks from consciousness, being absolutely non-objective, is brought to consciousness and becomes objective; in short, that the subjective constantly converts itself into object for itself.'[24]

Transcendental philosophy, then, asks the question 'How is knowledge possible?' To know consists, by definition, in this that one's representations correspond to things as they are in themselves. The philosopher begins with the very thing that he is obliged to doubt in virtue of this method. But he does not assert from the start, as natural man does, that one knows things as they are in themselves. He simply asks: 'Which are the conditions of its possibility?' Schelling's solution rests on a paradox: on the one hand, things according to immediate experience and certitude are what they are independently of one's knowledge. In that view, intelligence, in knowing, is merely passive, determined by the nature of things. The elaboration of that view is the task of theoretical philosophy. On the other hand, in all works of culture self-made representations of our own modify nature. In that view the world of things is determined by the representations, and things are passive with respect to a man's conscious will. The elaboration of that second view is the task of practical philosophy. In conscious willing and acting it is just the reverse. How, then, is it possible that one's representations depend on the objects while at the same time the objects depend on one's representations? The two facts cannot be thought together without contradiction except on the supposition that the activity that produces things be originally the same as the activity that works in conscious willing and acting. The same original activity that unconsciously produces things, as independent from one's conscious will, achieves them through men in a way that makes them dependent upon one's conscious will.

Transcendental philosophy, then, is at once and inseparably theoretical and practical. It is the unity of both. Combined with natural philosophy it leads to the following conclusion: 'Nature as a whole and in all its particular products must appear as a work consciously produced and yet at the same time as a product of blind mechanism: it is finalistic without being explainable in terms of finalism.'[25]

But how can one conceive that unity of unconscious and conscious activity? The archetype of it is found in man: in the creation of art. The whole universe is a work of art and the first principle of the whole is God, the artist. The crowning part of philosophy is a philosophy of art. God, although not reducible to nature, cannot be separated from it. Being the principle of universal artistic creation, He is not pure consciousness and light. There is in Him a dark side, as Schelling and other romantics learned from J. Böhme.

The later evolution of Schelling's thought is of no importance here, as it has nothing to do with Schleiermacher. It would be well to stop at this point and try to describe the philosophical world in which his thought moves.

The initial situation may be summarized as the opposition between Spinoza and Kant. According to Spinoza, God, the only substance, is not the world but the world is one of His manifestations. The infinite is in the finite and the finite is in the infinite. This conception is rather static. The procession of the finite from the infinite is not a process of evolution toward a *telos* or perfect realization. The world rests in God, as Goethe, a Spinozist in his own way, will put it:

> To God belongs the Orient
> To God belongs the Occident
> Northern and southern lands
> Rest in the peace of His hands.

According to Kant, on the contrary, as to all the philosophers of the Enlightenment, God is wholly transcendent and separated from the world. His relation to the world is not one of presence but of dominion. Man does not rest in Him, man has to obey Him. He is the law-giver. He commands. Men do not experience Him as a source of life, but postulate Him as a moral will above us and over against us. Religion is not a kind of abiding in Him, but an accomplishing of the dictates of conscience interpreted as divine commandments. The whole conception of Kant is dynamic. It is moral action directed toward a supreme end along the path of duty.

Romantic philosophy is an attempt to fill the gap between Spinoza and Kant, to unite in a great synthesis mysticism and moralism, the idea of God's all-penetrating presence experienced by man and the idea of history as a task striving after the actualization of a supreme good. Schleiermacher is an avid reader of both Spinoza and Kant.

The first attempt to bridge the gulf between Spinoza and Kant is the philosophy of Fichte. Fichte's system does not mean a one-sided continuation of Kant. The spirit of Kantianism is wholly conquered. God is no longer a commander who speaks to man's conscience. He is the innermost principle from which conscience in man springs: not so much the law-giver as the driving power of moral life. Man 'feels' Him as the 'I' of his 'I' in the very act of moral endeavor, and man's intuition of Him grows together with the intuition of self in the intensive and extensive progress of moral power and consciousness.

With Schelling the movement seems to swing back to Kant. The general scheme of his philosophy is conspicuously Kantian. On the one side is nature known by sense-perception and imposing a mechanical view of things (Kant's *Critique of Pure Reason*—Schelling's *Philosophy of Nature*); on the other side, a philosophy of subjectivity leading to a finalistic view of things (Kant's *Critique of Practical Reason*—Schelling's *System of Transcendental Philosophy*); and between both, a principle uniting the theoretical and the practical reason in aesthetic intuition (Kant's *Critique of Judgment*—Schelling's *Philosophy of Art*). For both Kant and Schelling the gap between the worldview of natural science and that of subjectivity cannot be reduced by means of reason. It can only be experienced in aesthetic intuition.

In Schelling's system, however, philosophy does not really go back to Kant. It moves farther from him in the direction indicated by Fichte. For Kant's philosophy is a philosophy of opposition, whereas the system of Schelling is a philosophy of identity. In Kant the way of thought that leads to the knowledge of nature is simply juxtaposed or opposed to the way that leads to moral and religious belief. Two different worldviews arise from the two enterprises of reason, and man must choose between them. If he opts for the view of conscience—the one reasonable thing to do—then aesthetic intuition can give him a model for thinking their ultimate unity. For Schelling, however, the starting point is not an opposition between knowledge of nature and moral belief, but between nature and intelligence, object and subject. The meaning of the latter term is coextensive with the whole activity of the subject, including conscience. Natural philosophy and transcendental philosophy are not just juxtaposed. Nature reveals itself to reflection not so much as an effect of intelligent action but as a kind of active intelligence itself going upward step by step toward its open and full realization in human consciousness. There is here a deep influence of the evolutive monadology of Leibniz. Human consciousness arises from nature because nature and intelligence are one at their source. Transcendental philosophy in its turn, reflecting upon the fact that knowing intelligence is determined by nature while nature is determined by creative intelligence, comes to the same conclusion that the deepest reality of both is the same. Intelligence is in nature and nature is in intelligence. They are in each other. This is the system of identity. Aesthetic creation presents man with a model enabling him to see not how both may be united in the scheme of an all-ruling transcending providence but how they are one in God at the very source of the double process by which God manifests Himself in creation.

Schleiermacher will go back to Fichte inasmuch as, in his philosophy, subjectivity and feeling become central in opposition to nature. But he will be with Schelling in conceiving subjectivity not as moral conscience but as something deeper of which moral, religious, and aesthetic experience are different determinations.

FRIEDRICH SCHLEIERMACHER (1768–1834)

Schleiermacher's personal background was frankly Pietistic. His parents were converted to the Herrnhuter Brethren, and he received his first education in the Herrnhuter college of Niesky and the seminary of Barby. Schleiermacher is profoundly marked by devotional pietism; it is the personal gate by which he entered into the world of philosophical and theological thought—hence the central place that feeling and religious experience will occupy in his philosophy. In 1790, three years before the death of Semler, he entered the university of Halle. He came into close contact with the romantic movement and was deeply influenced by his friend, F. Schlegel, with whom he shared a life-long admiration for Plato. He was influenced, too, by Kant, Spinoza, Fichte, and Schelling. Hegel, Schlegel, Schelling, and Schleiermacher belong to the same generation.

As with Hegel, there is something ambiguous about the thought of Schleiermacher, and it is difficult to achieve a final clarity about the ultimate meaning of their philosophies. Some interpreters exalt them as champions of true Christianity; others hold the view that in their thought Christianity is entirely swallowed by a rational philosophy. The issue is still outstanding. We have to take the risk of a choice. Happily it does not make an essential difference for the understanding of Schleiermacher's view on the development of doctrine.

The basic idea of his philosophy is that of the transcendental. Schelling is generally considered as its originator, but Schleiermacher claimed the right of paternity for himself: 'As if Schelling was the tenant of the domain of transcendental philosophy! I think I will not allow the right which is mine to be taken from me, nor will you.'[26]

Unlike Fichte, Schelling, and Hegel, Schleiermacher is above all a theologian. His point of view is determined by faith and his goal is the construction of a doctrine of faith, a systematic theology. His theological position is determined by his conviction that true philosophy and theology cannot contradict each other. There must be a harmony between them: 'The same members of that Christian community, which is the only thing by which the scientific form of the doctrine of faith comes into being and exists, are also those in whome speculative consciousness comes awake.'[27]

Two things come to light in this quotation: first, that the object of faith is something given from without; next, that it must always be interpreted. The rule of faith is not a book of many centuries ago but the actual belief of the community. One has no right to appeal to the Bible against what the present Church teaches. Such a principle is frankly anti-Protestant. It seems to betray a catholicizing threat, but it has nothing to do with Catholicism. Schleiermacher's conception of the rule of faith is already influenced by his philosophy. It seems positivistic because it simply starts with what the community actually believes. But that kind of positivism is already determined by a speculative insight. Faith is not a letter but a living spirit of which the NT is the first human expression. As history moves on, the self-expression of the Spirit, although fed by constant meditation on the past, grows and changes. The relation of man's present belief to the past is essentially one of interpretation. Starting with scriptural expression, the history of Christian consciousness is a dynamic tradition in which the expression of faith is continuously growing and changing along with the inner evolution of the Spirit. The first expression of that Spirit can be found in the Bible and is the theology of the NT. Faith lives in theology and moves with it. The dynamic historical reality of faith is tradition. What the Church now believes is the last link in a chain of reinterpretations of the past according to the development of the Spirit in us.

It is clear by now that Schleiermacher's doctrinal positivism is rooted in his speculative idealism. In his own thought the movement of tradition is going on. He now interprets the past in terms of the philosophy of the present age. His theology is not yet the form of belief of the community. But in his thought, sustained by parallel efforts of other theologians, the coming belief of the community in the making. The form of belief that dominates the religious consciousness of the community in a given generation he calls 'orthodoxy.' Orthodoxy is the immediate rule of faith and the starting point of theology. But the consciousness of the thinking, creative élite is ahead of the community in the onward movement of the Spirit. In comparison with orthodoxy the individual thought of the élite appears as 'heterodoxy. Heterodoxy does not have a pejorative meaning. Its meaning is only descriptive: that which is different from the form of belief still prevailing in the community. Heterodoxy slowly penetrates the community and will eventually become orthodoxy.

It is not true, then, that in the mind of Schleiermacher there is a philosophical theology along with a systematic theology. The two cannot be separated. To be sure, systematic theology is an attempt to give a coherent account of what the Church now believes and to understand it in the light of the evolution that led to the present stage. In that sense systematic theology is positive and historical. But the whole movement of theology is instinct with philosophy. The theology of the present day is the most recent link in a living chain that continues in the confrontation of tradition with contemporary philosophy. That philosophy itself is the present step in the movement of reflection that has always accompanied the life

H

of faith as its formal principle of interpretation. Theology is different from philosophy only in that it recognizes that from a certain moment in history the spirit lives and thrives under the impact of a definitive occurrence: the coming of Christ. Historic theology, then, is the systematic elaboration of what the present Church actually believes. It is the expression of orthodoxy. Philosophical theology, however, is the expression of heterodoxy, and its relation to systematic theology is the same as that of heterodoxy to orthodoxy. It is the elaboration and application of the principles that will aid orthodoxy to take its next step. Systematic theology starts with the past and moves toward the present. Philosophical theology starts with the present and interprets the past in such a way that the movement studied by systematic theology continues its course. We have to begin, then, with Schleiermacher's philosophy because his philosophy works out the principles of his theology.

The philosophy of Schleiermacher is transcendental. In order to understand what this means to him, it may be best to compare its logical movement with that of pre-idealistic natural theology. How does the mind discover God? According to traditional philosophy the existence of God is discovered by way of causality, i.e., at the end of the endeavor to understand the existence of those things experienced by the senses. The movement of thought is extroversive: from the things outside to their first cause, which is also beyond all things. In transcendental philosophy the reverse takes place. The movement of thought started by the encounter with nature does not go beyond nature in the objective direction but returns to its subjective origin, not by reasoning but by pure reflection leading to clarified intuition. The movement of thought is introversive: from thought, in which things initially appear, to its origin in the depths of its originating power. It does not ask, 'How is it possible that things exist?' but, 'How is experience or conscious life possible?' Before all experience and at the base of conscious life the transcendental is the unconscious source that creates the possibility of all experience. The awareness of the transcendental implies an awareness of God. God is the ultimate transcendental, experienced in the revelation of the subject to itself. According to traditional philosophy, then, God is the last objectively 'transcendent,' whereas according to the romantic idealists God is the last subjectively 'transcendental.'

Like Fichte, Schleiermacher calls 'feeling' the intuitive act by which one apprehends the transcendental in the exercise of the spiritual life. The life of the Spirit embraces thought as well as moral, religious, and aesthetic experience and activity. Unlike Fichte, he does not identify the transcendental with the source of conscience alone. The transcendental embraces in itself man's basic moral experience, but there is something deeper in it that is the first ground in man of the different kinds of experience, including conscience. This ultimate ground or first spring of all experience and conscious activity is called by Schleiermacher 'feeling,' in his later works 'immediate consciousness of self.' It is not, of course, a psychological category. One's empirical self-consciousness is mediated by one's awareness of things without. In the active and passive relations with the world we always know that what we call 'I' is that which receives the impact of nature and responds to it by active perception, attention, thought, choice, will, action. Ordinary consciousness consists in that implicit awareness of self in all its sufferings and doings. That existential awareness of self can be made explicit and objective by shifting the attention from object to act. But even then it is conditioned and mediated by one's relation to the outside. 'Immediate consciousness of self,' on the contrary, is not open to direct mental apprehension. We come to know it as the screen on which things can appear in such a way that their appearance leads to conscious apprehension. It is the basic condition of objective experience, in which the subject comes to itself. Objective experience, then, is the medium by which immediate consciousness of self is converted into a mediate empirical self-awareness.

Immediate consciousness of self is a priori determined by various possibilities of experience, i.e., possibilities of grasping intuitively values that are beyond the directly self-evident opposition of subject to object, proper to empirical consciousness. Such values are truth, duty, beauty, and also the divine. So Schleiermacher can say that 'devotion' (*Frömmigkeit*) is 'a determination of feeling or of the immediate consciousness of self.'[28] The term *Frömmigkeit* is untranslatable. It means the inner intuitive awareness of the divine dimension of all things. At the same time, however, it is also an attitude, a response of the subject to the revelation of the divine in his heart. Through active faithfulness the light of the divine shines brighter in man's experience.

Schleiermacher calls the object of the awareness of the divine or religious experience a 'feeling of unconditional dependence.' That which reveals itself as dependent is not only the particular subject but the whole in which his existence partakes. But dependent upon what? In the first place man feels himself dependent upon the whole to which he is united and with which he has to identify himself. But beyond this man is aware that the whole itself is dependent upon a beyond, irreducible to the world that circumscribes the range of his objective experience. 'That experience is most perfect when in our self-consciousness we identify ourselves with the whole world and nevertheless feel ourselves together with the world in a relation of dependence.'[29] So, the feeling of unconditional dependence upon God is given in and with a feeling of unconditional dependence upon the whole.

'Unconditional' means total, ultimate, absolute. With respect to the particular things of the world man is partly passive and dependent, partly active, making things depend upon him. With respect to the whole or God, man is wholly dependent. His freedom has no hold on the whole or on God. He is simply dependent in all respects.

What does 'dependent' mean in this context? Schleiermacher distinguishes between causal and teleological notions of unconditional dependence. The first is related to devotion as an awareness of the divine, the second to devotion as a duty of unconditional faithfulness. God is not only the ground from which man emerges, growing and flowering within Him. He is also the all-governing basic will that directs and orders man toward the accomplishment of a moral end, the end of the universe. In that way Schleiermacher unites the ontological 'in' of Spinoza with the ethical 'toward' of Kant. God is the 'beyond and in' of the source from which all things flow and also the 'beyond and in' of the *telos* to which all things go by the activity of man.

The next question, then, is how can one speak about the beyond, or God? The limits of man's objective experience coincide with the limits of the world. All his concepts and words are derived from that experience. How is he able to say something true about what is beyond the world? In applying his thought to the ultimate ground of all things and all experience, he comes to various concepts such as God (the Creator), Nature (the *natura naturans* of Erigena and Spinoza), Providence, or Fate. Now all these concepts are terminal concepts or 'limit concepts' (*Grenzbegriffe*). The limit in question is the limit of the world that circumscribes the range of an objective experience. According to their real meaning, then, the terms that denote God for man signify something within the limit: the whole or the world on which he is unconditionally dependent. But at the same time they point to what is beyond that limit. They do not represent it. Man does not apprehend it as he apprehends the things of the world. Therefore that second meaning is 'symbolic.' The theological concepts do not express the truth of God, but point to it by means of intra-mundane realities in which the reality of the 'beyond' shines through without making itself an object of separate apprehension.

Here Schleiermacher's version of the great idealistic scheme comes into sight. According to him, as was said above, God is not the whole of the world, but He shines through that whole because He is in it and it in Him. We can feel our absolute dependence upon Him as it shines through all things because we too are in Him and He in us (all the romantic philosophers are enthusiastic readers of the Fourth Gospel). We know that God is not reducible to the world, but we cannot objectify the distinction. We can only speak of Him in terms of the universe. God is the whole as beyond the whole. Man's dependence upon Him is not only causal but teleological. God is the beyond in the whole from which man originates, but He is also the beyond in the whole toward which the world is going through man's moral activity. So Schleiermacher can say that the divine whole is dynamic. God as the initial 'unity from which all opposition is excluded' is the *terminus a quo* and the power that drives man toward the conquest of the world by knowledge and cultural actualization. That world is the *terminus ad quem*, the final 'unity in which all oppositions are included.' From undifferentiated to wholly differentiated totality: this is the idealistic scheme.

This means that 'devotion,' or religion, as far as it is a life in accordance with the ethical exigencies, is not a rest in God but an energy that moves man from God to God. This is the framework within which Schleiermacher has to give a place to Christianity. Christianity is a religion in the same sense as all other religions. Every religion implies an attempt to realize the ideal world, inspired by the feeling of unconditional dependence. It is not simply culture, growing knowledge, and enlarging action. It is essentially 'the immediate consciousness of the unconditional in one's self, the immediate existential relation prior to the act of reflection, the immediacy of the awareness of the unconditional in our consciousness. Knowledge and action are consequences. . . . They are not the essence of religion.'[30] Tillich is right insofar as he means that thought and action are not religions except in the measure in which they follow from the feeling of unconditional dependence. But it would be well perhaps to add that action, too, belongs to the essence of religion as far as there is no genuine religion without consequent action. Religion is essentially a combination of 'resting in God' and 'acting from God.' Man's dependence on God is not only causal but also teleological, as Tillich himself admits.[31] Now the feeling of dependence is religious only insofar as it is an acceptance of dependence, and the acceptance of a teleological dependence upon God is already an active attitude toward realization of the *telos*.

All religions, then, are expressive forms of man's feeling of absolute dependence combined with patterns of consequent action. The essence is the same, though the forms of expressing it may be different. Christianity is the highest and definitive form of religion. This idea is common to the great representatives of romantic idealism. Let us proceed from the generic to the specific characteristics of Christianity.

The history of religious humanity is a slow progression from a state of doom to a state of salvation. The manifestation of man's unconditional dependence and of his relation to God and the whole, is revelation. The problem is how to interpret these terms? This is an all-important question. Schleiermacher's answer is greatly influenced by St. Paul and by his beloved Plato. He distinguishes two stages in the development of humanity and religion. In the first stage, the stage of doom, the flesh prevails over the spirit. Man is a prisoner of his sensual selfishness. He does not live in accordance with the requirements of his unconditional dependence which, being teleological, asks for a complete submission to the *telos*, the good of the whole. The dominance of the flesh means that man accords to his particular self and its gratifications a privileged position. This is proper to the first stage of the development of humanity. Moral life is a struggle to conquer the flesh and to bring it under the dominance of the spirit. To live in accordance with the spirit is to identify one's life with that of the whole and of God without according to the particular self any privileged position. The state of the predominance of the spirit over the flesh or of reconciliation with the universe and God—the one is the condition of the other—is the state of grace. Grace is the state in which man promptly accepts and fulfills the requirements of universal selfless love. The term *sin*, then, does not mean an originating act of freedom, but a stage of imperfection in the evolution of mankind. As Tillich puts it, 'According to this trend, sin is a shortcoming. It is not a "no" but a "not yet" . . . the "not yet" of man's spiritual development within an already fully developed bodily organism. The distance or the gap between these two processes is what we call sin. This condition is universal. It is the state of mankind universally.'[32] So too, salvation or grace is the state of fully developed spiritual life in which man is reconciled with the whole and God. In the state of perfection his sensuality and his spiritual self-consciousness 'would be wholly one, because every moment would begin in the spirit and end in the spirit. The flesh would only behave as a living link, a healthy organ, which does not bring about anything that is not initiated and accompanied by the spirit.'[33]

As the perfection of the universe is fully developed mankind, it is clear that reconciliation is not a feeling but a moral achievement by which the separation between man and man, caused by carnal selfishness, is overcome by selfless love.

In what sense, then, is it still possible to speak of a reconciliation through Christ? In Christ the transition from the state of doom to the state of grace is accomplished in such a way that he is and remains forever the ideal prototype of the new humanity that reveals God's essence of love in its own unselfish attitude of life. Redemption by Christ means that the devotional consciousness that is the essence of all religion is particularly stirred and enhanced by the impact of the historical Christ. For in Him is perfectly conquered 'the isolation of a carnal unity of life to which all consonant feeling for others and the whole remained subordinated.'[34]

Therefore Christ is the Son of God. In Him the love of God is revealed to the world. In Him the new humanity is initiated. Because He is the first and the perfect manifestation of the new being, forever unsurpassable, He is the head of the Church, i.e., the new humanity on its way to perfection. For the Churches or Christian organizations in which the Gospel is preached are only necessary instruments for the growth of the Church or of mankind in love. That Church is 'a whole in motion, susceptible of progress and development, but with one restriction—without which Christianity would disappear—namely, that it is not allowed to think that the Church of Christ could strive after or attain a perfection beyond that which is given in Christ. Each development cannot but be a better understanding and more perfect assimilation of that which is given in Christ.' Not a doctrine of Christ but the person of Christ is the rule of faith or perfect religious consciousness and life.[35]

In order to give an understandable account of Schleiermacher's position with respect to the problem of development of doctrine, it is necessary to place this in the general context of his philosophical system, and to give a general sketch of the historical background of German idealism. The thought of Schleiermacher is thoroughly systematic, but the principles of his systematization are not those of common sense. We cannot suppose them to be known. It would be better to say nothing about Schleiermacher than to give a short summary of his thought, which necessarily would lack all true intelligibility. One must go the whole way with him or let him alone.

Schleiermacher is the prototype of liberal theology. In judging him on this point a distinction must be made between the liberalism of his doctrine of dogma and the liberalism of his general system.

As to the first, the theological liberalism is manifest. The rule of faith is not a doctrine but a person: Jesus Christ. Jesus Christ, however, is not a rule by Himself, but inasmuch as He is the perfect manifestation of the Spirit who inspires the whole dynamic movement of history. Neither the doctrine of Christ nor a doctrine about Christ is the rule, but rather His personality as far as it presents the unsurpassable prototype of religion. If what reveals itself in Christ is not something that comes to man from without but something that grows from within, there is nothing in it that lies beyond the range of his inner experience. The supreme law, then, is the inner law, the Spirit who works in the history of humanity directing it toward its perfection. Christ is only an outer law insofar as He is the perfect historical expression of the inner law.

It is clear, then, that the development of Christian consciousness is not the gradual elucidation of a primitive doctrine, so that the doctrines of the past, although explained, reformulated, and enriched, are integrally conserved in the subsequent stages of their expression. To be sure, doctrines are necessary. The Spirit translates itself into doctrines. The NT is the doctrinal expression of

what Christ experienced and the Apostles experienced in Him. So
are the doctrines, too, that express the Spirit in later stages of its
growing illumination. But the relation of the present orthodoxy to
the orthodoxies of the past is by no means a relation of logical consistency. Logical consistency of whatever kind is only possible within the same system. The evolution of the Spirit, however, is
expressed in different systems, which succeed each other. So there
is no link of logical consistency between the theological interpretations of religious consciousness in the past and those that are
elaborated in one's own time. This is not necessary, for all human
concepts and propositions have an objective element. As such,
their real meaning does not properly refer to the divine absolute,
which is beyond objective experience, but only to the divine whole
of things in which the presence of the 'beyond' indirectly reveals
itself to immediate intuitive feeling.

That dogma or doctrine is not part of the permanent substance or
essence of Christian truth is a common view in all liberal theology. It
is what Newman will call the anti-dogmatic principle. With Schleiermacher, however, it appears in the context of a general system that
may be called liberal in another sense. The anti-dogmatic principle is not necessarily connected with a general system of that
'liberal' kind. Such a system has two characteristics: immanentism
and religious universalism. The two characteristics are not connected. Immanence means that all religion, including Christianity,
is the expression of an inner experience of some mystical kind,
proper to man as such, however dimly it may shine in the self-
consciousness of given individuals or groups. It follows from this
that Christianity is a religion in the same sense as any other religion
appearing in the evolution of religious consciousness. It may be
thought to be the highest and the definitive form of religion, as both
Hegel and Schleiermacher held, but then it is still the upper rung
of a ladder. This is universalism. Barth will represent the extreme
opposite of this kind of liberal theology: Christian truth can in no
way have its origin in man or human experience. It comes
exclusively from without. It does not grow from elements that
are present in all men and develop along the horizontal line of
history. It breaks into human existence vertically from above. It
must not be tested by reason or feeling. Man can only accept it by
the absolute submission or surrender of faith. Therefore Christianity is not a religion. Bringing salvation from outside, it cannot

be put simply on a level with other religions that try to achieve salvation from within. Faith is the negation of religion. All religions are false and unable to introduce man into the sphere of salvation.

According to Schleiermacher Christianity is the highest and the definitive form of religion because in it religious experience comes into its own and grows under the impact of Christ, the perfect realization of religious experience. But faith or consciousness of God 'is not produced from without, it is only roused from without. Within, it is as much potentially given as it is part of the universal finite consciousness of Being.'[36] Under the impact of Christ it grows in us out of elements that 'when human consciousness is seized by Christianity, do not disappear, but are fostered and promoted according to the measure of the capacity given to each.'[37]

G. W. F. HEGEL

Space does not allow a deep inquiry here into the system of Hegel, which is the most perfect achievement of philosophical liberalism. The system is very different from that of Schleiermacher, but their religious views are strikingly similar. According to Hegel, indeed, religion is the substance and center of life. It is the highest state in the evolution of the life of the spirit, or the 'Absolute Spirit' as he calls it, although not of pure thought. In religion the identity of the finite and the infinite is lived by man in spite of his alienation from the infinite in which the finite finds itself in virtue of its inherence in nature. In philosophy that identity is only thought. The Christian religion is the highest and the definitive form of religion because of its dependence upon Christ, who is the *Logos*, the Son of God. For He is the purest self-manifestation of the absolute mind. In Him the realization of the infinite in the finite—the supreme goal of creation—is perfectly actualized.

Hegel's view of Christ is related to the general principles of His philosophy: identity, alienation, and reconciliation by love, Considered in Himself, or, as Hegel says, in an abstract way, that is, without inclusion of or previous to His going out of Himself in creation God is the general Spirit. This spirit particularizes Himself in creation. The first stage of creation is one in which the Spirit is alienated from Himself in the non-spirit or nature. Nature is God but in the way of absolute otherness. The alienation is overcome by the dialectical process in which the finite spirit springing from nature realizes itself in history. As the general Spirit is alienated from Himself in the process of nature, so He comes back to Himself or is reconciled in the progress of the finite spirit. The finite spirit is the self-manifestation of the infinite Spirit. In the dialectical unfolding of nature and finite spirit God comes to Himself. He comes to exist not only in Himself but also for Himself. Previous to that process God contains in Himself the whole 'idea' or reality, but He is not the whole idea. He becomes the whole idea or His perfect self in creation only through the realization of the finite spirit. It should be remembered that for Hegel as for Schleiermacher Spirit (*Geist*) is not an intellectual subject that contemplates things —it is not a 'mind'—but the infinite, universal creative power of life, which ultimately realizes itself in full personal consciousness. The content of the Spirit is the idea. Both 'idea' and 'Spirit' have the same universal comprehensiveness.

Now there are three levels in the realization of the finite Spirit, each of which contains in itself the lower realizations, though transcending them at the same time. The first level is that of the subjective Spirit: inner conscious life as related to the subject. It may be studied by psychology. But the subjective Spirit of the individual gives rise to the objective Spirit or the objective struc-tures of community: family, state, society. In the objective Spirit the subjective Spirit is estranged from itself or depersonalized. Therefore the Spirit has to reconquer itself in the structure of the objective Spirit. This last stage, in which man is reconciled with the other in a fully personalized life, is the 'Absolute Spirit,' which unfolds itself progressively in art, religion, and philosophy.

Now the relation to the other in which men freely identify themselves with others and, in doing this, actualize their real independent personality, is love:

> In love all that is meant by the Absolute Spirit is given, namely, the reconciliatory return from one's other to one's self. That other, being an other in which the Spirit abides in itself, cannot but be a spiritual being, a spiritual personality. The true nature of love is a consciousness of giving up one's self, of forgetting one's self in the other but in such a way that in disappearing and forgetting one begins truly to have and to possess his own being.[38]

This is very clear. Each interpersonal relation of self-forgetting love is, as it were, a microscosm in which the whole divine process is reflected and at the same time actualized. God, the infinite, disappears and forgets Himself in the finite, which as nature becomes the other. But so doing, He gains Himself or realizes Himself through the progress of the finite spirit striving toward an absolute *telos*: the perfect community of persons. In that community the individual disappears in the other, and by so doing, realizes his full personality. In realizing ourselves we realize God or God realizes Himself in us. This is the meaning that Hegel himself gives to the word of St. John: 'God is Love.' He comments:

> For love means that two are distinct who yet are not simply distinct for one another. . . . I have my consciousness of self not in myself but in the other. This other, however, in whom alone I may have peace, . . . has, because he is thus outside me, his self-consciousness only in me. Both are that consciousness of their being outside each other and identical with each other. . . . This is love. . . . God is love, i.e., distinction together with nothingness of distinction. . . . This is the eternal idea.
>
> This eternal idea then is expressed in Christian religion as that which is called Trinity, that is, God Himself, the eternal triune.[39]

Here Hegel clearly states that the movement of self-estrangement or of going out into otherness in order to realize and to be oneself in the other (reconciliation) is an eternal process in God Himself. But in God, considered in the abstract, it is not actualized. It is actualized in time and space by the genesis of the finite spirit. Eternity and infiniteness do not add to temporality and finitude. They are of another order. But as such, as different, they are in one another. The realization in time and space is at the same time realization on the level of eternity and infinity. The infinite realizes itself in the finite and the timeless in the temporal.

Against that background the position of Christ in Hegel's system becomes understandable. Christ, who perfectly realized the essence of love in His personal relation to His fellow men, identifying Himself with them, is the perfect actualization of the infinite in the finite, the purest self-manifestation of the absolute. The Church, body of Christ, body of love, is the full realization of God. God rests, comes to peace in the community of love in which His being-in-Himself has completely become a being-for-Himself.

The almost unsolvable difficulty in Hegel's philosophy is how to understand the relation between religion and philosophy. In religion the absolute idea is wholly accomplished. But our consciousness of it is expressed in forms of representation. Without representations the heart is not touched, the will gets no strength. Our whole life in its ultimate truth is 'lived' or existentially exercised in religion that is not a part of life but the whole of it in its highest fulfillment. The philosopher as man cannot go beyond religion. Being finite and particular, it is impossible that representations concerning the infinite could give a knowledge of the infinite expressing its truth. They can only point toward the infinite. On the other hand, 'representation' is contradistinguished from 'concept' (*Begriff*). That to which religious man attains existentially is conceptually expressed in philosophy. In the dialectical movement of the Absolute Spirit, then, philosophy seems to be the definite stage in which religion in its turn is exceeded, realizing its own imperfect truth in a higher truth. According to Hegel, as according to Schleiermacher, the religious representations are only symbolic. But Schleiermacher does not go beyond that position whereas Hegel does so resolutely, saying that the symbolic truth of religion is *aufgehoben* (negated and preserved at once) in the truth of philosophy.

What does it mean? Could the relation between religion and philosophy be of the same nature as that which holds between the other links in the progression of the Spirit, and so end in absolute monism? At first sight it seems to be required by the logic of Hegel's system. But if one really understands the basic idea, it becomes highly improbable that this would have been the thought of Hegel. That basic idea is the identity of identity and non-identity, the 'coincidence of the opposites' (Nicholas of Cusa), the sameness of distinctness and indistinctness. If philosophy simply abolishes religion in itself, man comes at last to a static identity. It seems, then, that according to Hegel the final result of spiritual life must be a dialectical opposition of two poles, one representing the distinction or opposition and another representing the identity. If so, the final affirmation is the identity of two opposites: religion and philosophy. In religion man affirms the non-identity, the distinction. Man is not God. God is over against him as a 'Thou' to be attained in prayer and worship. In philosophy man affirms the identity. In the deepest ground of his being man is not distinct from God. Man's being distinct and nonetheless non-distinct is the same reality. As in love 'I' and 'You' are distinct and one, so in the creative love of God and our love of Him we are one in being distinct: as distinct as the infinite and the finite necessarily must be. This could be illustrated with most illuminating texts of Nicholas of Cusa and Meister Eckhart. God is not impersonal in the way things of nature are. He is not personal in the way finite spirits are. He is superpersonal in an all-inclusive way, and the love that unites finite beings in spiritual community is the revelation and reality of God's love for us and our love for Him. To love God and to love one's fellow man is the same thing. The love of God comprehends in itself the love of one's neighbor. In loving his neighbor man understands and realizes in himself the love of God. This may seem a bold interpretation. It can be questioned. But it cannot be denied that it is logical and can be substantiated by most impressive texts of Hegel.

THE ESSENCE OF LIBERAL THEOLOGY

Looking back on Schleiermacher and Hegel, let us try to extract from them some general principles of theological liberalism. First is the epistemological primacy of reason and science. In itself, ontologically, religion is superior to science. But in the order of knowledge, the truths of which man is certain by his own means cannot be contradicted by revelation or faith. If there is a conflict between reason and religious doctrine, the latter has to be adapted to the former and to be reinterpreted in its light. Revealed doctrine has no independent power of truth. Since the worldview of reason and science is subject to radical transformations, it follows that revealed doctrine is also subject to the same transformations. According to Schleiermacher and Hegel, the touchstone of truth is the speculative philosophy of idealism. Therefore Christianity has to be stated in terms of idealism.

Second is the nonessential character of doctrine. This principle follows from the first. If, in the course of history, Christianity has to remain the same, its historical identity cannot consist in an identity of doctrine but must consist in a continuity of a spirit, an experience or an attitude of life that is not bound up with the unavoidable variations of doctrine. Doctrines are intellectual factors loosely united into a consistent pattern and dependent upon the general worldview of a given culture or epoch. They form the various and successive scenarios in which man, the hero of the story, has to act his unchangeable basic character in different costumes and situations. 'Mankind is always advancing and man always remains the same,' Goethe said. The development of the same man or the same spirit in different intellectual stages may be conceived in an optimistic mood, as is conspicuously the case with Schleiermacher and Hegel. This is not essential. It might as well be thought of in a pessimistic mood, which looks at history as a progressive downfall from some 'Golden Age,' or in an indifferent mood, considering history as a perpetual flux of ups and downs. The only essential is the distinction between a non-intellectual kernel or substance that cannot be properly objectified and an intellectual objective husk of changeable accidents.

The third principle is symbolism. Without objectivation there is no conscious life. A definitive objectivation or doctrine is not essential, but that there be a certain objectivation is necessary. What religion or faith is about must somehow be expressed in representations and notions in order to enter man's self-conscious life. There is no mode of self-consciousness in a subject without a corresponding consciousness of an object. Moreover, an existential act or attitude cannot be justified and escape arbitrariness if one is not confident that in reality there is some foundation for it. But what founds the acts or experience cannot be properly objectified. It cannot be expressed in concepts and representations after the manner of man's knowledge of the world. Therefore the objective ideas that one forms in connection with the religious ultimate are by no means expressive of its truth. They are only pointers, fixing man's attention upon something that may shine through them, being apprehended intuitively together with them. Such pointers are symbols. Here we meet with an all-important problem: There is some truth in symbolism. It will be considered in the final critical synthesis of this investigation.

Fourth is the religious primacy of actual experience or interior happening. The questions that religion is called to answer are supposed to be basic and eternal problems of man. Therefore we are not the first to cope with them. Some exceptional religious geniuses and saints have experienced religious reality in an exemplary way. They have created symbols and have revealed their experience in their persons and lives. They have been occasions for others to have the same experience. The news of their experience has been diffused, interpreted, put in writing. Groups have been formed united in the same faith and in a definite social expression of that faith. Objective religions are then formed. Sometimes they grow into Churches with definite rules of faith and certain forms of authority. Various trends arise within them. They sometimes lead to divisions, either real schisms or sectarian groups. Thus each man comes to the age of reason within a religiously colored society and tradition. Such traditions, mediating in time between today and the creative genius of the past, are a kind of exterior rule. But they cannot rule a man simply from outside. They may point him toward possible experiences, invite him to open his heart to grace, aid him to understand his own experience if once it happens to him; but they are of no value as long as they are simply held as objective truth. They have to be converted into subjective truth, and the original experience has to be repeated in each man according to the measure that is given to him and taking the form of his own personal character. The inner experience or the subjective happening is the immediate rule of faith and conduct, and one has the right to express it freely within certain limits and to add one's own testimony to that of tradition.

Fifth is the universality of religion. If religion responds to questions that are part of man's common experience, then it may be expected that religious experience, too, will be a universal phenomenon. Christianity will be viewed as a species of the genus religion. It will be judged according to a comparative criterion, based upon a certain conception of pure and perfect religious experience and conduct. Christianity may be considered, then—as it usually is—as the most perfect religion for various reasons: because of the impact of the most perfect manifestation of religious experience, given in Christ (Schleiermacher), or because of the greatest purity and efficiency of its moral rule (A. Schweitzer) or because a unique significance is attributed to Christ as the mediator of the religious experience or salvation.

This last principle is not absolutely necessary. It certainly is the most natural assumption when the other four principles are accepted. But if one starts from certain presuppositions, as for instance, that salvation is the effect of a free predestination and election in which men have no part except through an encounter with Christ and a surrender of self to Him who is the Lord, then it is possible to place Christianity outside the genus of religion. The other religions may still be considered as expressions of man's anxiety and despair, of his longing for salvation, and of his attempt to attain salvation by his own means. But Christianity will be a different thing because in it alone occurs the event that opens the gate to salvation. Such seems to be the position of Bultmann.

LIBERAL THEOLOGY IN POSITIVISTIC GARB

How true it is that liberal theology, holding a transformistic conception of dogma, is itself subject to transformation, is strikingly illustrated by what happened after the 'breakdown of the great synthesis,' as Tillich calls it. All the causes of the dramatic reversal cannot be analysed here. Certainly man is always in search of something different; and after the climax of speculative idealism in the system of Hegel, he wearied of the lofty heights, so distant and different from the plains of common sense. Idealism is perhaps too unnatural to establish a lasting conviction. Moreover, post-Hegelian idealism divided into two opposite trends: the left-wing trend, leading via Feuerbach to Marx who formed a dialectical philosophy of his own that he called 'materialistic' and practical, in opposition to contemplative realism; and the right-wing, leading to a new kind of orthodoxy based upon a forced interpretation of Hegel's ambiguities and clad with idealistic vestments. After a while, of course, it became clear that the God of Hegel was but a sublime idea and not the living God who saves man from the despair of sin. Man, too, seemed to be reduced to a link in the majestic unfolding of the idea. Within the general framework of the system there was no real place for personal freedom and irreducible subjectivity. History seemed to be an unrelenting stream, irresistibly driven on by an impersonal spirit, in which the little whirlpools of individual persons had no real significance. The movement beyond Hegel to a religion of personal relationship with God was begun by the philosopher who was once his predecessor, then his rival, and afterwards his critic: Schelling.

Schelling never abandoned his speculative philosophy. But he realized that the last word of speculative philosophy was not the last word of man. On the contrary, at the very peak of speculation, the mind discovers that God as reached by rational thought is no more than an idea and does not correspond to the God in search of whom man has been driven along the path of speculative and practical reason. Man has to go the whole way of speculative reason in order to discover its utter insufficiency. At that moment the movement of thought is reversed and man looks around, seeking in the outer historical situation that which the game of immanent concepts could not yield. Thus speculative philosophy itself dialectically leads to a positive philosophy. Religion is no longer a stage in the inner unfolding of contemplative reason. It has to come from without, filling the void that speculative philosophy itself has revealed in us. The relation between philosophy and religion is still dialectical, not within the system itself, however, but between the system and existence.

> It cannot be doubted which kind of will it is that gives the signal to the reversal and thus to positive philosophy. It is the 'I' that we have left at the moment in which it has to abandon the speculative life and a last despair takes possession of it. . . . It is not yet freed from the inanity of existence that befell it and that it must experience more deeply after having tasted the knowledge of God. Only now the 'I' realizes the cleft between God and himself; he realizes how an apostasy from God, a being-outside-God, is at the bottom of all moral activity, making it doubtful. Then he has no rest or peace before the rupture is reconciled. No bliss can help him if it does not at once redeem him. Therefore he longs for God Himself. It is He whom he wants, the God who acts, who is a Providence, who, being Himself actually existing, is able to meet the actuality of apostasy. . . . In Him alone he finds the real highest good. The very meaning of contemplative life was none other than to go beyond the general to the personal.[40]

Reconciliation cannot be accomplished by man. It has to be bestowed upon him from without, through grace. It cannot be 'deserved nor proportionate, as Kant wished, but only undeserved, and therefore incalculable and superabundant.'[41] This means a return to Christian existentialism but dialectically springing, as it were, from the purest immanentistic essentialism.

S. Kierkegaard attended the last lectures of Schelling at Berlin. He opposed Hegel with an intensity equal to the attraction that his system exercised upon him. Personality, the most precious of all values, does not fit into the system. To become man is to discover the utter despair of existence, and to become a Christian is to make the leap to faith with a passionate subjective assurance, whose degree of certainty corresponds to the measure of objective uncertainty. The *nuda fides* is worked by grace alone and is not in need of any objective help, either rational or institutional. In this the paradox of Christian existence consists.

In their own time Kierkegaard and the later Schelling were not valued at their true worth. But their thought is a passionate outburst of something that was secretly at work in the semi-conscious depths of their contemporaries, and therefore their criticism of Hegel hit the mark, albeit in a negative way: they contributed to the defeat of the system, already dying from an inner lack of clarity and dissolving on both the left and right sides.

The dissolution of the great synthesis was only a negative cause of the momentous revolution that took place about the middle of the 19th century. Liberal theology, which is a spirit or a trend springing from the nature of man who always feels reluctant in the face of what seems to be irrational, had to seek another support. Such a support was offered by positivism. The first principle of positivism is not that science is the only rule of life. According to A. Comte, science is merely subservient to the good and the moral progress of man, and its pursuit can only be justified by this subordination. Morality is first. The unity of mankind in mutual love and service is the ultimate value and goal. But man's knowledge of what is cannot go beyond what can be proved by empirical verification. In Germany, a school of theologians arose who accepted the principle of theological positivism. They were averse to every form of mysticism or metaphysics and rejected the appeal to a special religious experience. There is only the immediate awareness or experience of being a person, i.e., a moral being or a moral call. To be man is to be called to overcome the inner and outer pressures of nature and to establish the reign of the spirit over nature in order to become free for a disinterested life of duty. But man feels himself incapable of realizing that freedom. He is captive in the grip of his egoism. This is sin. Such is the situation in which the message of the Gospel presents itself to him: a message of the forgiveness of sin through Christ. How can one be sure that the message actually occurred? There is but one way: objective scientific investigation. Religion is that which makes man capable of actualizing himself as a person. But in humanity as it is found in history, this is impossible without a forgiveness of sins. That forgiveness is really offered as something of which one cannot be sure except by historical proof. The epistemological background is Kant: empirical science and ethical consciousness are the only two things that can give support to human life. So Kantianism was at the bottom of that school of which A. Ritschl (1822–1889) was the leader.

It was A. Harnack (1851–1930) who gave the positivistic version of liberal theology its most perfect and successful expression. The publication in 1900 of his lectures on the essence of Christianity was a historic event. *What Is Christianity?* immediately became a theological best-seller. Harnack starts from the assumption that the answer to the question, 'What is Christianity?' can be given independently of any subjective attitude only by means of historical investigation. Not unlike Schleiermacher, he also supposes that Christianity simply pertains to the genus religion and is the outcome of a gradual development of ethico-religious experience: 'I am convinced rather, that at bottom we have to do here with something which is common to us all, and which in the course of history has struggled up out of torpor and discord into unity and light' (Harnack, p. 9). Further, in order to understand the nature of Christianity it does not suffice to go back to the Bible or to know the personality and the doctrine of its founder. 'We must look at the reflection and effects which he produced in those whose leader and master he became' (Harnack, p. 10). Nay, we have to follow the whole of its history, its living tradition, 'all the later products of its spirit' (Harnack, pp. 10–16). In this point, too, he follows Schleiermacher.

Harnack's conclusion may be stated in his own words: 'Gentlemen, it is religion, the love of God and neighbour, which gives life a meaning; knowledge cannot do it' (Harnack, p. 300). The great historian is not averse to knowledge, of course: but knowledge, although it has a certain relation to religion and faith, does not pertain to its essence. There is an element of knowledge in faith. It may be more or less comprehensive according to the inner development and subjective intelligence of the individual, but to the extent that it develops a doctrine it is not necessary for faith. 'The Gospel is no theoretical system of doctrine or philosophy; it is doctrine only insofar as it proclaims the reality of God the Father' (Harnack, p. 146). Religion is no more difficult to the uneducated or to those who are entirely engaged in the material things of this world than to the theologian. 'The christian religion is something simple and sublime; it means one thing and one thing only: Eternal life in the midst of time and under the eyes of God' (Harnack, p. 8). Therefore, nobody 'can fail to see it and distinguish it from its contemporary integument' (Harnack, p. 14). To the objection that the principle of 'Scripture alone' (Scripture to be interpreted by the individual under the inner guidance of the Spirit) leads to division and confusion, Harnack replies in an optimistic mood: 'Protestantism reckons—this is the solution —upon the Gospel being something so simple, so divine, and therefore so truly human as to be most certain of being understood when it is left entirely free, and also as to produce essentially the same experiences and convictions in individual souls' (Harnack, p. 275). There are different doctrines in Protestantism, 'but we do not wish otherwise,' we want even more freedom, 'more confidence in the inner strength and unifying power of the Gospel' (Harnack, P. 276).

From all this Harnack's position is clear. There are two aspects in religion: the interior and the exterior. The exterior is that of ecclesiastical organization, necessary to the proclamation of the Gospel; it implies doctrines, religious congregations, forms of worship, etc. The interior is that of individual faith. The first is subject to development and transformation; the second is the inner kingdom of conscience awakening and growing under the impact of the Christian message, 'its spirit leading from one light to another and developing higher forces' (Harnack, p. 11). It is strictly personal, grounded in experience. Therefore, 'it is only a religion which a man has himself experienced that is to be confessed' (Harnack, p. 148). Its life is moral strength and rightness: 'It is religion and the moral element that are concerned' (Harnack, pp. 147–148); 'The creed is to be nothing but faith reduced to practice' (p. 149). That interior factor is the formative element of the whole of life. The exterior forms of government, doctrine, and ritual, although determined by the historical and cultural situation, are only valuable insofar as they express interior religion, being enlivened and inspired by it.

Doctrines thus, as far as they pertain to the exterior social appearance of religion, are unavoidable. Our life does not flow from inner inspiration alone. We are living in a world, in an historical situation. In applying itself to moral action in a world of nature and history, faith must be objectified in terms of man's understanding of the world; it has to incarnate itself in a Christian worldview. In the formation of doctrinal structures contemporary philosophy and science have an essential part. They present man with the terms and categories by the means of which he devises his conscious image of that reality that is the domain of moral life inspired by religion. Doctrines, then, are unavoidable, and they unavoidably vary in the course of history according to the general state of philosophical thought and scientific knowledge. They constitute the exterior, changeable aspect of religion. They address themselves to man as the subject and maker of culture. The essential message of God's fatherhood, on the contrary, addresses itself to that which constitutes our very essential being. 'The essential elements in the Gospel are . . . "timeless." Not only are they so; but the man to whom the Gospel addresses itself is also "timeless," that is to say, it is the man who, in spite of all progress and development, never changes in his inmost constitution and in his fundamental relations with the external world' (Harnack, p. 149).

Harnack's views on the development of dogma, then, are most resolute and explicit. As an historian of dogma, he not only knows its evolution, but fully appreciates it. The dogmas of the patristic age are the outcome of the encounter of Jewish Christianity with Greek philosophy. They are the outcome of the second wave of Hellenization—the first being Gnosticism—that meant an unavoidable 'intellectualization' of the Creed. But the intellectual formulas of Trinitarian and Christological doctrine are not eternal rules. They no longer have any value for faith. They are not the proper object of any science of faith, but only of a neutral historical science. For faith is not the acceptance of a Christological Creed. Man has to live according to the Gospel in order to understand what the Gospel is about.

The position of Harnack may be summarized in the following two citations. Christianity 'is not a question of "doctrine" being handed down by uniform repetition or arbitrarily distorted; it is a question of life, again and again kindled afresh, and now burning with a flame of its own' (Harnack, p. 11). And further:

Either the Gospel is in all respects identical with its earliest form, in which case it came with its time and has departed with it; or else it contains something which under different historical forms, is of permanent validity. The latter is the true view. The history of the Church shows us that 'primitive Christianity' had to disappear in order that 'Christianity' might remain, and in the same way in later ages one metamorphosis followed upon another. From the beginning it was a question of getting rid of formulas, correcting expectations, altering ways of feeling, and this is a process to which there is no end. [Harnack, p. 14.]

LIBERAL THEOLOGY IN ENGLAND

Although liberal theology received its most perfect expression in Germany, England, with Chillingworth and the Cambridge Platonists, was the country of its origin. Semler was greatly influenced by English thought. Religious liberalism was always kept alive by the ecclesiastical party that would be labelled the Broad Church in the 19th century. But owing to the general character of the English mind, it remained predominantly practical. Liberals did not attach too much value to strict orthodoxy; they claimed the right of interpreting the Anglican formularies and rubrics in a broad sense and stood for freedom and tolerance. In the beginning of the 19th century, however, among the romantics, English thought came under the influence of German idealism. It is typical of England that the new views were not sustained by philosophers but by poets. The influence of German idealism was mediated by S. T. Coleridge.

English Romanticism was a passionate protest against the matter-of-fact philosophy of the Lockeian School. According to Wordsworth and Shelley there are two kinds of thought: on the one hand, practical thought, dealing with material things, aiming to master them and based on exact science; on the other hand, moral speculative thought, revealing the eternal nature of man. The former is the domain of reason, the latter of poetic imagination. Shelley explained the romantic view in a way that is as clear as it is beautiful and vehement: 'The cultivation of poetry is never more desired than at periods when, from an excess of the selfish and calculating principle, the accumulation of the materials of external life exceeds the quantity of the power of assimilating them to the internal law of human nature.'[42] For a poem is 'the very image of life, expressed in its eternal truth. . . . The great instrument of moral good is the imagination; and poetry administers to the effect by acting upon the cause. Poetry strengthens the faculty which is the organ of the moral nature of man in the same manner as exercise strengthens a limb.'[43]

The real philosophical genius of the romantic movement was S. T. Coleridge (1772–1834). He had visited Germany, made personal acquaintance with some of the leading poets and philosophers, and was greatly influenced by the mysticism of J. Böhme, by Herder, Kant, Fichte, and especially Schelling. The stars of Schleiermacher and Hegel had not yet risen, although, starting with Schelling, Coleridge's own thought on some points was not so far removed from Schleiermacher's.

One of the first principles of Coleridge is the necessary connection between philosophy and religion. Two tendencies are equally fatal: to reduce religion to philosophy and to separate religion from philosophy: 'As religion never can be philosophy, because the only true philosophy proposes religion as its end and supplement, so on the other hand there can be no true religion without philosophy, no true feelings and notions of religion about men at large without just notions of philosophy in the higher classes.'[44] This is a sound and well-balanced principle.

Coleridge shared with Wordsworth and Shelley the romantic loathing for the matter-of-fact and utilitarian philosophy that issued from Locke. But he resolutely rejected Wordsworth's appeal to the common sense of unspoiled nature against the fallacies of philosophy. False philosophy, he thought, can only be successfully fought by true philosophy. The true philosophy was not that of 'Understanding' but that of 'Reason,' which according to his conviction was characterized by fullness and harmony and appeared in history as an ever-recurring trend affirming and reaffirming itself in the face of various one-sided systems. The common sense of natural man supposed a sound philosophy in the upper classes: 'An accredited, learned and philosophic class . . . [is] an essential element in the composition of a civilized community.'[45]

The distinction between Understanding and Reason corresponds to the German distinction between *Verstand* and *Vernunft*. Understanding is the faculty of intermediate ends, and the philosophy based on it is that of the Lockeian kind, which tries to give an interpretation of the universe in terms accepted or deduced from sense-perception. Reason is the faculty of ultimate ends and has its origin in the deepest depths of self-consciousness. In his *Aids to Reflection* Coleridge speaks of 'The contra-distinction of Understanding and Reason, for which during twenty years I have been contending.'[46]

Coleridge's *Reason* corresponds to the *transcendental* of German idealism. Its originating act is the simple unconscious dynamism of the whole in man, preceding the particular activities of the mind including sensation, perception, and understanding, and rendering them possible. Sometimes Reason means the transcendental in its basic unity, corresponding to Schleiermacher's 'immediate consciousness of Self;' sometimes it stands for one of the determinations of the first undifferentiated whole: that which in conscious activity gives rise to philosophy. As such it is distinguished from imagination and, in a certain sense, from conscience and faith. Imagination, for instance, is related to 'fancy' as Reason to Understanding. This is akin to Schelling and Schleiermacher.

In philosophy, as in art, there is a general movement from the unconscious whole toward conscious wholeness or comprehensiveness. True philosophy is an endeavor to make actual intelligence coincide with reason. This is the general idealistic scheme. Being himself a poet of genius, Coleridge has described the presence and directing power of the whole in the genesis of a work of art in a way that seems forever unsurpassable:

> The poet described in ideal perfection brings the whole soul of man into activity, with the subordination of its faculties to each other according to their relative worth and dignity . . . by that synthetic and magic power to which I would exclusively appropriate the name of Imagination. . . . Good sense is the body of poetic genius, Fancy its drapery, motion its life, and Imagination the soul that is everywhere and in each; and forms all into one graceful and intelligent whole.[47]

Imagination, rooted in unconscious wholeness, is the power that makes man move as a whole, organizing all his faculties in order to produce a work of art that reflects in its objective wholeness and pleasurable harmony the wholeness from which it proceeds.

The relation between Reason and philosophy is strictly analogous to that which holds between Imagination and art. Coleridge distinguishes between primary and secondary Imagination. Considered as primary, it is prior to conscious will and thought, a participation by the finite mind in the infinite act of creation, the unconscious source. Considered as secondary, it coexists with will and thought: it is the directive presence of the whole in the process of artistic creation; it is executed by the consonant exercise of will, thought, and fancy. The same distinction applies to Reason: it is the unconscious source of man's search for truth and at the same time it is the controlling power of the whole process of knowledge, including sensation. For 'sensation itself is but vision nascent, not the cause of intelligence, but intelligence itself revealed as an earlier power in the process of self-construction.'[48] This is pure Schelling.

It is in the exercise of artistic creation and of truth-seeking thought that one has an intuitive awareness of the active and directive presence of Imagination and Reason. Reason is the source and principle of all searching after truth; truth, however, is essentially moral truth. Awareness of moral truth may be considered antecedently to moral life: then it is conscience or primary conscience. Or it may be at work during and after the exercise of good or bad moral decisions, taking the form of approbation or condemnation: then it may be called secondary conscience. If one's will coincides with the voice of conscience—Coleridge calls it the personal synthesis of Reason and will—it results in moral perfection or virtue. The highest synthesis is obtained when one's personal will entirely and unconditionally subjects itself to Reason, Coleridge calls this Faith. Insofar as pre-personal Reason enters into the synthesis, faith is light, an irradiation of the eternal Reason or *Logos* that is in God. As far as personal will enters into it, 'it must be an energy, and inasmuch as it relates to the whole moral man, it must be exerted in each and all of its constituents or incidents— it must be a total, not a partial, a continuous not a desultory or occasional energy.'[49] According to the essay just quoted, perfect faith or absolute fidelity to the will of God, perceived in the light of Reason, is the definitive form of what at first was defined as fidelity to one's own being. The immanentistic line must be brought out in the full.

Still, Coleridge is not an immanentist. Faith is not simply immanent Reason. He admits and affirms that the divine *Logos*, or Word, or Reason that shines in one's conscience has revealed itself in Jesus Christ as a redemptive Word. This is quite clear, for instance, from Coleridge's profession of faith in the first letter of *Confessions of an Inquiring Spirit*. Both manifestations of Reason, however, are correlative. The latter supposes the former and completes it. But we have good reason to think that according to Coleridge the aim of revelation is not so much to give us new information about the invisible as to renew in us the truths of conscience, obliterated by sin, and to reveal to us God's grace so that we may be able to overcome our selfishness and retrieve the glorious purity of our original being in righteousness, selflessness, and love. For righteousness is the realization in conscious intercourse of the sameness of 'I' and 'Thou,' given in the unconscious unity of transpersonal being. For 'the equation of Thou with I, by means of a free act, negativating the sameness in order to establish the equality is the true definition of conscience.'[50] This is dialectics of the most genuine kind: from an unconscious sameness to a conscious community of differentiated persons who have ceased to attach to their own 'I' a special importance and thus are free to live for others.

Coleridge towers as a lonely peak of speculative thought among the hills of England. There is no school connected with his name, but he exercised a considerable influence through the few who understood and appreciated his insights. Among these we find F. D. Maurice, now generally recognized as one of the greatest Anglican divines of his century. Maurice is the initiator of that mild and sober form of free theology that will remain the general characteristic of liberalism in England. Let us say at once that if the notion of liberal theology as defined here, is urged in the strictest sense, Maurice can hardly be labelled a liberal theologian. Here the equivocation of the term *liberal* comes to light. To Maurice, as to Coleridge, there was no true theology without philosophy. Theology was a kind of philosophizing in the light of Biblical faith. He greatly admired Plato: 'I never have taken up any dialogue of Plato without getting more from it than from any book not in the Bible.'[51] He also stood for the entire liberty of scientific investigation. He did not, however, despise doctrine, although orthodoxy was not so all-important with him. He fiercely opposed those who reduced faith to the acceptance of a Creed. This was particularly brought out in his attack upon H. L. Mansel on the occasion of Mansel's Bampton Lectures on *The Limits of Religious Thought*. Mansel attempted to defend orthodoxy with the weapons of philosophic skepticism: The knowledge of the Absolute and Infinite is made impossible by the very constitution of men's minds. From their very nature propositions about God are not speculative but regulative. They do not enounce truth as it is in God, but they give us such approximations to truth as may serve as a guide to conduct.

They are symbolic, not speculative. How, then, can one know something about God? Only from the revelation contained in the Scriptures and guaranteed by the evidence of miracles. Mansel's position is interesting as it comes very near to the religious epistemology that E. Le Roy will propound in the time of continental Modernism.

In *What is Revelation?* Maurice gave vent to his indignation and became engaged in an angry controversy. The truth concerning God, he contended, is neither speculative nor regulative but personal. Our conduct cannot be regulated by a truth if that truth is not properly known. We only know ourselves and our duties in so far as we know God. But that knowledge is not a speculative knowledge about God; it is a personal knowledge of God, given to us in what He does for us. God reveals Himself to us in the very act of creation and in the saving acts of Christ. Christian life is a personal response to that revelation. It is a living intercourse between persons; and in that intercourse, in that growing life of friendship, we come to know God better and better.

Faith, then, is a moral response of that whole person to God's active disclosure of Himself in Christ. The knowledge of God is not a dogmatic system constructed upon that personal revelation but a living knowledge inherent in it.

From such a position it necessarily follows that all dogmatic systems are of relative value and that if one clings to them as to saving truth, all systems become dangerous. Maurice holds 'a Catholic *system* . . . to be one of the greatest enemies of the Catholic *Church.*'[52] We live from a 'Tradition,' which is a growing treasure formed by the testimonies of those who have reflected upon the Bible and their experience of God and Christ. This tradition cannot be reduced to one of the many traditions of the different branches of Christendom. It is common and may be called—

> *the* tradition of the Church. As such we receive it and rejoice in it. But on this ground especially, that it is a continual protection against traditions, that when they try to force themselves upon us, we can always put this forward as a declaration that what we believe and trust in is not this or that notion, or theory, or scheme or document: but that it is the Eternal Name in which we are baptized, and in which the whole Church and each member of the Church stands.[53]

This tradition is expressed in the Apostles' Creed and the Nicene Creed, which the Church puts in the mouths of all its members. It is the true base of the ecumenical unity that is forcibly defended by Maurice:

> The English Church I look upon as merely one branch of the true Church; and every *system*, whether called evangelical, liberal, catholic, or purely Anglican, which has been invented by the members of that Church in former times and in our own day to express their notion of the Church I look upon as 'of the earth earthly' and as much carrying in it the seeds of destruction as the systems of the different sects which have revolted from her.[54]

From the doctrine of tradition it becomes very clear that if a man has to be judged according to his intentions, Maurice was not a true liberal. But it could be argued against him that the Creed that he considered to contain the *medulla* of the evangelical message was already a system—and a very definite one—and that it had to be interpreted in order to be understood. This must give rise to different 'systems,' which cannot be considered as accretions or additions to the Creeds but as attempts to get at their very meaning. Therefore, Maurice's doctrine concerning the Creed, which ranges him among the defenders of orthodoxy, is not altogether consistent with his view on the nature of religious knowledge. If personal knowledge of God includes the acceptance of the Creed, then it includes objective doctrines about God and His dealings with men; and if these doctrines are not merely 'regulative,' then they are 'speculative' in the sense that they objectively enounce in human language true propositions about God that as such are subject to the ordinary rules of logic. There is no escape from the dilemma of Mansel.

It is noteworthy that both Mansel and Maurice, in their attempt to defend orthodoxy, open the way to liberalism: Mansel through his agnosticism, which led him to ascribe to all religious notions a mere symbolic meaning; Maurice by denying that the personal knowledge of God implied a propositional system of truth about God.

English liberal theology will gradually develop in the second half of the 19th century under the joint impact of physical science and Biblical criticism. According to Maurice and many others, faith was a personal realizing of what God had done for us through Christ, as narrated in the Bible. The entire religious view is Biblical and Christocentric. The progress of natural science will destroy the firm belief in the Biblical miracles. Are they more than mythological stories invented by the first Christians in order to express their experience of the meaning of Christ? If so, what to think of Christ? Biblical criticism will show that the Scriptures are as human in their composition as any other books and are full of contradictions. How can one separate the kernel from the husk, the historical truth about Jesus from the accretions of human fancy and speculation? How can one be sure that Christ is the Savior of sinful man?

Again, it is in literature that we find the truest expression of the agonizing doubts that had to be overcome by the later Victorian theologians. After a long period of doubt Tennyson re-affirmed his faith as a pure faith, 'believing where we cannot prove' in the truth of a tale which narrates the saving deeds of God.

> For wisdom dealt with mortal powers,
> Where truth in closest words shall fail,
> When truth embodied in a tale
> Shall enter in at lowly doors.
> And so the Word hath breath and wrought
> With human hands the creed of creeds
> In loveliness of perfect deeds
> More strong than all poetic thoughts. [*In Memoriam* 36]

It is Maurice whom Tennyson greatly admired and who speaks here through the mouth of the poet but with undertones of doubt.

In the Victorian novel, *Robert Elsmere* (1888), written by Mrs. Humphrey Ward, the whole theological situation of liberalism is clearly pictured. In its own time it was a best seller and caused widespread alarm in orthodox circles. It relates the failure of the orthodoxy of a very active and socially-minded parson who tries to investigate the intellectual and historical foundations of his belief, and how he afterward reconstructed his religious worldview along liberal lines. When he consults an Oxford tutor on his vocation to the ministry he meets with the reply: 'One may as well preach a respectable mythology as anything else.' To his question of what mythology means he gets the answer: 'Simply, ideas or experiences personified.' He retorts: 'To the Christian, facts have been the medium by which ideas the world could not otherwise have come at have been communicated to man. Christian theology is a system of ideas, indeed, but ideas realized, made manifest in facts.' The tutor replied drily: 'How do you know they are facts?'[55]

The position of Elsmere is the religion of Maurice and Tennyson. But the doubt prevails: miracles are not historical facts. 'The witness of the time is not true nor, in a strict sense, false. It is merely incompetent, half-trained, prescientific, but all through perfectly natural. The wonder would have been to have a life of Christ without miracles. The air teems with them. The East is full of Messiahs. The resurrection is partly invented, partly imagined, partly ideally true.'[56]

The liberal reconstruction, then, comes to the idea of 'the image of a purely human Christ—a purely human explicable, yet always, wonderful Christianity. It broke his heart, but the spell of it was like some dream-country wherein we see all the familiar objects of life in new relations and perspectives.'[57] That perspective is optimistic in contrast to the gloomy Christianity of old: 'Half the tragedy of our time lies in the perpetual clashing of two estimates of life. The estimate which is the offspring of the modern Spirit, and which is forever making the visible world fairer and more desirable in mortal eyes: and the estimate of St. Augustine.'[58] Elsmere resigned as vicar and set to work in the London Slums. The conclusion is that 'God is to be sought in the soul of man, in the verifications of experience, and in the sacrificial giving of Christian love. All things change—creeds and philosophies and outward systems—but God alone remains.'[59]

Later, Van Buren will not go beyond this except that, starting with an absurd principle, he will contend that not even the word *God* can be used in a way that has any true meaning.

English liberalism had little impact upon the ordinary believer. Even in the intellectual circles it remained a small minority. Considered as a crisis within the Church of England, it soon passed, not, however, without having helped to bring about a sincere openness to the true results of physical and historical science. It was combatted with considerable success by such 'orthodox' writers as G. K. Chesterton. It also suffered from some congenital defects: it was too negative, too purely intellectual, too naive in its acceptance of certain 'modern' presuppositions that afterwards proved unsound and untenable, too arbitrary in its selection of the Gospel elements with which to sustain its views, too individualistic and divided. Later the 'liberals' joined forces in the *Modern Churchman's Union* and expounded their view in *The Modern Churchman*. Dean Inge became the central figure, but the liberalism of Inge himself was moderate, in the tradition of Maurice. Although opposed to dogmatism, he never doubted the divinity of Christ and His saving power. He described the tradition in which he stood as follows:

> A spiritual religion, based on a firm belief in absolute and eternal values as the most real things in the universe—a confidence that these values are knowable by man—a belief that they can nevertheless be known only by whole-hearted consecration of the intellect, will, and affections to the great quest —an entirely open mind towards the discoveries of science—a reverent and receptive attitude to the beauty, sublimity, and wisdom of the creation, as a revelation of the mind and character of the Creator—a complete indifference to the current valuations of the worldling.[60]

According to Inge the justification of our belief in Christ has nothing to do with Biblical miracles. Let Biblical criticism have its way! He was confident that enough of the substance of the Gospel would prove capable of withstanding all criticism. The true criterion of faith is that kind of personal experience that reaches its perfect expression with the great mystics. As for Maurice, so for Inge, Plato was the mystical philosopher who created the general spiritual atmosphere in which the meaning of Christ would reveal itself. Although ordinary Christians do not attain the heights of mystical experience, the inner life of every authentic man is traversed by flashes of light that allow him to understand the mystics and to acknowledge the invisible world to which they bear witness. Through the convergence of experiences the criterion of mystical experience becomes sufficiently objective:

> Those who have mounted higher are sure that they have been in contact with ultimate reality, and heard the voice of God Himself, or of the glorified and indwelling Christ. Ought we not to believe them? It is conceivable of course that they may be deceived; but if our highest and deepest experiences cannot be trusted, it is useless to seek for truth anywhere.[61]

MODERNISM

Harnack's *What is Christianity?* gave Loisy the opportunity to write his *L'Évangile et l'Église*. It presented itself as a Catholic reply to Harnack, but it was actually a Catholic version of liberal theology. It was a Catholic view insofar as it tried to establish the Catholic principle of authority. It has already been pointed out that the real difference between Catholicism and Protestantism does not consist in the doctrines of faith or grace but in the conception of authority. Unlike Protestantism, according to which the ultimate rule of faith is the Bible and the immediate rule its understanding by the individual mind under the guidance of the Spirit, the Catholic view states that, the Bible being the ultimate rule of faith, the immediate rule is its understanding and interpretation by the Church, voiced by an institutional authority. That was the principle that Loisy tried to defend by a philosophic understanding of the nature of man and history.

The essence of Christianity is not something purely interior, which has to be realized again and again in personal experience. It is itself social and historical. One cannot separate a religious inner core from a neutral husk of historical exteriority. In the collective life of the Church the essence of Christianity is not snowed under by a mass of extraneous materials but 'it remains alive in it under different forms which manifest its vital power' (Loisy, p. 170; Eng. trans., p. 179). The ecclesiastical, doctrinal, and liturgical factors are the structural forms in which the vital principle of Christianity manifests itself in the course of history. Vitality is a basic concept with Loisy, a key word. It is a power of continual adaptation to the changing historical situations in which a living unit has to exist.

Loisy tries to establish the Catholic principle by a philosophical interpretation of history that supposes a certain idea of man and human life. Man is a social being. He is determined by society not only in one or more respects but in his entirety. This does not exclude personal originality and an irreducible inner life. Nor does Loisy deny the continuous formative influence of personal freedom upon society and the course of history. But there is no inner part of personality, expressing the eternal nature of man and contradistinguished from an outer public part that changes with history. The whole of man's personal life is original. Man's exterior conduct expresses his inner personal life. Similarly, the whole of his personal

I

life is determined and colored by the social reality in which he happens to exist. Society determined the individual in the very springs of his originality. His ways of experiencing and feeling are no less influenced by his historical and social being as the categories in which he expresses them. There is no inner experience apart from language, for in language alone it becomes man's conscious experience. But language is a social reality. By thought and speech, in which experience becomes human and conscious, that experience is already engaged in a social historical milieu and pertains to it.

The same relation obtains between the Church with all its institutional aspects and the spirit or experience of Christ from which the Gospel proceeds. 'The Church is as necessary to the Gospel as the Gospel to the Church' (Loisy, p. 139; Eng. trans., p. 151). The Gospel is the permanent principle of religious and moral education and 'neither does the principle subsist without the society, nor the society without the principle' (p. 167; Eng. p. 177). The Church, then, is the living continuation of the Gospel. The Gospel was not a casual individual occurrence that gave rise to a society. It was a society from the start. Christ Himself founded a society and entrusted its government to the twelve with Peter as their chief: 'The first communities would not have been likely to survive without the rudimentary organization given to them by their founders' (P. 138; Eng. pp. 150–1). 'The Church was born and endured by the development of an organization, the lineaments of which were already outlined in the Gospel' (p. 135; Eng. p. 147).

What, then, is the spiritual substance embodied in the primitive Church? 'The message of Jesus is entirely contained in the proclamation of the coming kingdom and the invitation to do penance in order to have part in the kingdom' (p. 71; Eng. p. 86). Jesus cannot be understood apart from the historical situation that He shared with His hearers. He proclaimed the approach of the kingdom announced by the Prophets. That kingdom was not an invisible community but a visible form of society in which the existing conditions of social life would be destroyed and transfigured into a perfect society of eternal peace and immortal bliss, where the will of God would be done on earth as it is in heaven. The accomplishment of the kingdom is still to come. It is an inspiring hope, but it is also present among us by the coming of Jesus the Messiah and in us by faith and love. 'Its roots are interior: it lies like a precious seed in the soul of each believer; in that condition, however, it is hidden, rudimentary, imperfect. It awaits its perfection in the future' (p. 45; Eng. p. 62). Dispositions of love and forgiveness are not the kingdom itself, an invisible kingdom, but they are essentially related to the approaching glorious kingdom as a condition of membership when it will be in power.

However, the kingdom did not come soon. Gradually the eschatological tension relaxed and the relation of the Christian group to the kingdom had to be restated. The adaptation was required by the facts of history. The idea of the imminence of the kingdom had to be abandoned and the interregnum extended indefinitely, but the 'interim ethic' had to be maintained and the embryonic organization perpetuated in the form of a hierarchical Church. If it was to subsist, Christianity could not but reorganize itself under the rule of a readjusted faith: 'The faith in the resurrection of Christ; His invisible and lasting presence among His people; His eternal glorification; the continuous advance of the Gospel in the world; the regeneration of the world by Christianity; the anticipation of the kingdom of Heaven in the Church' (Loisy, p. 110; Eng. pp. 124–125).

It is clear that such a restatement of the Gospel was an entire transformation. According to Loisy, transformative adaptation is the very law of history and the power of the Church is seen in its infinite flexibility: 'Adaptation has been and always will be necessary to the preservation of the faith in the world' (Loisy, p. 168; Eng. pp. 177–178). This is impossible if the Church cannot move as a whole; and in the conditions of earthly existence, the Church cannot move that way except by the exercise of authority: 'Catholicism consists in receiving the actual interpretation of the Gospel by the Church as emanating from a divinely established authority.'[62] Authority, however, is only the mouth-piece of the whole ecclesiastical body: 'The whole development proceeds from the inner life of the Church, and the decisions of its authority only sanction and consecrate the movement of common thought and devotion' (Loisy, p. 169; Eng. p. 178).

The dogmas of the Church are the rule of faith. They are not the objects of revelation but its authorized elaborations. 'Revelation has for its proper and direct object the simple truths contained in the assertions of faith, not doctrine and dogma as such. Doctrine and dogma are said to be revealed because the primitive assertions of the faith are preserved in the authorized explanations of the Church.' Loisy is rather vague on the relation between dogma and revelation: 'The truths of revelation are living in the assertions of faith before being analyzed in the speculations of doctrine. Their native form is a supernatural intuition and a religious experience, not an abstract consideration or a systematic definition of their object.'[63] That which in the object of faith does not change, cannot be found in the original letter nor in any particular form of interpretation imposed by the needs of the time, 'but in their common ground, which cannot be expressed in human language by a definition adequate to its object and valuable forever.'[64]

Loisy left the Church soon after his condemnation. G. Tyrrell, although excommunicated, never thought of leaving the Church. To him, Catholicism always remained the only true form of Christianity. He sharply opposed liberal Protestantism. He felt intense irritation when the liberals praised him for his liberal tendencies. He could not stand the suggestion that 'Jesus is to Christianity only what Mohammed is to the Moslem' (Tyrrell, p. 268). According to his view, the essence of Christianity is the mystery of Christ: not the doctrine of Christ as expressed in Jewish symbols or a doctrine about Christ but the personality of Christ, who is the incarnation of the divine Spirit and who communicates himself to man in personal experience, dwelling in him and allowing him to partake of the same Spirit. Tyrrell's mystical view of religion and Christianity must be understood in order to understand the meaning of his doctrinal relativism.

The intellectual background of Tyrrell's interpretation of Christianity is a general theory of religion. All through its development from primitive myths and practices to its perfection in revelation, religion is of the same nature. Along with his awareness of the phenomenal world, man has a certain knowledge of the transcendent. 'The transcendent is not the spiritual as opposed to the phenomenal; but the whole as opposed to an infinitesimal fraction of possible spiritual existence.' (Tyrrell, pp. 207–208). That spiritual existence is a disinterested love of the universal good, striving for universality and comprehensiveness. It is the life of the whole in every part. As such the whole is Spirit or Personality. The organ of man's knowledge of the transcendent and its moral claims is his conscience. The mind, made for an existence-in-the-world, 'can never comprehend the Spirit and its universal end; yet it possesses a fractional knowledge of the transcendent, which it can perfect by analogies derived from its own narrow field of phenomena' (Tyrrell, p. 208). But the Spirit in us clamors for universal and eternal good.

It is important to note that the universal good is not conceived of in a Platonic way as a mere spiritual world. It includes sensible experience as well. It is the absolute fullness of life, a possession of the whole in the bliss of disinterested wonder and love. The development of humanity, which comprehends the development of nature, is the life of the whole, pulsing in all its parts and guiding them into a full possession of itself. Tyrrell's general idea calls to mind the great idealistic pattern of the German romantics and Coleridge.

In the growth of the Spirit in humanity there is a great turning point: the appearance of Christ. 'Conscience, that is first dimly felt as a mysterious influence interfering with and transcending the natural self and its laws, is revealed at last as the Spirit or Personality incarnate in Jesus' (Tyrrell, p. 273). The Spirit is Jesus. The 'Personality, the "I," that speaks and acts in Jesus, is the Spirit, though it speaks and acts through the limitations of a human organism' (Tyrrell, p. 263). Therefore He is all-perfect. 'Against the Spirit He had no freedom but only within the limits of the Spirit. If He could not sin it was because the Spirit cannot sin' (Tyrrell, pp. 262–263). In Him the Father has revealed Himself not in His fullness but insofar as God is inclusively the ideal image of man.

As the Spirit incarnate, Jesus is the Savior. Imperfect as man is, he can only progressively subject himself to the Spirit, but with the liberty of rebellion. Rebellion that separates him from the Spirit is sin. Christ saves man by communicating to him His Spirit through the mediation of His human personality. For Christ is more than an ideal of human personality; He is Himself a living human personality working on man's personality through His visible frame and life. Thus He communicates the Spirit through the visible form of His humanity. 'Personality is the end, and personality, mediated no doubt through external signs and symbols, is the means' (Tyrrell, p. 265). Jesus is the great sacrament and symbol of the divine life and Spirit. So Christ, giving His Spirit to man through the mediation of His visible personality, dwells in man because He is Himself the Spirit: 'The idea of Jesus as the divine indwelling and saving Spirit seems to me the very essence of Christianity. Faith in Christ never meant merely faith in a teacher and His doctrine, but an apprehension of His personality as revealing itself within us' (Tyrrell, p. 271).

Jesus the Spirit who communicates Himself through sacramental mediation of His human personality: this is the mystical kernel from which to start in order to understand the theological positions of Tyrrell:

1. His Catholicism is based on the sacramental principle: the unity of the spiritual and the phenomenal: 'Incarnation, embodied immortality, sacraments, external worship, a visible Church; all are founded in this correlative of the spiritual and the phenomenal' (Tyrrell, *Crossroads*, p. 208). The economy of the Church is the continuation of Christ.

2. His personalistic mysticism. Although he highly valued the sacramental function of the visible Church, he thought that it could be dispensed with in individual cases. This consoled him after his excommunication. In his *Much-Abused Letter* (London, 1906) he wrote to an imaginary friend: 'I think you agree with me, that though the one thing necessary is communion with the invisible Church, yet communion with the visible Church . . . is a great *desideratum*, is a condition of more fruitful communion with the invisible' (pp. 62–63). To be Christ-like and to be one in Christ with all Christ-like men is the one thing that is absolutely indispensable. To be saved is to be one in Christ through faith, and 'Faith is a seeing of God, not face to face but through a glass darkly: still it is a seeing for oneself: not a believing on hearsay . . . this vision is not a command but is given us; and that, most clearly in moments when we seem most filled with God' (*Much-Abused Letter*, p. 69).

3. His opposition to ethical liberalism. 'Now if we agree with liberal Protestantism in taking symbolically what the early Church took literally, we differ in taking it as symbolic of transcendental values and not of the moral order in this life' (Tyrrell, p. 145). Although Tyrrell shares with Loisy the conviction that the historical Jesus preached the imminence of the final kingdom and was consequently deceived, he furiously opposed those liberals who drew the conclusion that the apocalyptic Jesus should be dismissed, retaining only the lawgiver of the Sermon on the Mount: 'Judged by the text of life and fruitfulness, the symbolism of apocalyptic imagery is truer to our spiritual needs than that of Hellenic intellectualism' (Tyrrell, p. 209).

4. His historical indifferentism. The Bible as an account of the past may be left to historical criticism. To the faithful, Christ is not a figure of the past but a living personality. Insofar as He

belongs to history, i.e., to a definite epoch and culture, He does not interest us. We are concerned with Him insofar as He is the revelation of the eternal Spirit, and this is known not by historical research but by faith and actual experience: 'Certain concrete historical facts enter into our Creed as matters of faith. Precisely as historical facts they concern the historian and must be criticized by his methods. But as matters of faith they must be determined by faith, i.e., by their proved religious values.'[65]

5. His dogmatic relativism. 'We hold to the transcendent kingdom and, while not discarding the imagery, we recognize that it is an envelope and not the substance' (Tyrrell, p. 145). Images are more important than conceptual definitions, but both are only envelopes. They are never the substance. In *Through Scylla and Charybdis* Tyrrell had worked out with implacable logic his great dilemma: we must choose between the old orthodox and the new liberal theology, between the biological or organic view of development and the dialectical view. The Church speaks either from memory—and then the realities it speaks of are beyond experience and development can only be a process of deduction from a deposit of faith or a primitive doctrine—or it speaks from actual experience—and then the realities it speaks of are within every man, and development is the quasi-biological unfolding of a seed with all the mutations that are normally found in processes of natural growth. The dilemma defined for Tyrrell the position of the moment. At that time he did not himself choose between the conflicting points of view. Neither did he exclude the possibility of a synthesis; but he sharply criticized the attempts of Newman and W. Ward at a via media. It is clear that he was rather skeptical and that on the whole his sympathies were with the liberal view. In his last book he worked out his mystical and personalistic liberalism. Faith was a personal encounter with Christ, a mystical experience of His formative presence in man. Symbols and doctrines may change. 'We have long since outgrown those apocalyptic forms of religious thought in which the Spirit of Jesus first uttered itself as the Son of Man, the Jewish Messiah. But the Spirit itself we have not outgrown, and in us it seeks ever new forms wherein to clothe the same revelation' (Tyrrell, p. 267).

Loisy and Tyrrell are the most original and typical representatives of Modernism in the Catholic Church. They exhibit the imprint of Catholicism when they stress respectively the rule of authority

(Loisy) and the sacramental meaning of the visible Church (Tyrrell). They are marked by liberalism insofar as both of them exclude from the essence of Christianity all elements of religious doctrine, starting with the doctrine of Christ Himself, which was but an eschatological thought-form enveloping a substantial truth that could not be expressed in objective propositions but was present to experience as an idea working as a 'spiritual force and impetus,' not as 'an intellectual concept.'

There are other outstanding figures in Modernism. At the side of Loisy we find three great scholars who first followed him and later opposed him, often furiously, for his 'duplicity'; M. Hébert (1851–1916), who ended in a kind of humanistic pantheism; J. Turmel (1859–1943), who soon became an atheist but remained a priest in order to fight the Church from within and to take revenge upon it for having beguiled him in his youth into subjecting himself to illusions; A. Houtin (1867–1926), who became, in the end, the prophet of a new theism purified of all 'supernatural lore.'

In Italy Modernism was chiefly represented by A. Fogazzaro (1842–1911), the poet and novelist who always remained attached to the Church, and E. Buonaiuti (1881–1946), a college friend of Pope John XXIII, whom he assisted at his ordination. He was a zealous propagator of Loisy's ideas among the clergy and in spite of the severest excommunication (*excommunicatus vitandus*) never denied his catholic-charismatic idea of the Church. He lived long enough to think out the consequences of the Modernist position. The great revolutionary messages from which the higher religions have sprung, he said, never were doctrines but proclamations of sacral ideas pointing to prerational and spiritual values of human life, connected with such experiences as love, suffering, conversion, and death. The essence of Christianity is ethical. It is a call to free ourselves from all egoistic tendencies in order to live for our brethren, to be ready to sacrifice our lives for their good, following the example of Jesus Christ, and to wait for the coming of the kingdom of God. 'The conceptual translation of those values in the formulas of dogma and in the hierarchical construction of ecclesiastical discipline, uniting the groups formed by these new values, came afterwards.'[66] They are unavoidable for a social and proselytizing religion, but in themselves they are incurable defects, always threatening with death the fervor of faith. The real power of the Church does not lie in the system but in the Spirit. In order to survive, the Church must always restore the balance between charism and syllogism, faith and discipline.

Contemporary thought here means that which has been affected by the experiences of the two world wars. Before the First World War liberal theology was characterized by a placidly optimistic mood. It seemed self-evident that evil was but a kind of immaturity and imperfection and that the historical progress of humanity should always be for the better. To those who profoundly experienced the First World War all optimism of that kind could only appear superficial and naive. The First World War was the 'Shaking of the Foundations.' It revealed the destructive and demonic forces hidden in the depths of the soul and always ready to break into the open, the primitive dragons that sleep for a while in their caverns, but always may awake and destroy the world with their breath of fire.

In the new situation liberal theology had to shift its ground. The main inspiration of the new liberal theology came from A. Schweitzer, especially from his book *Die Mystik des Apostels Paulus* 1930). He reproached the followers of Harnack for confining the life of faith and justification to the inner and timeless sphere of experience, isolating it from the inspiring idea of the kingdom of God, which has to come from without, although already working through us in our never-failing attempts to realize in this world the ideal of Christian love.

The positions of the new school were most ably expounded by U. Neuenschwander in *Die neue liberale Theologie*. The new liberal theology agrees with the old in its fundamental principles: the entire acceptance of all the acquisitions of science, including the results of unhampered Biblical criticism; the rejection of all 'mythological' dogmas such as the doctrines of the Trinity, the two natures in Christ, satisfaction, and original sin; the principle of tolerance; the ethos of disposition and of openness towards the world, as distinguished from the casuistic ethos of deeds and self-centered preoccupation with one's own salvation.

The most important point for this study is the conception of revelation and faith. Revelation does not imply any heteronomy. Always and everywhere it is at work in man's existential relation to the world, although in such events as the appearance of Christ, there may be a greater concentration of it. But it never presents itself merely from without; it cannot be known first and afterward acknowledged: 'The acknowledgment of revelation comes before the knowledge of its content, not the other way around.'[67] Faith consequently is 'a subjective act . . . not an intellectual but an existential acknowledgment.'[68]

Nevertheless, the new liberal Protestantism differs from the old in that it can no longer believe in a one-sided optimistic view of things. Ultimate reality presents itself as an inscrutable abyss. There is in the world, in man, and in God Himself a dark side that is beyond human comprehension. The history of the world is not the immanent growth of the kingdom of God. But man can work in the world with an eye to the kingdom, doing his best to establish a state of peace and justice. Christ is the revelation of divine love inviting man to live according to the requirements of the kingdom.

> God's coming out from the complete enigma of the *coincidentia oppositorum* in order to show us the direction; the light that shines in the dark; the appearance of the *deus revelatus* in the *deus absconditus*; all this we call the event of Christ. The event of Christ is the announcement and the realization of divine love as the unambiguous eschatological power in the divided world, pointing us to a meaning.[69]

The attitude of the new liberalism is that of a non-speculative *docta ignorantia* with regard to the ultimate nature of things but amidst the encircling gloom Christ is our 'kindly light.'

The same experiences that awoke liberal theology from the happy dream of historical optimism led to a far more important event in the history of Protestant theology: the radical revolution of the so-called dialectical theologians against the religious views that came from Schleiermacher. Dialectical theology stressed the infinite difference between God and man. Against the presuppositions of liberal theology it opposed two presuppositions of its own, a negative and a positive one complementing each other. According to the first there is no way that leads from natural man to God. Religion considered as a self-directing movement of man toward God is condemned as impossible and to attempt it as idolatrous. According to the second, God manifests Himself to man as a saving God through Christ, and through Him alone, so that the only knowledge man has of God is what is disclosed in the Bible.

This is a fundamental point on which Bultmann fully agrees with Barth. But he differs from Barth in asserting that in man himself there must be, previous to the hearing of the Word, an opening by which the Word might enter human existence. In describing that point of contact, Bultmann makes use of Heidegger's philosophy of existence. It must be noted, however, that Bultmann's conception of this point of contact in man radically differs from what liberal theology says to the question. It is not a special religious faculty or a sensibility to the divine. The relation of a natural man to God is one of contradiction, but contradiction precisely is not an absence of relation but a wrong relation. By his contradiction man is wholly alienated from God and consequently from himself and his fellow men. Hence the point of contact is the wound of rebellion that infects the whole of human existence. '*Man in his existence, man as a whole is the point of insertion*. And therefore it is true that in man there is no "religious" organ that is receptive to God's word in a particular way.'[70]

The role of Heidegger's philosophy in the theology of Bultmann is very different, then, from that of idealism in the theology of Schleiermacher. The latter interprets Christian doctrine positively in terms of his philosophy. The former does not interpret the message in philosophical terms at all, but he makes use of Heidegger's existential analysis in order to bring to man's consciousness the meaninglessness of his existence and to make him ask for a meaning. To ask for a meaning in a situation of meaninglessness is to ask for God and 'to ask for God is the same thing as to ask for myself.'[71] Without such a questioning about one's own existence man is unable to hear the Word of God. In that sense self-understanding (*Selbstverständnis*) is already a pre-understanding (*Vorverständnis*) of the Christian message.

Bultmann's existential analysis brings to the fore the contradictions in which man is enlaced. He is aware of his limitation and contingency, and this plunges him into the distress of daily life moving toward its inescapable end. Man has clear intimations of truth and beauty, desiring to take hold of them, but even the highest moments of insight and delight wear away. He longs for love but is confined within the walls of insuperable isolation. He hears within him the voice of conscience, but the same voice condemns his incurable sinfulness.

In such a situation God must appear as a dark and fiendish

power that thrusts man into the despair of existential contradiction. Faith is a radical reversal by which man hopefully turns to God, believing that He forgives or takes away sin and opens for man the possibility of a new existence. What do sin and new existence consist in? 'Sin is not immorality but consists in man's pretension to exist by himself, to dispose of himself, to take his life in his own hands. It is *superbia*, the desire to be like God.'[72] That will of 'self-existence' locks him up in himself and makes it impossible to go out and to live for others. Consequently, the new existence is a giving up of self-will, committing of one's life to God alone, accepting existence as an existence for others: 'The New Testament mentions and faith acknowledges an intervention of God through which alone surrender, faith, love, or authentic human life become possible.'[73]

It is interesting to note the similarity and the difference between Bultmann and Schleiermacher. To both of them salvation is a transition from selfishness to selfless love. But according to the latter that transition, which in the course of history begins with Christ, is a stage in an immanent process of evolution through the growth in humanity of the Spirit, who from the start is working in all things. To Bultmann, however, the transition is a dramatic turning from a state of existential and sinful estrangement from God to a new existence in love worked in man not from within but from without.

According to Bultmann, then, the existential revolution is effected by an act of God, namely revelation, to which man freely responds by the act of faith. What, then, does revelation mean and in what does faith consist?

Revelation is not something that took place in the past. It always happens here and now to the individual. To be sure, something of decisive importance happened with Christ. His significance is eschatological. He is 'the crisis, the turning-point of the aeons. Through Him our history acquired the possibility of being qualified by love instead of hate.'[74] What happened in Christ forever offers to mankind the possibility of a new existence. Therefore, 'grace and forgiveness are nothing else but the fact that the history in which we exist is qualified through the crisis that took place in Christ. We are asked whether we are willing to belong to the new aeon of love or if we prefer to stay in hate and death.'[75]

Consequently revelation is not a doctrine about God and salvation handed down from the past. It is something that may happen to us when hearing the kerygma or message. The hearing of the kerygma is the only essential condition for faith and conversion. The kerygma proclaims that the new existence, which manifested itself in Christ, becomes a possibility here and now through God's grace of forgiveness. Revelation, accepted by faith, does not add any new knowledge to the store of man's religious conceptions. It is not an objective piece of information but an existential happening and asks for an existential decision. The existential happening of revelation is accomplished by God who makes the word of the preacher a word for me, compelling me to a decision for or against.

For the same reason Christ in the flesh, or the historical Jesus, whose life is recorded in the writings of the NT, is not something to be concerned about. Bultmann indulges in the most radical skepticism in matters of historical criticism. Let the bridges burn. It does not affect him. As historical facts, the life, death, and Resurrection of Christ are of no interest to the believer. Leave the facts to the science of history. The only thing that matters is the meaning of Christ who is here and now revealed through the mediation of the kerygma. The meaning of life is not to be found in history. 'The meaning of history always lies in your present. You cannot perceive it as an observer but only in your responsible decisions. In each moment slumbers the possibility of being the eschatological moment.'[76] The only thing that matters is *that* it happened, not *how* it happened or how it can be proved. One should not look in history for Christ, the crucified and glorified Lord. 'Christ crucified and risen comes to meet us in the word of the preaching and in nothing else.'[77] This does not imply that it is unimportant whether the events occurred, but that we recognize them not through historical investigation but in the very act of faith, which is at once an existential act of apprehension and a decision.

Faith, then, is both an act of apprehending or being apprehended and an act of surrender, a decision. It is not an apprehension on which the decision then follows in time as an act of free choice: 'Faith does not at all rest on a decision which I can think over. It is a decision, i.e., in the act of hearing I have already decided how I hear.'[78] This decision about the *how* is made possible by my self-understanding, the understanding of my situation, but it is not caused by it.

The text does not give me knowledge of any astonishing discoveries, or of things already existent but hitherto unknown to me; it imparts no knowledge of unknown incidents. But possibilities of my own self are disclosed to me which I can understand only insofar as I am open to my possibilities and will to let myself be open. I cannot simply accept what is said as information; for I understand it only by affirming or denying. This does not mean that I first understand and then take a position. The understanding comes about only in affirming or denying. . . . Understanding, therefore, is always simultaneously resolve, decision.[79]

Revelation and existential faith are strictly correlative. The *fides quae creditur* cannot be separated from the *fides qua creditur*. To reduce faith to the acceptance of an orthodox doctrine (*fides quae creditur*) proposed from without and to deduce the *fides quae creditur* from within, from a religious experience or act (*fides qua creditur*), as Schleiermacher tried to do, are two enterprises that are equally absurd. The objective moment is only grasped in the existential acts and the existential act cannot happen except as determined by its object proposed by the preaching. Hence the importance of preaching in the theology of Bultmann. The fundamental law of preaching is adaptation. If it be true that man is an historical being, living under intellectual conditions determined by the whole situation of human life and its corresponding worldview, then it follows that the message cannot reach him as long as it is not proposed to him in terms of his own age and culture. The task of interpreting the word of the message in present-day language is the proper object of theology. From its very nature theology is hermeneutical: an endeavor to translate the Gospel in such a way that it can be heard by contemporary listeners. Theology is not faith, for faith is not in our power. Theology, on the contrary, 'is nothing else but a scientific reflection on our own existence as determined by God: it is thus a scientific unfolding of something which is already there in simple faith.'[80] It belongs to theology to work out the kerygma in contemporary language. The success of the preacher will not depend on the power of his personality but on the quality of his theological training.

The hermeneutical task of theology has a negative side. Bultmann calls it 'demythologizing.' The way in which the Christian message is proposed in the writings of the NT is connected with the historical background of a mythological worldview: the world is constantly interfered with by mysterious entities that come into it from below (hell) or from above (heaven). Patristic theology interpreted the Gospel in terms of Platonic metaphysics, adapted to the Hellenistic milieu. Such worldviews are definitively antiquated. Man can no longer live and think in a world made of myths. The message has to be freed from all mythological or metaphysical elements and proposed in terms that match the scientific worldview of the present. This does not imply that the substance of the Gospel is tied to the world of contemporary science. That world too may pass away. But in order to be heard, the theological way of proposing the Gospel must now take account of the modern worldview. The essence of revelation and faith, which is a happening, does not depend on any human self-understanding or world-understanding. The only thing that matters and that can never be demythologized is the existential happening in which man recognizes and accepts the forgiveness of sins and enters into the new aeon of Christ and love.

Looking back on the position of Bultmann it can clearly be seen that by his radical rejection of all forms of immanentism or mysticism, he cannot be reckoned among the supporters of liberal theology. But it is equally evident that by reducing the essence of Christianity to the existential happening of revelation and faith, removing from it all dogmatic propositions, he is aligned with liberalism. Bonhoeffer clearly pronounced the verdict: 'Bultmann would seem to have felt Barth's limitations in some way, but he misconstrues them in the light of liberal theology, and hence goes into the typical reduction process (the "mythological" elements of Christianity are dropped and Christianity is reduced to its "essence").'[81]

In a posthumous work already quoted, P. Tillich says: 'I feel that on most points I am on Bultmann's side. But he does not know the meaning of myth.'[82] The comparison between Bultmann and Tillich is perhaps the most convenient way to approach the latter's thought. The analogies are striking enough, but in each similarity there is also a profound dissimilarity owing to a radical difference in their philosophical outlook. Bultmann radically opposes Schleiermacher, whereas Tillich is, as he says, 'thoroughly on the side of Schleiermacher'[83] in opposition to dialectical theology. Or rather he tries to transcend the opposition between the two types of theology, as he says in *The Protestant Era*.

The first point concerns the general conception of philosophy and theology and their relation to science. For both Bultmann and

Tillich there is a radical distinction between science, historical and physical, on the one hand, and philosophy with theology, on the other hand. Science has to do with the establishment of facts. It gives information about things of the world. The object of philosophy and theology is not a category of facts but the implications of an existential experience the truth of which is entirely different from any kind of factual truth. Therefore, 'science has no right and no power to interfere with another dimension.'[84] But Tillich differs widely from Bultmann in defining the nature of philosophy and its relation to theology. Philosophy is not an analysis of human existence although such an analysis is part of it. Its proper subject is 'Being' or 'Ultimate Reality,' which is the true object of man's 'Ultimate Concern.' Being is not a particular object alongside the objects science is interested in. It is that which gives meaning to all objects and human endeavors because it is the creative power that works and manifests itself in them all. Now the object of faith is the same. Faith is the state of being ultimately concerned; its object is God or Absolute Being. But the attitude of the philosopher toward Being is different from that of the theologian. Philosophy strives for objectivity. To be sure, the genuine philosopher is ultimately concerned, but as far as he is a philosopher his starting point and aim are not a personal commitment but 'a clear and detached observation of the way ultimate reality manifests itself in the processes of the universe.'[85] Therefore, its tools are concepts and its truth consists in true concepts concerning the ultimate. Theology, however, is *fides quaerens intellectum*. Its starting point and aim are a definite commitment (e.g., the Christian commitment), and it points to the ultimate by means of symbols in which the ultimate is existentially reached. This calls to mind Hegel's distinction between religion and philosophy. It follows, then, that revelation, although it may come to man through historical facts, is not a revelation of facts but of meanings that could as well be disclosed in other facts. Faith, in its turn, includes certitude about its historical foundations—certain facts—'but faith does not include historical knowledge about the way in which this event took place.'[86] If historical research demonstrated that there was never a man called Jesus and of Jewish origin, then 'he had some other name' and 'we should then go to some other city;' for 'the personal reality behind the Gospel story is convincing. It shines through.'[87] So he can say with Bultmann, 'I am a great sceptic with respect to historical research into the life of Jesus.'[88] That we are sure of the existence of Christ, Tillich explains by means of a distinction between facts and their reception. 'The event includes both the fact and the reception. The fact has the power of impressing itself on the disciples in such way that historical images occur.'[89] The fact can be attained in the records of the impression it made, even if the fact in its historical concreteness cannot be established by historical science.

The knowledge of faith is not informative. Revelation is a breaking in of the infinite into the finite, a manifestation of ultimate reality in certain occurrences. Now the infinite or ultimate reality is something we always know because it is working in the very springs of conscious life (this is Schleiermacher's 'transcendental'). It is possible not to acknowledge it expressly, or even to deny it. It may be connected, too, with relative values such as a particular nation or party—this is idolatry—but it is always recognized implicitly in the very fact of being ultimately concerned. Revelation, then, which makes the infinite recognizable in an existential experience, does not add to one's information. The only new knowledge acquired in revelation is the consciousness of its own experiential happening: 'Knowledge of revelation is knowledge about the revelation of the mystery of being to us, not information about the nature of things and their relation to one another. Therefore the knowledge of revelation can be received only in the situation of revelation, and it can be communicated—in contrast to ordinary knowledge—only to those who participate in this situation.'[90] Bultmann could subscribe to this, but his theological background is entirely different.

Revelation always takes place here and now; it is not history. The facts that have revelational value may belong to the past—thus the event of Jesus. However, they only acquire the value of revelation in the act of their meaning being apprehended and recognized by faith; this is in accordance with Bultmann. But the facts that convey the revelation of the ultimate may be of any kind because the ultimate is at work in all things and events. It may 'cut into the temporal . . . by elevating a piece of it out of the ordinary context of temporal things and events, making it translucent for the divine glory.'[91] 'You may encounter it in one sentence of a book or of a conversation or of a lecture, or even of a sermon. Or you may be grasped by the truth in an encounter with a piece of nature-beauty and its transitoriness; or the encounter with a human being

in friendship and estrangement . . . ; or in an encounter with yourself in the sudden insight into the hidden strivings of your soul . . .'[92]
Some facts such as the appearance of Jesus in history have a privileged revelational value. But the ultimate may reveal itself by any
channel of experience. This entails that there be revelation and faith
in other religions as well as in Christianity. Such a position runs
counter to dialectical theology, according to which Christ is the
only fact in which God's forgiveness addresses itself to man, so that
faith is only possible as a response to the proclamation of that fact.
The humorous note in the quotation just given ('. . . or even of a
sermon') indicates how Tillich relativizes the value of preaching.

Revelation addresses itself not only to individual minds,
inviting them to conversion, but also to groups or generations,
manifesting itself in the existential experience of a line of action
by which they collectively respond to a given situation. Such was
the movement of Christian Socialism for the generation of Tillich
himself in Germany after the First World War. All this is closely
connected with the immanentistic and dialectical view of history
as presented by Hegel and the romantic idealists. History is the
dynamism of creative being guided by the immanent spirit that somehow realizes itself in the rhythm of action and reaction.

Tillich comes very near to Bultmann in his stress on the apologetic function of theology. Tillich, like Bultmann, is deeply concerned with the problem of how to bring to men the message
of salvation. He employs a Socratic method in order to make
them conscious of their actual situation of estrangement and to
make the question of God arise from their own hearts. This is an
application of what he calls the principle or method of correlation, a general principle with Tillich and the backbone of his
theological system. It determines the method of reconciliation of
opposites and has something to do with the dialectical method. Man
is entirely dependent upon God, who is entirely independent of
him. But through creation God gives to man freedom and independence, and thus He makes Himself dependent upon man: we
are men-for-God but He makes Himself God-for-us. In that correlation man freely answers God's acts, and God reacts upon that
answer provoking new responses from man. This becomes particularly clear in the relation between God and man in the situation of
faith. 'Man is the question, not the answer. It is equally wrong to
derive the question implied in human existence from the revelatory

answer. This is impossible because the revelatory answer is meaningless if there is no question to which it is the answer.'[93] Therefore, 'symbolically speaking, God answers man's questions, and under the impact of God's answers, man asks them. Theology formulates the questions implied in human existence, and theology formulates the answers implied in divine self-manifestation under the guidance of the questions implied in human existence. This is a circle which drives man to a point where question and answer are not separated.'[94] In formulating the questions of man, the theologian acts as a philosopher; in formulating the answers of God, he acts the part of the theologian. But the two enterprises never mix together. 'As a theologian he does not tell himself what is philosophically true. As a philosopher he does not tell what is theologically true.'[95] Question and answer meet and match, but they remain independent and cannot be deduced from one another. This is strikingly similar to Blondel's method in *La philosophie et l'esprit chrétien*; but Blondel, who is a philosopher, calls his method a properly philosophical method whereas Tillich, the theologian, awards the whole enterprise to theology. The general similarity to Bultmann's apologetical theology is evident, but how different is the systematic context!

The two theologians also hold similar views concerning the question of sin and salvation; but here too Tillich tries a via media between Bultmann and Schleiermacher. Man and the whole of his historical life, collective as well as individual, incessantly spring from infinite Being together with all the things of nature. The state of salvation consists in the unbroken harmony with the whole. Harmony on the level of the person is love; but through the relative independence of his free will, man may go astray and sever himself from the universal fountain of Being. This is the condition of fallen man. 'Sin means the power that separates from God; it is a demonic power.'[96] That separation is threefold: man is separated from the ground of his being and at the same time he breaks the harmony with the universe and is separated from his fellow men and from his own being, which is only 'true being' to the extent that it is rooted in 'Being itself.' The state of sin is a state of nothingness. Sinful separation from God is a state in which man finds himself—symbolized by the myth of original sin—before he accomplishes it by his own sinful actions. Sin is not only a perversion of the will but also of man's whole consciousness and knowledge.

Salvation, then, consists in a universal reconciliation operated by the recovery of man's 'being in God.' That recovery is the 'New Being.' It is a conversion of the will together with a change in man's view of things and especially of other persons: 'There is only one way to know a personality—to be united with that personality through love. Full knowledge presupposes full love. God knows me, because He loves me; and I shall know Him face to face through a similar uniting, which is love and knowledge at the same time. . . . In love, the seeing face to face and the knowledge of the center of the other I are implied.' Because man's love in historical existence is always imperfect his knowledge is also imperfect: 'A little light and much darkness; a few fragments and never the whole; many problems and never a solution; only reflections in the mirrors of our souls, without the source of truth itself; that is the situation of our knowledge.'[97] The difference from Bultmann is evident.

In an earlier quotation we read 'symbolically speaking, God answers man's question. . . .' This brings up the most characteristic piece of Tillich's religious epistemology. Like Jaspers in *Die Frage der Entmythologisierung* (Munich, 1954), Tillich reproaches Bultmann for his elimination of myths. In doing so, however, he, not unlike Jaspers, shifts further in the direction of radical liberal theology. For Bultmann there was one essential point that could never be demythologized: the decision for or against authentic existence under the impact of Christ, who assures the forgiveness of sin and the possibility of entering the new aeon. Tillich objects: 'This is a symbolic or mythological way of speaking.'[98] In other words, all that man says about God is mythological. God is not a particular being but Being itself to which all beings symbolically point:

> If God as the ground of being infinitely transcends everything that is, two consequences follow: first, whatever one knows about a finite thing one knows about God, because it is rooted in Him as its ground; second, anything one knows about a finite thing cannot be applied to God, because He is, as has been said 'quite other' . . . The unity of these two divergent consequences is the analogous or symbolic knowledge of God. A religious symbol uses the material of ordinary experience in speaking of God, but in such a way that the ordinary meaning of the material used is both affirmed and denied. Every religious symbol negates itself in its literal meaning but it affirms itself in its self-transcending meaning.[99]

This text is particularly clear. Its pure epistemological tenor does not essentially differ from the doctrine of Aquinas on the analogy of the divine names. But the ontology in which it is rooted is entirely different, and this entails all-important consequences, as will be shown presently.

Is there no proposition about God that is not symbolic as, according to Bultmann, there is a content in faith that cannot be demythologized? It seems that the statements of Tillich on the point are not wholly consistent. For in Volume One of his *Systematic Theology* he writes: 'The statement that God is being-itself is a non-symbolic statement. It does not point beyond itself. It means what it says directly and properly.'[100] In the introduction to Volume Two, however, where he restates his fundamental assertions in the face of criticism, he says that the only non-symbolic assertion about God is 'the statement that everything we say about God is symbolic.'[101] The solution seems to lie in some passages in his later work on the meaning of the word *God*: 'God is symbol for God. This means that in the notion of God we must distinguish two elements: the element of ultimacy, which is a matter of immediate experience and non-symbolic in itself, and the element of concreteness, which is taken from our ordinary experience and symbolically applied to God.'[102] This settles the question. All propositions about God, because they objectify the logical subject and the predicate, giving them a concreteness that fits only finite beings, are symbolic. Only the intuition to which they symbolically point is not symbolic. 'Being itself,' then, is as symbolic as 'God.' This is the same, of course, as Schleiermacher's doctrine of limit concepts. They properly signify something inner-wordly, but symbolically they point to a beyond that cannot be objectified.

This is the crucial point of Tillich's theology: on the one hand, all finite things and events, because they participate in infinite Being, may become revelatory symbols pointing man to that Being and to his participation in it; on the other hand, no finite being or event is able to represent God in a non-symbolic way. This carries momentous consequences in Christology. It is impossible that in Christ the infinite itself should enter into history as identical with a finite person in a way that is qualitatively different from the participation that is proper to all finite persons. It is impossible that real happenings, such as His life, death, and Resurrection, should have a revelatory meaning different in kind from other events in

which God discloses Himself: 'All the actions, past, present and
future . . . are symbols taken from our daily experience, and not
information about what God did once upon a time or will do
sometime in the future. Faith is not the belief in such stories, but it
is the acceptance of symbols that express our ultimate concern in
terms of divine actions.'[103] And: 'If Christ—a transcendent, divine
being—appears in the fullness of time, lives, dies and is resurrected,
this is an historical myth.'[104] Jesus is only unique through His sinlessness: 'In the picture of the New Testament we have temptation
and tragedy, but we have no estrangement from God in any moment
in the life of Jesus as it is pictured.'[105] 'For this reason I have called
Jesus as the Christ the center of history. I mean that here, at one
decisive point, the relation between God and finite man was not
interrupted.'[106] 'There is no convincing theological reason to say
that some saints did not attain to the same sinlessness as Christ.'[107]
This goes beyond even Schleiermacher and seems to imply that
despite his denials Tillich's theology is but a philosophy of religion
with a special preference for Christian symbols or myths. The
Christian symbolic tales or myths about Christ are true not in the
literal exoteric meaning, which common sense attaches to them, but
in a symbolic esoteric meaning, which the sophisticated philosopher reads into them.

But then, of course, it must theoretically be possible that
Christianity, as qualified by Christ, should pass away in the course
of history without losing its essential identity. Myths cannot be
made, cannot be invented. They have power over man, he has no
power over them. But in the changing conditions of historical
existence they may die, as for instance in Protestant Christianity the
'Virgin cult' and 'the doctrine of atonement in terms of the substi-
tutional suffering.'[108] Why not the whole story of Christ? Tillich
can by no means justify the assertion that the myth of Christ is
immortal.

The system of Tillich is on the whole entirely consistent. It
rests upon his existential dynamic ontology according to which
Being cannot rest in itself but has to enter into existence, i.e., a
temporal, contingent way of being. Being contains 'non-being' in
itself, and therefore it cannot but go out of itself in creative action
by which it constantly asserts itself and overcomes its own non-
being. Such is Tillich's interpretation of Schelling's ontology. The
whole movement of finite existence is the continuous and necessary

self-expression of Being itself. Therefore, the pattern of its development is determined by the nature of its own immanent movement. God is not that sovereign independent being resting in its own inner life and freely creating the finite world as an expression of love. He does not remain really independent with respect to His creation. Therefore, He cannot freely enter into its development as if from without, i.e., in a way not determined by the inner necessity of His immanent process in finite being. Therefore, salvation history and the appearance of Christ cannot be conceived of as free deeds of God that vertically interfere with the horizontal immanent movement of history. Incarnation and Resurrection are symbols and myths, attached to certain facts. The significant tales did not happen as narrated, i.e., as real supernatural events.

Tillich is a metaphysical theologian, but his metaphysical views are those of idealism. This makes all the difference between Tillich and, say, Thomas Aquinas. According to both of them one can signify the reality of God only by means of representations taken from the order of finite being. The reality they point to (*res significata*) properly belongs to God, but the finite representations that necessarily determine man's way of signifying God (*modus significandi*) cannot be properly ascribed to God; and therefore they must be denied in the very act of using them as indicators. To both theologians finite being is a participation in infinite being. The act of creation is not a magical trick calling forth the world of things from a nothingness outside God. Men are not distinguished from God in virtue of the being they have, but in virtue of that lack of being that constitutes their finiteness. But Tillich seems to explain creation by a non-being at the heart of Being itself so that Being has in itself a necessity of creation that does not depend on its own sovereign will. Being lives in becoming. To Thomas Aquinas, however, God is pure being, pure act or power of being. He has in Himself a perfect infinite life. If He is necessarily and unchangeably God, and consequently Creator—for His being Creator cannot be contingent in Him—it is not because something in His nature, independent of His will, makes him Creator. As absolute being He is absolute freedom. If He cannot but be Creator, it is because His being absolute freedom is the same thing as His being perfect love. If this is so, then God may initiate an economy of salvation reuniting sinful and estranged man to Himself in a way that, looked at from below, seems to interfere with the immanent course of things established by Himself. This is the historical Incarnation of God. It seems to be a vertical interference or an interference from without only in reference to the course of creation. For the meaning of creation is the perfect manifestation of divine love. Therefore, it is an anthropomorphism to say that the Incarnation, even literally conceived, interferes from without or vertically with the process of creation. Redemptive Incarnation is not so much included in creation as creation is included in the Incarnation. For the supreme revelation of God's love is the aim of creation and consequently its true and final reality. What is called creation independently of Incarnation is entirely directed toward that Incarnation and has no final meaning without it. Therefore, Jesus is not only the center of history but as the redeeming God He is also the circumference including in itself the whole of history and nature. Here, then, two ways of metaphysical thought, that from the start determine the relation between the finite and the infinite in different ways, confront each other. Tillich's liberal theology depends on his metaphysical preconceptions. If he tried to bridge the gulf between Schleiermacher and dialectical theology, between immanentistic mysticism and existential transcendentalism, he did not really succeed. He did not go beyond Schleiermacher.

If one starts with the liberal principle that as a source and a rule of knowledge faith has no rights of its own but must simply be accommodated to the philosophy of the day, then every turn in the philosophical mood of this civilization will bring about a new type of liberal theology. Consequently it was to be expected that the predominant trend in contemporary Anglo-Saxon philosophy, the so-called Philosophy of Analysis, which sprang from a protest of common sense against idealism (Moore) and from the logical positivism of the school of Vienna, should produce its own variation on the theme of liberal theology.

The main influence at work behind the new theological movement is that of the philosopher L. Wittgenstein. His personal thought was characterized by a sense of clarity combined with mysticism. In his *Tractatus logico-philosophicus* he argues that among the general statements about reality only those of experimental science are meaningful because they alone can be verified. But he adds that there is an unspeakable reality that can only be attained by silent intuition. The principle from which he started was the 'verification principle,' according to which the meaning of any statement is given by the method of its verification. If so, moral statements too seemed meaningless. But this contradicts common sense. Therefore, Wittgenstein in a posthumous work, *Philosophical Investigations* (1953), corrected his definition of the verification principle or changed it to the principle of use: the meaning of any statement is given by the way in which it is used. This is rather vague. The common-sense interpretation of the principle would be that the use of a proposition is determined by the object it is used to signify: and then it is an innocent truism. The real point, however, is this: How to determine what a given sentence states? To specify the use of a sentence is to describe the situations, the states of affairs by which the statement it expresses would be verified. Probably Wittgenstein himself went beyond that stage of his philosophy, but it is difficult to determine.

In 1955 R. B. Braithwaite published a lecture *An Empiricist's View of the Nature of Religious Belief*, in which he applied the principle of use to religious statements; he reduced them to moral statements. Moral statements do not express emotions but intentions to act in a certain way. Consequently, 'the meaning of a religious assertion is given by its use in expressing the asserter's intention to follow a specified policy of behaviour.'[109] Religious statements differ from moral ones in that they refer to a whole system of which any particular statement is representative. In such a system, objective statements do not mean to say something about reality, but only about the intention to act according to a certain rule. Thus the Christian's assertion that God is love (agape) declares 'his intention to follow an agapeistic way of life.'[110] In order to realize the meaning of a man's pattern of behavior, he expresses it in the concrete form of stories. For the Christian the regulative stories are those of the Bible. One need not assert their historical truth but rather live according to their exemplary moral value. Thus, 'a religious assertion, for me, is the assertion of an intention to carry out a certain behavior policy, subsumable under a sufficient general principle to be a moral one, together with the implicit or explicit statement, but not the assertion, of certain stories.'[111]

T. R. Miles criticized the reduction of religious statements to moral statements. Objective religious statements points to something beyond one's moral intentions, but what that beyond is cannot be properly expressed in forms of human thought: 'His [Braithwaite's] stories are "mere stories", whereas here I am offering a doctrine not of "mere parables" but rather of silence qualified by parables."[112] This was rather an improvement on the original view of Wittgenstein.

In the meanwhile, a discussion was begun on the meaning of the statement of God's existence, starting from the new assumptions of the Philosophy of Analysis. It began with a paper of Prof. J. Wisdom on 'Gods' in *Philosophy and Psychoanalysis* (Oxford, 1953), contending that the factual assertion of God's existence could not be verified but that it nevertheless was meaningful and could be true. Its acceptance or rejection was a matter of feeling. He illustrated the impossibility of verifying such a statement by a parable about two explorers who find in the jungle a clearing that somehow seems to be a garden. One of them believes, the other disbelieves, that there must be a gardener. They wait and watch. No gardener shows up. 'Perhaps it is an invisible gardener,' the believer says. So they set up an electrified barbed wire fence. Nothing happens. Then the believer supposes that the gardener must be intangible too, without any sensible properties. The original statement is gradually qualified in such a way that at last it is beyond all possible verification. The parable led to a discussion between A. Flew and R. M. Hare published in *New Essays in Philosophical Theology*.[113] The former concluded that religious assertions, taken as statements about 'how things are,' are meaningless. Hare agreed to the point, but added that the Christian statements are not statements about 'how things are,' but something similar to those presuppositions that direct man's way of thinking, feeling, and acting without being verifiable or falsifiable, as, for instance, man's trust in nature's continued uniformity. They express man's slant, or 'blik' as Hare calls it, man's way of viewing existence as a whole connected with the basic attitude toward it.

A different approach was worked out by Ian T. Ramsey. He confronts the question. 'To what kind of statement does religion appeal?'[114] He answers that in certain situations objective structures of experience suddenly reveal a 'beyond' that is intuitively grasped. The objective structures do not contain the beyond, but in actual experience they point man toward it. Such objective structures may be real happenings or images suggested by linguistic symbols. Religious language is made up of objective statements that may become to the reader or the hearer an occasion for such an 'odd discernment,' bringing to the light of consciousness an intuition beyond the imagery. In a later work he calls this discernment 'cosmic disclosure' because in order to be religious the structure or pattern of reality disclosed by the imagery or the stories must have a universal significance, i.e., a significance that is related to the world as a whole and may be grasped by anyone in certain situations. So he says that 'the reference of any and every cosmic disclosure, i.e., a disclosure which is restricted to no finite pattern of spatio-temporal events as its centre, is the same, viz. God.'[115] Such a disclosure always implies a personal commitment. Certain tales evoke a discernment 'from which the commitment follows as a response.'[116] The situations, then, in which religious language functions may be called situations of 'discernment-commitment.'

Theology has to analyze the logical status of religious language and to present its objective 'models' in such a way that the disclosure may take place: 'The central problem of theology is how to use, how to qualify, observational language so as to be suitable currency for what in part exceeds it—the situations in which theology is founded.'[117] Thus, speaking of the significance of the Cross, various models are used, such as 'justification,' 'substitution,' 'satisfaction,' 'reconciliation,' 'redemption,' 'propitiation,' and 'expiation.' These models, if applied literally according to ordinary logic, describe procedural transactions, 'a species of atonement engineering,' and as such they become absurd. They are only models or 'metaphors,' to be used in such a way as 'to point us to a cosmic disclosure around the Cross and to give us hints for reliable talking about what is disclosed.'[118]

The word *God* functions in a way similar to the word *I*. I cannot be separated from its context. It therefore connotes more, and that 'more' cannot be described. So too—

> for the religious man 'God' is a key word, an irreducible posit, an ultimate explanation expressive of the kind of *commitment* he professes. It is to be talked about in terms of the object-language . . . but only when this object-language is qualified, in which case, this qualified object-language becomes also currency for that odd *discernment* with which religious *commitment, when it is not bigotry or fanaticism, will necessarily be* associated.[119]

This is something altogether different from the position of Braithwaite. Ramsey does not mean that the 'stories' are only

expressive of a commitment or intention but that they point to a
disclosure of real structures on which commitment follows. Neither
does he mean that the Cross of Christ around which the cosmic
disclosure happens is not to be held as an historical event. The
intuition evoked by the models supposes the fact but reveals its
significance. Lastly, the cognitive element in the disclosure is not
only the objectified model but the model together with the significance that is disclosed by it. A religious statement or dogma, being
an inadequate expression of a deeper reality, may be conceived of as
true and unchangeably true, not as to the particular model that is
used, but as to the combination of different possible models with
what is disclosed and intuitively grasped in them. For these reasons,
Ramsey has nothing to do with liberal theology.

Not so with Paul van Buren. He takes from Ramsey the idea
of 'disclosure-commitment'; but what is thus disclosed is not conceived by him as a deeper metaphysical dimension of the real, but
only as 'the Christian's historical perspective': a way of viewing
history in the light of a faith in the possibility of a social pattern for
men who, under the contagious impact of Jesus, have become free
to exist for one another. Van Buren substantially agrees with Braithwaite's view that religious statements are assertions of an intention
to act in a certain way, assertions in the garb of certain stories. But
'we would clarify the "intention" with such words as "discernment
and commitment;" and we would define the "certain way" as a
response to and a reflection of the way of Jesus of Nazareth' (van
Buren, p. 145). The intention, then, is not a mere choice but a
choice or commitment arising from a personal experience or discernment and that discernment-commitment leads to a way of
viewing things and history as a whole (Hare's 'blik'). The objective
element round which it takes place is not a set of stories but an
historical fact: the life of Christ and the impression it made on His
disciples. Here van Buren comes near to Tillich, although his
language is altogether different. According to Tillich, Christ was
the sinless man who never was separated from the ground of Being
and consequently never fell into selfish isolation from others. Van
Buren simply says that 'this man . . . though fully man and in no
sense "more than a man," is not to be confused with other men.
He stood apart from them for the very reason of his solidarity with
them: he was the one man who truly existed for others' (van Buren,
p. 54). Tillich says that Jesus must be an historical person, but the

methods of history are insufficient to verify the historical facts about Him. His personality shines through the impressive power He exercised on His disciples so that historical images occurred. Van Buren says that something happened with Jesus and because of this the disciples were changed and 'caught up in something like the freedom of Jesus himself, having become men who were free to face even death without fear. Whatever it was that lay in between, and which might account for this change, is not open to our historical investigation. The evidence is insufficient. All we can say is that something happened' (van Buren, p. 128). That something is an event that led to the 'story' of Easter.

The theology of van Buren is entirely Christocentric whereas that of Tillich is rather theocentric. 'Whatever men were looking for in looking for "God" is to be found by finding Jesus of Nazareth' (van Buren, p. 147). The difference is significant. The philosophical presuppositions of Tillich are those of idealism. God, or 'Being itself,' cannot but be the central notion. Van Buren, however, starts with the use-principle of Wittgenstein; therefore, a sentence about God cannot have any meaning to him. If indeed 'statements of faith are to be interpreted, by means of the modified verification principle, as statements which express, describe, or commend a particular way of seeing the world, other men, and oneself, and the way of life appropriate to such a perspective' (van Buren, p. 156), then the use of the word *God* in any statement is either meaningless or misleading: 'The word *God* has been avoided because it equivocates and misleads. It seems to be a proper name, calling up the image of a divine entity, but it refuses to function as any other proper name does' (van Buren, p. 145).

It is said that this is not atheism. Indeed, if atheism is the negation of the proposition 'God exists,' then van Buren cannot be an atheist because according to his principles any proposition about God as a divine being is meaningless. The proposition 'God does not exist' is as meaningless as the proposition 'God exists.' But it is meaningless precisely because all talk about metaphysical entities is nonsense. What all men understand when they hear the word 'God' (*id quod omnes intelligunt Deum,* as Thomas Aquinas says) is a divine being or a transcendent creator. If van Buren is to be judged according to common-sense language, it is difficult to see in what sense he really differs from an atheist. It is not agnosticism because any proposition in which agnosticism is formulated is nonsensical too. The only possible escape would be to say that the possibilities of language are not coextensive with those of reality, that there is or may be a 'beyond language,' about which one must be silent. 'Undoubtedly Jesus believed he was obeying some "one," whom he called the "Father," but the Gospel of John, as well as the logic of language, forces us to silence before all questions concerning that "one" ' (van Buren, p. 148). This is, of course, a contradictory statement because, according to John, the Father was undoubtedly a divine being, whereas according to van Buren's logic of language it is not only impossible to say something about the some 'one,' but it has no meaning at all to use the word *Someone* for the 'X' that Jesus believed He was obeying. If there is a mystery that shines through Jesus and about which no significant proposition can be made, if one accepts van Buren's verification principle, why could it not be indicated by the word *God*, even if it could not be conceived as a some 'one'? For Tillich also the word *God* does not point to a divine being existing along with other beings. He is Being itself. Why does van Buren not say that there is a mystery beyond language that is not the man Jesus Himself but that shines through Him? The only answer seems to be that his philosophy does not admit of such a mystery and that he considers the realm of language to be coextensive with the realm of consciousness or, perhaps, of what exists. Again, what is the difference between such a position and atheism?

Most puzzling about van Buren is the way he accepts his presupposition. 'We set out upon this study with some acknowledged commitments to what we called "Secular thought," and we said that secularism, as we were using the term, is grounded in empirical attitudes in some way' (van Buren, p. 83). To him, the verification principle, which he thinks is the head and front of the Philosophy of Analysis, seems to be a presupposition of the modern mind expressing the empirical attitude he alluded to. Why does he accept these presuppositions? Not so much, it would seem, because they are simply true as because in his estimation they must be the presuppositions of mankind in the present epoch of its evolution, determined by technology and the whole industrial process. Here he seems to make two blunders. First, secularism, considered not as an idea in the head of some philosophers but as a social fact, implies a refusal not of metaphysical beings but of some ways of relating them to human existence. Moreover, that existing secularism is not

even the actual attitude of the greatest part of contemporary mankind, even if 'mankind' refers only to the intellectual élite. This
has been brought to light by recent sociological investigations.

Next, the appeal of van Buren to the Philosophy of Analysis in
justifying his acceptance of the verification principle, as understood
by him, is by no means to the point. His principle of verification was
formulated indeed in the early stage of that philosophy and still
persists in some quarters; but it is vigorously attacked by a good
many of the Anglo-Saxon empiricists, and it is rather on the defen-
sive. This clearly appears from *Clarity Is Not Enough,* a collection
of *Essays in Criticism of Linguistic Philosophy,* mostly by supporters of that very philosophy. J. N. Finlay, for one, in 'Use, Usage
and Meaning,' subjects the use-principle to a devastating criticism
at least in its radical form, which tries 'to buttress a priori doctrines
as to what we must or cannot mean.'[120] C. K. Grant remarks that
'the verification principle is by no means beyond question, as is
now generally recognized.'[121] Even its main champion, A. J. Ayer,
grants that it 'suffers from a vagueness, which it has not yet been
found possible to eradicate.'[122] B. Blanshard entirely rejects it and
concludes: 'It is idle to tell us, on the strength of a preconceived
theory, that statements which everyone has been making for centuries and everyone recognizes as significant are really meaningless.'[123] It is at least naive, then, that a theologian should feel obliged
to construct a theology without God on so weak a basis in order
not to lose the audience of his believing flock.

From van Buren's general position there follows a definite view
on the subject of development. He amply treats the development of
Christology. The NT, he says, was written by men who had received,
along with the contagious experience of Christ's freedom, a new
perspective on life. But 'they proclaimed the good news in the form
of cosmological assertions about the world and the human situation which are meaningless to secular man. To affirm those assertions is to deny the character and tendency of modern thought
which the believers share with the rest of their society' (van Buren,
p. 157). This seems to imply that on the occasion of a 'something'
that happened and that was not the bodily Resurrection of Christ,
the disciples underwent an experience of contagious freedom,
which they expressed in the mythical tale of the Resurrection.
Now, the psychological process thus supposed is so improbable as
to be practically impossible. The disciples did not express a 'some-

thing' in the form of the Resurrection story; that story was the very thing that they believed in, considering it as the only foundation of their faith and their new view of history. It does not make sense to say that the disciples were equipped with brains that worked according to certain laws of perception and logical thought different from ours. Even primitive men do not think according to irrational patterns different from those of a citizen of New York. When they tell myths they know very well that they are not talking history. 'Specialists have been forced to recognize that there is a unity in the structure of man, and that the suggestion of an intellectual split which would separate one group of mankind [the primitives] from the other [the speaker *cum suis*] is quite artificial.'[124] It would be very curious that a man like Paul should have been beguiled into believing that a myth of his own creation was really an historical fact, as he obviously did.

It is the superficial manner of interpreting a truth worked out by contemporary philosophy that is all wrong: the truth that man is not simply a piece of nature but a piece of history written by himself in the context of nature and with the tools of nature; that he thus creates his world, a world of interpretations, and his way of existing; that there are shifts, and often radical changes, in his world and his pattern of life and thought; that the course of history is irreversible. It is insane, however, to conceive the great historical stages of human development as closed compartments, so that a man can no longer think the things that were thought by past generations. The myth-maker, the metaphysician, and the empiricist always dwelt and still dwell together in the same man. One of them may take the lead for a time, but no one of them can expel his mates. In every generation there are acute minds in whom one of those fundamental functions of eternal man prevails. All great poets are myth-makers; all really great philosophers are metaphysicians; all genuine scientists are empiricists. I do not say that they are exclusively but only that they are predominantly such. They represent the basic structures of the human mind. Their work may be disjointed, their influence limited, their views distorted by one-sidedness—the original sin of the thinking animal—but the functions are forever together and are potentially there in every man.

This fundamental insight van Buren fails to acknowledge. He does not find fault with the NT mythologists: they could do only what they did, living as they did in a cultural epoch in which it was impossible to distinguish experiences pointing to facts from experiences leading to myth-creating activity. Nor does he quarrel with the theologians of the patristic and medieval ages who tried to give a clear rational expression, in terms of a Hellenistic metaphysic, to the Christian interpretation of what happened in Christ. They achieved for their own age what had to be done, and they did it admirably well. But Christ can no longer be thought of as a substantial though unconfused unity of divine and human being. The assertion of Christ's human nature means that He must be spoken of in the language proper to the history of a mere man. The assertion of His divine nature has to be placed 'in the context of language appropriate to a freedom which has been contagious, and to the historical perspective which arises from a discernment situation' (van Buren, p. 168). In so doing, "we have found no simple correspondence between patristic christological terms and those of our own interpretation. There is a logical equivalence, however, of these two interpretations of the New Testament witness to Jesus Christ' (van Buren, p. 168). This is a muddle if ever there was one. The only thing that really mattered for the Fathers was the assertion that Christ was an eternal being, God in the same sense as the Father (*consubstantialis Patri*) without excluding His being a real man in the same sense as each of us, and that this union was required for man's salvation and was not 'a freedom to exist for others,' although it implied this, but a union with God, which, although it implies consequences for this present life, was no less than an eternal divinization. The logic of their language was such as to enable them to make such assertions. Between their Christology and that of van Buren there is no logical equivalence at all. If 'hermeneutic' be—as it is with van Buren and many others—the art of interpreting texts in such a way that the very meaning of those texts is dropped, then it would be better not to use the term *interpretation*, which means just the opposite according to common sense and the great philosophers who worked out the epistemological status of hermeneutic.

In van Buren, then, the liberal or transformistic conception of the development of doctrine reaches its most radical and most questionable expression.

K

CHAPTER NINE

The Theological Theory of Development

The relation between the logical theories of scholasticism and the transformistic theories of liberal theology is one of dialectical opposition. The difference is clear. According to the former theories, revelation is conceived of as merely propositional. What is communicated by it is a number of statements about God. These statements were given to mankind at a definite time in history, so that the Church in preaching the Gospel only speaks from memory. Faith, insofar as it is no more than faith, is not an experience but an intellectual assent given to a Creed. There may occur a kind of experience along the path of spiritual progress, faith being perfected by the gifts of intelligence and wisdom, but ordinary faith as related to its material object, or the elements of knowledge, is the acceptance of a doctrine and nothing else.

According to the latter theories, however, revelation is a spirit or a dynamic and directive idea that works in the inner regions of unconscious and conscious life, bringing forth fruits in the social world through the hidden power of its inspiration. Revelation considered in its essential nature is in no way a communication of propositions. It is an actual personal experience. Its relation to the past is only a relation to a person, Jesus of Nazareth, in whom the Spirit broke through and became manifest either for the first time or in an exemplary way, forever unsurpassable. To preach Christ is not to demand an assent to propositions about Him, but to confront men with His historical personality and the experience that shines through it, to point the hearer to the possibility of an experience and to invite him to make it his own. Conversion is not an intellectual change in doctrinal commitments but an experience that

changes the heart and consequently one's whole attitude toward
life. Of course, there are elements of doctrine. For without a doctrine there is no unity in the preaching of the Gospel and the social
structure of common life. However, doctrines are no more than
intellectual patterns. They are not expressions of faith itself in the
sense of objective truth, but they create a Christian worldview
inspired by faith and structured according to the cultural milieu
with its scientific knowledge and its philosophical interpretation of
the world and man. They are objective patterns in the same way as
social life-patterns, changing according to the stages of scientific
knowledge and industrial progress. These life-patterns as well may
be and ought to be expressions of faith and of the attitude of love
commanded by faith.

The opposition between the two positions just described is
dialectical, i.e., their relation to one another is not simply one of
historical parallelism. They are closely connected with each other
in a way that is called dialectical. They create and sustain each other
by their very opposition. The word *dialectic* means that within the
spontaneous movement of an undifferentiated original unity,
opposites are generated which tend to exclude one another yet at
the same time seek by their very nature a synthesis, that is, a reconciliation or restoration of unity on a higher level of greater differentiation. It is not necessary to adhere to a definite philosophy in
order to acknowledge the fact that a kind of dialectical structure
is proper to the movement of history. Whatever may be the philosophical explanation of the dialectical nature of the movement of
history, the immediate psychological causes have been very well
described by great minds such as Schlegel, Coleridge, and Newman.
In the realm of thought the possibility of dialectical opposition is
grounded in the very nature of human knowledge. Man's knowledge
of things is abstract: he cannot take in at once or encompass in one
view the whole of reality or of one of the minor wholes that are
part of reality, hence the possibility of a partial or one-sided
view. One works out one's idea of reality, picking out certain aspects
for attention and turning a blind eye to others. When the consequences of such a position are worked out at sufficient length, its
inadequacy will be felt in due course and confirmed by difficulties
in its practical application. Then an immanent revolution takes
place; the neglected aspects emerge in forms of reaction or protest. Carried away by its own impact, however, the movement of

reaction is in danger of falling into the opposite extreme. Thus one-sided views confront one another. In virtue of their one-sidedness, they tend to run away from each other. In virtue of their intrinsic complementarity, each is attracted to the other; they seek to reunite in their original unity.

If the possibility of dialectical opposition is founded in the abstract nature of human knowledge and thought, its actualization is no less influenced and fostered by human passion, weakness, pride, and stubbornness. Man, the rational animal, is almost by definition the exaggerating animal. This characteristic is rooted in the abstract nature of knowing, combined with the passional nature of his willing. When once he has made up his mind, adhering to certain views and acting upon them, man easily becomes a partisan, insensible and blind to truths and values that are beyond his perspective. He cannot enter into the views of his opponents; he cannot see as they see. The conflict hardens his mind, and thus opposite factions or tendencies arise that continually generate one another by the very fact of their contradiction. Such is the case in the relentless contemporary conflict between progressive and reactionary groups within the life of Catholic theology and public opinion.

This, then, is man's aboriginal weakness, the 'original sin' of his mind, as Schlegel calls it, so admirably expressed in the words of Coleridge: 'Every reform, however necessary, will by weak minds be carried to an excess, which will itself need reforming.'[1] This explains the to-and-fro movement of conflicting tendencies, each in turn overcome by or prevailing over its antagonist, failing to see the other's part of the truth. Whenever history notes this kind of pendular rhythm one may be sure that its origin lies in human weakness and that fresh efforts towards synthesis and comprehensiveness are required. The 'weak minds' Coleridge alluded to are not characterized by a lack of intelligence—they are often very acute and logical—but by a lack of that wisdom that is rooted in intellectual comprehensiveness and mental dispassionateness.

Looking back on the history of orthodox scholasticism and liberal theology with respect to this dialectical opposition, it is not difficult to discern a pendular rhythm in their historical relation. This is particularly clear in Protestant thought, where orthodox and liberal tendencies take turns in the lead, engaged as they are in unrelenting combat. In scholastic theology, where the traditional training has preserved a common ground, it is only after a certain time that an opposition is seen between two extreme forms of logical explanation, continually opposing one another and searching for reconciliation in a *via media*. It is only since Modernism that opposition has arisen again and again between classical orthodoxy and liberal trends of religious thought within the Catholic Church. Until Vatican Council II the liberal movement had simply been repressed by ecclesiastical authority, but it always emerged under new guises. Therefore men must consider the possibility of a middle way and look into history for precedents.

One final remark lest we be misunderstood. The description here of the dialectical interplay between conflicting opposites should not be taken to mean that those men who stood for logical or transformistic theories of development were unbalanced. What is true of movements as a whole cannot be said of the individuals that partake in them. Man is a social, historical being. He is not a separate self. His entire personality is embedded in a tradition. There may be many reasons why a given thinker who somehow feels the inadequacy of a system and is inclined, therefore, to tolerance and mildness does not succeed in freeing himself sufficiently from entangling traditions and acquired habits of thought. He is not able to make a new synthesis for himself and his fellow men. It is possible to have a keen pre-reflective sense of the whole without being able to escape one-sidedness on the level of explicit and constructive thought.

There are other possibilities, too, one of which must be mentioned. Two interpretations of the whole may be fairly comprehensive, including the major aspects of human experience, yet nonetheless remain radically incompatible. It is possible that two philosophies are entirely at variance with each other not so much by reason of the choice of those aspects of reality they emphasize as because of a significant difference in first principles that are not due to a lack of comprehensiveness but to different points of departure from which the whole is approached and consequently to different methods of arranging its various aspects in some order. The ultimate reason is that human thought is always thought and not reality. Therefore, worldviews aiming at comprehensiveness are not passively received and conceived in the mind but actively constructed from a certain point of view. The 'perspectiveness' of human thinking is incurable. It is possible, then, to look at the whole from different angles without turning a blind eye to some of its essential aspects. Such a difference exists, for example, in the opposition between the philosophy of Hegel and that of Thomas Aquinas. Both are characterized by comprehensiveness, but they remain forever irreducible to one another.

It is not necessary to go deeper into that question of ultimates. Let it suffice to see that the dialectical process, owing to the human deficiencies here described, is an historical and understandable fact and that the quest for a synthesis is not only necessary and fruitful but has its antecedents in history.

THE GERMAN CONTRIBUTION: CATHOLIC ROMANTICISM

It would have been amazing if the great philosophy of German idealism had exerted no influence on the (then) contemporary Catholic thought. The two forces met, indeed, and it is the historical merit of the Catholic Faculty of Theology, incorporated in 1817 into the University of Tübingen, to have produced the fruits of the dialogue between idealism and traditional Catholic theology. To be sure, there were other minds who attempted a synthesis. Fr. Schlegel, a leading genius in the development of romantic thought, became a Catholic in 1808, and in his later writings he worked out a kind of Christian philosophy that in its own way is very important for this inquiry. He is now gradually being recognized as one of the most acute and comprehensive minds of that epoch of the giants; he was certainly the most learned. The difference between Schlegel and the School of Tübingen is that Schlegel entered the Catholic Church at a mature age and had to assimilate the Catholic tradition to which he entirely subjected himself, whereas Drey and his disciples started with that tradition and tried to rethink it in the light of romantic idealism.

Schlegel is a most original genius and in order to appreciate his views one must understand some of his basic notions and distinctions. He characterizes his own philosophy as a philosophy of life, based on the whole of human experience and opposed mainly to the philosophy of reason (*Vernunft philosophie*), which proceeds from rational ideas and does not leave the realm of ideas. It is his basic conception that life is a concrete many-sided experience of reality, growing to clarity through a process of thought in which all the human faculties, springing from their original unity, must work together. Understanding alone cannot reach truth. Man as a whole is engaged in the process, and the attainment of truth supposes in the thinker an inner harmony of all his faculties.

The basic structure of all knowledge, natural as well as supernatural (they cannot be adequately distinguished), is of the same nature, although that sameness is a sameness of analogy. There are always three stages: outward or inner 'perception' (*Wahrnehmen*) leading to 'experience' (*Empfindung*). Through experience the truth, which in perception presents itself phenomenally to the mind, becomes an inner awareness of the reality itself. There is a growth in experience guiding one into 'spiritual contemplation' (*das geistige Anschauen*). Spiritual contemplation results from the fact that the truth that is felt or experienced is made explicit in language, thus becoming a clearly illuminated object to the inner eye and something that can be communicated. It is evident at once that such a description of the process of knowledge is relevant to the question of development. Faith begins with the exterior perception of the revealed Word, it becomes an experience of the reality, conveyed by that Word, and it tends to grow in us toward a full explicit knowledge, the object of which, although contemplated indirectly and not in the clarity of vision, is nonetheless an object of inner spiritual sight.

The meaning of a few terms must be explored more deeply. In living thought there is always a contact with the real. This is why it is knowledge. In all thought there is knowledge, however vague or undifferentiated. In all thought, even in erroneous thought, there is a pre-reflective implicit awareness of the real as a whole. Thought tries to unfold its riches into a living system of concepts. It may disfigure the content through one-sided explanations. Thought never succeeds in covering the whole of the implicit richness of real experience, but it strives toward it as toward a limit. The perfection of knowledge man strives for is called *idea*—the term is cognate with *ideal*—and the starting point, the first turning toward it is called *belief* or *faith* (in German there is but one word). All thought is a movement from faith toward knowledge.

In Christian religion, faith is the acceptance of the message presented from without under the influence of God, the sole origin of truth. Divine grace gives man the inner experience of that which is spoken of. Faith then is already an inchoative mode of knowledge. It is an assent combined with a living experiential awareness of the saving reality. Through thought, faith tends to convert itself into knowledge. This is clearly Augustinian and matches Anselm's definition of theology as 'faith seeking understanding.'

Hence the affirmation of Schlegel that faith and knowledge are not separated from nor opposed to each other but are related to each other as a beginning to its perfection: 'As to the order and succession, in the broad domain of all natural outer and inner experience, faith is rather a beginning striving after a developing, and not yet fully accomplished knowledge.'[2]

As faith cannot be separated from knowledge, so 'experience and revelation considered as the given contents of all knowledge are also inseparably connected with each other. The former is related to the latter as an outer appearance to an inner power, as a visible frame to an enlivening vital principle, or inner kernel of light for which the frame functions as an organ or bearer or as a wrapping or clothing.'[3] It is clear that revelation, no less than faith, has a general and a particular meaning. All knowledge, whatever may be its perceptual origin, has, as far as it becomes an inner experience, its real origin in God. Christian faith, responding to the Word of God (perceptual origin), immediately comes from God insofar as it is a contact with the realities of salvation. Schlegel emphatically states that faith depends on a tradition going back to an historical revelation. But that which was outwardly revealed, being now continued in tradition, must be revealed within man in order to cause the sight and assent of faith.

A second point in Schlegel's philosophy, equally important for this subject, is his critical insight into history and its dialectical structure. Although a certain consciousness of the real as a whole is inherent to all thinking, explicit thought may interpret it in various one-sided ways. Schlegel distinguishes six types of one-sidedness that may disfigure the truth. Each of these types is determined by the dominance of one of the basic faculties of man. The deepest root of the tendency toward one-sidedness is the sinful disruption of human consciousness. Divine redemptive faith alone is able to restore man to his original integrity. Through the continual interplay of those trends of one-sidedness history shows a dialectical structure. Schlegel with his immense philological and historical erudition mapped out a general philosophy of history, in which the non-Christian cultures and their religious ideas were each interpreted as dominated by a particular type of one-sided interpretation of reality. The whole of history dialectically moves toward

Christianity. But the same movement goes on in the very history of thought within the Christian culture. There are three stages in Christian understanding. The first results from the simple attempt at bringing together the elements of Christian faith. The second results from its confrontation with error or heresy; the perception of actual or possible error enhances the clarity and distinctness of man's consciousness of truth. Lastly, through the dialectical process, man becomes aware of a possible perfection of knowledge in which all the opposites should be reconciled. This is the 'idea' (*Idee*). Schlegel gives an admirable general description of the inner dynamic structure of the development of ideas and doctrines. By the power of his faith combined with the comprehensiveness of his genius, Schlegel rejoins and revalorizes the main stream of Catholic tradition. He did not write an *Essay on the Development of Doctrine*, but in his philosophy of faith and his insight into the dialectical structure of history all the elements are given for a well-balanced theory to explain how tradition retains its identity in a process of continuous development.

The founder of the School of Tübingen was J. S. Drey. In his thought the basic characteristics of the school are clearly displayed: a dynamic idea of revelation and a dialectical conception of tradition. Not unlike Schleiermacher, who greatly influenced him, he holds that the rule of faith is not something of the past but the present state of the tradition. That present state is the outcome of an organic growth in which all the factors work together like members of the same body enlivened and directed by an inner spirit. In Christian tradition that inner spirit is the Holy Spirit. Through His Spirit God Himself unfolds in the course of history what He had planted in its soil at the time of revelation. Therefore, the historical revelation and the subsequent tradition together form one continuous process, and what thus grows is a system, a unity in multiplicity: not a unity made by abstract logical relations but a living unity effected by a guiding, all-pervading principle of organization. Schlegel's conception, which is no less organic that Drey's, is clearer on that point: the principle of unity that vivifies and guides the system in its growth is an initial and not yet articulated knowledge of revealed reality in its wholeness.

Drey particularly stresses that the moving principle in active tradition as well as in revelation is God Himself. This does not exclude, however, the importance of the human contribution. The factors that enter into the dialectical process are man's inborn striving for conceptual clarity, the dialogue with culture, the progress of the sciences, the different nations, each with its own spirit, and especially the historical oppositions against Judaism, Hellenism, and heresy. As in the thought of Schlegel, the Church, according to Drey, comes to the full consciousness of its system only through the necessity of defining its position in contrast to heresy: 'In the midst of those movements which constantly cross one another in the struggles and shiftings of opinion, the invisible Christian spirit attains its goal: a growing perfection in the unfolding of revelation, a greater coherence in the system of faith.'[4] The free interplay of those conflicting influences would inevitably lead to total confusion if God had not provided a social body, the Church, which is the system incarnate as it were, unfolding and framing itself from within. Although the particular role of the doctrinal authority is not stressed, Drey, whose thinking is within the general view of Catholic ecclesiology, certainly implies the hierarchical function in the self-ruling movement of the body of the Church. He is too engrossed in his original idea to deal explicitly with its juridical aspects.

The most illustrious representative of the School of Tübingen is J. A. Möhler. He is greatly dependent upon his master and shares with him the organic conception of the Church and its tradition. But he surpasses him through his profound historical knowledge of the Early Church and the comprehensiveness of his mind.

Möhler's first work, *Die Einheit der Kirche oder das Prinzip des Katholizismus* (1825), is generally considered one of the most important contributions to the subject and requires here a brief analysis of its content. The primary idea is the Romantic idea of organic unity. The Church is a unity in multiplicity. That unity in multiplicity is characterized by intrinsicality and wholeness. By *wholeness* he means that, in all its manifestations, the Church lives and thrives as a whole. The development of doctrine is an aspect of that comprehensive growth, and the development of individual dogmas is vitally connected with the whole system of truth that guides the life of the community. By *intrinsicality* he means that the visible structures and their development are but manifestations of an inner principle or power of spiritual life. It is the inner principle that creates its forms. Doctrinal life, too, with its propositional expression and systematic coherence is governed from within by the one Spirit that vivifies the Church. That Spirit is the Holy Spirit. Möhler's view of the Church, like that of Drey, is mainly pneumatological.

Doctrinal tradition, then, is governed from within by the same Spirit who gave the revelation and who inspired the Scriptures. Tradition is the continuation of the same life that began with revelation. The primitive Church is not conceived of as an ideal to which the Church must return. It is the original reality in which the fullness of life is already given, but as a seed that has to develop in the process of time. Tradition, then, is not only an historical phenomenon that can be studied in documents. It has an inner mystical side: 'That spiritual power of life which is transmitted and inherited in the Church, is the tradition, its inner, mysterious side, beyond any power of perception.'[5]

The Spirit guiding the whole life of the Church from within works its exterior manifestations in and through the Christian people, which is the Kingdom of God. The medium through which the development is accomplished is not a part of the Church, not even its hierarchical authority, but the whole body of the community, vivified and guided by the Spirit. For even authority is not so much viewed as established by an exterior historical act, but is rather considered as an organ, flowing from the inner power of the Spirit, and called to exercise an indispensable function in the social and historical life of the Church. To be sure, Möhler does not deny the establishment of the ecclesiastical authority by Christ, nor does he diminish its importance. But in accordance with his organic view of things he stresses not so much the external juridical relation from the top downward as the inner vital relation from below upward.

In a certain sense, Möhler answers Schlegel's conception of the general process of development. The active principle is the Spirit, but what is worked by the Spirit is present in the Church at first as an unreflecting sense of truth, an 'inner core of consciousness' (*intimus conscientiae fundus*). Möhler distinguishes between two modes of consciousness:

The contemplative, reflective and the contemplated, active and living, the latter providing the first with its matter. Such is also the case with Christian consciousness. To be a Christian is something which has to be lived. The Christian must have absorbed Christianity in his consciousness. Previous to Christian investigation a Christian matter has to be given on which reflection can be exercised.[6]

That which is believed and afterward analyzed by reflection must become a part of the Christian's being. It is not enough that it should be present to the mind in the way of objective information. The message has to be converted into existential truth:

> That which is positively given, when once it has been assimilated by us, provides the matter of which the activity of the mind may take hold in order to produce a scientific structure, and hence the Christian philosopher of religion differs from the simple believer not by the content of his knowledge but solely by the form taken by that which is common to both. The relations of all the particular elements of faith to one another and to the whole become clear to the former, or he at least tries to clarify them; the faithful as such has become for himself an object or reflection; faith, unconscious at first, has become conscious.[7]

It seems clear that according to Möhler the object of reflection in the Church, leading to intellectual clarification and propositional systematization, cannot be thought of as merely a set of original doctrines. It has to be conceived as a whole that materially is a Creed but formally is an inner personal relation to that which the Creed points to. The spiritual assimilation of Christian truth consists in a conversion of that truth from the condition of exterior verbal notification to a condition of living contact with the indwelling reality, worked in man by the grace of God. The message or Creed becomes an object of authentic Christian thought only as far as it is subjectified by becoming a personal communication with the real. Through that mediation the verbal deposit of tradition, which by its very nature could only be imperfect, and always will be, becomes an inner deposit of living faith. Through its power of realization faith embraces the whole in a non-propositional way. Thus the truth of the message acquires a new dimension, which it cannot have except in personal life. Therefore, the Christian combines in himself an assent to the objective message with a subjective apprehension of its real mystery, and so it becomes true that, as Möhler says, the Christian makes himself an object of reflection, providing that reflection with a material of inexhaustible richness.

Such a conception of faith in its relation to reflection naturally leads to an historical view, which in agreement with the general spirit of German Romanticism will be thought of as a dialectical process. Since the central idea of Möhler and Drey is the idea of life, it must be expected that it will be combined with that of growth. 'Since Christianity is a new divine life given to man and not a dead concept, it is subject to development and elaboration.'[8] The form of growth, however, is not only determined by inner impulses and tensions but also by outer influences and resistances. The inner tensions that occasion the dialectical movement are conflicts or differences between epochs, stages of culture, national characters, generations, families, individual idiosyncrasies, etc. The external resistances that especially compel the Church to clarify thought are the heresies.

In later years the idea of a living Church continued to be present to Möhler's mind. There is, however, a shifting of accents. The objective elements are emphatically stressed over and above the subjective elements described in the masterpiece of his youth; but there seems to be no substantial change. His later views perfect and complement his early intuitions and must be judged in the light of the particular circumstances and intentions of the individual works in which they occur. Möhler's second masterpiece *Symbolik oder Darstellung der dogmatischen Gegensätze der Katholiken und Protestanten nach ihren öffentlichen Bekenntnisschriften* (1832) is a comparative study of confessions. It is understandable that in a book of this kind the objective factors characteristic of Catholicism (dogma and authority) will be particularly stressed. He emphasizes, indeed, the historical origin of doctrinal tradition going back to Christ and the unchangeableness of dogma remaining the same under different forms. But these views do not contradict those of *Die Einheit der Kirche*. To say that in the course of history the content of faith remains the same while the form is subject to change is a vague formula that can be understood in any sense: from Bossuet's immobilism to dogmatic transformism. It depends entirely upon the interpretation of the terms. If the term *content* is interpreted in the sense of what in English could be termed *proposition* as opposed to *sentence*, Bossuet's sense is indicated. If, on the contrary, one means by *content* the unspeakable presence of a creative experience, considering all external manifestations to be the *form*, one is on the side of Schleiermacher. Möhler's statement, then, has to be interpreted in the light of the whole of his work, which is the only true and adequate context of any thinker's particular utterances. It seems clear that the true meaning of Möhler lies somewhere between these extremes. The most natural interpretation that presents itself to the critical mind is that the unchangeable content is a definite object, imperfectly expressed in the ancient documents but always fully understood by the faith of the Church, while the changing form is a clearer expression and a further explication of the primitive doctrine. That process of new expression combined with further explication cannot be understood without the mediation of a subjectifying and realizing faith. That Möhler so strongly emphasized the objective historical character of tradition is not at variance with his earlier stress on the role of subjective assimilation. It is rather a sign of his comprehensive and balanced genius. This is confirmed by the occurrence of statements in his later works reminiscent of his initial views. So in his *Neue Untersuchungen* in which he defends his *Symbolik* against Baur, he says: 'Development cannot but be an unfolding of something which from the start is given in its fullness, in such a way that the later originates from the earlier and this positively in living gradualness of transition.'[9]

The same can be said of the shift of emphasis from the 'from within' by the Spirit to the 'from without' by the historical Christ in explaining the origin of tradition and ecclesiastical authority. There is no contradiction between, on the one hand, the statement that from the beginning and all through its existence tradition and authority continuously flow from the indwelling Spirit, and on the other hand, the strong affirmation that tradition has its origin in the doctrine of Christ and the Apostles and that the hierarchical structure of the Church is due to an historical institution by the Lord. For all that Christ and the Apostles said and did was said and done in the Spirit who exercises in the order of salvation everything that in the general order of creation is attributed to Providence. We should firmly hold that the unity of the historical and the charismatic is the essence of true Christianity.

J. E. Kuhn was the successor of Möhler in Tübingen. His emphasis is on tradition, and he restricts the object of his reflection to the doctrinal side of development. Geiselmann has pointed out that the main influence on Kuhn is not the Romantic trend of German idealism but its rationalistic form as worked out by

Hegel and the idea of 'spirit' (*Geist*), not the idea of 'life.' There was yet another and decisive influence, namely that of Schlegel, the greatest of Hegel's adversaries and critics. A simple comparison suffices to make it clear.

Kuhn has to face several adversaries who contradict one another. First, consider rationalism and strict Biblicism. Against the former he must sustain the unchangeableness of doctrine; against the latter he defends a distinction between the immutable content and the shifting form of tradition. The rule of faith, he contends, is not the Bible but the tradition in its present stage. This idea of Schleiermacher was also held by Kuhn's predecessors. Tradition, not the dead letter of the past, is the compelling force of the development, although it must be tested time and again by comparisons with the inspired sources. This supposes, of course, that faith is a kind of knowledge. Next, he has to do with the rationalism of the Enlightenment and that of speculative idealism. Against the first he stresses the special divine element in revelation; against the second, which conceives religion and revelation as a stage in the return of the Absolute Spirit to itself, he emphasizes the human side of the tradition.

Development, then, according to Kuhn is an historical fact. But a priori one can ground its possibility and prove its necessity. Development is possible because the knowledge of faith is human in its expression, while its object is of such a fullness that all endeavors of human thought can never exhaust its content. It is necessary because the way of expressing revealed truth must be affected by historical relativity. The Apostles, whose word is the perpetual rule of what is to be said, were dependent on a given language of a particular culture. Starting with the apostolic message and traversing different cultures and epochs the dogmatic tradition is not weakened but clarified.

In his way of determining the nature and the dialectical structure of development, Kuhn comes so near to Schlegel that the likeness can only be explained by the hypothesis that the theologian of Tübingen is dependent upon the philosopher of Vienna. This is particularly clear in Kuhn's correction of the general scheme of Hegel's philosophy. According to Hegel, the dialectical movement of the spirit has its origin in the general undetermined idea. Perception and ideation are only connected with imperfect stages of the process that leads to the full identity of the infinite Spirit with itself. Kuhn must deny this, and he sees the starting point of the dialectic in an empirical fact: apprehension. As to Schlegel, so to Kuhn the life of Christian thought begins with an apprehension of the reality that speaks to him through the word. Faith begins as a form of immediate knowledge of its object. Progress, therefore, is not a progress of the real or of the object itself—a progress of which the thinker makes himself a passive witness in the attitude of reflective contemplation. It is a progress in the knowledge of the real—knowledge that begins as an immediate consciousness of a special object, presented from without by the message and worked from within by the Spirit. Perception is 'the basis of all truth to the finite mind, its deepest ground beneath which there is no further beyond. Consequently it is the starting point of the dialectical process.'[10] Hence, 'the source and proper norm of the dialectical development of dogma is, on the one hand, the substantial content of the Christian truth which is given in the apostolic tradition and immediately present at any time to the faith of the Church; on the other hand, the Spirit of truth who works through the organs of the Church.'[11] Therefore the homogeneity and consistency of the development has not to be proved. It is warranted by the Spirit who speaks in and through the Church. The general parallelism with the position of Schlegel is evident. Faith is from the beginning a supernatural perceptive knowledge of the revealed reality. The dialectical movement of thought is no more than a clarification of that initial knowledge. The knowledge of faith is the beginning and the end: 'That knowledge abides in faith itself, it goes out from faith, remains in faith throughout the dialectical process, and comes back at last to the faith of the beginning.'[12]

Kuhn distinguishes between the development of faith and the development of thought about faith or theology. Both are equally dialectical; but the first starts with empirical perception and proceeds along the empirical level, progressing toward an empirical concept, or a concept that is the reflected expression of the initial perception, while theological development considers what is given in the light of necessary truths and principles of reason. Its goal is a speculative concept. The two processes of development are distinct but not unrelated. For the endeavors of speculative theology are important factors in the process of dogmatic development.

In living faith there is a supernatural perception striving after a perfect understanding of itself—this calls to mind Anselm's *fides quaerens intellectum.* Indeed, the basic impetus, driving forward the development of doctrine, is the natural tendency of the mind to clarify and organize its perceptions and intuitions. But in the life of history other factors are at work, giving to the process its typical dialectical structure. These factors are the different ways in which the original perception is translated into concepts by the efforts of thought and imagination. There is already a difference between the representations by which each Apostle tried to express his perception of faith. Even within the work of one Apostle different models occur that try to express in forms of human thought different aspects of the inexhaustible dogma.

It is not always easy to reconcile the various representations pointing to the same indivisible reality. Hence tensions come to the fore that sometimes lead to oppositions and heresies. Christian dogma is viewed in different aspects, and the attempt to overcome the contradictions brings to light in explicit formulas the various aspects of dogma. Thus the knowledge of what faith apprehends is gradually determined: 'The general indeterminate expression in which a truth of faith is apprehended becomes distinct by the elimination of possible contradictory conceptions. Thus the content of faith is exposed in a more determinate and unambiguous way and its expression becomes sharper.'[13] In the course of development, Kuhn says, the content remains the same but the form changes. It is very clear what he means. The content is what faith apprehends in a preconceptual way, the changing form means not only that better equivalent formulations are substituted for imperfect images but that there is an objective progress on the level of conceptual apprehension. The clear doctrine of the disciple confirms the earlier interpretation of the master's meaning.

THE ENGLISH CONTRIBUTION : J. H. NEWMAN

The doctrine elaborated by the School of Tübingen immediately leads to the thought of Cardinal Newman. His theory of development of doctrine is surprising for its originality and its thoroughness. Unlike the German thinkers analyzed in the previous section, the idea of development was not suggested to Newman by a general philosophical tendency in which he participated. It did not arise in his mind as a part or aspect of a more comprehensive religious view connected with the philosophy of the day. It is impossible to trace his insights back to definite historical influences. As Father Tristram, who spent a long life on the study of Newman, wrote: 'We can affirm without hesitation that Newman derived the idea of development from no other source than his own mind.'[14] Moreover, Newman's personal bent was altogether different from the spirit of metaphysical idealism. He rather disliked such philosophical constructions, considering them to be abstruse and unreal. He was inclined to distrust all notional systems built upon abstract a priori principles, not derived from experience. The substantial correspondence between his conception and that of the school of Tübingen is therefore all the more remarkable.

It cannot be doubted that he was influenced by the empirical tradition of his country, and it is necessary to go deeper into the nature of Newman's empiricism. He shared with Locke and Hume the general tendency not to say more than could be allowed by the facts. But he widely differed from them as to what could be considered as pertaining to the domain of facts. In his philosophy the notion of experience is not narrowed down to sense experience and to consciousness as determined by it. If experience is defined as the awareness of what is immediately given and by reference to which any assertion has to be justified, then according to Newman, experience is not limited to the data that can be verified by an appeal to the witness of man's common faculty of sensory apprehension. Such things as moral conscience pertain to the domain of experience no less than to the perceptions of the senses, although the truth of its existence and of its inner injunctions cannot be verified in the same way as the existence and qualities of a tree or the behavior of an atom in a given experimental situation.

Newman could have spoken this way defending the rights of conscience by saying that its dictates are as much to be reckoned among the data of immediate experience as are the data of sense perception. He could have described both in the same terms although with analogous meanings: just as, according to the testimony of sense experience, one perceives things and not only phenomena, so that the sensations through which one communicates with the things are to be interpreted as impressions that the things make on the sensory organs, so too the dictates of conscience bring one into contact with an invisible and personal Reality and must be interpreted as impressions of His will on men's souls.

The picture of the process of sense perception that functions in this context as a comparative model in order to describe the way of conscience is now considered very defective. Indeed, man perceives things—on that point all agree as long as the thinking is not highly sophisticated—but there is no evidence that the perception of them is caused by impressions of whatever kind made by those things upon man's body. This is a natural interpretation, but it collapses when considered seriously.

All this, however, is of no real importance. Newman might be misled by traditional models of thought that are unable to express his true meaning. He is wrestling with inadequate tools for the expression of his intuition. One can now see that his notion of experience is itself different from that of the empiricism of his day. Experience is not that kind of operation by which one receives the first elements with which ideas are constructed, combining them into propositions and inferences according to the laws of formal logic. Experience is not so much an immediate knowledge of separate elements presenting themselves to consciousness in definite patterns available and demonstrable to all men with normal senses and sound judgment, and which are the same for every man whatever may be the condition and the stage of his individual personality. Experience is a living whole of conscious life. It grows; it admits of various degrees of clarity and depth according to the development of one's personality. That development is guided not only by an increase of information and intellectual knowledge but also by personal dispositions and moral attitudes. The attainment of truth in matters of ultimate concern and moral conduct is more than a question of brains, intellectual sagacity, and mental application. It is also a question of moral earnestness, fidelity to the voice of conscience, right conduct, openness with respect to all the intimations of truth that present themselves in one's daily intercourse with things and persons. Genuine experience supposes an openness toward experience, a humble will to accept its lessons and its guidance, a restraining of willfulness, impatience, and pride. Man moves as a whole. His true convictions are not self-made products of his mental operations but fruits that slowly grow in a receptive mind. Truth does not so much depend upon correct reasoning. 'All depends on which set of principles you begin by assuming.'[15] First principles are not proved. 'They rule and are not ruled.' Generally one takes them for granted so that one accepts them without making them objects of reflection. One thinks and acts from them, one does not think of them. 'They are hidden for the very reason they are so sovereign and engrossing.' The principles a man starts from will depend on who he is: 'They are in short the man.'[16]

This basic view of Newman is frankly personalistic. Man thinks as a whole. His experience contains his sensory life as a part of one of its functions. Man cannot reduce experience to sense perception without beguiling himself into deceptive abstractions. Such a personalistic view may be called radical empiricism, i.e., an empiricism that refuses to take a part for the whole or to give a priori a privileged status to one of its components or aspects. That kind of empiricism is a leading epistemological idea in contemporary philosophy.

> Fundamental to any empirical philosophy, we believe, is an ideally objective and inclusive view of experience. While it may be granted that what is 'found' in experience is determined in part by some regulative view of 'the whole,' nevertheless the empiricist may strive to avoid any undue emphasis upon any one aspect of experience which would distort his view of the whole. . . .
>
> We believe that a broader view of experience is more empirical, that it is more faithful to the heterogeneous, complex and ongoing affair which is man's life in nature. That process . . . is not exclusively 'physical' or 'psychical,' 'objective' or 'subjective,' 'quantitative' or 'qualitative,' 'individual' or 'social,' cognitive, affective or volitional. Rather it is all of these as it is 'immediately had,' and any exaggerated emphasis upon any of these elements is based upon a false abstraction of the living whole.[17]

This is not Newman speaking, but Newman could have subscribed to this.

Experience, then, is a process of gradual clarification and expansion of a comprehensive view of things. All the elements or functions of conscious life cooperate in it in a measure greatly determined not only by their own nature but also by such personal factors as temperament, moral attitude, and individual history or destiny. It is guided by unconscious influences as well as by conscious orientation. It may deviate from its original course because of the impact of sudden insights flashing upon the mind and making one see all things in a new light, or by secret choices of freedom that gradually work out their effects in the living growth of the mind. One is aware of it as a whole, though one fails to see all its factors distinctly; and a spontaneous judging and controlling power is at work in it, which like the 'magic eye' of an automatic electronic device silently checks the rightness of the thought-process. Newman calls this the 'illative sense.'

The foregoing description is all-important for understanding Newman's theory. His basic idea of development is a faithful translation in general terms of something that he saw at work in his own experience and that he brought to light by efforts of personal reflection with no aid from without. If it is true that Husserl's program of 'going back to the things themselves' is the very mark of a great philosopher, then Newman is to be considered as an outstanding genius in the history of human thought.

It must be clear by now why Newman, in spite of his empiricism or, better perhaps, because of the proper nature of his empiricism, 'proves to have had perhaps the most comprehensive, detailed and integrated view of things—in the sage's sense—of any English writer of his century.'[18]

If that view is called a system, the meaning of that term must be qualified so that it does not convey the idea of a logical construction that, starting from general principles supposed to be evident or demonstrable to any mind that is able to understand them, develops along the straight ways of a formal inferential method. It is rather a living synthesis that has proceeded 'among the encircling gloom' of man's mysterious condition and has grown out of the seeds of his personal conscience by the path of fidelity to experience as a whole, yet brightening step by step under the scrupulous eye of an honest and critical self-examination. Newman is constantly aware that man is surrounded by a world of mystery. Cautiously and attentively he advances in the dark, guided by his own inner light, and though the clouds are never dissipated, his view enlarges and brightens so that he can distinguish a general pattern sufficient to lead him on. This makes clear why, although starting from opposite points, Newman, guided by his own experience, and the theologians of Tübingen, trying to fit the truth of a definite system into the pattern of their religious thought, came to similar conclusions. Their leading idea was the same; the idea of wholeness and the spontaneous growth of conscious life. That they came to the same insights by such different ways and independently of each other is a fact that might justify a certain confidence that there is a good deal of truth in their views.

Although the idea of development was derived by Newman from his own experience and reflection, the problem of doctrinal development would probably not have become so paramount in his thought had it not presented itself to him as the central problem in the development of his own convictions. The facts that he tried to explain and justify by his theory of doctrinal development formed indeed the main obstacle to the great decision of his life. For reasons that need not be gone into here, the leader of the Oxford Movement, at the acme of his religious influence in the Church of England, came to doubt the truth of his position. That position was based on the assumption that the Church of the Fathers was the ideal, the supreme rule of Christian truth and life. On that assumption it seemed to him that the Church of England, being a via media between two deviations from the ancient rule, namely the Protestant by dogmatic indifference, the Catholic by corrupting additions to the deposit of faith, was the true heir of the spirit of the ancient Church. In order to make his case he set himself to study the old documents intensely. Gradually the features of the ancient Church took shape before his inner eye. But when, looking around in the religious world of his own day, he tried to identify that face among the existing confessions, he slowly realized that the Catholic Church of the Continent rather than the English Establishment reflected the truer image of the past. He could not, however, accept the Roman religion because it still seemed to him that in it the principle of dogma—the most basic principle of the Oxford Movement—had been corrupted by later additions that were not conformable to the rule of antiquity.

It is in that personal situation that the idea of development came within sight and gradually grew more distinct. He had been struck by the fact that in the first centuries of Christian history some Fathers and great ecclesiastical writers had spoken of the Son and His relation to the Father in a sense that came near to subordinationism. It seemed clear, then, that the doctrine of Trinity as defined by the Councils of Nicea and Constantinople was not distinctly understood and professed in pre-Nicene times and that the most august truths of Christian faith had been shaped in the mind of the Church by a gradual process of development. Consequently, it was necessary to qualify the Vincentian Canon ('what has been believed everywhere, always, and by all') in such a way that the sameness of faith in the course of history was not to be conceived as a static immutability but as a dynamic continuity. Tradition does not exclude an increasing distinctness in man's apprehension of its objective content. On the contrary, 'from the nature of the human mind, time is necessary for the full comprehension and perfection of great ideas' (*Development*, p. 29). Development becomes a sign of vitality: 'In a higher world it is otherwise, but here below to live is to change, and to be perfect is to have changed often' (*Development*, p. 40).

Once this idea was firmly grasped and accepted, it was easy to foresee the consequences. If development must be excluded, then the Council of Nicea cannot be justified and the very principle of dogma is endangered. If it must be admitted, then a post-patristic development of doctrine becomes probable, and it could be that the Council of Trent was no less justified than that of Nicea. Thus the theory of development removed the last obstacle on Newman's way to Rome.

A distinction must be made between Newman's idea of development and his theory. The former is the object of a descriptive analysis; the latter takes the form of an argument. The idea of development is one part of a more comprehensive description of the processes of human thought. It cannot be understood apart from its general context. The theory, although understandable by itself as to its particular point, nevertheless presents itself within Newman's religious worldview as a link in a more comprehensive argument by which he justifies his Catholic conviction. In Chapter 7 of his *Apologia pro vita sua* he drew the broad lines of his general apologetical position. The description of the idea comprises a twofold analysis: of human thought in the individual mind, and of the social processes by which ideas develop in the course of history. The argument is twofold: a theological and a controversial one.

How, then, do ideas develop in the human mind? In the last of his Oxford University Sermons, dealing for the first time in an extensive way with the problem of development, Newman describes the process as a gradual clarification, differentiation, and articulation of an idea by way of reasoning. *Reason* is a general term, embracing in its meaning all the possible operations of discursive thought. *Idea* is the object of a mental intuition that is at first grasped as an indistinct whole and strives toward clarification by means of reflection, analysis, and inference. In the process itself the idea is always present *per modum unius* as a directive intuition. Therefore, it is at the same time its source and its result: 'The idea which represents an object whether real or supposed is equal to the aggregate of its possible aspects' (*Development*, p. 34). Because one can never succeed in making explicit all the aspects of a great idea, the term *idea* finally signifies an ideal toward which one's knowledge tends without ever reaching it completely.

It can safely be said that the idea as Newman understands it in his earlier works generally corresponds to the object of what in his *Grammar of Assent* he calls real apprehension. Real apprehension is distinguished from notional apprehension. A word that stands for a thing can evoke in the mind either a concrete reality known by experience or a general notion abstracted from other experiences or known by teaching. The name of a town, for instance, means to the native a congeries of concrete experiences, united somehow by his recollecting imagination into a general picture. For the stranger, however, who never visited the town, its name only evokes a set of general notions: an agglomeration of houses, streets, shops, churches, etc., as he has seen in so many other towns. This vague representation may perhaps be enriched with general descriptions such as 'big,' 'fine,' 'on the sea-shore,' etc., which he has learned from others or read in books.

Not all objects of real apprehension are ideas in the sense stated above, but all true ideas are objects of real apprehension. They are present to the mind as objects of direct experience. But ideas are objects of mental and not of possible sensuous apprehension. The 'idea of a university,' for instance, is not the sum total of its buildings but the ideal pattern of an educational institution. In order to be able to analyze it one must first experience it, having participated fully in its life and aims.

Real apprehension, then, may be called an analogical expression. It points to different classes of objects in different ways. However, it always means an apprehension of something real, actually or ideally, present to us on the ground of experience.

A few examples will illustrate the analogical nature of real apprehension, so as to be able to understand its final application to the way in which faith apprehends its object. In reading the works of a great author knowledge may grow on two different levels: that of his philosophy and that of his personality. One may give primary attention to the objective system of his thought, a combination of general notions that are understandable to all those who have learned them. It may be, however, that one is mainly concerned with his personal style and peculiarities so that his words come to the ear as spoken by a man with a unique personality. He thus becomes familiar, and one recognizes him by his language as one recognizes a friend by his walk. His language is 'the expression of that one person's ideas and feelings . . . proper to himself, in the same sense as his voice, his air, his countenance, his carriage, and his action are personal.'[19] The way in which one apprehends another's system is notional, and the knowledge one obtains of it is directly communicable. But one's personal apprehension of his peculiar character is real and cannot be directly communicated.

Another well-known example is the apprehension of God through conscience. Conscience is a moral sense and at the same time a sense of duty. As a moral sense it is a faculty of immediate discrimination between good and evil in the same way as the aesthetic sense is a faculty of immediate discrimination between the beautiful and the ugly. It is possible to work out the dictates of the moral sense into a system of ethics. But unlike any other sense, conscience considered as a sense of duty makes one apprehend its judgments as *imperatives* addressing the will and requiring uncon-ditional obedience. As such it 'carries on our minds to a Being exterior . . . and superior to ourselves . . . and in proportion as we listen to that Word, and use it not only do we learn more from it; . . . but its very tone is louder and more authoritative and constrain-ing. And thus it is, that to those who use what they have, more is given; for, beginning with obedience, they go on to the intimate per-ception and belief of one God.'[20] As in the style of an author one recognizes his personality, so in the authoritative 'style' of one's con-science one comes to apprehend an unseen Teacher, the Master, just, holy, helpful, all-seeing, and omnipresent. This example illustrates the personal and active character of real apprehension. God is present in one's conscience; but if that conscience is not obeyed, one's apprehension of Him gradually fades away. If, on the contrary, one is faithful to His voice, apprehension of Him grows in clarity and personal intensity.

Real and notional apprehension are distinct and irreducible. But they are not unconnected. They are like two dimensions of a single knowledge. They may go together in the same act. When

Aeneas, referring to Dido, says: *varium et mutabile semper femina*, he states a general proposition, but at the same time he 'realizes' its meaning in a concrete experience. They are also complementary:

> To apprehend notionally is to have breadth of mind, but to be shallow; to apprehend really is to be deep, but to be narrow-minded. The latter is the conservative principle of knowledge, and the former the principle of its advancement. Without the apprehension of notions, we should for ever pace around one small circle of knowledge; without a firm hold upon things, we shall waste ourselves in vague speculations. However real apprehension has the precedence as being the scope, and end and the test of the notional; and the fuller is the mind's hold upon things on what he considers such, the more fertile is it in its aspects of them, and the more practical in its definition. [*Grammar*, p. 34]

This touches the heart of the matter with regard to the problem of development. Dogmatic propositions may evoke in the mind divine realities of which we have through God's illuminating grace an experiential apprehension; or they may represent notions that can be clarified and related to one another by theological thought. Faith is based on a real apprehension; theology on a notional apprehension. On the one hand, then, dogmas considered as notional propositions, and theology, working out their ramifications and consequences, are necessary for the purity of living faith. Dogma with its conceptual clarity and critical determination sharply focuses the eye of faith on its true object, preventing it from running wild and being distorted by uncontrolled products of the imagination. For what one subjectively 'realizes,' as Newman often repeats, may be real or considered to be such. On the other hand, realizing faith is necessary for a true notional apprehension of what it is about. In order to analyze rightly an idea or an object of real apprehension, it must be seen as a concrete whole. According to the depth and firmness of his hold on the realization of faith, the theologian will be able to distinguish more aspects and to apprehend and relate them to one another without departing from the truth. 'Such a one . . . is able to pronounce about the great sight which encompasses him, as about some visible object; and . . . is not inferring abstraction from abstraction, but noting down the aspects and phases of that one thing on which he is ever gazing'

(*Grammar*, p. 316). Because notions are abstractions, they never represent the whole thing. Therefore, if a man does not constantly have before his mind the realities he is thinking about, a point may be reached where 'the notion and the thing part company; and then the notion, if still used as the representative of the thing, will work out conclusions, not inconsistent with itself, but with the thing to which it no longer corresponds' (*Grammar*, pp. 46–47).

Faith is based on a real apprehension. By itself, however, it is an assent. Such an assent has its proper characteristics that distinguish it from an assent following upon a mere notional apprehension. A notional assent, not accompanied by a firm hold on the real, is an assent of the intellect alone, and by its own power it generally does not rise above an opinion. Real assent, on the contrary, 'being concerned with things concrete, not abstract,' is given under the impact of 'objects which kindle devotion, rouse the passions, and attach the affections; and thus it leads the way to actions of every kind, to the establishment of principles, and the formation of character, and is thus again intimately connected with what is individual and personal' (*Grammar*, pp. 90–91). Therefore faith is not only an intellectual assent given to propositions but a real personal conviction, containing in itself the attitudes that correspond to the nature of its real object. Faith is an act of the whole person: man's answer to the revelation of God and his salvation through Christ. Therefore it is in itself an act of personal acceptance, adhesion, confidence, and surrender.

Faith is not only an act that every believing individual performs in the secret of his heart; it is also a participation in the faith of a community. We believe within the fold of the Church, the communion of the Saints. Theology, too, is a common undertaking of the Christian community. In the thought of the Church the real apprehension of faith has two complementary properties: a negative one and a positive one.

The life of faith preserves the work of the theologian from one-sided and superficial systematization. In trying to understand the spirit of the Fathers and the great doctors of the Church, we find that they are conspicuous for their intellectual prudence. They are thinking, as it were, surrounded by a mystery in which their life participates and of which they feel the unspeakable presence. They act as brain cells in a growing body of tradition. They are aware of the distance separating their concepts and words from the august reality that they try to express. Therefore, the Fathers did not create brilliant systems all of a piece, but 'they were intently fixing their minds on what they taught, grasping it more and more closely, viewing it on various sides, trying its consistency, weighing their own separate expressions. And thus if in some cases they were even left in ignorance, the next generation of teachers completed their work, for the same unwearied anxious process of thought went on' (*Development*, p. 367). Real apprehension, then, is the guarantee of theological prudence.

At the same time, the presence of the real in the process of tradition impresses on the mind of the believing thinker the right principles that will spontaneously lead his thought, and in the light of these principles, the real gradually unfolds it different aspects. One aspect points to the other and thus the whole develops in its various aspects, expanding, as it were, its riches within a consistent pattern. Thus real apprehension is the source of theological richness.

It is possible now to describe briefly the process of development itself as it takes place in the believing mind of the Church. As was pointed out above, the process of development is a process of reasoning. However, reasoning for Newman is a manifold, subtle, and intricate activity. It covers the whole realm of discursive thought, including not only deductions but also that kind of induction by which the concrete is determined by seeing the convergence of independent probabilities, as well as other processes, too subtle to be noticed, which are at work in the living act of the mind under the guidance of the illative sense, which controls the whole process *per modum unius*.

Newman always emphasizes that the activity of reasoning, by which ideas in general and Christian doctrine in particular are developing, is not a deliberate operation of the intellect but the spontaneous working of an innate power of expansion within the mind.

The question indeed may be asked whether a development can be other in any case than a logical operation; but, if by this is meant a conscious reasoning from premises to conclusions, of course the answer must be in the negative. An idea . . . grows in the mind by remaining there; it becomes familiar and distinct, and is viewed in its relations; it leads to other aspects and these again to others, subtle, recondite, original . . . and thus a body of thought is gradually formed without his recognizing what is going on with him. [*Development*, pp. 189–190]

Newman's position is succinctly described in the following quotation: 'In investigating and determining, the mind progresses by a freer activity of thought and by means of a more subtle instrument and it is often hardly conscious of its own exercise and of its results.'[21]

Faith, then, is an assent to dogma, but an assent grounded in a real apprehension of the heavenly things to which the human forms of dogmatic language point. As such, the object of assent is the real, apprehended in the notional; and assent itself, beyond its being an intellectual acceptance, is in the first place a subjection to a reality. The development of dogma is not so much a logical working out of first propositions, as a propositional clarification of a knowledge that, through the medium of these propositions, communicates with the real. Thus the point of departure of the development is not merely propositional. It is a comprehensive awareness of the real—and the real is always the whole—through a propositional expression that may be very partial and always remains inadequate. The comprehensive intuitive awareness of the whole and the propositional expression cannot be separated, but the former always exceeds the latter: one could not know a friend on that deeper level where 'heart speaks to heart,' if one did not see and hear him. In the same way faith could not attain to its real object on the level of supernatural communion without the mediation of dogma.

But the real apprehension, having for its object the real and consequently the whole, always exceeds the notional, which by its very nature is always abstract and partial. The real apprehension may be as perfect when accompanied by a notionally undeveloped and even defective expression as when pointed out by a more fully developed and more correct and adequate elaboration. Therefore faith, in its essential act, is not more perfect in the later Church, which has more explicit and precise dogmatic views than in the Church of former times when the form of the message was still primitive and notionally incomplete, 'St. Hilary and St. Irenaeus could use expressions or make statements about the Holy Trinity or the Incarnation, which the great subsequent Catholic development of doctrine afterwards discarded, without failing in a real apprehension of the doctrine itself.'[22]

Development, then, is in the first place an expansion in the believing mind of a real comprehensive view of its divine object. But that development does not take place except through the mediation of dogma, which in its original form was a message articulated in a primitive Creed. Without dogma there could in the beginning be no apprehension of faith, and afterward there can be no notional expansion of that real apprehension except through the mediation of dogma. The development of faith, considered as a real idea, cannot be separated from the development of the doctrinal content of a primitive Creed.

O. Chadwick's interpretation of Newman's position has to be corrected. He says that according to Newman 'the original revelation is unique: it was given *partly* in explicit doctrine, *partly* in feelings which were left to be subsequently drawn out into doctrines.'[23] Therefore, the further development is not a development of a primitive Creed but of a wordless impression given together with it and different from it in its content. It follows that development brings to light such doctrines as were not contained in the primitive Creed. Fresh revelations were added in the course of time and 'if it were established (for example) in catholic theology that revelation ended at the death of the last Apostle, Newman's theory could hardly survive without a restatement so drastic as to leave it almost unrecognizable.'[24]

The error here lies in the 'partly . . . partly.' According to Newman there is no question of indistinct feelings added to doctrines but of a real apprehension of the whole through a partial notional apprehension of the same, pointing to that whole. Revelation enters the world as a message about the meaning of Christ, the saving Incarnation of the Word promised by God through the Prophets. All that the Church now believes or ever will believe is contained in the inspired records of what happened in Christ. Nevertheless, although entirely contained in the primitive Creed, the content of revelation is not explicitly unfolded in it. Through illuminating grace, revelation, presented to man by the words of the message, impresses upon the mind of the faithful and the Church a real idea of the whole, imperfectly represented yet completely indicated by the scriptural message: 'One thing only has to be impressed on us by Scripture, the catholic idea and in it they [the dogmas] are all included.'[25] Development, therefore, is not only the expansion in the mind of a wordless 'idea-impression' but at the same time and in the same measure the explication of the content of the original message. That idea-impression is the living medium through which reflection unfolds the content of the message in a way that is faithful to its concrete fullness. It may be said, then, that the same process of development considered as a whole is as well a clarification of a presence of that whole to realizing apprehension as it is an elaboration of what is contained in the primitive message. In the process of development, the former functions as a medium to the latter, as the latter is a medium to the former. Both processes are in one another; they are one. Therefore the process, being guided by a real apprehension through which the whole is present to the mind, cannot be reduced to verbal reasoning. There is more in it than can be justified by formal logic. But at the same time the process will not be illogical or irrational. Reflection will afterward be able to show that the various points are related to one another in such a way as to form a consistent pattern. The dogma of the mother of God is closely related to the dogma of the Incarnation. The dogma of the Immaculate Conception fits in perfectly with the general idea that Mary is the true human mother of God, that she freely assented to the Incarnation and has therefore been united divinely to her Son in the whole work that she freely assented to by consenting to be His Mother. At the side of Him who is immaculate by the power of His divine nature men contemplate her who is immaculate by pure grace, pointing thus to the closest connection with God in the order of grace, combined with the infinite distance from God of even the highest perfection of which nature is capable by grace. The same dogmas are also harmoniously related to other doctrines, such as the Christian idea of the Church. Thus variously illustrating and emphasizing one another, all dogmas, old and new, form together one harmonious and consistent pattern according to the principle of the 'analogy of faith.'

Development of doctrine, then, is a continuous organic process of life by which the realizing faith of the Church expands itself into intellectual consciousness under the guidance of its illative sense, which is itself guided by the all-penetrating presence of the Holy Spirit. There may be imperfections and even material errors in its expressions, but the Spirit gradually leads the Church into the fullness of truth. Such a development is to be distinguished from an application of logical devices to a set of original propositions. The process uses reason but largely goes beyond it. There are spontaneous processes in it that later will be found to be in accordance with the rules of formal logic. For 'we think in logic as we talk in prose.' But the process as a whole cannot be described in terms of verbal logic, and some movements in it may seem incongruous for a time but will be corrected afterward. 'Nor do those enunciations become logical, because theologians afterwards can reduce them to their relations to other doctrines or give them a position in the general system of theology.'[26]

How is it possible to show that later doctrines are true developments and not corruptions of the original Creed? Not by the rules of logic, of course, for the process is by its very nature superior to such rules, although partly in accordance with them and never contradicting them. Therefore the only guarantee of true development is supra-logical. It is the guidance of the Holy Spirit who is present in the Church and works in it as a supernatural 'illative sense.' The Spirit is infallible. His guidance is infallible and that infallible guidance is at work in the Church as a whole. But in the social reality of the Christian community it must have an external spokesman whose declarations in certain circumstances are for all Christians the immediate criterion of what pertains and what does not pertain to the fullness of objective faith.

This Catholic theological solution is argued by Newman, especially in his *Essay on the Development of Christian Doctrine*, on the ground of a realistic sociological analysis of the life of an idea in a society. For the social life of the Church, although supernaturally inspired, conforms to the general laws of social life.

When a living idea, which entails a whole pattern of life, creates a society and enters into the minds and hearts of its members, it inevitably becomes the focus of constant and various preoccupations, leading to different views according to differences of character and situation. From their very nature human beings will tend to interpret the Christian idea from different points of view according to their personal character and their needs and inclinations, according also to their historical position in a given nation, a given culture, a school, a social or intellectual class, a religious or political party, or, finally, in the social structure of the Church itself. Hence, since partiality and one-sidedness are an innate feature of humanity, conflicting interpretations soon will confront one another, and the struggle begins. In the face of opposition, the confronting parties tend to overdo their respective positions. This leads to extremism and violent controversies. The peace of the community is disturbed; a general state of confusion sets in. Clear and sober minds try to find intermediate solutions in which the conflict is overcome by a synthesis of the partial truths that are to be found on both sides. Generally, free discussion is unable to bring about reconciliation and peace. The authority of the Church has to intervene. The Church as a whole has a feeling of the truth but does not know how to formulate it, how to answer the objects and arguments. Time is necessary for some points to become clear. They are discussed in local and then ecumenical councils, or an appeal is made to the sovereign pontiff. After due consideration clear formulas are created in which the Church recognizes its true meaning. They are solemnly defined and received by at least the greater part of the community, and peace is restored in the Church at large.

From the beginning, and independently of any philosophy, Newman read in the facts themselves the dialectical structure of the history of ideas. In his first great work, *The Arians of the Fourth Century*, he described how the Christological controversy had its origin in an opposition between two theological schools: Antioch and Alexandria. The former considered Christ mainly from the point of view of the Synoptic Gospels; and saw in Christ a man, just like ourselves, upon whom the gift of divinity had been bestowed. He was a man who received divinity. The latter looked at Christ in the light of St. John's Gospel and saw in Him the eternal Word who took flesh. In both positions the truth of Christ was endangered. The Antiochenes tended to separate the divinity and humanity of Christ in such a way that Christ was reduced to a loose juxtaposition of two beings. The Alexandrians, however, tended to confuse the divine and the human side of Christ so that the human side seemed to be reduced to a temporal modification of a divine subject. In the first position, the true divinity of Christ, the man, was endangered, and when asserted in a one-sided way, led to Nestorianism. In the second, the true manhood of Christ the God was obscured, and this eventually led to the Monophysite heresy. In the Council of Ephesus the first danger was warded off, and in the Council of Chalcedon definitive formulas were reached in which the unity of substance and the duality of natures were equally safeguarded.

L

In the description just given, the social reality of dogmatic development is merely viewed from without. It should not be forgotten, however, that the life of the Church, although subject to all the laws of social and historical existence, is more than human. It is vivified by the indwelling Spirit who according to the promise of Christ will in due time guide it into all truth. The Church is entirely human. As such it conforms to the laws that govern the existence of any human society. But at the same time it is entirely divine because the Spirit of Christ is the true inner principle of its life. Therefore, it seems natural to Newman that the way in which the Spirit infallibly guides the Church from within should have its expression in the external social structure of the Church. The idea of a doctrinal authority that externally guides the Church and under given circumstances settles its dogmatic problems in an infallible way through a special charism bestowed upon it for the occasion, is entirely in agreement with the wisdom of God who guides all things according to their nature.

Here, then, is the theological argument of Newman's theory of development. How can one be sure that a given point that came to the fore in later times is contained in the primitive deposit? Logical rules are by the nature of the case insufficient to bring about a definitive answer. They may lead to probabilities and go a part of the way, but they generally do not procure indubitable certainty. Moreover, even if individual minds or particular groups could be convinced, they could not impose upon the Church at large. Finally, taking account of the social tendencies just described, which inevitably lead to schisms and divisions by the working of human weakness, one-sidedness, and partiality, it seems evident that the unity of faith cannot be maintained except by the institution of an authority recognized as infallible by the community. It appears, then, that the infallible authority of the *magisterium* determines which accretions of doctrine are true developments, and which have to be rejected as corruptions. At the same time it raises a dogma from the condition of subjective truth, actually believed by at least a part of the Church, to the status of objective truth, which must be believed by all members of the Church.

According to Newman, then, in order to make sure that a given development is true to the original deposit, a declaration by the Church is a definitive and sufficient criterion. It is not necessary to prove by reason or history that later dogmas are contained in primitive teaching. As long, however, as the Church has not reached an infallible judgment, a theologian is allowed to argue against any disputable point with no blame being attached to him. In his later works Newman repeatedly says that freedom of thought is the best policy and that the Church should take action only when its inner peace is really endangered.

Therefore, in his *Essay on the Development of Doctrine* he does not attempt to prove that the actual developments accord with the original truth of the Gospel. The theological argument is enough. If he discusses some particular points and especially the privileges of the mother of God and the infallibility of the Church, he does so only in order to confirm by actual evidence an insight gained by theological reasoning and to remove some of the difficulties felt by his Anglican coreligionists.

In the second part of his book, however, Newman works out a philosophical and controversial argument in order to show that the general identity of Christian doctrine in the course of history can be plausibly argued on purely rational grounds. It is rather important to understand the true scope and nature of this argument. It is not Newman's intention to work out norms by which to prove that separate points are true developments. He is anxious to show that since the Church is a living body, moving as a whole, it is possible to establish 'that modern Catholicism is the legitimate growth and complement, that is, the natural and necessary development of the doctrine of the early church' (*Development*, p. 169). This he undertakes by working out seven notes or criteria of true development, taken from the general analogy of uncorrupted life: 'Taking this analogy as a guide, I venture to set down seven Notes of varying cogency, independence and applicability, to discriminate healthy developments of an idea from its state of corruption and decay' (*Development*, p. 171).

It is clear that Newman is working with a model of growth taken from nature and therefore easy to grasp. It should be emphasized, however, that the model is no more than a metaphor and has to be dealt with as such. Newman does not presume that the life of the human mind or society develops according to the same biological laws as the life of a tree. The general idea of life is realized in wholly different ways, which present, however, some general characteristics that lead men to refer to them by the same term. The general likeness between mental and natural life justifies the use of the latter as a guiding image to describe the former. 'The metaphor is an intellectual device by which we succeed in bringing within our reach that which is more remote. By means of what is nearer to us and easier to master we are able to get into intellectual contact with what is more distant and more difficult to control. The metaphor is an extension of our intellectual arm, it is a kind of logical fishing pole. . . .'[27] This is the kind of logic by which Newman's argument is to be judged. He always has a keen, direct, and comprehensive awareness of the mental and social phenomenon he is analyzing. But he brings it into focus by means of the metaphor of natural growth. This may be dangerous in less intelligent people; but in a mastermind who is constantly aware of the particular idea that he is talking about, it is the most adequate of methods.

The first criterion of genuine development of an idea is called 'the preservation of type.' The development of doctrine is an aspect of the full concrete life of the Church, in the same way as the development of one's convictions is an aspect of the total growth of one's personality. By severing the intellectual process from the whole life of the Church one falls into distorting abstractions since the Church, too, moves as a whole. If, then, the general characteristic or type of a person or a community remains constant through the course of time, it is a sign that their guiding idea has not been corrupted in the process. If the type of the whole is uncorrupted, it may be presumed that the development of its idea has also been genuine.

To Newman this first criterion is all-important. He devoted more than a hundred pages to its application. It is closely connected with his own spiritual way. The deep change in his conviction concerning the true form of Christianity was indeed occasioned by his gradual realization that in modern times the characteristic features of the ancient Church that he considered to be the test of genuine Christianity were to be found in the Church of Rome.

The second note is the 'continuity of principles.' It was made clear earlier what Newman means by 'first principles.' He distinguishes them from doctrines: 'They are the man.' They may change, but then the man too changes. Therefore they do not so much develop as govern and determine the development of one's convictions and opinions. They are the hidden forces and supreme masters of one's mental growth. They constitute a pattern. They express in the form of practical rules a basic experience of man. A man's true moral principles, for example, are the expression of the experience of conscience. Hence it follows that the continuity of principles is a more important note of true development than the identity of doctrines. If the problem of doctrine presented difficulties insoluble until now, the evidence of an identity of principles could be reassuring.

In the same way, it may be said that the true first principles of Christianity constitute the Church. The identity of principles is the inner side of what appears in the preservation of type. Those principles form together a consistent pattern. They are the expression of the basic experience of faith: the redemptive Incarnation of the eternal Son. In his *Essay on the Development of Christian Doctrine* Newman enumerates nine principles among which the principle of dogma has the first place. Later he added a tenth: the principle of development itself.

The third note is 'power of assimilation,' already spoken of in another context. A healthy organism grows by absorption of extraneous elements. The stronger its health, the more easily it assimilates these elements into its own life. By so doing, it loses nothing of its selfhood. On the contrary, it makes and perfects its own being and originality. In the same way, a healthy idea, a true view of life, is able to incorporate in its synthesis all elements of truth, whatever may be their philosophical context or origin. Therefore, the ability to assimilate other ideas is a sign that the assimilating idea is strong and healthy enough to develop its own content by taking up into its synthesis the most heterogeneous elements.

The fourth note is 'logical sequence.' We have already noted that it does not consist in the logical nature of the concrete process by which an idea advances, but in the coherence that afterward may be found in its results.

The fifth note is called 'anticipation of the future.' If it is true that there is an inner harmony between the later developments and the original idea, it may be expected that they will be anticipated or foreshadowed from the beginning in allusions or occasional statements that point to them.

The sixth note is 'conservation of its past.' As the present is anticipated in the past, so the past will be conserved in the present, not in a static and material way but in a dynamic way. As the child is conserved but cannot easily be recognized in the full-grown man, so in a more developed intellectual pattern early doctrines may be conserved in such a way that they cannot be discerned at first sight.

The last note is 'chronic vigor.' All ideas and institutions that are moving in time are naturally subject to processes of decay and enfeeblement. But as a healthy and strong organism soon cures and restores itself from within by its own vitality, so too a healthy social body will overcome its periods of decline by its own inner power. Such resistance to the ravages of time is a token of spiritual vitality and selfhood.

THE RUSSIAN CONTRIBUTION: VLADIMIR SOLOV'EV

Solov'ev, whom Mgr. D'Herbigny called 'a Russian Newman,' came to the conclusion that there was no essential difference between the great Churches of East and West, and worked for their union. Later after being silenced by the Holy Synod, he never abandoned his thesis that both East and West had their proper values, which should never be rejected, and that being complementary both would gain by a union.

One of the main difficulties that he had to surmount while working out the idea of the ecumenical Church was the fact of dogmatic change, which Orthodox theologians objected to in Roman Catholicism. Solov'ev dealt with it in the first part of an unfinished work on *The History and Future of the Theocracy* (referred to henceforth as *Theokratie*). His adversary, T. Stojanoff, declared that all possibility of *rapprochement* was excluded because, whereas the Eastern Church conserved the Christian truth, the Roman Church had developed it. Solov'ev argued that in the conditions of earthly existence it is impossible to preserve the truth from false interpretations except by developing it. The magisterial definitions 'are not new revelations but only new manifestations of one and the same unchangeable truth under aspects which up to then had not been clearly and distinctly perceived by the consciousness of the Church' (*Theokratie*, p. 415).

Solov'ev clearly demonstrates that saints such as Justin and Theophilus of Antioch had expressed themselves in a way that proved that the relation of equality between the Father and the Son was not a clear idea in the first centuries of the Church; if it was, they would have been heretics. The dogmas of Nicea and Constantinople were developments. He also proved that the Fathers of the 4th century accepted the idea of development. Solov'ev's case, as that of Newman, was with the Fathers.

Solov'ev's idea of development is dependent on German idealism, which he had criticized in his first great work, *The Crisis of
Western Philosophy*, and on Möhler, whom he admired. But his
main source is the idea of *Sobornost* by which Orthodox theologians
characterize their conception of the Church in opposition to Roman
authoritarianism. The meaning of the term, derived from *sobor*
(assembly), is very rich. It not only points to the synodical structure
of Church government, but includes the idea of a certain ontological unity. The whole life of the Church, in all its manifestations,
is the expression of one idea, which precedes, accompanies, and
penetrates it, working in it as an inner principle of cohesion.
Therefore in its outer life, too, the Church moves as a whole, and
although its decisions are made and pronounced by the synods,
these decisions have force only because and insofar as they express
the sentiment of the whole Church. Because we are one in Christ,
all the movements of the Church have to be accomplished in a spirit
of cooperation, agreement, and peace.

The central idea of Solov'ev's thought is the idea of 'God-
manhood, the union of God and creature' (*Theokratie*, p. 419). The
economy of salvation and the meaning of history is the perfect
actualization of the union, awaited by the entire human race,
promised to the Chosen People, and accomplished in Christ. The
union of God and man in Christ is the archetype of the ideal
humanity that all men are naturally striving after and toward which
the whole of history is guided by God's providence.

Therefore, in dealing with the problem of development,
Solov'ev repeatedly emphasizes that the whole Christian revelation
can be reduced to one single idea, the consciousness of one single
reality: the Christ-event. 'The one single dogma, the one truth which
contains in itself all other truths is the truth of the God-man, who
appeared in the flesh, rose from the dead, was exalted in heaven and
poured out the Holy Spirit on his disciples' (*Theokratie*, p. 421).
The essential act of faith by which we accept that single dogma is
'faith, living and concrete to which all abstract determinations are
alien' (*Theokratie*, p. 431). Hence: 'In that one single dogma all
those dogmatic truths and definitions which afterwards gradually
achieved clarity in the consciousness of the Church, becoming
unassailable parts of its dogmatic teaching, were already contained.
But in primitive Christianity those partial dogmas had not yet come
to clarity in the consciousness of the Ancient Church' (*Theokratie*,

p. 427). 'They were all inferred from it according to need by the teachers of the Church' (*Theokratie*, p. 430).

Two points must be elucidated concerning the nature of the process. It is a process that is at once human and divine. This is the basic idea. In God there is no change: consequently, the development of doctrine takes place on the human level. Man is by his very nature a being of development. His receptiveness to truth is subject to change. The truth of God does not change in the process, but 'to those changes in man's receptivity, relative changes in the effectiveness of the divine powers unavoidably correspond, that is insofar as that effectiveness is conditioned by human receptivity' (*Theokratie*, p. 416). The active principle, then, is the working of the eternal truth in a mind characterized by a changeable receptivity. If the life of dogma were divine only, no change could take place. If it were only human, there would be no immutability in the ongoing development. Consequently,

It is impossible to ascribe the definitions of the ecumenical councils exclusively to the relative powers of man. For they have a character of unconditional obligation. . . . Such a contradiction can only be avoided when one holds to our conception according to which in all the decisions of the ecumenical Church, performed by its legitimate representatives, neither the divine powers nor the human are separately at work, but the God-manly nature of the ecumenical Church itself in which the divine and the human principle are inseparably united without confusion. To the extent that they are dependent upon the divine principle those definitions express the unchangeable truth. To the extent that they follow from the human principle, they do not express that truth in its perfect fulness; and on that account they are perfectible by acts of the ecumenical Church which unveil other aspects of the same truth. [*Theokratie*, pp. 477–478]

If the godhead is in and by itself absolutely unchangeable, whereas humanity is in and by itself subject to various changes, then the God-manhood unfolds itself in a regular way. This means that it preserves its essence and its basic structures without any mutation, while at the same time it grows not only in its exterior range but also in its inner fulness and in the perfection of its expression in all the spheres of its existence [*Theokratie*, p. 476]

The second point that has to be considered is that of the laws that rule the process of development. Solov'ev always describes it as a kind of reasoning or inference. But it is clear that the word *reasoning* is to be taken in a very loose and general way. The example given is always that of the way in which St. Paul infers from the Resurrection of Christ man's own future resurrection. The former is uncontested from the beginning. It belongs to the one single object of the original Christian message. 'The latter truth, however, only becomes *indisputable* to the faithful when the qualified teacher of faith has manifested the inner connection of that truth with the fact which constitutes the original revelation; thus demonstrating that the former is *implicite* contained in the unchallenged content of revelation, and inferring it from the latter' (*Theokratie*, p. 430).

The idea of reasoning has to be qualified by the model of organic growth. From the nature of Solov'ev's idea itself and also because of his dependence on German Romantic sources, it was to be expected that the image of natural growth would be emphasized. He says indeed that developments arise 'in a way similar to that in which the parts and organs of one indivisible being gradually come out from the original, hardly perceptible yet fully real and internally determined, living seed, and become distinct' (*Theokratie*, p. 420). Although the declarations of the Church are occasioned by the rise of heresies, 'the living organization of the Church is directly at work here, elaborating its forms and separating those elements that are damaging to its wholeness' (*Theokratie*, p. 477).

THE FRENCH CONTRIBUTION: MAURICE BLONDEL

The intellectual situation in which Blondel wrote *Histoire et Dogme* is of particular interest. In his first and greatest book, *L'Action*, and the subsequent controversial articles, all written before the Modernist crisis, he had criticized the current apologetic methods that were more Lockeian than Catholic. According to that apologetic, the truth of Christianity must be proved by purely objective arguments based on verifiable facts, such as miracles and the fulfillment of prophecies. Blondel argued that the method did not work, as Lacordaire and Cardinal Dechamps had already experienced, and that from its very nature—its extrinsicism and dependence on logic—it could not work: first, because it made the possibility of personal belief and salvation dependent 'upon proofs which I cannot directly control by my own means,'[28] and which are now plausibly challenged by unbelieving critics; second, because a man cannot turn to a religion if it does not answer the basic problems of existence. Blondel pretended that even the defenders of the extrinsicist method were not convinced by their own arguments that they 'really but unconsciously rested on better reasons which indistinctly influenced them although, as a rule, they were not able to recognize and expound them.'[29]

Against the extrinsicist method Blondel opposed his 'method of immanence.' He constructed a most remarkable and profound philosophical analysis of human life considered under its volitional and active aspects. In all the movements of the will, directed toward the various possible goals of the present existence, a basic existential will reveals itself, ever striving beyond those empirical goals after an ultimate goal where it may come to rest as in its true and ultimate perfection. That basic will be called *volonté voulante*, distinguishing it from the *volonté voulue*, meaning by this that every exercise of the will (*volonté voulue*) was propelled and directed by a will that was not a special act but a dynamism that constituted the nature of the will itself (*volonté voulante*). That deeper will, active in experience, before all conscious acts determined by deliberation and choice, is to be found in and at the bottom of every act of personal self-orientation.

Blondel's analysis proceeded dialectically and ended in the conclusion that the object to which the *volonté voulante* was directed was something that transcended the actual range of the *volonté voulue* and was therefore necessary but impossible: necessary because man could not attain his proper ultimate perfection without it, impossible because it was beyond the reach of his human powers.

The practical conclusion was that no other way was left to a man who had reached that point than to assume an attitude of expectation, looking around for a solution that could not come except from without. In that situation the Christian religion presents itself to him as a message of salvation, and he finds himself invited to try its inner truth in practice by the test of the *volonté voulante*. Thus, by way of contemporary philosophy, Blondel rediscovered the old Christian idea of man expounded in the introductory remarks to Chapter Three of this study.

A second controversial situation opposed Blondel to the

'immanentism' of the Modernists, which when combined with historicism led to the rejection of the historical validity of such central facts as the Resurrection, and to an interpretation of Christian development exclusively in terms of an historical method that reduced the reality of history to its phenomenal side consisting of demonstrable facts. This led the Modernists to deny any special divine intervention in the course of history and to reduce the origin and development of Christianity to a process produced solely by the immanent forces of man and nature.

With regard to the problem of development Blondel is fighting a war on two fronts. On one side there are the conservative extrinsicists who accept without proof or inquiry that everything now believed must have been believed by the primitive Church because, as they assume, the infallibility of the Church is established by extraordinary facts such as miracles and fulfilled prophecies. Their uncritical a priori position prevents them from a serious examination of the evidence and from being really interested in the matter. The modern historicists, on the opposite side, reduce Christian history to a series of demonstrable facts succeeding one another according to the general immanent law of human history.

Against the former Blondel argues that the origin and progress of Christianity are of the nature of historical facts and that their historicity—that they took place according to the general laws of history—is an essential aspect of their reality. Against the latter he objects that the reality of what happens in history exceeds the purview of an exact historical method. The real is infinitely rich and intricate. A positive science can only describe one exterior aspect of its real object. It uncritically trespasses its limits when it takes its own abstract results for the real whole.

How is it possible to reconcile theology and history, the thesis of immutability with the sense of history? 'The active principle of the synthesis lies neither in the facts alone, nor in the ideas alone, but in the Tradition which embraces within it the facts of history, the effort of reason and the accumulated experiences of the faithful' (*History and Dogma*, p. 269). The deposit of faith is more than the message of the Gospel. It is an original, supernatural happening, the appearance of Christ in history, continued by the Holy Spirit in the life of the Church. This is the Christian presupposition and no science of history can reasonably disclaim it. What is called development of doctrine, although worked out in the sphere of the intellect, is only an aspect of a total process in which Christianity under the impact of Christ and guided by the Holy Spirit is engaged as whole. There is a dialectical relation between the facts, the thoughts and the experiences that present themselves to consciousness as the fruits of faithful action, all of them united in one single process. The source is not something that vanished in the past and is now only remembered. Tradition 'no doubt relies on texts, but at the same time it relies primarily on something else, on an experience always in act which enables it to remain in some respects master of the texts instead of being strictly subservient to them' (*History and Dogma*, p. 267).

Development of doctrine, then, is a process of dynamic conservation: 'I would say that tradition's powers of conservation are equalled by its powers of conquest: that it discovers and formulates truths on which the past lived, though unable as yet to evaluate or define them explicitly, that it enriches our intellectual patrimony by putting the total deposit little by little into currency and making it bear fruit' (*History and Dogma*, p. 267). The letter of the Gospel is only a part of the deposit. 'It is the guardian of the initial gift insofar as this has not been entirely formulated nor even expressly understood, although it is always fully possessed and employed; it frees us from the very Scriptures on which it never ceases to rely with a devout respect: it helps us reach the real Christ whom no literary portrait could exhaust or replace, without being confined to the texts' (*History and Dogma*, p. 268).

Here it must be emphasized that Blondel's solution of the problem of development rests on his 'Philosophy of Action,' probably the most important Catholic contribution to the philosophical thought of the day. The basic idea is the same as that expressed in Newman's statement that 'realizing is the very life of true developments;'[30] 'developments, arising out of a keen and vivid realizing of the Divine Depositum of Faith' (*Apologia*, p. 209). For according to Newman, the process of realizing is not so much a matter of the intellect as of the whole active personality, real apprehension being an impression made by the real on the mind, condition by daily efforts to live and act according to its claims. In order to realize God through conscience, man must be faithful to the inner voice. In order to realize Christ, man must live according to His word and example.

Blondel, however, worked out the idea by a philosophical

analysis unsurpassed in the history of thought. Time and again he repeats that developments arise out of a contact with the real Christ who invites men by faith and faithful action. As he says:

> Doubtless they could never be discovered by a doctrine which had no feeling for these elements contained in the moral and religious life which are not unconscious and irrational, but subconscious and unreasoned, which are provisionally and partially irreducible to explicit thought. But where a philosophy of action is concerned it is an entirely different matter: for this studies the various regular, methodically determinable ways by which a clear and formulated knowledge succeeds in expressing, more and more fully, the profound realities on which it feeds. [*History and Dogma*, p. 272]

Thus 'tradition presents the conscious mind with elements previously held back in the depths of faith and practised rather than expressed, systematized or reflected upon' (*History and Dogma*, p. 267).

What then is the test of true development? Certainly it is possible to show that later developments are internally connected with primitive doctrines, but these intelligible connections cannot be reduced to deductive relations between premises and conclusions according to the model of Aristotelian logic. Therefore 'the infallible *Magisterium* is the higher and really supernatural guarantee of a function which has its natural foundation in the concert of all the powers of each Christian and of all Christianity: *viribus unitis docet discendo et discit docendo semper*. Divine assistance ensures the normal, indefectible exercise of this essential function' (*History and Dogma*, pp. 277–278).

BARON FRIEDRICH VON HÜGEL

Von Hügel's could well be described as a cosmopolitan contribution. Of German and Scottish origin, born at Florence, he lived in England and was as equally well-read in German and French as in English philosophy and theology. Although a personal friend of the leading Modernists he was himself as orthodox a Catholic as ever one could be. His intellectual sympathy was principally with Blondel, although he was not really dependent on the French philosopher. He resisted stubbornly to the end of his life that kind of scholasticism represented by W. G. Ward, who thought it possible to enclose the whole truth, and nothing but truth, in a clear system of notions, propositions, and inferences.

Il n'y a que le tout qui soit intelligible (Blondel). Wholeness is the leading idea of von Hügel. The only object of true knowledge is the whole, i.e., the concrete; in order to get at it, man has to move as a whole; the process by which knowledge grows is a process of organic unity not only in the individual but also in society. From the first act of perception to the highest flight of mystical intuition there is a constant continuity. In a letter to A. Thorold he makes a distinction between: 'a certain aboriginal, dim but most real sense of realities of all kinds, especially of the Reality of God' on the one hand, and their reflective systematic elaboration on the other. 'And so far we can say that not only all Science but especially all knowledge begins with intuition—a certain Mysticism if you like' (*Life of von Hügel*, p. 337). We know the whole from the beginning and the processes of thought try in vain to exhaust its riches.

Another distinction is made 'between what is clear in and to the consciousness of the individual mind, and what, over and above this, is more or less dimly, unrecognizedly operating within and upon it' (*Life of von Hügel*, p. 336). Man's knowledge begins as a dim consciousness; that dim consciousness operates in the process of clarifying thought. Such thought is an essential condition of clear consciousness; the total content of what man dimly apprehends always transcends the range of clear notional elaboration.

In contrast to a mind such as Ward's 'there are other minds which see truths as intensely luminous centres, with a semi-illuminated outer margin, and then another and another, till all shades off into utter darkness. Such minds are not in the least perturbed by even having to stammer and to stumble' (*Life of von Hügel*, p. 330). Von Hügel's 'dim real sense of realities' clearly corresponds to Newman's 'idea' or realizing apprehension.

If the object of thought is the real in its concrete wholeness, the act, too, is a personal act, an act of the whole man. On the front page of his book de la Bedoyère places the following life-motto of von Hügel himself: 'More and more to live the spiritual life, increasingly to penetrate into the living Realities it reveals, and to express my discoveries, infinitely deepened, extended, tested, and standing by those of others, as faithfully and fearlessly as I can: this alone I can strive to do.' This is characteristic of a man who was all of one piece in his life and his thought.

Thought, according to von Hügel, is intensely individual and personal. That which matters cannot be directly communicated by means of notions, but must be experienced and thought out for oneself. Notional knowledge alone is never convincing. Von Hügel is deeply impressed by 'the apparently insurmountable individuality of all that affects us, and the equally insurmountable non-affectingness of all that is clearly and certainly transmissible from any one man to another.'[31] That thought is personal means, in the first place, that all the human energies and faculties have to collaborate in the growth toward truth: 'Man's personality, the instrument of all his fuller and deeper apprehensions, is constituted by the presence and harmonization of a whole mass of energies and intimations belonging to different levels and values; and not one of these can . . . be left aside or left unchecked by the others, without grave drawback to that personality.'[32]

If the individual character of all genuine knowledge is emphasized, its social and historical dimension is no less fully acknowledged. All individual thought is a participation in the efforts of a thinking community, and the thought of each generation participates in one movement extending from the past to the future. True knowledge goes from the concrete person to the concrete whole: 'something concrete which, being always more or less organic or personal, only develops in its relations to other organisms and individuals.'[33] As all the parts of a person make an organic whole, which as a whole enters into the search for truth, so the persons of one generation as well as succeeding generations are united into one social and historical organism striving after an ideal of knowledge that will never be entirely reached. The earnest worker in any field of research comes to the discovery 'that his work was largely limited and permeated by ignorances as to its subject-matter and passing modes of thought and feeling as to its appropriate categories; and hence, that to remain operative at all, it has to be sifted out, reinterpreted, transformed and incorporated by other minds and generations, who in their turn on the eternal quest, are as certainly doomed to a similar noble disappointment and unrest.'[34] This is a magnificent description of the general process of historical development, and it applies to the development of doctrine in the Church.

The last point to be examined is the role of ecclesiastical authority. In the painful situation in which he lived, von Hügel emphatically distinguished between infallible authority, the movements of Catholic public opinion, and the machinations of certain Roman or ultramontane circles. But he entirely accepted the rule of authority, centered in the See of Peter, as not only instituted by Christ but also necessary for the Church. This clearly results from his essay on 'Institutional Christianity or the Church, Its Nature and Necessity.'[35]

A PROTESTANT CONTRIBUTION: KARL BARTH

Karl Barth represents the extreme reaction against all forms or specific views of liberal theology. Whereas the liberals start with the principle that Christian doctrine should continuously be adapted to the discoveries of science and the current insights of philosophy, Barth proclaims the absolute independence of Christian truth and even ignores the problem of adaptation to the minds of contemporaries. Whereas the liberals conceive Christianity as the most perfect or divinely enhanced expression of a religious experience at work in all the religions of the earth, Barth simply denies that in sinful humanity there is any true knowledge of God independent of Christian revelation. There is no true way from man to God except by the coming of God to man. He even condemns Christianity as far as it has become a 'religion.' All religion is idolatry. Moreover, there is in man no 'capacity for God.' Even the possibility of knowing God, even man's receptiveness to Him, is caused by God alone, by the grace of His revelation. Whereas liberal theology excludes dogma from the essence of Christianity, Barth holds that by its very nature the Word of God as addressed to man becomes dogma and that the acceptance of dogma is an essential factor in all genuine faith. Because man can only reach God through dogma, dogmatic theology, which sifts out the dogmas from the written word of God, clarifying and systematizing them, is absolutely necessary. If dogma, conceived as a definite truth about God and His saving acts, is not essential, then theology has no meaning at all.

Theology, then, is an independent intellectual enterprise, making use of all the resources of language—for dogma is an expression of divine revelation in linguistic forms—but with no dependence upon the methods and results of autonomous human thought. The scriptural data are for the theologian what the data of sense experience are for the physicist. The theologian only aims at fitting the scriptural data into a system. Therefore Barth's disciple D. Bonhoeffer criticizes his theology as an *Offenbarungspositivismus*, a positivism of revelation.

Of course, Barth is not the sole representative of strict dogmaticism. Such an attitude was originally proper to the whole movement of dialectical theology. But Barth remained faithful to his extreme position. Brunner and others came to admit a universal religiosity, based on a diffuse natural revelation, while Bultmann entirely departed from the principle of dogma. For this reason and because of the magnitude and clarity of his *Kirchliche Dogmatik*, consideration is here limited to Barth. It would also be interesting to study the anticipations of Barth's question on the point of dogmatic evolution. In English theology, for instance, one should read the two volumes of H. D. McDonald's *Ideas of Revelation: An Historical Study* (New York, 1959). It is interesting to note that what he says for instance about Charles Simeon (1759–1836), an Evangelical, already points to the later solution of Newman; but it would take too much time to collect all the fragments.

According to Barth, revelation and faith are strictly correlative. The way man conceives the one necessarily entails a corresponding way of understanding the other. Revelation is in the first place the 'Word of God,' which has its ruling human expression in Scripture or the 'word of God.' The two have to be distinguished. The 'Word of God' is in itself beyond all creaturely powers of comprehension. It is God Himself in the act of His self-communication. That self-communication is not only a communication about God, but also and principally a communication of God. The scriptural 'word of God,' however, is not an act but a document in which the original happening of the Word of God is recorded in human words. Dogma is the whole content of the Word of God as expressed in the scriptural records, that dogmatic theology tries to extract from Scripture, exposing, clarifying, analyzing, and systematizing it by all the means of the intellect. Ideally considered, Dogma would be coextensive in its content with the 'Word of God,' a perfect replica of the Word in the human mind. But we can never exhaust it. The dogmas of man are never coextensive with Dogma. The dogma's, then, are the ecclesiastical propositions that try to express man's knowledge of the Dogma, while dogmatic propositions are theological statements that try to analyze and define as distinctly as possible the dogmas of the Church with a view to a growing explication of Dogma.

There is, then, a continuous and homogeneous movement from dogmatic theology toward the Word of God by the means of dogmas that try to express Dogma. 'Dogmatic propositions, dogmas and Dogma have this in common; taken together they are not the truth of revelation, but Dogma is, and the dogmas and dogmatic propositions aim at being . . . on the way to the truth of revelation' (*Church Dogmatics*, pp. 307–308). 'Truth of revelation' is to be understood as the reality of revelation or the self-revealing reality or the Word of God. The proper, although ideal, object of dogmatic theology is not formally the 'truth of revelation' but Dogma, which, being an idea in man, is not the Word of God itself but tends toward it. The Word of God is that toward which faith tends through the mediation of Dogma, as Barth argues, quoting St. Thomas.

Dogmas, the actual expression of Dogma in the Church, although growing in distinctness and verbal clarity, will never succeed in expressing the whole of Dogma. 'If we knew about Dogma, if we had Dogma, then we would know and have the Word of God itself in a definite and definitely indicated form and manifestation of Church proclamation, because Dogma is Church proclamation in real agreement with the Word of God. But a theology which would assert its knowledge and possession of Dogma would be a *theologia gloriae*, which ought not to claim to be the dogmatics of the Church' (*Church Dogmatics*, p. 308).

It is clear by now that Barth's 'Dogma' somehow corresponds, on the level of theology, with 'Idea' in Newman's sense, Blondel's 'realizing knowledge,' or von Hügel's 'dim but most real sense of realities.' Its origin is divine, but the way it functions in theology is the same as the way the realities just mentioned function in a general theory of knowledge. It is present and already at work in the first stage of human consciousness; it leads theological thought in its efforts to clarify its object; it forever transcends all dogmatic or theological achievements. Dogma is the content of what the Church preaches, as far as it corresponds to the Word of God expressed in the Bible; but in dogmatic preaching it is never fully expressed. The preaching impresses Dogma on the believing mind, but in defective dogmatic expressions. In the act of believing man assents to Dogma, tending toward the Word of God, but the object of that assent is only imperfectly represented by the explicitly formulated dogmas.

Barth's general theory of the development of dogma is luminously articulated. By theological reflection on Dogma—the proper object of dogmatic theology according to Barth—the body of ecclesiastical dogmas continually grows or may grow toward an unattainable fullness.

Up to now this study has dealt only with the objective aspect of the process. A consideration of the subjective side is equally necessary, for one cannot attain transcendent Dogma, reaching toward God's Word and Truth, except by a personal act of faith.

As modern theology in general and dialectical theology in particular emphasize, Barth too holds that revealed truth is not genuine truth as long as it is only notionally apprehended and assented to. As long as it does not become truth for a man in a personal apprehension and acceptance, he does not really know it. Dogma is 'a truth, which we may possess as a truth only by its being told us by God, and by the acceptance of it being impossible otherwise than by the decision of a definite attitude to what is said to us. . . . a dogma . . . is a doctrinal proposition . . . but a proposition which can teach us and be a dogma only so far as it goes forth from God . . . and comes to us in the act of obedience . . . [it] goes forth in a divine, comes to us in a human decision' (*Church Dogmatics*, p. 311). Therefore, 'it must first [not in a temporal but in a logical way] be believed and only then and in that way can it be known as truth. *Credo ut intelligam*' (*Church Dogmatics*, p. 314).

In the foregoing text, what is added to the exterior proposition seems to be no more than an injunction addressed to the will. Is it also an illumination of the mind? In order to answer the question Barth's theology of faith must be probed more deeply. Faith is an acceptance of Dogma. Before the act of faith, Dogma as expressed in the dogmas is no more than a set of naturally understandable propositions—understandable in a notional sense! But the apprehension (*Erkenntnis*) of God's Word is only possible to man in 'the event (*Ereignis*) of the Word of God' (*Church Dogmatics*, p. 226). *Apprehension* means here true or real apprehension as distinguished from a mere knowledge about the message. Men apprehend the Word of God only when it hits them in their existence. Now the event through which the notional message becomes an apprehension is, considered as terminating in man, an experience (*Erfahrung*), and considered as going out from God, a call (*Anruf*). This experience is both an apprehensive and a volitional act (compare the doctrine of St. Paul and St. John as systematized by St. Thomas).

It is a self-determination of man, but such a self-determination is only possible and actually accomplished through a determination by God: 'Our very self-determination is here subordinate to a determination by God, and our self-determination requires this determination by God in order to become an experience of His Word' (*Church Dogmatics*, p. 229). Barth is concerned with the absolute primacy of grace. Man cannot even know how faith happens or that faith is possible except in the act of faith itself. Faith is an absolute beginning and as such it is worked by God in the way of a *gratia operans*, as St. Thomas would say.

> In faith as real experience through the known Word of God, the control passes as it were to acknowledgment of the Word of God, which we regarded as the concrete form in which it is experienced by men. No matter in what perfection or imperfection of form human action, regarded as acknowledgment, may take place, in faith it is the right, the accepted, the acknowledged acknowledgment, not because man in himself has the power of, not because he has of himself succeeded in, achieving this right acknowledgment, but because what he actually can and does compass is acknowledged by the acknowledged Word of God, not as self-determination, but as self-determination determined by the Word of God. Let us hold on to the fact that faith is experience, a concretely fixable temporal act of this man's or that, the act, in short, of acknowledgment. [*Church Dogmatics*, p. 263]

Attentively considering that the act or acknowledgment of faith is both a volitional and a cognitive act whose object is not a set of formulated dogmas but the living Dogma that shines through its imperfect expressions and sets man toward the Word of God, it clearly results that the nature of the apprehension does not remain notional but becomes real in the act by which God causes in man the experience of faith. That experience is not only an experience of being addressed by God but also an experience of God Himself in His act of addressing man, which is the event *hic et nunc* of revelation. God's Word in the concrete is Christ, and the experience of faith is real, not just thought to be so, because men experience Christ: 'But it is the Word, it is Christ, to whom faith is related because he gives himself as object to it, who makes faith into faith, into real experience' (*Church Dogmatics*, p. 263).

It is not difficult to see that Barth's conception of the development of dogma is a theological one. We do not, of course, mean by that expression that he accepts an infallible authority as the concrete criterion of true development, but that for him the process is not a mere logical operation of the intellect but a growing apprehension of the content of Dogma, grasped *per modum unius* by the mind under the gracious impact of the Word of God.

A COMPARATIVE SYNTHESIS

That from the beginning of the 19th century so many great philosophers and theologians, however different their background and their way of expressing their ideas, came to the same basic insights into the process of dogmatic development, and this is an original way and in most cases independently from one another, is at least a striking fact. It betrays a gradual change in the intellectual climate of Western culture: a new way of understanding the nature and working of human knowledge and thought. It was an effort required by the historical situation to overcome the opposition of what may roughly be called the realistic and the idealistic conceptions of knowledge. According to the first, represented by the prevailing philosophy of the *Aufklärung*, knowledge proceeded by a generalization from the facts, given in sense experience, and thence by deduction from the statements obtained by such generalizations. According to the second, the philosophy of gross common sense, building upon the foundations of sense information, had to be broken through in order to get at the point of departure and the method of true philosophy. That point of departure was an idea not derived from without by means of sense experience but present in the very source of spiritual life, constituting it, and dialectically comprehending all sense experiences in the process of its self-realization. According to the romantic type, the idea, although reflected in the representations of objective thought, could not in itself be objectified. It had to be lived and immediately experienced in the individual consciousness, and the whole life of the subject was active in the process of its self-clarifying actualization. According to the rationalistic type, most purely represented by Hegel, the whole process was objective, not in the way of sense perception but in the way of pure ideas or concepts, and the moral subject was as such not involved in the dialectical progress of the undifferentiated idea toward the all-comprehensive articulate system. The philosopher was a mere contemplator and had only to follow with his mental eye the divine genesis of the universe, which was identical with the unfolding of the idea in his own consciousness.

The general idea of development as a necessary process from an imperfect and unrealized toward a perfect and fully realized state has undoubtedly been worked out in German idealism. The Christian thinkers studied in the course of this chapter had to defend the originality, the otherness, the irreducibility of a Christian revelation that entered into history not from within, as a stage in the general movement of dialectical evolution, but from without, by a free decree and initiative of God's mercy. With the exception of Newman, all of them were more or less influenced by the great movement of idealistic philosophy, including even Karl Barth, who in his harsh protest against liberal theology was deeply influenced by his opponents, whom he knew so well.

The first point to be justified, then, was that *fides est ex auditu.* Faith, the beginning and source of Christian life and salvation, does not flow from man's own inner powers within the process of his spiritual evolution. It is a beginning brought about by God, received by man in his encounter with His Word as it is preached by the Church. It is a knowledge of God and of His gratuitous dispensation through Christ, a knowledge that comes to man through the senses. That knowledge cannot begin except as a kind of awareness of something that stands before man and comes to meet him as an independent reality. It is occasioned by a contingent exterior happening that he perceives and that conveys to the mind a definite meaning.

The whole problem, then, is one of determining what is properly and ultimately perceived in the message of faith and consequently what the nature of faith consists in. The general answer, given by all the authors considered, is that the material object of faith-perception, although it presents itself in dogmatic propositions, is not properly these propositions, considered as notionally communicable pieces of information, but the reality itself that these propositions point toward. The material object of faith, although articulated for human understanding in the form of abstract propositions, cannot be reduced to these propositions. Man's inner perception goes beyond them and reaches the real itself, the Dogma, of which man is aware *per modum unius* and which contains in its fullness not only those dogmas that are actually known but all possible dogmas that may gradually but never exhaustively be explicated from the original impression. In assenting to that whole, conveyed to man's consciousness by propositional forms, man assents to all the possible dogmas, however imperfect the actual state of dogmatic knowledge may be.

Solov'ev and Blondel, especially, draw attention to the fact that the original truth of faith is the proclamation of fact: the saving facts connected with the appearance of Christ. In the fact of Christ as apprehended and assented to by faith, all possible dogmas are already implicitly contained. Blondel, together with Möhler and von Hügel, especially emphasizes that this concrete fact, with the fullness of its meaning, has preconsciously to be lived by the whole person before it is acted upon and discerned by analyzing reflection.

Schlegel, Newman, and Kuhn, although supposing the influence of a previous moral attitude, emphasize the intellectual and intuitive nature of the first originating act by which the object of faith is apprehended. Subsequently all the powers of man are stirred up by the impact of the real; hence the person moves as a whole—or as a harmonious whole, as Schlegel would emphasize—in revealing to the inquiring mind the riches of the original inner perception.

Kuhn, Newman, von Hügel, Blondel, and Barth point to the fact that the original idea or Dogma is not only the primitive datum, the point of departure of the process of clarification, but also that it is present in the process itself as a guiding principle, as the object of reflection, and as an ideal that intellection is always striving after without ever comprehending its inexhaustible fullness.

Solov'ev, Drey, Möhler, Kuhn, and Blondel explicitly state that the proper rule of faith is not the Bible, a document of the past, but the present doctrine of the Church, which is the actual stage of a living process that began in the OT, grew toward Christ, who is the fullness of objective revelation, and continues to grow in the mind of the Church by way of a living tradition.

Newman and Barth, under the influence of their respective situations, which made them face dogmatic relativism in its initial (Newman) and its final (Barth) stages, were particularly keen on the dogmatic principle according to which true faith, although transcending the propositions in which its object presents itself, is not possible without dogma conceived as a definite unfalsifiable truth about the saving God.

All the authors considered here, except perhaps Karl Barth, conceive the development as a dialectical process, going on through the synthesis or reconciliation of oppositions that arise in the course of interpretative thought. Some of them mainly or exclusively bring to the fore the challenge of heresy. But others, especially Schlegel, Kuhn, and Newman, lay bare the general causes that are part of human nature: the natural tendency of the mind to conceptualize and to analyze its experiences; the abstract character of our knowledge; the tendency toward one-sidedness leading to controversial incomprehension and narrow-mindedness.

In Kuhn, Newman, Solov'ev, Blondel, and von Hügel the general view is worked out that development is inevitable and necessary because the expression of faith is human and that all the manifestations of man are characterized by historicity. It is not true, then, that development arises only through the contingent appearance of heresy in a life of faith that would otherwise go on in Arcadian peace. Revelation received in human minds and hearts, necessarily from the nature of the case, causes the restless intellect to strive after a perfect comprehension of the divine gift. Faith, *quaerens intellectum*, has in itself the impulse toward development. The possibility of heresy is rooted in that spontaneous movement of analytical interpretative thought.

With this is connected the general idea that development, although traversed by efforts of deliberate reflection, is on the whole a process of spontaneous mental growth. Its proper figure is not that of a ratiocinative operation but that of a spontaneous unfolding of the different aspects of an idea which rather suggests a comparison with natural growth. The image of the organic is cherished by almost all the authors studied, but as applied to the life of the mind it was analyzed with particular acuteness by Newman.

Lastly, some Catholic thinkers, especially Möhler, Kuhn, Newman, and Blondel, strongly emphasize that the sole definite guarantee of true development is not to be sought in logical tests but is given by the faith of the Church itself and especially by its infallible organ, the hierarchical magisterium.

PRESENT POSITION IN CATHOLIC THEOLOGY

The view on the development of doctrine advocated by the theologians and philosophers in whose works its evolution and various presentations were studied here, we call 'theological,' as opposed to 'logical' and to 'transformistic.' In opposition to the logical theories, the theological view does not describe the phenomenon of development as a chain of inferential operations, verified by strict logical rules, but as a broader process in which a gift of judgment and consequently the living faith of the believer works as a concrete rule. The results of that process, although not conflicting with the rules of logic, cannot be reduced even in retrospective consideration to the relations of abstract intelligibility that connect them with one another in a homogeneous systematic pattern. That position, especially in the thought of Newman and Blondel, is justified by a general philosophical insight into the real ways of man's thinking activity. But the properties of that complicated process, moving on as a growing center of light with a semi-illuminated margin that fades away at last into the darkness of mystery (von Hügel), are enhanced in the development of Christian doctrine by the mysterious and supernatural character of its object and of the way it is apprehended by faith.

Theological theories are also opposed to transformistic theories in that they simply accept the special origin of that revelation which is the object of theology. They take faith as a supreme and independent rule, not subject to reason as to a higher critical norm. Theology accepts its own starting point and its principles from revelation. Reason is used only as an instrument to work out in a critical and consistent way the specific content of that revelation. Revelation with its definite content that cannot be explained away by reason—although presented in a form that is subject to reformulation—has to be accepted simply as irrevocable truth; this is the 'principle of dogma' that is denied by liberal theology.

If the rule by which to judge the development of doctrine is neither a logical device nor the philosophy of the day, it follows that development must have a rule of its own. That rule is accepted by faith: the rule of doctrinal authority. The magisterium expresses and declares the ecclesiastical sense of faith that is itself guided by an inner supernatural rule: the Holy Spirit, working in the Church as a whole and assisting its leaders. These leaders are appointed by Him through the voice of the Church to be the successors of the Apostles to whom Christ once entrusted the government of His community. Because this rule works in a supernatural way that can only be recognized by faith, it follows that its acceptance is a second reason why the theory under discussion may be called theological.

There are two reasons, then, why a theory of development may be characterized as theological: the theological understanding of its process and the theological nature of the norm by which its truth is to be judged. Of course, if one does not accept the rule of a lasting living authority and thinks, as Barth for instance does, that the appeal to Scripture is able to work somehow as a sufficient criterion, the solution that he gives to the problem may still be typically theological because of the first reason.

The theological theory gradually penetrated Catholic theology and came to supplant the once-current logical explanations. The main reason for this change in Catholic thought has already been dealt with in the critical survey of the logical theories. No logical device is able to cover the facts that history has brought to light. Moreover, the logical theory rests upon the unreal a priori assumption that a living progress of thought, if it be true, must be the working out of a mental operation that is in itself syllogistic or reducible to formal logic.

The theological theory has had its pioneers in Catholic theology, most of them men of recognized genius. The basic idea or intuition that they try to work out is demonstrably the same, as can be seen from the investigation here. Their general background, their terminology, may differ greatly. They do not emphasize the same aspects equally nor are they equally aware of all that is involved in the problem. But the intellectual pattern is unquestionably the same.

This examination concludes with a general historical outline of the growing influence that the theological view has exercised in recent Catholic theology. It will be brief and will not dwell on the separate contributions of the various authors. This has been done admirably well by G. E. Meuleman in *De Ontwikkeling van het Dogma en de Rooms katholieke Theologie* (Kampen, 1951) and by H. Hammans in *Die neueren katholischen Erklärungen der Dogmenentwicklung* (Essen, 1965). The way in which the question is introduced is in many cases the same: all other theories fail to cover the facts or to correspond sufficiently to the requirements of faith. Therefore one must look for another solution along the lines prepared by such thinkers as J. A. Möhler and Cardinal Newman. Newman is the main source. At first, theologians felt uneasy before

Newman's thought, which was so conspicuously essayistic and non-scholastic. They set out to translate and rethink his views in scholastic terms, trying to correct them and to fit them into their traditional system. This often resulted in a more involved reconstruction of the logical theory. Even Marín-Sola thought he had done justice to the essential meaning of Newman. Gradually, however, a deeper change set it. Catholic theological thought became freer and more critical toward the traditional schemes of neo-Scholasticism.

In the 19th century the theologians who had to prepare the definition of the Immaculate Conception had already come under the influence of Möhler and Newman. G. Perrone was rather vague; but his great pupil, C. Passaglia, came very near to a new type of solution not uninfluenced perhaps by St. Thomas' concept of faith. He does not distinguish between an unchangeable objective, and a changeable subjective, faith. In one respect both are unchangeable, in another, both are subject to development. This development is a transition from an immediate and unreflected but real apprehension to a mediate and reflective but notional apprehension. The point of departure is not so much a set of propositions as the reality apprehended in them and in which all possible dogmas are already implicit. Faith is already a participation in the things man hopes for, and the life of faith guides him deeper into the truth, making possible new ways of explicating its content.

The First Vatican Council, in reproving the views of A. Günther, dealt with the problem in a significant way. That devout priest devised some theological views, building on a philosophy of his own, inspired by contemporary idealism. The reason why revelation is necessary does not consist in the fact that its truth transcends, by its own nature, the powers of human understanding. It is necessary because of the weakness of human thought caused by sin. It is not supernatural as to its essential content, only as to the way in which it is given to man by a special intervention of God. Revealed truth consists in a few facts and basic insights, which are the germ out of which Christian reflection develops the doctrines of faith with the aid of the Holy Spirit. The Apostles had only an imperfect explicit knowledge of the content of revelation. The Fathers expanded and corrected their views with the aid of a given philosophy. Medieval theology improved upon the Fathers using the instruments of another philosophy. In later times a new interpretation would be required in accordance with a better philosophy, of which Günther himself tried to elaborate the basic insights. The definitions of the Church are necessary in order to sift the grain from the chaff in a process partly determined by man's sinful condition and to establish the official doctrine of the Church in a given epoch.

There was a real danger of relativism in Günther's idea of the relation between philosophy and revelation. He seemed to imply that revelation, working only as a corrective within the progress of natural human thought expressed by philosophy, had no content of its own really distinct from that of philosophy and that its meaning had to be reinterpreted in accordance with the higher stages of philosophical developments. Hence it followed that the definitions of the Church, although ruling the faith of the Church for the time being, could in a certain sense be reconsidered and corrected by later declarations. The Council in condemning Günther appealed to the Vincentian canon, but clearly admitted the principle of development in a very broad and general sense. It excluded only this: that the meaning of what was once declared by the Church could be altered in the course of time according to new philosophical principles of interpretation.

When dealing with the theology of the 19th century and the anti-Modernist reaction it has been noted that some theologians tried to keep away from any logical theory and variously conceived the development of dogma as a transition from an indistinct to a more distinct or from a partial to a more adequate apprehension of what is given from the beginning. However, they did not devise a real theory of development.

In this context three theologians must be mentioned who appealed to Newman and came to a better understanding of his meaning. The first is H. de la Barre. While he adhered to a propositional interpretation of dogma and its development, he emphasized that the process of dogmatic development was different from that of a purely rational development because its point of departure, the 'Christian idea,' being a revealed mystery, was different from that of natural thought. Hence its results, expressed in the declarations of the Church, are of the nature of a 'transcendent fact.' If so, then the process, too, 'is not exclusively amenable to the human laws of any other doctrinal evolution. The magisterium steps in as a superior principle: it is a guiding principle, the soul of the doctrine, just as the principle of life directs the evolution of an embryo.'[36]

Complementing de la Barre, J. V. Bainvel stressed the point that tradition in the Church cannot be reduced to what may be detected in its literary monuments. Tradition goes beyond them as a living reality that works in the collective consciousness of the Church. What lives in tradition and constitutes the object of theological reflection is one single reality, apprehended by the Apostles, and by the Church after them, as a 'basic intuition.' In that whole the later dogmas were already apprehended by the Apostles as facts, not as truths. In the course of time they became formulated doctrines. Here, Bainvel obviously goes too far and does not rightly interpret Newman, who would not have admitted that the Apostles apprehended the dogma of the Immaculate Conception as a fact. Newman rather holds that as a fact and as a truth it was implicit in the one Christian system, confusedly apprehended as a whole.

Deeper still was the contribution of P. Rousselot. He knew Newman but combined his insights with the Thomistic doctrine of faith in a most original way. The main ideas of Rousselot were these: (1) all the possible points of faith form together an organic unity in which they are all correlative to one another, so that to know a part is already to know all of them; (2) the total object of faith is apprehended by an intellectual view, the eye of faith, caused by the supernatural light of faith; (3) therefore a greater grace of faith gives a surer eye to discern and judge the truth of faith, because of it men know the truth and the truths of faith *per modum connaturalitatis*, as St. Thomas says; (4) the knowledge of faith may, on the plane of discursive and analytic thought, remain indistinct, while on the plane of inner apprehension of *auditus interior* it may be more complete than the reflective notional apprehension of a great theologian: a mystic and even an ignorant Christian may enjoy a more exact view of Christian truth than a theologian who has less faith; (5) therefore, the development of dogma in the Church is a translation of that vision of faith in terms of rational thought. In accepting the later dogmas we do not believe new articles, but we know more explicitly the content of the old articles whose aspects form a unity.

In the question of development, as also in the question of the rational justification of faith, Rousselot combined the ideas of Newman with the Thomistic doctrine of the *lumen fidei*, but he did it in such a way that his personal view did not entirely agree either with that of Newman or with that of Thomas Aquinas. His contribution to the question could not exercise a great influence because his explicit remarks on the point were published only in 1950.

It is only at the end of the 1930s that the controversies began that would lead to a definitive break-through in the theological solution. They were stirred by L. Charlier's *Essai sur le problème théologique* (1938). Starting with the idea that the proper and formal object of theology is God Himself, considered in the mystery of His self-communication, Charlier first concludes that faith is not in the first place an acceptance of positions in human language, but a supernatural communion with the self-revealing God Himself, pointed to by means of the revealed word. Revealed truth is primarily a real happening and secondarily an acceptance of doctrine. Hence the revealed truth transcends theology, systematic as well as historic. Neither speculation nor history can give a sufficient guarantee that a given point of doctrine is part of revealed truth. The only guarantee is the Church itself in which Christ lives and whose preaching is a living tradition that comprehends and transcends both Scripture and the history of dogma. If this is true, then as the word is only a cognitive aspect of a reality that happens in the Church, so the development of doctrine, too, is only a cognitive aspect of the expansion of Christ's life in the Church. As in the first, so in the second case, the only possible guarantee is the supernatural authority of the Church. Reasoning and historical investigation are by their very nature unable to do it.

A year before the publication of Charlier's original book, two great scholars of the Thomistic School, M. D. Chenu and H. D. Simonin, had made a step forward in the direction of the theological solution of the problem by considering it in the light of St. Thomas' doctrine concerning the *lumen fidei*. They invoked the authority of St. Thomas in order to establish that the deepest reality of faith is not an assent to dogmatic propositions but a communion with the reality that those propositions indicate. Consequently, progress in the understanding of faith cannot be reduced to a logical connection of propositions, although on the plane of human expression such connections may be found. The progress of dogma in the Church is a supernatural process by which a supernatural awareness of the material object of faith expands in the thought of the Church, assisted by the Spirit and in due time declared by the magisterium.

In that process, discursive thought according to human rules is only auxiliary. The whole process is a process of faith: within faith, in the light of faith, and toward the goal of faith, the reality of which man already possesses in a dim way under the veil of faith. Its movement cannot be covered by processes of logical inference, and the declaration of the Church is a necessary supernatural rule by which to discriminate between true and corrupting developments.

It is difficult to summarize the contemporary debates to which more than fifty theologians since World War II have contributed. The discussion became particularly animated on the occasion of the definition of the Assumption. Therefore this study will not give an account of the particular opinions put forth by the various contributors, but will simply attempt to explain the outstanding ideas that arose in the course of the last decade.

The problem of the development of doctrine is a very comprehensive and complicated one because it is connected with so many other central problems of theology: the nature of revelation, the place of Christ in revelation, the sense of Scripture as God's Word and the special requirements of its true interpretation, the relation between divine truth and its human expression; also, the nature of faith, the way it apprehends its object, the possibilities and means of its progress in the human mind; and the nature of the Church, the way tradition lives in it, the relation between its life as a whole and its doctrinal tradition; the relation between the hierarchical social institution, expressed in forms of human culture and organization, and the inner supernatural reality of the mystical body; the working of the Spirit who guides the Church into all truth.

As to the nature of revelation, different aspects, often presented in different ways, have been differently emphasized or estimated. Some theologians lay special stress on the character of fact. What is manifested in revelation is not so much a propositional doctrine about God and Christ, but God Himself, unveiling His mystery in the coming of Christ and his saving activity. That fact with its meaning is still present and open to the faith of the Church as it was to the faith of the Apostles. With Christ, objective revelation is in a certain sense completely achieved. The special charismatic apprehension and explication of that fact by the Apostles is the divine word that defines the meaning of the fact. In the fact of Christ, combined with the words of the Apostles, objective revelation comes to an end. But as that fact is an inexhaustible mystery open to the sight of faith, it is apprehended in a way ruled by the apostolic interpretation but not fixed by it. By contemplating that fact and reflecting upon it, an infinite progress of faithful understanding is possible in which no new truths are added to the apostolic deposit but new articulations are distinguished in it. This point was stressed by N. Sanders, H. Rondet, and others.

F. Taymans, following Charlier, insisted on the point that the reality through which God reveals Himself is the hidden life of Christ in His mystical body. Christ progressively reveals Himself in the Church. Development of doctrine is a continuous growth of the consciousness that the Church has of its own inner mystery.

There is an element of truth in this view, but if it is taken separately, unconnected with the first, it might become misleading because it suggests the idea of a continuous revelation. It is better to say, then, that the growing consciousness that the Church attains of its own mystery in the course of time is not an immediate explication of that ever-present mystery but one that is objectively mediated by man's apprehension of the historical Christ as described in the Gospel and interpreted by the apostolic generation.

K. Rahner and H. Schillebeeckx, agreeing with the preceding authors that revelation is a divine self-communication through Christ, emphasize especially the proper supernatural character of that self-communication, considered as a self-gift of God. If revealed truth could be reduced to a number of propositions about God, man's apprehension of their meaning could not transcend the range of what human language is able to convey. There would be no proper self-communication of God. In order to be a special supernatural communication, the propositions must come to man in such a way that through them he attains God Himself. Therefore, revelation must be of such a nature that a true apprehension of what it intends exceeds the limits of what human language is logically capable of expressing. In other words, faith cannot be an assent to human propositions caused only by an actual grace operating in the will. It must be caused by a divine light, the light of faith, which connects men with God's self-revealing reality in a way that is strictly divine. Hence it is evident that by the very nature of the formal or proper object of faith, development of doctrine cannot be a logical operation on propositions. It must be formally grounded in and guided by the light of faith or inner revelation. The process necessarily escapes an adequate control by logical rules.

Other authors, among them H. de Lubac and M. Köster, stress the point that even in natural human knowledge there is a pre-propositional, global apprehension of its object that gradually becomes explicit and articulate in an analytic rather than strictly inferential way. Similarly, under the impact of God's reality upon the mind through the illuminating grace of faith, man apprehends His revelation as a whole, and development of doctrine is a gradual translation of that global apprehension into forms of human language. Once more, this is a valuable insight; but it must be corrected by the essential complementary view that in the post-apostolic Church the global apprehension, although effected by an inner light, is, on the level of conscious knowledge, mediated by a message that comes from without; so that in relation to the conscious life of faith the object of that apprehension is ruled by the scriptural word and the dogma of the primitive Church. The basic and essential pattern of what in faith presents itself to the believing mind after the manner of explicit knowledge is determined by the dogmatic content of the primitive message. It must be stressed that if the development of doctrine is rather an analysis and description of something present to the mind in its wholeness, the essential condition of its being convertible into explicit human knowledge is its being presented to man in the form of a message. It is the proper characteristic of faith that it is both a real apprehension, or a mysterious contact with a supernatural concrete whole, brought about in man by a divine light, and an assent to a verbal proposition reaching man from without and enabling him to grasp it in a human way and to assimilate and use it in his conscious life. The inner divine contact and the outer message are two essential aspects, neither separable nor confused, of the one theandric reality of revelation and faith.

Therefore, some theologians refuse to accept the idea that an immediate supernatural contact with self-revealing reality is essential to the point of departure of doctrinal development. Man certainly apprehends the reality of revealed truth but only through the medium of conceptual propositions. Against this, however, it might be objected that according to the general structure of human knowledge, mere notions cannot help man to apprehend a reality. They cannot go beyond abstractions. A reality cannot be truly reached through images or concepts derived from realities of another order. They may be true in their own way as metaphorical

M

or conceptual pointers toward a reality, but they cannot make one apprehend that reality itself. Only when linked to an immediate contact with the real are they able to function as clear windows through which is seen a given aspect of the real. If supernatural faith attains to the divine itself, then it must have its origin in an immediate supernatural contact with the divine. Only on the condition that notional communication and a real impression go together is it possible that development of doctrine may be more than logical deduction. We must hold to the theandric conception of faith: a communion with God in the light of God, given from above, together with a communication reaching us by way of human teaching. Through the doctrine, which is its incarnation, the object of supernatural intuition comes within the range of articulate human apprehension.

In connection with the problem of development of doctrine a new question has been discussed in recent theology: that of the *sensus plenior* of Holy Scripture. Scripture is an expression in human words of something that God intends to communicate to man. Any word is a word of somebody to somebody. To the listener it means what the speaking subject means by it; at least it should be so. What then does God mean? How does one determine the sense of His word as addressed to man?

The word of God is addressed to the intellect, having a sense that, as with any written message, can be determined by critical investigation; but it primarily addresses itself to faith with a sense that the believer as such is asked to discern. The full sense of Scripture is that which the inspiring Spirit intends to convey to the believing reader. That sense goes beyond the literal sense, which is only the surface meaning available to a non-participating critical reading. The believer is asked to grasp, in and through the letter, the Spirit or the full meaning of what God who speaks is trying to convey to him. K. Rahner points to the fact that even in ordinary language, as distinguished from formal scientific language, there is an area not sharply delineated that is part of what the speaker communicates although he does not say it formally. So it is with the language of the Bible. God, speaking through the Prophets in a way that is limited by their personal and cultural power of expression, communicates things that are not sharply brought into focus by the prophetic word. On both the objective and the subjective side, then, the side of the speaker and that of the listener, two levels of meaning must be distinguished: what the Spirit communicates and the believer is expected to understand, and what is bound up with the limited faculties of prophetic expression and constitutes in its limitation the object of critical exegesis.

The fuller sense is 'a sense chiefly "intended" by God and not, or at best imperfectly, intended by the sacred writer; a sense, however, which depends on the letter of the text and consequently is not extracted from it by way of allegory.'[37]

An adequate exegesis cannot be limited to the critical literary study of the Bible texts. It must try to get at the full meaning of what God communicates through the Bible. In order to be up to its task, exegesis must be theological, using critical text-exegesis as a tool.

The problem of the *sensus plenior* has been dealt with very well by R. E. Brown in *The Sensus Plenior of Sacred Scripture* (Baltimore, 1955). P. Benoit prefers not to oppose the *sensus plenior* to the literal sense but to conceive of it as a second literal sense contained in the words of Scripture, and essentially of Scripture viewed as a whole in its successive stages throughout which God Himself explains and perfects the expression of His meaning. One must distinguish, says Benoit, between the subjective progress of human understanding and the objective progress in the course of which 'God Himself gives a deeper explanation of His Word, recasting it in the successive stages of His revelation.'[38]

To this, however, one must answer that whatever may be the technical meaning of the expression *sensus plenior*, the Word of God, in the sense of that which God tries to convey through the inspired medium, transcends by its very nature, when viewed in its dimension of fullness or depth, the Word of God in the sense of that which the words of the Bible expressly state, even if the scriptural word is considered as a literary whole. Therefore, the total synthetic impression that the believing Church, by listening to the scriptural word and meditating on it, receives from God is richer and fuller than that which any literary study can derive from it. The apostolic inspiration that constituted the tradition prolongs itself in the inspiration by which the Church is able to explicate the tradition in such a way that there is not only a more intense subjective penetration, but also a more extended objective apprehension.

This touches the process of development itself. Is that process to be conceived of as a strictly supernatural clarification and articulation of a dim comprehensive intuition, impressed by God upon the mind of the Church through the grace of faith? Or is it, in the main and with due qualifications, still to be conceived of as an inferential process starting from propositions?

Three types of answers are possible: (1) development of doctrine is a supernatural process in which there is no place for logical operation, although theology may find afterward a kind of logical connection between its results; (2) development of doctrine is basically a process of human reason, although in practice led and sustained by the light of faith; (3) development of doctrine essentially participates in the nature of both a supernatural process and a logical operation.

The first position was held by de Lubac, von Balthasar, and most clearly by H. D. Köster. The way of thinking that leads to the development of dogma is not logical, starting from explicit statements, but strictly supernatural. The believing mind under the inner guidance of the Spirit gradually distinguishes particular points in a reality that as a whole is present to faith: 'On that assumption it is possible that the Church comes to certainties of faith which neither logically nor historically can be demonstrated in the deposit of tradition, but which—we cannot say it otherwise—did come to light through a supernatural sense of the real.'[39]

The second position was held by C. Dillenschneider and worked out by E. Dhanis. Dillenschneider emphatically states that the point from which the development of doctrine starts must be a formulated truth and that, accordingly, it must proceed as a kind of discursive reasoning. However, it cannot be reduced to a process of ordinary logical inference. In the Church there is by faith a subjective contact with the revealed reality, but through the mediation of a doctrine objectively proposed by ecclesiastical authority. Therefore, the human logical process is inwardly complemented by an uncontrollable divine logic, which in the believing community works as a sense of faith. The sense of faith is 'the intuitive supernatural sense of the believer, grounded in the power of his faith and the gifts of the Holy Spirit. By that sense he is able to discern, in communion with the Church, the potentialities of the deposit of revelation, objectively presented to him by the doctrinal authority.'[40] The expression *divine logic* is infelicitous; the word *logic* suggests the idea of controllable rules of thought, according to which concepts are brought together in propositional judgments and in patterns of reasoning. But the higher rule, according to which the process of development escapes the strict control of those rules that all human thought must obey, is supralogical and can only paradoxically be called a divine logic. It is better, then, to use a more general term, such as *divine rule*, a supralogical principle that guides the Church into new insights through such inferential processes as exceed the range of strict inferential logic. The sense of faith, then, is a kind of divinely ruled 'illative sense.' Notice that the use of *sense of faith* and similar expressions has been variously limited: it is attributed to the individual or to the mass of simple folk or to the whole Church including the theologians and the magisterium or, in a special way, to the organs of doctrinal authority itself.

The most elaborate form of a theological solution, trying to preserve the propositional character of revelation and the logical nature of its development, has been propounded by E. Dhanis. He too starts with the Thomistic doctrine of faith. Faith is an assent to propositions, but it is moved by a dim awareness of God as the origin of those propositions. That awareness is given in an effective movement, corresponding to an attraction on the part of God. In virtue of that supernatural attraction one discerns in a direct non-conceptual way God as revealing Himself in those propositions, or in other words, the actual witnessing of God. To witness, however, is a mode of speaking. In speaking man always conveys to other minds something that is present in his own mind. Different modes of speaking are specified by different moral injunctions to act in a definite way with regard to what is said. Thus, witnessing is a communication of a truth asking for faith. Revelation is a communication of truths by God, asking men to accept them as coming from Him whose testimony is possessed in the attraction or the light of faith.

Dhanis' point is that the range of that to which God invites men by His attraction has a wider extension than that which is explicitly expressed in the original word of revelation. God invites men to accept the whole truth into which His Spirit will guide them. That whole truth comprehends all that is somehow truly comprehended in the immediate revelation and can be known mediately by any method of discursive thought. The witness of God inviting men to faith formally extends itself to that whole truth: 'His witness directs faith toward a fullness of truth of which the seed is what he has said explicitly.'[41] To revelation, then, formally attested by God, all those truths may belong that are inferred from its explicit utterings, even if a natural premise be involved in it, or if, from the point of view of reason, the inference be only probable or persuasive. The authority that certifies for man that a given inference of whatever kind is thus formally attested by God is not the authority of natural reason but the authority of the magisterium of the Church. That authority is not independent of the rules of human thought. It must be able to indicate in the sources the presence of its later declarations. But in determining with certitude that a given statement, although it cannot be convincingly inferred from the sources, is nonetheless truly revealed, it complements the work of reason in a supernatural, divinely warranted way.

Dhanis made an excellent point in trying to show that a demonstrable logical structure of some kind must be inherent in the process of development. But he would be contradicted if he denied that such a logical structure operates within a supralogical process that is grounded in an immediate contact with the revealed reality, continually present to living faith as a dim vision, apprehended *per modum unius*. Even the natural growth of man's convictions is directed by a dim undifferentiated and prereflective apprehension of the real concrete whole that is explicated by his efforts of analytical reflection. In applying that general model to the growth of doctrine in the Church, the ordinary ways of human cogitation are not excepted from it. However, the development of doctrine is different from that of natural thought for two reasons: (1) because the object that is dealt with is not an object of natural experience but of an experience that can originate only in a free self-communication of God, who infinitely exceeds the range of natural experience; (2) because God, who is both the object and the active source of the experience of faith, is also active in the process of its notional clarification, guiding and assisting it by His Holy Spirit in that divine way that makes the process infallible, although human thought and reflection are particularly inadequate to its object. Perhaps Dhanis did not sufficiently penetrate his own profound view of attraction of faith. If God, in His effective attraction, immediately communicates Himself to the individual believer as the source of the message, it is not clear how He can make Himself felt as actually attracting without including a dim knowledge of that which attracts. A dim knowledge of God as attracting must imply a dim apprehension of His attracting reality. An awareness of God as actually inviting man to belief must be accompanied by an awareness of that to which He invites and attracts man. A direct affective experience of the formal object of faith cannot be separated from an affective experience of its material object. The *prima veritas* is dimly and supernaturally apprehended as *quo* and at the same time as *quod*.

Therefore, it is better to hold with Rahner and Schillebeeckx that there is an inherent logical aspect in the process of development but that the process as a whole is pervaded with and directed by a divine beyond, guiding the Church into conclusions that cannot be adequately controlled by reason. According to that position, the proper task of the theologian, who tries to analyze the object of faith by means of natural reason, is a part of the process of development. The theologian not only orders the results of the process in a coherent pattern afterward; he participates in the process itself by his rational endeavors to distinguish the various aspects and implications of revealed truth. 'We think in logic as we talk in prose' (Newman). The laws of logic are working in the process of living thought before they are detected and systematized in a special science by reflection upon the spontaneous processes of the mind. Therefore, the tentative deductions of the theologian are not only a subsequent systematization of the results of the process; they are part of the process itself insofar as they illuminate and make explicit the aspects of logical coherence that are inherent to a developmental event that nonetheless goes beyond them. It would be impossible to discover afterward a logical connection with the results of development if its structure itself were a-logical. Of course, as Newman would warn, the process of development does not itself become logical—in the sense of proceeding by comparison of propositions—simply because theologians may *post factum* reconstruct its results into a logically connected system. The living process, although partly influenced by abstract theological efforts, is, as a whole, a concrete vital growth of self-differentiating apprehension guided by an inner principle that is light and life.

To conclude, that which is common to all theological theories of development is the position that the ultimate criterion of true developments is the magisterial declaration of the Church, whatever way the starting point and the process of development be described.

CHAPTER TEN

A Theological Reflection

The subject, development of doctrine, has been considered here on the basic assumption that history is the proper mode of human existence. As he emerges from nature, man is only a possibility that universal nature refuses to actualize further according to the unconscious laws of biological evolution. Man has to actualize himself by his own efforts and at his own risk, guided by thought and insight. Man, as Ortega y Gasset put it, is a drama of which he is both the author and the hero. This is true on all levels: that of an individual, of a civilization, and of humanity as a whole. The present state of culture, which is the sum total of human acquisitions, represents the present phase of man's becoming and constitutes his proper world. Man's self-actualization by personal effort is embedded in the development of a culture. He is the product of tradition and must continue its development by his own creativity. To be sure, a personality cannot be reduced to its elements of natural or cultural inheritance. Human freedom implies a personal responsibility for what man is. Great creative personalities have been formed in lower stages of civilization, and in higher stages the multitude still tends toward inertia. The constant struggle between an upward movement of creative progress and a downward movement of inertia belongs to the very structure of history; each prevails alternately, leading to flourishing conditions or to conditions of decay.

Human thought participates in the general nature of human history. It is the intellectual aspect of history, and its documents reflect the ideas by which man has been guided in his efforts toward the realization of himself and his world. As will be seen further on, man's personal thought is penetrated by tradition. He has to think for himself, but in doing so, he cannot but continue the movement of tradition, accepting it or trying to correct it or to change its course. The thought of a generation contains in itself the whole history of its cultural past, and present problems can rightly be understood only in the light of their historical antecedents. Therefore, one cannot separate historical from systematic thought. In trying to understand the history of philosophy or theology one philosophizes or theologizes in the truest sense of the word. This implies, of course, a definite conception of what historical understanding is. This will become clear further on, in the final sections of this chapter. Let it suffice to say now that present-day problems of philosophy and theology cannot be conveniently stated except in the light of their history, and that attempts to solve the problems of one's time imply the task of interpreting the past.

The present effort, then, to understand the history of development of doctrine has not been an introduction to a personal attempt toward its solution, but a necessary part of it. In trying to get at an historical understanding of what has been said about the development of Christian doctrine, there has been a constant awareness of the problem today, an exchange of views, as it were, with the great thinkers of the past. The concluding part of this study is an attempt to continue their efforts in the light of the general intellectual situation of the present time.

The development of Christian doctrine is a special instance of a general phenomenon: the development of ideas in human history. It has characteristics of a particular kind, but still it proceeds according to a general pattern. Therefore, this chapter will first outline a general philosophy of knowledge and its development. Because the proper characteristics of the development of Christian doctrine follow from its dependence on a special revelation, assented to by faith, the chapter will deal with some basic questions about revelation and faith. The process of dogmatic development itself will be described; and the chapter will conclude with an attempt to understand the problem of development in the light of contemporary discussions about the problem of hermeneutics.

KNOWLEDGE, THOUGHT, AND DEVELOPMENT

Knowledge is the appearance of what is. In knowledge the real becomes apparent or evident to the knowing subject. This is the very

M*

notion of knowledge. To the appearance there corresponds on the part of the subject an act of apprehension. There is, however, a full apprehension that attains to the concrete, and there is a partial apprehension that only reaches the abstract. The terms *full* and *partial apprehension* do not mean complete and incomplete distinctness of a view, but its total or partial comprehensiveness, whatever may be the degree of articulation.

Full apprehensive knowledge is a personal act. Man acts in it as a whole, guided by his inner personal freedom. It is a moral act. The fullness of the real object is only attained by the wholeness of the knowing subject. This means that if intelligence is compared to a mirror, it is a very curious kind of mirror. It is not a passive mirror. It is the instrument of a free mirroring subject whose receptive attention is directed and predetermined by a free moral project, which creates for reality the possibility of appearing. This is what Max Scheler means when he says that although man only knows by his intelligence, it is love, however, the basic act of personality, that unveils what thus appears to the intellect. The real, or truth, is always present and presenting itself to man; but in order to appear or to become manifest to man, he has also to create it.

The words *truth* or *reality* do not mean here the multitude of things and objects as they surround man, coming within or disappearing from the scope of sense perception, but rather existential truth, or such truth as gives meaning to the whole of things and to one's own existence. To exist is to be passionately concerned with existing, to be in search of a meaning that fulfills and justifies existence.

Meaning and existence are mutually correlative. True meaning is not subjective or dependent on man. It must be objective, founded on reality. If not, it is only an illusion of meaning. Therefore, existential truth is truth in the fullest sense of the word. Man attains it insofar as he knows a meaning, independent of his subjective contingent existence. Such knowledge may be dim and imperfect, never attaining to a fully lucid comprehension. It may dwindle into partial and finally into total darkness, as von Hügel says. But however dim, it is always comprehensive or full in the sense of related to the whole. As a contingent and conscious being, man cannot create the meaning of his own contingency. Meaning or truth, which saves his contingent existence from utter meaninglessness and despair, is something that unveils itself as having validity by itself, not by man's approving it. It is a gift that man must humbly and thankfully receive. In that sense it creates his existence giving truth and reality.

On the other hand, however, man must create within himself what is thus given to him. Just as existence becomes true through objective meaning, so through existence, objective meaning becomes true. For truth, however independent its content may be of the subject, has to become truth for a knowing subject in order to exercise that function in virtue of which it is called truth. It does not, however, exercise that function without the active and free collaboration of the subject. That collaboration is not so much a special act as a commanding attitude, present in all human acts. One may clarify its meaning by such words as love, openness, availability; or one may call it an anticipation or an a priori will for the good. For in the order of meaning related to existence, truth is also the good. The basic attitude of truthful existence is thus a selfless will to let things be as they are, to accept their existential meaning whatever it may be. If, then, the recognition of truth is an act of the free person, exercised within the moral project of a life for the good, then it is evident that—to employ the expression of Bishop I. T. Ramsey—*discernment* cannot be separated from *commitment*. Commitment is already anticipated in the basic moral act which conditions the discernment.

In opposition to full truth, which is the object of a personal apprehension and which is at once a gift of the self-unveiling absolute object and an accomplishment of the self-creating contingent subject, there is a partial truth, a form of diminished truth resulting from an act by which the intellect abstracts itself from the fullness of personal existence in order to face dispassionately that which beyond any possible doubt impresses itself on the mind as irrefragable. Consequently, as the intellect abstracts itself from the original unity and fullness of the active person, so too that which comes within the scope of apprehension is an abstraction from the unity and fullness of the original appearance. It may be called the 'phenomenal.' The unity of the original appearance is broken into a multitude of phenomena, sensory or mental, which are registered by the mind, conceptualized, and ordered into a system of abstract generalizations. F. von Baader has clearly explained the two senses of abstraction and their mutual correspondence. Abstract or notional knowledge of an object corresponds to an act by which the intellect abstracts itself from the original fullness of life or experience. This completes what Newman says on the subject of real and notional apprehension. Real apprehension comes first. It is the full and the most original way of knowledge. Notional apprehension follows. It analyzes and combines the various aspects that the original experience presents to the mind. Baader relates this to the personal attitude of the knowing subject who either participates in the fullness of experience or separates himself from it in order to become a pure intellect. This explains the true nature of what Newman calls real and notional assent. Real assent is always commitment because in the act of apprehending the real, one has already decided for it in virtue of the antecedent project within which the real appears as such. Notional assent, however, is by itself no more than a purely intellectual acceptance of something as true. It does not entail commitment because in the act of apprehending, the intellect has abstracted itself from the basic act of personality.

This does not mean, of course, that notional knowledge, however diminished when compared with the real, is not justified or useful in its own way. Phenomena of whatever kind are true aspects of the real. The real appears in the phenomena. They point to the real. Therefore the operation by which the intellect conceptualizes what appears, may go on being related to it. Within the existential striving toward truth it may function as an effort toward clarification. By an act of *kenosis*, or self-sacrifice, separating itself from the fullness of experience, the intellect may become an instrument in man's striving toward a more conscious possession of what experience conveys. An artificial separation for the sake of a special end may be accomplished without losing contact with the original wholeness and fullness that it intends to serve. It may be said, then, that existential truth embraces in itself the possibility of notional or scientific truth. Existential truth is the original fullness. Theoretical truth is an abstraction obtained by a partial emptying of that fullness in order to achieve clarification. It will forever remain the merit of Newman and Blondel that they refused to oppose *real* and *notional* as incompatible; they related them to each other as two movements of a single process rooted in their dialectical opposition and unity.

The working of intellectual reflection, which by its very nature abstracts itself from existential recognition, although not necessarily severed from it, is indispensable for direct communication by means of statements about the real. This does not mean that verbal statements are the only means of communicating experiences to one's fellow man. There are forms of indirect communication by symbols that may disclose a cosmic or all-comprehensive meaning in one flash of intuition. Personality, too, embodying and displaying existential values, has by itself an eminent power of communication. The person thus becomes a living symbol in which the truth is existentially disclosed and grasped. The creation of symbols is the first and basic way of expressing one's apprehension of existential truth. Poetic language comes before prose. The symbolic expression is more directly related to the original appearance of meaning, being the first, more spontaneous, and more congenial mode of expressive activity. In a certain sense true symbols are not created by man. They are revealed to him in the very act of rising to consciousness as expressions of what shines through their transparent selves. An artist may work them out and enhance their revealing power by the magic of words and forms, but he is more their instrument than their master.

Symbols do not, however, explain what appears in them. Through symbols existential truth takes possession of man; they make him realize such truth. But the mind, in its turn, must take possession of that truth; and this it does by becoming an inquisitive intellect, analyzing, defining, comparing, in order to elaborate a conceptual frame that tends to become a coherent system. In so doing the mind creates in the apprehension of truth a definite clarity and articulate distinctness. It also gives truth a more direct verbal expression, which enables one to communicate it by way of explanation and teaching.

THE DANGERS OF CONCEPTUAL THOUGHT

This, of course, necessary as it may be, is an enterprise beset with dangers and difficulties. By intellectual reflection man tries to master the truth that first has mastered him. But the mind has a tendency to refuse to be mastered in order to become the sole master of things. Wisdom asks to be satisfied with an inadequate possession of what first possesses man. Man must humbly accept his being possessed by truth in the very act of his trying to master it for himself. Truth has to be venerated as a master that transcends man's capacities to grasp it. If the intellect severs itself from the existential self-revelation of truth; if it tries to reduce truth to an intellectual system in which it is entirely within the intellect's power of understanding; if it clutches avariciously and irreverently at truth; then the communion of mind with the appearance of the real breaks off, and the intellect retains only a verbal clothing of something that escapes from its grasp, as Joseph escaped from Poti-phar's wife, leaving his garment in her hand.

As was pointed out above, what appears in the existential relation is the real, the concrete, and consequently the still undivided whole. It is a fact known by experience that before any intervention of man's analytical powers, he himself has a kind of direct consciousness of what afterward becomes an object of reflective consideration and abstractive division. That consciousness may be called a feeling, meaning by this not a subjective state but something like an indiscriminate intuition of objective reality accompanied by an affective attitude toward it. It is affective because in the act of apprehending existential truth, the 'I,' or the person, still moves as a whole in which affection and moral appreciation are not separated from cognition. This object of totalizing consciousness, which has here been called, with Newman, the *idea*, is present as a constant focus in the discursive activity of conceptual thought about it. Such thought is an activity by which the various possible aspects of the idea are gradually made explicit to the mind. But this kind of clarification, operating on a different level from that of direct existential experience, is by its very nature inadequate. It is unable to lay before the mind's eye the whole of the idea in the form of conceptual propositions. The idea, although present in reflection and worked on by it, always remains beyond its reach. Existential or real apprehension comes from insight that possesses man completely; theoretical or notional apprehension comes from one's attempt to grasp an idea in that imperfect way proper to the human nature and condition. Therefore, the same idea that precedes and accompanies discursive reflection is also its ideal end, toward which it strives without ever exhausting it. The presence of the idea, existentially known to the intellect but still inviting it to further exploration, explains the restless movement of the *cogitatio*. We should not seek if we had not somehow found, and we should cease to strive if that possession were perfect.

From this it follows that thought is always in danger of deforming truth, veiling it under a false clarity that pretends to cover the whole. Notions, though pointing to the real, are not commensurate with it; they are of a different order. Hence it is possible that notion and reality part company. One may become absorbed by notions and words, and cease to focus on the original idea. The difficulty is that we must keep an eye on both, moving dialectically from the one to the other within a steady comprehensive view of the whole process.

Decline inevitably occurs if one does not constantly and humbly return to the real idea, subjecting oneself to its rule and accepting its transcendence. Reasoning will be true to the real to the extent that one keeps a firm hold on its presence in prereflective awareness. This means that thought too is a moral and responsible act of the free subject, because one's faithful apprehension of the real is conditioned by an attitude of humble submission. The same free moral attitude that makes the appearance of the real possible is also the first inner rule of truth in notional explanations. In relation to human knowledge the truth is the good and the real is the moral. To be faithful to intellectual truth implies keeping a right attitude toward existential good. We may add, with Newman, that the firmer one's hold on the real, the more fertile will be one's conceptualization of it and the more faithful will be one's reasoning about it.

By its very nature and by the conditions in which it is exercised, the role of conceptual thought is ambivalent. If it remains in close relation to the existential appearance, the concept becomes an open window through which reality shines. However, if it cuts itself off and tries to grow independent and self-sufficient, it becomes a closed door concealing reality from one's apprehension. Of course, the opposition is not so absolute. There are various degrees of transparency or opaqueness according to the degrees, respectively, of receptivity to what is beyond or of self-centered lack of availability. According to the depth of one's real knowledge one will be protected against the temptation to mistake a pattern of concepts for reality itself and will be aware of the distance between what is conceived and what appears in it; one will be anxious to be faithful to the whole and not to disregard important features of its appearance, and will not be satisfied with easy generalizations, looking away from the presence of the whole and concentrating upon our logical machinations; and finally, one will always concentrate on the real idea and always be disposed to correct the inadequate endeavors by which one tries to translate that idea into objectifying language.

The wrong relation of conceptual thought to the full appearance of the real is that of one-sidedness. This originates when the thinking subject exclusively concentrates on one aspect of the real idea or on one consistent pattern of such aspects, disregarding others that do not seem to fit the pattern. The mind then separates those aspects, converts them into concepts, replaces them by linguistic devices, and tries to reconstruct the whole in its own isolated consciousness by impersonal, technical methods of inferential thought.

This is not an altogether conscious process. It is directed by a selective attitude of the mind, rooted in one or other inclination of the person. In a fully balanced person all the faculties are working together in harmonious unity. Consequently he is equally open to all the aspects of reality corresponding to those faculties. Most persons, however, are not thus balanced. Their peculiar bent is determined by the prevailing influence of one faculty, and this leads them to select from the full appearance of reality those aspects that correspond to their inclinations. There are matter-of-fact and imaginative, voluntaristic and meditative, ratiocinative and intuitive, extrovert and introvert minds. The complete human mind seems to be splintered in its individual realizations. How this comes about is difficult to explain, but that is the way it is; and it is the duty of every person to try to correct his spontaneous bias. This is not only an intellectual but a moral task. The most basic inclination of man is toward inertia. He easily consents to follow the spontaneous tendency of his mind or to be led on by it without resistance. Only a serious love of truth enables him to scrutinize the very springs of his thought in order to control them, to purify them, and to correct their natural course. A growing subjection to truth is required to inspire that constant moral discipline that frees man to fix his gaze on the objective whole in spite of his natural tendency to swerve away from it by subjective partiality. Man thinks as a whole; hence, in order to attain to the objective fullness of the appearance of truth, he has to acquire that kind of morally directed personal wholeness that conditions his capacity for integral truth. If, as we have said, man's apprehension of existential truth is a personal moral act, it follows that his capacity for such apprehension is a moral virtue, a kind of *holē dikaiosynē,* to speak with Plato, a comprehensive rightness that can only be acquired by a constant moral and intellectual discipline. Perhaps, as Schlegel says, man is in need of grace to restore in him the original unity and completeness disfigured by sin.

The tendency toward one-sidedness is manifest not only on the plane of individual thought but also, indeed more so, on the plane of collective thought. Individual thought is immersed in the various social milieux in which man finds himself. To say that men think as wholes implies that they think as members of a more inclusive social whole, and they think, indeed, as members of a family, a class, a school, a party, a nation, a culture. One's intellectual tendencies are determined not only by individual bent but also, and no less, by the social setting in cultural space and time. It is on the social plane that thought most clearly manifests its tendency toward one-sidedness with all the consequences thereof. The various systems that confront each other in the arena of human thought seem to be characterized by the predominance of certain principles that betray a one-sided approach to reality: materialism and idealism, empiricism and rationalism, existentialism and conceptualism. There is a rhythm in the history of philosophies and world views caused by a constant opposition as various points of view alternately dominate intellectual life. This is the famous dialectical movement so conspicuous in human history. All trends are constantly mixing in the struggle of ideas, but some of them emerge victorious for a time and later become submerged again to gather new strength for a fresh start toward the top, and reappearing in new garments and under new names.

Ordinary semi-intellectual people are particularly sensitive to intellectual moods and fashions. They do not think for themselves but follow certain beliefs without much personal reflection or judgment, partly by accident—because they are caught in a given current of thought—and partly from certain unconscious inclinations. Such assents to fashionable ideas, which sometimes succeed one another in the limelight of public opinion as rapidly as film stars, sports champions and popular singers, are hardly assets at all. Newman calls them 'professions':

> Professing to understand without understanding. It is thus that political and religious watchwords are created; first one man of name and then another adopts them, till their use becomes popular, and then everyone professes them, because everyone else does. Such words are 'liberality,' 'progress,' 'light,' 'civilization,' such are 'justification by faith only,' 'vital religion,' 'private judgment,' 'the Bible and nothing but the Bible' . . . all of which in the mouths of conscientious thinkers, have a defi-

nite meaning but are used by the multitude as war-cries, nick-names, and shibboleths, with scarcely enough of the scantiest grammatical apprehension of them to allow of their being considered really more than assertions. [Grammar, pp. 43–44]

We could add an impressive list of contemporary watchwords, such as: 'secularization,' 'death of God,' 'Christianity without religion,' etc. This characterization holds not only for a vague would-be intellectual multitude but also for philosophical and theological writers and speakers: 'Many a disciple of a philosophical school, who talks fluently, does but assert, when he seems to assent to the *dicta* of his master, little as he may be aware of it' (*Grammar*, p. 43). The world is greatly led on by currents and counter-currents of ideas that, however serious and deep they may have been in the minds of their originators, are degraded by epigones and by a multitude of sympathizers and supporters into unreal words, sentimental myths, and insincere ideologies. In our own time, characterized by the democratization of thought and learning, the phenomenon of an anonymous tyranny of philosophical and religious watchwords supported by the weight of numbers is particularly conspicuous. Never perhaps in history have such large numbers of men professed so boldly and understood so little as today. It is a real danger to culture and to religion. All real thoughts are threatened with submersion and dissolution in a cacophony of words.

Social thought is constantly nourished and influenced by the thinking of individuals. The decline from the full appearance as a whole to various one-sided conceptualizations on the plane of individual thought is continued in conflicting movements on the social plane. By reason of the anonymous power of parties and multitudes, individual consciousness of the original revelation of meaning is easily obscured by thickening clouds of words, and man is alienated from his true self by the superegos of the various social worlds that claim his loyalty. Moreover, society is the field of those passions that create parties. Parties generate parties by the violence of their opposition. Dialogue degenerates into dispute. The respective positions are hardened through exasperation. Men no longer understand one another, not for lack of intellectual endowment, but for lack of that serenity of mind that is the highest moral virtue in the field of thought because it generates and sustains that capacity and willingness to listen so indispensable for mutual understanding and fruitful conversation.

THE PROBLEM OF AUTHORITY

Therefore the cause of truth in the world as we know it is linked with the cause of authority. There must be an authority of some kind for without it there is anarchy, and anarchy in the world of man means crippling confusion, dissolution, and in the end, death. This is as true on the level of ideas as it is on the level of political government. One of the distinctive marks of this century is that authority is founded on personality and not on institutions. This is especially true in the world of intersubjective communication, and is of the utmost importance there. But it is no longer true in the large public world of social coexistence, where the range of personal authority is generally restricted, and the conditions of social existence are such that it is improbable that the bearers of true wisdom will get a hearing from the violent and noisy congregation that fills the public scene. Therefore personal authority, which in an ideal world would be the only rule, cannot function in the tumult of real social life. Authority must be supplied publicly, however unsatisfying, imperfect, and dangerous its exercise may be. Where the ideal solutions cannot work, one must be satisfied with the solution that, however imperfect, is able to make the best of it.

In fact, human nature, as it appears from the general facts of history, has always created a form of authority as imperfect as our common existence. This is tradition, a social deposit formed by a slow spontaneous selection of accumulating experience and by many lessons of trial and error. From the nature of social existence, tradition in all civilizations is always represented by special social organs that preserve it and pass it on. To be sure, tradition too is beset with dangers, originating in the human tendency to one-sidedness. Those who take the side of tradition, especially its institutional representatives, often tend to see only the duty of conserving, ignoring the duty of guiding. Once more, a basic tendency of human nature is the tendency toward inertia; on the plane of ideas, this means keeping to the acquisitions of the past and defending the old safe truths of the fathers. Merely to conserve does not impose great intellectual efforts. But, like it or not, tradition is a living movement in which new ideas and insights appear in the light of new situations created by history. Tradition is the intellectual side of history. By its very nature it is creative, forming as it does the great adventure of man's quest for truth and meaning.

Those who represent tradition betray their office if they know only the products of the past. They have to know, by continuous efforts of sympathetic and critical understanding, the ongoing movement of the restless mind in order to judge its results not only in the light of the past but also in the light of the existential appearance of truth, ever present to the mind and inspiring its continuous endeavors of expression, as it once, in the beginning, provoked the first stammerings of awakening mankind. Truth always possesses man as a whole, in spite of his erroneous or defective efforts to possess it by converting it into a world of speech, controlled by self-conscious life. The endeavor to focus truth more sharply, to make it explicit, to state it more precisely and correctly, is not only our individual duty but a common responsibility of human society as it goes on thinking within the community of living tradition.

It is not the intention here to solve the general problem of authority. But it was necessary to state it clearly in order to understand the Catholic view of authority as related to the development of doctrine.

Thought is, in the first place, existential and receives the full appearance of objective meaning in the living context of a moral project that conditions the possibility of such an appearance. The contact with existential truth, present to the mind as a unity, as the inner testimony of the real, is the basic and all-embracing condition of knowledge; it is present in the theoretical thought itself in which the intellect clarifies the existential truth by analysis and synthesis of the various aspects that reality is able to unveil to such consideration. Neverthless, necessary as it may be, the self-abstraction of the intellect from its existential basis is dangerous. It creates an opposition between real or existential and notional or theoretical apprehension and thought. This opposition implies the danger that notional thought shall be separated from real perception, so that the mind, cutting off its basic relation to the full existential appearance, finds itself shut up in its inner subjective world of concepts and words. Concept and word, originally the means to introduce the real into the sphere of conscious life, become a pictured veil that hides the real from sight. The true relation between the existential contact with the realm of reality and meaning on the one hand, and on the other hand, the intellectual enterprise of aspectual analysis and synthesis, is a relation of dialogue or dialectical union. In this dialogue both retain the characteristic of mutual opposition, while they illuminate each other by movements alternating between withdrawal and union. Conceptualizing reflection creates, as it were, clear windows through which we may attain definite views of reality, but realizing existence conditions the visibility of the real through those windows. If our contact with the real through existential apprehension weakens or disappears, then the windows become blurred, only dim figures that the imagination interprets are seen, and at the end one is left with no more than the forms of his concepts. This leads to the phenomenon of one-sidedness. The real is replaced by abstractions and words; by a process of reasoning which, at the extreme, becomes merely verbal, a system of words is created that is mistaken for a reconstruction of the real. The clarity of such a system is only a formal clarity of logical relations; the real content dwindles into total obscurity. Of course, this limit is seldom reached. In most cases the separation of the intellect from personality or existence results in a biased view that is mistaken for the whole for lack of sufficient control by full undistorted experience. On the social plane this results in oppositions between narrower worldviews, engaged in a constant struggle for power. These oppositions are enhanced and hardened by the various passions through which human pride breaks into the world of thought. A dialectical movement sets in, driven forward by contradictions, and seems fated to result in confusion and intellectual anarchy if it is not counterbalanced by an efficacious authority. When the sense of tradition and authority is lost, real progress becomes impossible and the specter of intellectual barbarism appears on the horizon.

REVELATION AND FAITH

The foregoing philosophical meditation provides a basic insight by which to understand the development of doctrine in the Church. There is a close relation between human thought in search for meaning and Christian thought that starts with an acceptance of meaning by faith. That relation is twofold: a relation of continuity and of analogy. The former does not directly pertain to the subject of development, but it has to be stated carefully. Revelation is addressed to man. Its answers are not related to new questions, added to the basic questions that arise from man's existential needs.

They rather present themselves as the only satisfying answers to the basic questions of human life. In his quest for existential truth, man has to confess at last that the truth that he is able to discover by reflection on his ordinary experience does not give the ultimate satisfying answers to these questions. What he finds does not seem to be what he is seeking. His questioning existence goes beyond the answers that he finds in his experience. Therefore, existence as such is looking for a new appearance of meaning, not included in existence, and for which the term *revelation* is ordinarily used.

The term *revelation* must be taken in a specific sense. In contemporary philosophy, and even theology, it is used in senses that are more general. The appearance of existential truth is not compelled by our intellectual endeavors, but precedes them as something that is present by itself, although we may not be aware of it. This presence, too, which always possesses us and which in given situations may burst into one's mind with a flash of recognition, is often termed revelation. Those especially privileged moments in which the truth reveals its presence are often indicated by that word. To the full appearance of meaning or the full content of the existential presence of the real undoubtedly belongs the reality of God. Certainty about the existence of God is not gained by the reasoning mind, although such reasoning may clarify His existence to one's consciousness. The reality of God is given in the full appearance of existential truth. It possesses man before all efforts to take possession of it by articulate and reasoned knowledge. If, then, God is a personal being, one may suppose that the discovery of His presence in one's consciousness is not merely an act of the apprehending subject but also an act of God who thus reveals Himself in human experience. This leads to the idea, broadly acknowledged in contemporary theology, of a general revelation of God along the common roads of experiential thought. It may be dim, uncertain, vacillating, distorted by human interpretations, but still it is there. As such it is the background of the special revelation that Christians believe in. In the history of Israel and especially in Christ the hidden nature of God has been unveiled and clarified in a way that transcends the limits of what common experience is able to discover but at the same time does not supersede the general revelation. It illuminates it from within, it brings to man's knowledge such features of God and such characteristics of His attitude toward man as are sufficient to give that complement of ultimate meaning that existence needs and seeks in existential thought and reflection.

This is very important for our investigation. If the Christian revelation is really an inner specification of the general full appearance of existential truth, it is probable that the way it works will be analogous to that of existential apprehension and thought. Christian revelation, although simply beyond the scope of experience that constitutes our being as human, appears as a special determination of its object, and consequently it will be primarily an object of existential or real apprehension and only secondarily an object of notional analysis and conceptual clarification. This conceptual clarification will be historical and surrounded by the same dangers that have their origin in human weakness, one-sidedness, and passion. If Christian revelation is thus given by God through a special intervention of His saving mercy, it becomes probable that the same mercy will direct the historical process of man's understanding of it by a special guidance and that, on the social plane, the way it controls the dangerous currents of conflicting ideas will be an authority of a special nature.

This anticipates in a general way the distinctive characteristics of the Christian's intellectual movement toward the possession of that divine truth that had previously taken possession of him in the simple apprehension of faith. The difference, then, between the general revelation of philosophical truth and the special revelation of theological truth is twofold: first, Christian revelation comes to man through a message that interprets some contingent facts of history; second, he enters into it by a personal aid of grace, bringing about the discernment and the assent of faith in the individual and the Church. The special nature of Christian revelation consists, on the one hand, in the fact that it is met objectively in the acts of and the events surrounding a contingent historical person, Jesus of Nazareth, interpreted in a primitive message. On the other hand, man perceives its meaning subjectively and assents to it subjectively by an inner gift of what Christ Himself called the Holy Spirit, whom He would send to His followers and to His Church after the end of His visible historical presence.

The first characteristic, then, of Christian revelation is that it comes to man through a special contingent medium: the historical appearance of Christ, whose meaning is interpreted by a message, a good news, recorded in the Bible and impressed on mankind by the continual preaching of the Church. This is an objective factor that works on the public scene of social life by way of historical action. Christian revelation is not simply a new appearance of saving truth within the general appearance of existential truth. To be sure, it is this; but the inner event is normally conditioned by the outer event of hearing the message and confronting it in a given social situation. As it is a special personal self-disclosure of God in a free gesture of saving initiative, it is also given in a special contingent happening that is not a natural event in the ordinary course of things. To the free and personal character of salvation not contained in God's general revelation corresponds the contingent character of its manifestation according to a pattern of historical events.

REVELATION AND TRADITION

The role of facts and words in the process of revelation must be examined more closely. That Christian revelation comes to man through facts and words is a special case of what normally happens in the revelation of existential truth. Christian revelation is different, of course, in that it is linked up with a privileged series of historical facts and with a privileged message that is believed by reason of its inspiration to have a divine origin. This, its specific character, corresponds to the nature of the case. But it must be remembered that contingent happening and language also play a important part in the way man becomes conscious of the appearance of ordinary existential truth.

Every person by the very fact of his existence is addressed by the full appearance of existential truth. But language is not a neutral, indifferent stock of words, simply available to every individual in order to express his ideas in his own way. On the contrary, before any attempt to express it personally on the ground of personal insight and thought, the meaning of life is already interpreted by others. This is what living tradition consists in. Man is not simply confronted with tradition as a thing exterior to himself. By the fact that from his early years he has learned a given tongue in a given community, he is the unconscious heir of a world of ideas by which he spontaneously interprets the meaning of things. The way he views and interprets existence in the world is determined by others, by innumerable generations, who have created the living languages in their attempt to express on various levels the appearance of the real. Living language is charged with definite meanings. In learning the mother tongue man comes to understand life as it is understood by his family, milieu, class, nation, generation, and culture. Living language as a whole is a kind of general message by which the appearance of truth in consciousness is conditioned from without. In an individual's first personal encounter with the problem of meaning, his mind is not naked but clothed with a language that already anticipates the way meaning will appear to him.

There is, then, a similarity between the way the general existential truth originally comes to man, raising questions and impelling him to look for answers, and the way Christian revelation comes, offering ultimate answers to the basic questions. Both are *ex auditu*. They come to man through language.

Of course the language of words is never a language of mere words. The communication of existential truth, insofar as it is true to the mind of the speaker, is a commentary on something that also reveals itself in his conduct and countenance. Living language, as a bearer of meaning, cannot be entirely separated from life, which reflects that same meaning in patterns of conduct. A language is a function of a culture, of a general social pattern of human life. A culture is the incarnation of a spirit, and as such it visualizes for the understanding mind the philosophy that underlies its common ways of behavior and speech.

As a human being man is inwardly confronted with the general appearance of meaning in a situation determined by a common way of life, which finds its expression in common language; so too, as a Christian, he is inwardly confronted with saving truth in a situation determined by the exterior facts of Christ and His Church, explained by the words of Scripture and preaching. To go even further, without the language, which is received from the cultural community, the awareness of existential meaning would not be awakened in the consciousness of the individual. This does not mean that language causes the presence of truth to man. Truth is present to him by itself. It only means that the gift of language, received from without, awakens his consciousness of that presence, conditioning its appearance. Man's inheritance of spoken thought points him toward the presence of existential truth, perhaps in a very imperfect and distorted way. He needs a kind of language to point his consciousness toward existential truth. It pertains to the very nature of the human condition that man becomes aware of the immediate presence of truth only through the medium of an expression that is not his own and that in the very act of awakening him to truth may falsify it by wrong or distorted interpretations. In a similar way through the light of faith, by which man is born of God, Truth, and the Spirit, as St. John says, saving truth is inwardly present, but man's awareness of it is conditioned by hearing the testimony of Christ, the Apostles, and the Church. The living language of the Church, addressed to man in the message, points him toward the real presence in him and to him of the mystery of salvation. His way of becoming conscious of that mystery is determined by the word he hears. Therefore, it greatly matters whether that language is true to the mystery to which it points, lest in the act of guiding man's consciousness it would misguide, falsifying the very truth it is intended to impart.

The word of God, then, as it comes from without, is not the proper cause of the presence to man or the apprehension by him of the saving truth. This truth is present and reveals itself to man by itself. That is what the light of faith is for. The light of faith is in man's mind the seal of the First Truth, as St. Thomas says. Through the light of faith, God, the saving reality, is present to the mind, and man is adapted to the recognition of its appearance. The message, however, is an actual condition of its becoming an object of conscious apprehension to man. When an object of knowledge is not present through the senses, man cannot consciously and explicitly apprehend it without the medium of human expression created by him or received from without. To be sure, there may be a presence of real meaning to the mind in a subconscious and implicit way. That presence may even direct human behavior after the manner of an instinct. But it does not become an object of conscious apprehension except in an act of expression. Heidegger rightly says that the self-revelation of Being not only originates in man the human word that expresses it but is also accomplished in the act of expressing it. Revelation is terminated in man's mind by its human expression. In its expressive translation, revelation, considered as received by man, takes place. If he does not receive revelation in the full prophetic way, i.e., in a way that creates in the individual the images or concepts through which it becomes conscious, then revelation has to address itself to him through an expression that is communicated from without. The difference between the prophetic light and the light of faith is that the former allows the prophet to create the expression in which the revelation of God is accomplished in him, whereas the latter does not allow the believer to create the original expression of what he believes, but only to recognize the presence of self-revealing reality through an expressive medium that comes to work in him when he learns it by the sensible perception of words, or of acts combined with words.

This part of our reflection is concluded with the following points. First, as to the exterior fact, which conditions conscious apprehension of appearing truth, there is a certain similarity between the apprehension of that general existential truth whose presence constitutes man's being man, and the apprehension of that special existential truth whose presence in the light of faith determines his actual vocation to become a Christian. Man is initiated into the mystery of existence by cultural tradition carried on by living language; he is initiated into the mystery of salvation by the tradition of the Church, originating in the prophetic inspiration of chosen individuals and carried on through history by documents of the past and by preaching. Second, there is a difference, in that in the former case both the inner appearance and the outer initiation are universally available, the first being essentially connected with the individual nature and the second with the social nature. In the second case, however, both the inner appearance of divine truth in the light of faith and the outer initiation by the hearing of the message are contingent, the first being given to the individual by a free grace, the second reaching him through a special proclamation.

It was impossible to deal with the role of the message in the origin of faith without referring constantly to the second point in which faith, as an apprehension of a special revelation, differs from the apprehension of general existential truth. Let us now consider more carefully that second point: the proper nature of the apprehension of faith. According to St. Paul and St. John a new spiritual birth is required in order to acknowledge the truth of the message. In the second chapter of 1 Corinthians St. Paul argues that the carnal selfish man must be changed into a spiritual man according to the image of Christ in order to perceive and to understand the things of the Spirit or the mind of God by a participation in Christ's understanding. Being born from the flesh and the will of man, St. John says, a new birth from God, from the Truth, from the Spirit is needed in order to be able to become children of God, seeing Him in Christ, knowing His Truth, and acting in accordance with it. For St. John, Truth is Reality. To know the Truth is not to be convinced by arguments that some statements are true, but rather to be aware of the real by the presence and appearance of the real itself. The capacity for this is rooted in a new being, a new gift of life, which is eternal life. That God is Love, giving in Christ eternal life to His elect is St. John's basic idea. Eternal life, however, is not something in the future but something that is already man's in faith and love. Faith and love are the acts in which eternal life in man is properly exercised. They spring from a source of eternal life in him, leading him on toward its fullness, a fullness that does not yet appear but eventually will be revealed as being a likeness to God.

To recognize God in Christ, or to come to Christ, to come to God through Christ, is the act, as it were, in which the new birth takes place. But no one comes to Christ if not attracted by the Father who sent Him. To be sure, faith does not happen without a hearing of the message. St. John calls it 'testimony.' That faith or divine knowledge is conditioned by hearing the witness is another of the basic ideas of St. John. To witness is to say what one has seen. Therefore Christ, who is eternally in the Father, knowing and possessing all that the Father knows and possesses, is the first direct witness. The Incarnation of the Word is the coming to man of the testimony of God. The Apostles too are able to witness because through the grace of the Father they have recognized Him in the person, the words, and the works of His Son. After the departure of their master they will receive the Spirit who will guide them into the fullness of truth, enabling them to witness together with the Spirit or through the power of the Spirit in them. The Spirit will impress upon their minds the Truth so that they will become able to bear witness to Christ in a free way in spite of the contradictions of the unregenerate world.

In the originating act of faith two things are closely connected: the exterior witness through the word of the preacher and the interior witness through the indwelling Spirit. The word of God to man must become a word in man. We have His testimony in us. The hearing of the external testimony is not enough. No one believes or comes to Christ except by the attraction of the Father who teaches him interiorly. By this interior attraction that teaches, man receives the word or the testimony of God. St. John clearly insinuates that the exterior testimony only introduces man, by the way of a condition, into a possession of the truth. The proper cause of divine truth in man is the Holy Spirit, the divine anointing that makes man know all things in such a way that exterior teaching is no longer necessary.

The interior anointing has at once the nature of a teaching and that of an attraction. Somehow the cognitive and the effective factors are most closely connected. The Gospel of St. John repeatedly states that in order to recognize God in Christ man's works must be good. He who does not escape from the power of the flesh or selfishness is unable to see the light. He does not apprehend the meaning of Christ and His works. The new birth implies a moral regeneration. Therefore faith cannot be separated from love. To have faith is to do the works of love. Rebirth, faith, and love are one and the same thing, the dynamic reality of the new being. To have one of them implies the possession of all. They condition one another. They form a kind of organic unity. They exist in mutual dependence on one another. As they exist together, they also perish together. A moral dimension of life is necessary to the apprehension of truth, antecedently as well as consequently. The antecedent conversion to God is the effect of His inner activity insofar as it is an attraction, while the appearance of the truth comes from the same activity insofar as it is a teaching. This must be theologically interpreted according to the analogy of our general knowledge of existential meaning. As all existential meaning only appears in the light of a moral thrust, awakening man to truth and to the deepest questions of life, so too the new divine meaning, which gives the answer to these deepest questions, only appears within the moral impetus of a life according to the claims of love. Therefore, faith too, the discernment of the truth that introduces man into eternal life, entails by itself a commitment to its works, the works of disinterested love.

The conclusion may be stated in the following points. First, there is a general analogy between the way that existential truth, which makes us men, and divine truth, which makes us children of God, exercise their inward appearance. In both cases the appearance of meaning is inwardly conditioned by a moral dimension, and its apprehension entails personal commitment. According to Thomas Aquinas, faith originates in man as an instinct. In it the discernment of value and the movement toward it are one. But this faith is completed in him by an act of intellectual assent under the influence of the will. This will prolongs the initial movement of the divine instinct by a personal decision that, although aided by grace, is an act of freedom, the freedom of the children of God.

Second, analogous as they are in their general structure, their difference is no less striking. The possibility of existential truth is a possibility of human existence as such, whereas the possibility of divine truth is created in man by a special gift of grace, the gift of eternal life. For this is what eternal life consists in, that men know the Father and Jesus Christ, His messenger.

Third, however distinct they may be by their very nature, general and special revelation cannot be so separated that the first is conceived as merely a gift of nature and the second as a gift of grace. We have to take very seriously the statement that the revelation through Jesus Christ gives to man the true ultimate answer to the questions that are awakened by his perception of all true existential appearance. Therefore the moral dimension that conditions the first appearance of true meaning must be considered as an initial grace that points man, by the existential questions it raises in him, to the answer that God will bring in His time through the appearance of the Truth incarnate in Jesus Christ. It is not without reason that some philosophers and theologians have also called faith the subjection to the prereflective apprehension of the full appearance of truth in its still indistinct form. Of course it is only analogically so. This is not faith in the theological sense of the term. But it is a kind of pre-understanding in the form of a question of what will really be understood in the form of a response when, addressed by the exterior testimony of Christ, the Father will attract and teach us interiorly. It is difficult to conceive that the graceful God is absent from the general good will that conditions true awakening to human self-consciousness.

REVELATION, PHILOSOPHY, AND THEOLOGY

There are three senses of the word *revelation*. The first is that of general revelation, an aspect of the full appearance of existential truth by virtue of which man attains to the level of true manhood. The second points to the historical event culminating in the appearance and testimony of Christ by virtue of which God manifests His Being as a Being of love that promises and gives eternal Life. The third is that of the inner testimony of the Holy Spirit or the light of faith, by virtue of which men come to see and understand the meaning of Christ, entering into the sphere of eternal Life and able henceforth to live and act like children of God imitating the love of the Father.

These three senses of the term are closely connected. As the second prolongs the first, so the third prolongs the second, albeit in a different way. General revelation is a preparation for what is intended by the second and the third. It is a preparation in that it makes men feel and see the mystery of existential meaning as a focus of existential questions. Thus it makes one look expectantly in the direction from which true answers may come. It makes one able to understand, at least by way of an antecedent condition, the divine answers when they come, and to recognize, by way of subsequent confirmation, that they truly respond to the first questions of existence. To work out the relation between general revelation thus understood and the message of Christ is the proper study of apologetic theology.

The second and the third sense simply cannot be separated. The historical revelation is completed in the inner light of faith. To reveal is to unveil a secret to someone. Without its efficacious relation to an addressee, revelation is not revelation at all. Therefore, a condition without which the meaning of an exterior revelation cannot be grasped necessarily pertains to the integral notion of revelation itself. It is a basic truth of Christianity that the exterior testimony of Christ and the Church cannot be duly apprehended except by the inner testimony of the Holy Spirit. The inner revelation terminates in the individual the act of divine self-communication witnessed by Christ, the Apostles, and the Church. The essential conditions of its termination are part of any kind of speech whatsoever.

Roughly, philosophy is the intellectual clarification of that which is given in the first appearance of existential truth, while theology is the intellectual clarification of that which appears in Christian revelation. Theology is related to the object of faith as philosophy is related to the general object of existential awareness. For two reasons, then, as we have seen, special revelation cannot be separated from the general revelation. First, the new meaning that appears in Christ is an inner clarification of the original meaning that appears in existence, raising the basic questions of human life. Second, the moral openness toward the appearance of existential meaning is already brought about by a preparatory grace directing man toward the acceptance of its completing gift. Therefore, as general revelation is related to special revelation, so in a similar way philosophy will be related to theology. Answers must somehow be given in the same terms as those of the questions to which they respond. It follows that the theological intellect, in elaborating the various aspects of the idea revealed in Christ, will make a certain use of the categories that philosophy has invented in order to clarify the general appearance of existential truth. Faith is independent of reason, i.e., the exercise of philosophical reflection, but theology in which faith seeks understanding cannot be wholly indifferent to the toils of philosophy. It follows, too, that one must accept the existence of a Christian philosophy, meaning by this not a philosophy that should take into its work specific elements of faith but a philosophy that by being faithful to a preparatory grace unfolds its thought in accordance with its own original object.

THE STARTING POINT OF DEVELOPMENT

The development of doctrine begins in the Christian revelation, exteriorly presented by the message of Christ, interiorly assimilated through the working of the Spirit of Truth, and appearing against the background of general revelation. The first thing to say, then, is that reflection, leading to notional statements about the Christian revelation, comes to operate as naturally within the realizing view of faith as within the existential apprehension of meaning. Within the movement of faith seeking understanding, the intellect acquires a certain independence in order to objectify what the person believes and to analyze its various aspects. The general structure of the conceptualizing process of Christian thought, the scientific form of which is called theology, is not different from that of existential reflection, the scientific form of which is philosophy. Its relation to the prereflective appearance of truth is the same. Faith is real apprehension. It is a free personal act that engages the whole man. To the concreteness and wholeness of the subject in the process of knowing corresponds the character of concreteness and wholeness of the object in the happening of its appearance. As in prereflective existential apprehension, so in faith the reality that appears is the whole, however dim and inarticulate it may be to the intellect. In faith as in existence truth is present to man by itself. The proper characteristic of human existence is that by its own nature it is self-illuminating. Existence moves in the light of existential truth. From the start man is possessed by that truth, however much it may be distorted and obscured by the interpretations resulting from the activity by which he tries to gain conscious possession of it. In a similar way faith is self-illuminating. Through the light of faith the saving truth possesses man. It is immediately present to man as a whole, although his conscious apprehension of it may be partial, inadequate, and more or less distorted by his conceptualizations. In Christian thought, as generally in human thought, conceptualizing reflection is an endeavor to embrace with intellectual consciousness what embraces us in its pre-intellectual appearance. This does not follow from an attitude of pride, although pride may work in its distorting and devastating effects. It simply springs from a natural tendency toward clarity, which in its genuine form is inspired and led on by a devout striving to penetrate the mystery that encompasses man. That striving of faith seeking understanding is the origin and impetus of theology.

What appears to man in the light of faith is always complete and perfect, but his existential apprehension of it is always imperfect because his spiritual eye is weak. The light of faith, then, is perfect to the extent that within it, saving reality is present to man, but it is imperfect to the extent that its appearance to man depends on his subjective receptivity. Man may realize more and more the real that is immediately present. This is a question of fidelity and growing holiness. There is a growth of the light of faith that is not caused by reflection but conditioned by action. The real becomes more and more real to those who love it and obey its claims on them. The knowledge of faith grows by its own inner light, penetrating more deeply the believing subject if he is faithful and actively responsive to its demands. That growth is a growth in depth. It has nothing to do with theological clarity or distinctness. The faith of the most ignorant believer may be more perfect than that of the greatest theologian. There is, however, a certain correlation between them, as will be seen presently.

On the contrary, man's conceptualization of what is present to the vision of faith is by its very nature always inadequate and imperfect. It belongs to another level, as was said above. It does not function within the possessive movement by which the real penetrates more deeply into the subject, but functions within the possessive movement by which the human subject, according to its nature, tries to clarify its consciousness of the real by distinguishing aspects, defining notions, comparing judgments, and thus constructing a

N

richer and more comprehensive system of conceptual thought. The process of conceptual clarification has a growth and development of its own. It is growth in another dimension: that of clarity and breadth, not that of existential penetration and depth.

There is, however, a correlation between the two modes of growth. That which conceptual reflection tries to clarify in its own way and with its proper means is the very object of real apprehension itself. Through notional analysis the object of faith becomes more conscious, more distinct. Human consciousness is a speaking consciousness. Consciousness takes possession of its object by pointing or being pointed to it through the medium of a language, either concrete and symbolic or abstract and conceptual.

Symbolic language and conceptual language function on two different levels of consciousness. Symbolic expression comes first, as in the development of humanity as a whole, imaginative thinking precedes conceptual thinking. Images are the first and basic language of humanity. The first and direct expression of awareness of a world of meaning, shining through the world of immediate sense perception, is the image that focuses the eye on the appearing meaning. In a psychologically immediate way man communicates with the self-revealing meaning in the transparency proper to images. A representation of the imagination, whether expressed or not in a creation of art, becomes a true image or symbol by acquiring that quality that makes it point to a meaning by its own transparency. Imaginative thought is closely connected with the process of realization. We realize a deeper meaning by concentrating on the symbol by means of which we bring it into focus. In the case of ultimate meaning, moral attitudes and actions are essential conditions of a growing realization, but images are spontaneous media or technical means by which consciousness is directed toward the real. Therefore, devotion uses symbols rather than concepts.

Conceptual thought prolongs imaginative thought, although on a different level. Symbolic consciousness is rather contemplative and ecstatic: man is beyond himself in the real that fills him with the experience of meaning. Conceptual thought draws man back into himself and is discursive; he concentrates on the thoughts that have been formed in his mind, arranging them and relating them to one another in a logical pattern.

At this point the relation between real apprehension, living in vivid images, and notional apprehension, expanding in conceptual ramifications, becomes clear. Through realizing apprehension, communion with the real becomes closer and deeper. The danger inherent in all conceptual thought is that of losing sight of the very object that man tries to bring to the clarity of consciousness, and thus of being locked in the magic circle of self-made concepts. That danger is warded off by the firm grip of reality on the mind. Through the intensity of real apprehension, conceptual thought remains concentrated on its true object. The real unveils to the analyzing mind ever-new aspects of its inexhaustible richness. Consciousness of the incommensurability of the real and the notional does not weaken. One is not beguiled into mistaking the constructions of the intellect for the structure of reality. Thus the realizing eye of faith guarantees to the theological thought its realism, richness, and prudence.

What has been said about existential or real apprehension in relation to conceptual thought also applies to the image. Symbolic and conceptual thought operate on two different levels of consciousness. This means a discontinuity, but there is continuity as well. Symbolic thought naturally goes over into conceptual thought when a certain stage of human development is reached. This does not mean, however, that conceptual thought supersedes and replaces symbolic thought. Conceptual thought is a new dimension in the development of a process that can never disown its origins. Without the working of the imagination by which man fixes his gaze on such meanings of reality as are not present to the senses, reality and thought easily part company, and thought degenerates into a logical game with words. In a well-balanced mind the symbolic media of realizing thought are always vividly present at the very heart of the concepts. A leading image is like a focus from which rays of clarifying thought part in different directions unveiling different aspects to the searching mind.

There is, however, another side to the problem. The help of the imagination is indispensable, but in the act of using it, it has to be disciplined and channelled. Imagination is not only the source of a well-directed symbolism; it is also a source of free association, which easily runs wild especially when it enters the domain of the invisible. Imagination may lead one away from reality just as much as one-sided conceptualizing and reasoning. It is therefore in need of direction by a trained and disciplined mind. When in the development of consciousness man has once reached the stage in which the fixed constellation of leading symbols begins to dissolve, the indispensable function of the imagination has to be controlled by reason.

In the world of higher meaning, then, the ideal is a balanced condition in which the realizing imagination, which presents to reflection the richness of the real and prevents it from disintegrating, on the one hand, and conceptual thought, which analyzes the appearance of the real and prevents imagination from getting lost in unbounded fantasy, on the other hand, are closely united with one another in constant interaction. In religion this is realized in practice in the unity of preaching and symbolic action. The sacraments are the highest things in religion, Goethe said. A happy combination of the sacramental and theological principles is conspicuous in some older forms of Christianity, while in certain kinds of Protestantism the absence of the sacramental principle has led to a dry intellectualization of religion, devoid of any true spirituality —as many Protestants avow. The renewed sympathetic interest in religious symbolism, myths, and mysticism witnessed in recent literature seems to mean that modern man is aware of the danger that he finds himself in through the loss of the symbolic element of thought. Modern man is increasingly aware that a serious effort has to be made to recover that dimension of symbolic depth without which the world degenerates into a dull combination of scientific abstractions and utilitarianism.

To this could be added that the notional elaboration by which man obtains a relative intellectual mastery over the world of meaning is necessary for an ordered practical life. In primitive humanity the thrust of life is directed by the great symbols of primitive culture according to patterns that work by way of instinctive intuition. Once that stage is passed a well-ordered view of life according to a conscious pattern of means and ends naturally requires a well-ordered worldview according to a pattern of intellectual clarity.

THE PROCESS OF DEVELOPMENT

In the light of these considerations the development of Christian doctrine as it springs from its *terminus a quo* and as it proceeds toward its *terminus ad quem* becomes fairly understandable. The process of development, then, can be viewed as it proceeds from what is originally given or as it proceeds toward its proper end.

Regarding the first, it is clear that the point of departure of the process that leads to development is neither exclusively a message about saving truth nor exclusively an immediate presence and appearance of that truth in the light of faith. It is both at once in a specific combination. As a social and cultural being man necessarily focuses the appearance of truth through the medium of a tradition that possesses him before he possesses it. His relation to tradition is somehow analogous to his relation to truth in its immediate presence to him. He is possessed by it and formed by it before the first attempt to think for himself. As was said above, existential truth also possesses man before his first attempt to take possession of it. There is then a certain similarity.

Developing thought in the Church proceeds from a kind of intuitive awareness of saving truth as a whole, explained by a Christian tradition that goes back to the historical event of Israel and Jesus Christ, charismatically understood and expressed by the Prophets and the Apostles. Saying this does not confer on it a special epistemological status altogether different from that of philosophical thought. Of course there are differences, as will be seen presently, but the general structure is the same. A distinction must be made between the immediate presence of existential or salvational truth and the way its appearance is consciously apprehended by the human subject. That it appears is determined by the immediate presence and action of truth itself; but the way in which it is perceived is determined by the tradition of the period. Therefore, although in both cases truth is immediately present by itself, either from the nature of human existence or by a special gift of illuminating grace, it is not apprehended in its independent purity, but in and through the interpretations that hold the mind by the force of tradition. Tradition is not something that merely exists outside man and with which he has to deal. Tradition is also within him. It is an essential dimension of being because man by his very nature is— though not exclusively—a product of a culture that is transmitted from generation to generation by the living working of tradition. Christian tradition, then, thriving in Christian life and preaching, is related to the apprehension of truth that appears in the light of faith in the same way as cultural tradition is related to the inner appearance of existential truth.

The difference between the two may be stated as follows. Cultural tradition as far as it is merely cultural—in fact, Christian culture is also shaped by the influence of revealed truth—has grown out of the common human experience and its interpretation by the intellect, whereas the Christian tradition proceeds from a special revelation connected with definite historical facts and an original interpretation whose truth is divinely guaranteed. The light in which the common appearance of truth is apprehended by man is the light of his common nature, whereas the light in which saving truth appears to man is a special light, the light of faith in which the saving God makes Himself present to our immediate affective apprehension: *Dieu sensible au cœur* (Pascal).

The kinds of similarity and difference that were noted in the process of development, viewed from its point of departure, are also found in the same process viewed in itself. In itself the development of doctrine is a process of discursive thought, or of reasoning, if you like, but in the broadest sense of the word. It is not a process of verbal reasoning in accordance with the rules of Aristotelian logic. It is the progressive analysis of an idea, which is ever present to the mind in its indistinct wholeness. By dwelling in the mind as an object of constant care and consideration, it gradually displays to the intellect its manifold aspects. In this it is not driven by intellectual curiosity but by vital interest. One's attention is constantly drawn to it in the context of an existence that is concerned with its meaning and seeks to understand it. Our being absorbed by it is not an effect of intellectual application, but of vital necessity. It is the intellect, however, the instrument of clarity, that notes down within the existential context the various aspects, defining, distinguishing, comparing them with one another, establishing the mutual relations by which they form a coherent intelligible pattern or system that reflects, as far as it does, the original and ever-present idea. Viewed in its vital aspect, development presents itself as a spontaneous, largely unconscious growth; viewed in its intellectual aspect, it is the result of a deliberate and conscious application of the mind. Ideas grow in the mind by remaining there. Their expression spontaneously ripens in the unconscious or semi-conscious regions of the mind. They are pre-formed, even in their conceptual and linguistic expression; clear insights and formulas suddenly rise up in one's consciousness, and then reflection may intervene, spontaneously or by deliberate application, in order to steady one's view of them, to work them out, to compare them with other insights already possessed and to fit them into the general pattern of the conscious worldview. Concepts are partly born in the mind and partly made by the mind.

Man never has complete control over that kind of thinking just described. Of course, as in a very broad sense it is a kind of reasoning, so in an equally broad sense it is a kind of logic. The different parts and articulations are somehow related to one another in such a way that they make an intelligible pattern. We see its consistency as a whole by what Newman calls the 'illative sense.' But we are often unable to determine the exact nature of the different relations by which the various parts are fitted into the comprehensive view. There may be different kinds of inductive or deductive inference. The analysis of the human mind and its thinking processes is not yet fully achieved by the science of logic. Aristotle has described some of them. Modern logic has discovered other kinds, or sub-variations. Perhaps man will never be able to formalize entirely the functional relations that link together the various articulations of actual thought; but the process of thought goes on by itself. It has a structure that is to be investigated, not made. Man is not allowed to judge its rightness exclusively by those rules that are entirely under his control. Thought, ruled by the appearance of truth, is not exclusively of man's own doing. It also possesses him before he comes to survey and more or less control it by reflective analysis and orientation. The mind is as mysterious as the world. In the living exercise of thought the mind is present to itself in a way similar to that in which existential truth is present to it. The results of logical analysis are as inadequate to the living process of thought as the results of phenomenological or metaphysical analysis are to the appearance of existential meaning. Even the most refined pattern of logical rules is but a rough replica of the way in which living thought makes its way under the direct guidance of its illative sense.

From this it follows that all true philosophical thought, however technical, is to a certain extent supra-logical, if 'logical' means 'proceeding according to the rules of formal logic.' Once more, in saying that the development of doctrine in the Church considered as a living process is supra-logical but not illogical, we are not claiming for it a special status. The difference is that the idea that develops through it is not the general mystery of existence in which man finds himself by the fact of being man, but a deeper level of mystery to which he has access only through a special light. It is more above him; and therefore the ways of development in the Church, guided by the Spirit, will be still more recondite than the general development of thought in humanity. Its supra-logical character will be more prominent.

Another question concerns the relation of the process to its norm of truth. In this respect the dissimilarity is more striking than the resemblance, but there is a resemblance. In both cases the direct norm of truth is its own appearance. In both cases there is an indirect norm: tradition. On that point, however, there is an important difference. In the philosophical interpretation of life tradition is not a norm by itself. It is wise and necessary to take account of it, but it is not necessary to conform to it because it is tradition. By reason of human nature tradition is a part of the mind. Willy-nilly, man is a traditionalist. He cannot cast off tradition in order to make a philosophy entirely of his own. Even if he rebels against it, he is unconsciously in its power. Moreover, it is not very probable that a cultural or philosophical tradition, which in the course of many centuries has selected and collected the fruits of what so many thinkers of genius have produced, will simply be false. From the beginning men have thought within a common basic condition of existence ruled by the same presence and appearance of existential truth. There may be tensions and contradictions between various trends and schools. In fact philosophical tradition is a continuous struggle among one-sided, impoverished, or simplified worldviews. One may be more true than the other, but the actual human condition being what it is, it is neither acceptable that one of them will be the whole truth nor probable that one of them will be devoid of all truth. A wise man will take impartial account of the various currents that clash within the restless stream of tradition. He will continue the dialogue of philosophies, equally removed from presumption as from skepticism. There is truth, and man may find abundant truth in tradition; but it would be a kind of intellectual insolence or naiveté to imagine that he might possess the truth in its entirety and purity. The process has to go on. Time and again he has to make a fresh start, reflecting on the problem of existence in the light of tradition and in a spirit of philosophical ecumenism that is as necessary for the good of mankind as religious ecumenism is necessary for the well-being of Christianity.

It is true, then, that even in the field of philosophy, tradition has an important part. When there arrive on the scene of history generations that neglect or despise the heritage of the past, the return to barbarism has begun. Nevertheless a traditional doctrine has no authority simply because it has been repeated by masters of the past. It is always open to criticism. We may come to conclusions that are at variance with statements of the past. In expressing our views, the rule of the self-appearance of truth is in no way subjected to the rule of tradition. In Christian tradition it is otherwise. The tradition of faith dates back to definite public facts of antiquity that are known through historical information. These facts have a definite meaning, stated in prophetic words whose truth is forever guaranteed to us by God. Subsequent dogmas or doctrines may state them more precisely, elaborate their consequences, make them explicit, clarify them by a reflection that, guided by them, dwells upon the ever-present mystery of faith. But later doctrines are never allowed to contradict or to obscure what was undoubtedly intended by the primitive tradition that came to life in the preaching of the ancient Church and in the inspired documents of Scripture.

Every doctrine of faith accepted by Christians must be equally true to a message of the past as to the present appearance of saving truth in the light of faith. We cannot appeal to the present appearance of truth against anything that is clearly intended by the *traditio constitutiva*. If thoughts and sayings do not conform to the rule of antiquity, it is a token that neither do they agree with what God shows to the believing mind by the light of faith. The inspired Word understood by the Church always represents the whole of Christian truth, however imperfect or perfect the stage of its expression may be. Man always says more than what he says. In matters of ultimate meaning, what he succeeds in saying always implicitly refers to a universe of meaning that he is aware of without being able to put it into words. In the act of speaking, i.e., of directing his thoughts to others, man says not only the words he actually pronounces but also the totality he intends to say. Thus the Word of God in its original linguistic expression tries to communicate something to man, which although truly expressed *by* it is not entirely expressed *in* it. The whole that is immediately present to man in the light of faith is entirely signified by the scriptural Word although it is not entirely rendered by its verbal translation. What in Scripture is thus present as a whole is called *Dogma* by Karl Barth, and it is never entirely grasped in the dogmas of the Church although it is always entirely addressed to man by God.

We conclude, then, that the development of doctrine is not partly a reasoning from an imperfect primitive message and partly an elucidation of an intuitively present idea. It is entirely both at once. The whole process is both an attempt to express an interior vision that always exceeds such attempts and an attempt to make explicit what is entirely intended by, although not entirely uttered in, the words of Scripture. For the integral or full meaning of what is said under prophetic inspiration is the same mystery that is also present in the extraordinary light of prophecy and in the ordinary light of faith. The relation of the later stages of dogma to the primitive stage is not only such that it cannot contradict it but also such that it must fit into its doctrinal pattern. It is the proper task of theology to work out a system in which primitive and later dogmas are related to one another in such a way that they harmoniously and intelligibly fit into a pattern, the main lines of which already appear in Scripture.

The development of Christian doctrine in history is not isolated in itself and separated from the general movement of human thought. It does not flow along a tranquil canal, but mingles with the vast turbulent stream of cultural tradition. It lives in constant interaction with the whole of human thought, influencing it and being influenced by it. Therefore it is subject to all the conditions that a good sociology of thought discovers in the general history of ideas. It is not an exclusive business of saints, keeping aloof amidst the floods of sinful humanity. Minds very different in their formation, culture, tendencies, or disposition are engaged in reflecting upon the vital truth offered to them by the Christian tradition. These differences, as we have said, are not only intellectual; they are rooted in character. If man thinks as a whole, his individuality is determined by the whole of his personality. That personality has not only an individual but also a social dimension. Original as man may be, he is always a child of his time, his culture, his nation, party, and family. Therefore the whole dialectical process provoked by the clash of one-sided views and angry oppositions will also mark the course of doctrinal history in the Church. The general structure of religious thought in the Church is not different from that of philosophical thought in the world at large.

There are differences, but they do not belong to the description of the process but its hidden nature, which is an object of faith. The prophetic origin and authority of the message, the light of faith, the working of grace, are not descriptive characteristics. We believe them. So too the inner guidance of the Spirit, who continues in the mind of the Church the illuminating activity initiated by Him in the light of faith, is not a descriptive trait of the process of development. We believe it.

This also applies to the authority that separates corruptions from faithful developments in the course of time. It has been pointed out that the situation of fact in the history of human thought cannot but raise the problem of public authority. Human nature itself provides a kind of public authority: the cultural tradition and the body of teachers that represent it. In the same way, the tradition of faith, presented by the testimonies of the past and by the preaching of the Church, is as it were a natural public authority in matters of faith. The difference is that Christ, at least according to Roman Catholic faith, has provided His Church with a teaching body that represents in a special way the authority of tradition. To be sure, the dogmatic tradition of the Church in its present phase is the supreme authority. Councils and popes cannot declare something to be part of faith that is not in accordance with tradition or not given in it. Making use of the natural processes of human thought, the Holy Spirit brings to maturity in the Church such dogmatic insights as are in accordance with His revelation and light. But in the actual course of history the work of the Spirit is constantly immersed in an impure stream of defective and willful thought. In making use of the natural resources of the human mind, the Spirit does not destroy the natural tendencies to deviate in the Christian community as a whole. Therefore it is believed by Catholics that Christ, who sent the Spirit, has established in the Church an exterior social authority that in certain circumstances is enabled, through the assistance of the same Spirit, to settle disputes in the Church by decisions whose truth is guaranteed by His invisible authority. The end is like the beginning. The course of development begins with a special revelation addressed to the world by divinely inspired persons. The testing of its fruits is made by a special authority exercised by a divinely assisted body of teachers.

DEVELOPMENT OF DOCTRINE AND HERMENEUTICS

Our theory of the development of doctrine in the Church unavoidably raises the contemporary problem of hermeneutic. As G. Ebeling put it:

The different verdicts on the question whether the tradition has to be assigned interpretative or supplementary character hang together with the divergence of views on the nature of interpretation. But according to the view of the Roman Church the tradition naturally contains nothing that contradicts Scripture and is not provided for at least in germ in it. The concept of development, on which the discussion of the Catholic concept of tradition concentrates itself, therefore involves the hermeneutical problem.[1]

Hermeneutic is a reflection on the problem of the interpretation of texts. To interpret is to determine what an action or statement really means. It is not about the meaning of things but about the meaning of such human products as are intended to express or to communicate something: statements and actions, works of art, and texts. Modern hermeneutics concentrates on the problem of how to get at the understanding of old texts, especially such texts as belong to different cultures or to earlier phases of one's own culture. In theological circles the problem has been vividly discussed in connection with the question of understanding authoritative texts of the past, especially the Scriptures.

The questions that the science of hermeneutics asks are: What is the nature of interpretation? How does it proceed? How are its limits determined? The contemporary concern with hermeneutics is the consequence of a growing insight into the historical nature of man. Historicity is an essential law of man, including his consciousness and thought. The human world is not a world of bare things and facts. The things and facts enter man's world to the extent that they are assumed into a world of meaning through which he views them. A world of meaning is like a pattern of features, picturing the countenance of the real as far as it is turned to us. Utimate meaning or existential truth is in a certain sense always present to man; but it only enters into his conscious, active life through certain activities of expression or interpretation that are always inadequate and may be more or less one-sided or partly wrong and partly right.

A distinction must be made between two senses of the word *interpretation*. In the primary sense it means the basic activity of human thought; it may be called *interpretation of things*. In the secondary sense it means the reflective activity by which man tries to get at the real meaning of existing interpretations of things; it may be called *interpretation of texts*. This implies a limitation for the sake of the present investigation. There is also an interpretation of works of art, which in itself is no less important than the interpretation of texts. We shall not refer to it, however interesting it may be, because it does not fall within the strict scope of our subject.

Interpretation of texts—the proper object of hermeneutics—is an interpretation of interpretations. Consequently the nature of the former depends on the nature of the latter. How human statements about the meaning of things—*things* is a vague term that signifies the whole of what is somehow within the range of one's experience—are interpreted will depend on how one sees the relation between the expression of meaning and meaning itself. The first question is the meaning of meaning. Some existentialist philosophers think that the interpretation of things is not ruled by an appearance of meaning that imposes itself on man. They think that all meaning is subjective, i.e., not something to discover but something to create by the existential project. If this be true, then the rules according to which ancient texts must be interpreted will be wholly different from those that are required by the present position about the presence and appearance of existential meaning. If one starts from the assumption that meaning is merely a human creation, then the link between past and present interpretations of things is only one of succession in time. That succession may be explained as a dialectical process of some kind. But from the point of view of a subjectivist conception of values, the nature of the dialectical process itself will be altogether different from what it appears to be from the point of view that past and present interpretations of things are attempts to express an apprehension of meaning the appearance of which constitutes human nature. In holding to the insight that existential truth as a whole is present to all men, we have already decided on our answer to the fundamental question of hermeneutics. We have stated the point of departure or the first principle of its solution.

To say that the same existential truth is present to all men does not mean that the whole truth simply lies open to all men or that it lies open to all of them in the same way. For, as we have insisted, conscious apprehension of it only happens in an act of expression, which, however true, can only be defective. Therefore the approach of truth, not only in the thought of the individual but also in that of the community, has to be viewed as an endless pilgrimage toward itself. The common truth that possesses all men tends to be gradually apprehended and possessed by men, although the process will never come to an end. This is the way in which truth is truth for a finite mind. If truth or being is considered, not as an hypostasis outside the mind but as a transcendental presence that is only actualized in understanding, then truth or being must be said to be finite and contingent. If truth is only truth to the extent that its possession of the mind is converted into a being possessed by the mind, then truth in humanity is a constant becoming, a contingent history. It is an illusion to think that truth, as far as it enters human life, is a timeless structure of an objective world that lies open to the reconnoitring of a timeless intellect capable of knowing truth entirely if only man makes the effort to clear his mind. It is a definite acquisition of contemporary philosophy, in opposition to the Cartesian assumption, that subject and object are equally and simultaneously involved in a finite process of self-becoming. Truth in the human mind endlessly tends toward itself without ever coming to rest in itself.

This does not mean that there is no infinite or necessary being, but that the possible knowledge of such a being by the human mind is a finite, contingent, and progressive happening that, always reassumed and carried on, never comes to a stop in the course of history. Existential truth, then, as far as it is transcendentally present and mentally intended, is always the same, but as to the mode of its appearing to man and being signified by him, it is always changing and becoming. This does not mean that a statement that is true at one moment or in a given stage of history may become untrue afterward. There is always truth and falsehood in tradition. However, to the extent that a tradition contains truth it can never be falsified in its further course. If it can afterward be falsified, it has never been true. To be sure, this truth is but a human truth, subject to the conditions of human existence. Therefore it can always be completed, enriched, expressed in new ways. But to the extent that it is true, it is true forever. If a re-examination of a saying entails the negation of what is clearly and consciously said and meant by that saying, then it is not an interpretation. Interpretation may bring to the fore elements of meaning that are not expressly said but implicitly intended by the mind in its inadequate efforts toward the whole truth. These new elements may seem to modify the pattern of what previously was apprehended by the mind, but the former elements of truth, which are thus transcended in the new pattern, can never be disavowed by it. Interpretation may go beyond the given truth but never against it, lest it cease to be an interpretation. If, for instance, the words of Chalcedon that Christ is perfectly and truly man in the same sense as all men are, but also perfectly and true God in the same sense as the Father is, are declared to mean that Christ is only a higher achievement of man—as is the contention of van Buren and others—then we are faced with a negation and not with an interpretation.

An interpretation, though going beyond what is said, must conserve in itself what is explicitly meant by the statement. This is a first rule, following from the very nature of interpretation. It at once introduces our proper subject: the interpretation of the authoritative texts of the Christian religion. Christian tradition, considered in a general way, according to a purely sociological description, has carried in itself many errors, which have been eliminated in the course of history or will be eliminated in the future. But, insofar as it goes back to historical facts that come down through an interpretation the truth of which is divinely guaranteed, later interpretations can never entail a negation of what is clearly meant in the original documents. The relation between the later interpretations of the sacred text and the interpretation of the facts by the sacred text can only be one of further explication of what is ultimately meant, although incompletely expressed, by the text itself. And if the truth of some further explications is equally divinely guaranteed, although in a different way perhaps, then the process of developing interpretation, going on without end within history, is never allowed to contradict or eliminate one of those elements of truth that were acquired in the previous course of tradition. Dogma is a statement held by the Church to be divinely guaranteed. Consequently the development of dogma in the strictest sense is the development of Christian tradition along the hermeneutical path, insofar as that tradition carries with it a number of statements that cannot be falsified by subsequent interpretation. The development of dogma is the backbone and the substance of the Christian tradition. Theological thought, concentrating upon the Christian mystery as it is present in faith and apprehended by means of its traditional expression, may offer to the Church new elements of believing insight, but as long as these insights are not divinely ratified, they are not parts of the substance that cannot possibly be denied by further theological interpretation.

Tradition is a living historical whole. The theological problem of hermeneutic not only relates to the interpretation of the Scriptures that give the first interpretation of the salvific facts, but also to the interpretation of all further dogmatic interpretations that form the living substance of tradition. These interpretations form a chain. The original interpretation of the Christ-event now comes to us through a whole chain of later dogmatic interpretations. The Christology of Chalcedon is an interpretation of the Christology of the NT which is itself an interpretation of a pre-scriptural tradition that was current between the experiences of Easter and Pentecost and the time in which the writings of the NT came into being. The Scriptures are already an enlargement on the views of the original witnesses. Chalcedon is a further enlargement on the Biblical view. But the form of the original witness about Christ, the Biblical image of Christ, and the formulas of Chalcedon about Him are different stages in one and the same effort to express one and the same vision of Christ impressed on the mind of the Church by the light of faith. Because the vision, which all formulas tend to express, always exceeds them, there is no reason why these efforts should ever cease. It must be held, however, that the scriptural testimony about Christ is true to that of the eye-witnesses who discerned in the light of revelation the true meaning of Christ. Those eye-witnesses would have recognized in the further scriptural stage of Christological expression what they really meant. So too the formulas of Chalcedon are true to the scriptural witness; and the writers of the NT, if they had gone through the history that led to Chalcedon, would have recognized in its sharply outlined statements a further clarification of that same vision of faith that they tried to put into words. Hence, those who are living in the present stage of tradition must not go back to one moment of the past, the pre-scriptural, the scriptural, or the conciliar, but in order to determine their own place within the ongoing movement of tradition they must go back to the original message through the whole chain of authoritative interpretations. We may try to reconstruct exactly the primitive message through Biblical criticism. We may try to get at the Christological view of the Bible within the strict mental limits of its authors, determined by their historico-cultural situation and expressed in the letter of their works. Such enterprises are useful and good. They are even necessary. They clarify our knowledge of the different stages that the process of development has gone through, and this helps us to understand exactly our own position in its present stage. But whoever intends to reintroduce the Biblical view as an appropriate theology for our own day only betrays that he has no understanding at all of the true nature of historical existence. A contemporary theology cannot go back; it can only go onward, consciously prolonging the ongoing impetus of tradition.

GENERAL CONCLUSIONS

To state it succinctly, we have arrived at several insights, which are:

1. In matters of ultimate meaning human thought is an attempt to take possession, by expressing it, of an existential truth, the presence and possible appearance of which constitutes man's proper being. Such attempts are imperfect by reason of the ontological finiteness of the thinking subject. Therefore development and improvement of expression are possibilities rooted in the nature of things. Christian thought, then, is an attempt to take possession, by expressing it, of a saving truth, the presence and possible apprehension of which, founded in the light of prophecy or faith, constitutes human existence in a new dimension, that of salvation. The expression of what appears to faith, i.e., revelation, cannot but be inadequate, because the receiving subject is still affected by the limitations of his ontological imperfection. Hence, a development in the understanding of revelation is a possibility that follows from the nature of the case.

2. The actual apprehension of existential truth is an act of the whole person. In this act moral determination is as essential as intellectual application. Discernment necessarily implies commitment. Consequently, the actual apprehension of saving truth is too an act of the person and not an act of one of his faculties. Without moral openness and engagement, saving truth cannot actually appear to man. Therefore the discernment of revelation in the light of faith necessarily implies the commitment of the believer by the act of faith.

3. The human way in which saving truth is actually apprehended in the act of expressing it is conditioned and determined by the historical situation. There is no human apprehension of meaning that is not conditioned by a concrete contingent situation. Even the

o

first apprehension of the meaning of Christ by the Apostles was conditioned by their contingent historical situation as determined by the expectations of Israel founded in prophetic tradition and also by the contemporary position of their people within the Roman Empire. There are two factors, then, in the situation conditioning the way in which the truth of revelation appears to the believing mind and is apprehended by it: the tradition of the past, which inevitably and in a large part unconsciously molds his way of apprehending and expressing the truth of revelation; and the present condition, which in function of its own needs and questions invites him to prolong the tradition in a certain direction.

On the one hand, then, we have to enter into the tradition; we have to make it our own. We have to rethink it for ourselves by a kind of personal application equal to that of our predecessors who shaped it in the course of time. But we can never free our minds from it because those minds are already possessed and framed by it before their first acts of conscious self-orientation.

On the other hand, the dialectical movement of history continually creates new situations. A new historical situation, however, sheds a fresh light on the existential or saving truth already apprehended in its existent expression. Thus new aspects of that truth may come into sight, inviting and impelling man to give them due expression and to determine their proper place within the pattern of tradition.

4. In the course of its historical movement, tradition is constantly attested by documents that are added to the treasure of objective culture. Hence the term *tradition* has a twofold sense: the living movement of thought through the chain of generations (subjective tradition) and the sum total of the documents in which the various stages of the living movement are attested (objective tradition). Since linguistic expression is essential to conscious thought, the interpretation of tradition is essentially, though not entirely, an interpretation of its past documentation. This raises the problem of hermeneutic. The nature of interpretation is determined by the common condition of human thought. Human thought, past and present, is influenced by the transcendental presence of existential truth. From the nature of the human condition real thought is an attempt to express the same existential truth that our ancestors tried to express. Hence the interest of an ancient philosophical or religious document is not only a detached historical interest; it con-

cerns present existence. In interpreting a text we are trying to express with the help of the text a meaning that is present to us as it was to the thinkers of the past. To those of the present as to those of the past that meaning has the same vital interest. What they really meant and intended to say transcends what they actually said. The meaning that thus transcends the letter shines through the letter and constitutes, as it were, its dimension of depth. Such, too, is the general relation of the believing thinker to the sacred documents of the past. Aided and directed by them, he reassumes the task of expressing what they meant but did not succeed in expressing adequately. The same movement goes on along the hermeneutical path.

5. In objective Christian tradition some documents (Scripture, conciliar formulas, ecclesiastical definitions) have a privileged status. Their truth is guaranteed to the believing mind by the Holy Spirit who inspired them. Therefore it may rightly be said that the later dogmas are included in the *sensus plenior* or the full sense of the Scriptures. Since the Spirit inspired the attempts of the canonical writers to express the appearance of saving truth, He intended to say not only what was explicitly understood by the sacred writers but also the whole meaning toward which their words were pointing. What the Spirit says through the sacred author is free from the limitations of the latter's consciousness and of his capacity of expression. Further, since the Spirit guides the Church into all truth, it is clear that He is at work not only in the primitive interpretation of the facts but also in the dogmatic growth that results from later interpretations of the texts. Christian hermeneutic is ruled by the belief that the Holy Spirit is at work in the whole history of salvation, in its ecclesiastical as well as in its pre-ecclesiastical phase. The beginning is the end. What the Spirit meant in inspiring the Scriptures is the ideal Dogma to which all dogmatic interpretation is tending.

6. The interpretation of the sacred text, like the interpretation of any other text, supposes an intellectual and a moral participation in the undertaking of the writers whose works are under scrutiny. As to the intellectual participation, it implies an effort of comprehension and an effort of explanation. The interpreter must place himself in the situation in which they were writing, trying with them to think the same thoughts they tried to express. By so doing he takes them into his own thought. This implies that he agrees to be ruled by them,

because they perhaps saw things that the interpreter would not perceive alone, and because their situation was perhaps more suitable for discovering some aspects that his own situation tends to conceal. This holds as true for the interpretation of Plato as for that of St. John. The theologian has, of course, another and a peremptory reason to let his mind be guided by the sacred text: its divinely guaranteed truthfulness in which he believes. On the other hand, the interpreter has to fix his attention upon the meaning intended by the ancient writer, which partly exceeds his power of expression, limited as it is by his personal capacity and his historical situation. In so doing, the interpreter is not only disposed to learn something from the writer he is explaining, but he also applies his own lights, conditioned by his own situation, to an understanding of the existential or saving truth, which goes beyond what the writer was explicitly aware of. According to a well-known theological formula, tradition, since the end of public revelation, is *conservativa et explicativa* with respect to the *traditio constitutiva*: it preserves, and therefore it has to comprehend it in itself; it explicates, and therefore it has to go beyond it, guided by its light and by the light of faith in which saving truth continues to be present to the Church.

7. Our participation in the tradition is also a moral one. In order to share with the sacred writers in their discernment we must participate in their commitment. The light of faith cannot be separated from the assent of faith. The light of faith, in which saving truth appears, only shines in those men who commit themselves to its claims. Therefore the true and full interpretation of the sacred text is strictly theological. It is an act of the believer seeking to understand not only what comes to him by way of history but also what is present to his faith through illuminating grace.

8. The development of doctrine is a social phenomenon. All factors at work in the history of Christianity are also at work in the history of its self-understanding and self-interpretation. This implies that the negative factors of one-sidedness and passion, leading to division and disruption, are as active in the history of Christian thought as in that of humanity in general. If, then, a definite truth, historically determined by God, has to be preserved in the process of its divergent interpretations, the idea of an institutional authority, equally determined by God and enabled by Him to settle controversies of interpretation, is as natural to the mind as the idea of an historically revealed truth itself.

Notes

NOTES TO CHAPTER ONE

1. R. Draguet, 'L'Evolution des dogmes,' *Apologétique*, ed. M. Brillant and M. Nédoncelle (Paris, 1937), p. 1167.
2. A. Fox, *Dean Inge* (London, 1960), p. 169–178.
3. L. E. Elliott-Binns, *English Thought 1860–1900 The Theological Aspect* (London, 1956).
4. C. D. Broad, 'Two Lectures on the Nature of Philosophy,' *Clarity Is Not Enough*, ed. H. D. Lewis (London, 1963), pp. 49–50.

NOTES TO CHAPTER TWO

1. C. D. Broad, 'Two Lectures on the Nature of Philosophy,' *Clarity Is Not Enough*, ed. H. D. Lewis (London, 1963), p. 59.
2. B. Blanchard, 'The Philosophy of Analysis,' *Clarity Is Not Enough*, p. 105.
3. J. H. Newman, *Lectures on the Present Position of Catholics in England* (Dublin, 1857), p. 26.
4. H. G. Gadamer, *Wahrheit und Methode* (Tübingen, 1965), p. 261.
5. J. Ortega y Gasset, *Ideas y creencias, Obras Completas*, 5th ed. (Madrid, 1961), vol. 5, p. 384.
6. V. Tapié, *Chateaubriand par lui-même* (Paris, 1965), p. 85.
7. H. H. Price, 'Clarity Is Not Enough,' *Clarity Is Not Enough*, pp. 34–35.
8. Broad, 'Two Lectures on the Nature of Philosophy,' p. 49.
9. *Ibid*.
10. Newman, *Lectures on the Present Position of Catholics in England*, p. 261.

393

NOTES TO INTRODUCTION TO PART TWO

1. J. H. Newman, *Oxford University Sermons* (London 1884), p. 337.

NOTES TO CHAPTER THREE

1. A. Méhat, *Etudes sur les 'Stromates' de Clément d'Alexandrie* (Paris, 1966), p. 441.
2. W. R. Inge, *The Philosophy of Plotinus* (London, 1941), 2:19.
3. M. Harl, *Origène et la fonction révélatrice du Verbe Incarné* (Paris 1958), p. 288.
4. *Ibid.*, p. 161.

NOTES TO CHAPTER FOUR

1. A. Oepke, 'Revelation in the Old Testament,' Kittel *ThW* (Eng.) 3:573.
2. W. Eichrodt, 'Offenbarung im A.T.' RGG³ 4.1600.
3. Oepke, 'Revelation,' 3:573.
4. J. Keulers, *De brievan van Paulus* (Roermond, 1953), 1:198.
5. R. H. Lightfoot, *St. John's Gospel: A Commentary* (Oxford, 1956), pp. 287–288.
6. V. Morel, *De ontwikkeling van de christelijke overlevering volgens Tertullianus* (Bruges and Brussels, 1946), p. 181.
7. *Ibid.*, p. 186.
8. *Ibid.*, pp. 155–157.
9. C. Mohrmann, VigChr (1951), p. 11.
10. Summary adapted from R. Hanson, *Origen's Doctrine of Tradition* (London, 1954), p. 116.
11. *La Jeunesse d'Origène* (Paris, 1936), p. 268, n.2.
12. Hanson, *Origen's Doctrine of Tradition*, pp. 51, 97, 116.
13. *Contra Celsum*. 1.7. ed. H. Chadwick (Cambridge, 1953), p. 10.
14. J. Lebon, ed., *Lettres à Serapion*, SourcesChr 15 (Paris, 1947); 57–58.
15. K. Federer, *Liturgie und Glaube* (Freiburg, 1950), pp. 108–109.
16. *Ibid.*, p. 114.
17. F. Marín-Sola, *L'Evolution homogène du Dogme catholique* (Fribourg, 1924), 2:133.

NOTES TO CHAPTER FIVE

1. *Oeuvres théologiques et grammaticales de Godescalc d'Orbais*, ed. C. Lambot (Louvain, 1945), p. 100.
2. H. D. Simonin, 'La théologie thomiste de la foi et le développement du dogme,' RevThom 40 (1935): 544.
3. *Ibid.*, p. 548.

4. See M. Grabmann, *Die philosophische und theologische Erkennt-nislehre des Kardinals Matthaeus von Aquasparta* (Vienna, 1906), p. 157.

5. See P. Tihon, *Foi et théologie selon Godefroid de Fontaines* (Paris and Bruges, 1966), pp. 42–46.

6. *Ibid.*, pp. 92–93.

7. See P. De Vooght, 'La Méthode théologique d'après Henri de Gand et Gérard de Bologne,' RechThMed 23 (1956): 78–79.

8. R. Aubert, 'Le Problème de la foi dans l'œuvre de Pierre Olivi,' *Miscellanea historica Alberti De Meyer* (Louvain, 1946), p. 630.

9. R. Guelluy, *Philosophie et théologie chez Guillaume d'Ockham* (Louvain, 1947), pp. 220–258.

NOTES TO CHAPTER SIX

1. H. Jedin, *History of the Council of Trent* (St. Louis, 1961), 2: 52–98.

2. See R. Struman 'La perpétuité de la foi dans la controverse Bossuet-Jurieu 1686–1691,' *Revue d'histoire ecclésiastique* 37 (1941): 145–189.

3. A. Arnauld, 'Seconde défense des professeurs en théologie de la faculté de Bordeaux,' *Oeuvres compltes*, vol. 21 (Paris, 1775-81) p. 167.

4. 'Histoire des variations des églises protestantes,' *Oeuvres complètes*, vol. 14, ed. F. Lachat (Paris, 1862–66), p. 3.

5. *Oeuvres complètes*, 13: 223–224.

6. *Ibid.*

7. 'Première instruction pastorale sur les promesses de l'Eglise,' *Oeuvres complètes*, 17: 111–112.

8. *Le vrai système de l'Eglise et la véritable analyse de la foi* (Dordrecht, 1686), p. 509.

9. *Lettres pastorales adressées aux fidèles de France*, troisième année (Rotterdam, 1686–89), p. 125.

NOTES TO CHAPTER SEVEN

1. *Opusculum de conceptione B. Virginis* (Venetiis, 1594), folio 71 verso.

2. *In 1 Sent*, Prologus, 1.2.3, ad 4 contra Scotum, *Defensiones theologicae divi Thomas Aquinatis* (Turin, 1900), vol. 1, p. 17.

3. *In dialecticam Aristotelis* 1.2, ad 7 (Salamanca, 1574), p. 91.

4. *De locis theologicis*, 12.2 (Salamanca, 1563), pp. 390–391.

5. See E. Marcotte, *La Nature de la théologie d'après Melchior Cano* (Ottawa, 1949), pp. 150–159.

396   *Notes*

6. *In I partem D. Thomae,* 1.2 ad 3 (Barcelona, 1934), p. 21.
7. *Commentaria in I partem D. Thomae,* 1.2 (Venice, 1602), p. 7.
8. *Cursus theologicus* (Paris, 1879), vol. 11, p. 48.
9. *Ibid.,* p. 55.
10. *Ibid.,* p. 57.
11. *Ibid.,* p. 69.
12. *Ibid.,* p. 58.
13. *Ibid.,* p. 69.
14. *In I partem D. Thomae* 1.2.5 cap. 3 (Lyons, 1631), p. 15.
15. *L'Evolution homogène du dogme catholique,* 2d ed. (Fribourg, 1924), vol. 2, pp. 163–165.
16. *In I partem D. Thomae* 1.8 (Barcelona, 1934), p. 83.
17. *In 2am 2ae D. Thomae* 1.7 (Salamanca, 1585), pp. 85–86.
18. *Ibid.,* 1.10, pp. 130–131.
19. Juan Martinez de Ripalda, *De fide* 8.3n.37 (Lyons, 1652), pp. 101–102.
20. *De Fide* 6.3 n.10, in *Opera Omnia* (Paris, 1858), vol. 12, p. 174.
21. *De Fide* 3.11 n.11.
22. J. Alfaro, 'El progreso dogmatico en Suarez,' *Problemi scelti di teologia contemporanea* (Rome, 1954), p. 118.
23. Gütersloh, 1949–54.
24. G. Perrone, *De immaculato Beatae Virginis Mariae conceptu an dogmatico decreto definiri possit disquisitio theologica* (Milan, 1852), p. 105.
25. C. Pesch, *Glaube, Dogmen und geschichtliche Tatsachen, Eine Untersuchung über den Modernismus* (Freiburg, 1908), p. 185.
26. *Die neuern katholischen Erklärungen der Dogmenentwicklung* (Essen, 1965), p. 120.
27. M. Tuyaerts, *L'Evolution du dogme* (Louvain, 1919), p. 86.
28. 2 vols., Fribourg, 1924.

NOTES TO CHAPTER EIGHT

1. St. Axters, *The spirituality of the Low Countries,* trans. Donald Attwater (London, 1954), p. 68.
2. K. S. Latourette, *Christianity in a Revolutionary Age,* The Nineteenth Century in Europe (London, 1959), vol. 1, p. 209.
3. E. Hirsch, *Geschichte der neuern evangelischen Theologie* (Gütersloh, 1949), vol. 2, p. 115.
4. A. Macintyre. 'The Logical Status of Religious Belief,' *Metaphysical Beliefs,* ed. A. Macintyre, and R. G. Smith (London, 1958), pp. 198–199.
5. R. L. Colie, *Light and Enlightenment: A Study of the Cambridge Platonists and the Dutch Arminians* (Cambridge, 1957).

6. *Ibid.,* p. 15.
7. Wharton MSS, 943, fol. 859. See R. Orr, *Reason and Authority: The Thought of William Chillingworth* (Oxford, 1967), p. 82.
8. *The Religion of Protestants* (London, 1727), p. 159; quoted in Orr, *Reason and Authority,* p. 83.
9. H. More, 'An Explanation of the Grand Mystery of Godliness,' *Theological Works* (London, 1708), p. 363.
10. *Ibid.,* p. 364.
11. R. Cudworth, *Sermon to the Honourable House of Commons,* 1647; quoted in Colie, *Light and Enlightenment,* pp. 47–48.
12. B. Whichcote, 'Sermons,' *The Works of Benjamin Whichcote* (Aberdeen, 1751), vol. 2, p. 387.
13. B. Whichcote, 'Sermons,' *Works,* vol. 1. p. 168.
14. R. Cudworth, 'Sermon to the Honourable House of Commons,' *The Intellectual System of the Universe* (London, 1820), vol. 4, p. 303.
15. J. Locke, *An Essay Concerning Human Understanding,* ed. R. Wilburn (London, 1947), p. 333.
16. I. T. Ramsey, 'Introduction' to J. Locke, *The Reasonableness of Christianity* (London, 1958), pp. 16–17.
17. T. L. Bushell, *The Sage of Salisbury: Thomas Chubb* (New York, 1967), p. 18.
18. J. S. Semler, *Lebensbeschreibung von ihm selbst abgefasst* (Halle, 1781), vol. 1, p. 96.
19. G. E. Lessing, 'Uber den Beweis des Geistes und der Kraft,' *Werke,* ed. L. Zscharnack (Berlin, 1925–35), vol. 23, p. 44.
20. J. G. Fichte, 'Erste Einleitung in die Wissenschaftslehre,' *Werke,* ed. F. Medicus (Leipzig, 1911–12), vol. 3, p. 18.
21. 'Die Bestimmung des Menschen,' *Werke,* vol. 3, p. 351.
22. *Ibid.,* p. 350.
23. *Ibid.,* p. 346.
24. F. W. J. Schelling, 'System des transcendentalen Idealismus,' *Werke,* ed. M. Schröter (München, 1927), vol. 2, p. 345.
25. *Ibid.,* p. 349.
26. F. Schleiermacher, *Briefe,* ed. L. Jonas and W. Dilthey (Berlin, 1861), vol. 30, p. 233.
27. F. Schleiermacher, *Der Christliche Glaube* 28.3, 7th ed. (Berlin, 1960), vol. 1, p. 160; Eng. trans. H. Mackintosh and J. Stewart, *The Christian Faith,* paperback reprint ed. (New York, 1963), vol. 1, p. 122.
28. *Der Christliche Glaube* 3.4, vol. 1, p. 14; Eng. trans., vol. 1. p. 10.
29. *Ibid.,* 46.2, vol. 1, p. 228; Eng. trans., vol. 1, p. 173.
30. P. Tillich, *Perspectives on Nineteenth and Twentieth Century Protestant Theology* (London, 1967), p. 108.

31. *Ibid.*, p. 98.
32. *Ibid.*, p. 113.
33. Schleiermacher, *Der Christliche Glaube* 66.2 (Berlin, 1884), vol. 1, pp. 347 ff.; Eng. trans. vol. 1, p. 272.
34. Schleiermacher, 'Der Christliche Glaube 101.2, 7th ed., vol. 1, p. 98; Eng. trans., vol. 2, p. 433.
35. F. Schleiermacher, 'Der Christliche Sitte,' *Schleiermachers Werke,* ed. O. Braun and J. Bauer (Leipzig, 1910), vol. 3, p. 169.
36. F. Schleiermacher, 'Psychologie,' *Sämtliche Werke,* ed. L. George (Berlin, 1862), vol. 3.6, p. 547.
37. Schleiermacher, *Der Christliche Glaube* 29.1, 7th ed., vol. 1, p. 161; Eng. trans., vol. 1, p. 123.
38. G. W. F. Hegel, 'Vorlesungen über die Aesthetik,' *Sämtliche Werke,* ed. H. Glockner (Stuttgart, 1928), vol. 13, p. 149.
39. G. W. F. Hegel, 'Vorlesungen über die Philosophie der Religion,' II, *Sämtliche Werke,* vol. 16, p. 227.
40. F. W. J. Schelling. 'Mythologie oder Darstellung der rein rationalen Philosophie,' *Schellings Werke* (Munich, 1928), vol. 5, p. 748.
41. *Ibid.*, p. 749.
42. P. B. Shelley, 'Defense of Poetry,' *Political Tracts of Wordsworth, Coleridge and Shelley,* ed. R. J. White (Cambridge, 1953), pp. 105–106.
43. *Ibid.*, p. 102.
44. S. T. Coleridge, *Philosophical Lectures 1818–1819,* ed. K. Coburn (London, 1949), p. 264.
45. S. T. Coleridge, 'The Statesman's Manual,' *Political Tracts of Wordsworth, Coleridge and Shelley,* ed. R. J. White (Cambridge, 1953), pp. 83 and 85.
46. S. T. Coleridge, *Aids to Reflection* (London, 1904), p. 160.
47. S. T. Coleridge, *Biographia Literaria,* ed. E. Rhys (London, 1906), pp. 166–167.
48. *Ibid.*, p. 148.
49. S. T. Coleridge, 'An Essay on Faith,' *Aids to Reflection,* p. 349.
50. *Ibid.*, p. 344.
51. *The Life of Frederick Denison Maurice Chiefly Told in His Own Letters,* ed. F. Maurice, 3d ed. (London, 1884), vol. 2, p. 30.
52. *Ibid.*, vol. 1, p. 308.
53. F. D. Maurice, *The Prayer-Book Considered Especially in Reference to the Romish System* (London, 1848), p. 147.
54. *Life of F. D. Maurice,* vol. 1, pp. 306–307.
55. Mrs. H. Ward, *Robert Elsmere* (London, 1888), vol. 1, p. 99.
56. *Ibid.*, vol. 2, pp. 18–19.
57. *Ibid.*, vol. 2, p. 24.
58. *Ibid.*, vol. 1, p. 196.

59. *Ibid.*, vol. 2, pp. 74–75.
60. W. R. Inge, *The Platonic Tradition in English Religion* (London, 1926), p. 33.
61. W. R. Inge, *Mysticism in Religion* (London, 1947), p. 149.
62. A. Loisy, *Autour d'un petit livre* (Paris, 1903), pp. 205–206.
63. *Ibid.*, p. 200.
64. *Ibid.*, p. 201.
65. G. Tyrrell, *Lex Orandi* (London, 1903), p. 169.
66. E. Buonaiuti, *Storia del cristianesimo* (Milan, 1942), vol. 1, p. 15.
67. U. Neuenschwander, *Die neue liberale theologie* (Bern, 1953), p. 34.
68. *Ibid.*, p. 38.
69. *Ibid.*, p. 95.
70. R. Bultmann, 'Anknüpfung und Widerspruch,' *Glauben und Verstehen* (Tübingen, 1952), vol. 2, pp. 120–121.
71. R. Bultmann, *Jesus Christus und die Mythologie* (Hamburg, 1958), p. 60; Eng. trans., *Jesus Christ and Mythology* (New York, 1958), p. 53.
72. R. Bultmann, 'Die Krisis des Glaubens,' *Glauben und Verstehen*, vol. 2, p. 11.
73. R. Bultmann, 'Neues Testament und Mythologie,' *Kerygma und Mythos* (Hamburg, 1954), vol. 1, p. 40; Eng. trans. by R. Fuller, 'New Testament and Mythology,' *Kerygma and Myth* (New York, 1961), p. 33.
74. R. Bultmann, 'Zur Frage der Christologie,' *Glauben und Verstehen*, vol. 1, p. 106; Eng. trans. by L. Smith, 'On the Question of Christology,' *Faith and Understanding* (New York, 1969), vol. 1, p. 137.
75. *Ibid.*, p. 110; Eng. trans., p. 140.
76. R. Bultmann, *Geschichte und Eschatologie* (Tübingen, 1958), p. 184; Eng. trans., *History and Eschatology* (Edingburgh, 1957), p. 155.
77. Bultmann, 'Neues Testament und Mythologie,' p. 46; Eng. trans., p. 41.
78. Bultmann, 'Zur Frage der Christologie,' p. 108; Eng. trans., p. 139.
79. R. Bultmann 'Die Bedeutung der "Dialektischen Theologie" für die neutestamentliche Wissenschaft,' *Glauben und Verstehen*, vol. 1, p. 127; Eng. trans., 'The Significance of "Dialectical Theology" for the Scientific Study of the New Testament,' *Faith and Understanding*, vol. 1, p. 158.
80. Bultmann, 'Zur Frage der Christologie,' p. 89; Eng. trans., p. 120.
81. D. Bonhoeffer, *Letters and Papers from Prison* (London, 1966), p. 110.
82. P. Tillich, *Perspectives on Protestant Theology* (London, 1967), p. 228.

83. *Ibid.*, p. 91.
84. P. Tillich, *Dynamics of Faith* (New York, 1958), pp. 81–82.
85. *Ibid.*, p. 92.
86. *Ibid.*, p. 89.
87. P. Tillich, *Ultimate Concern* (London, 1965), pp. 146–147.
88. *Ibid.*, p. 145.
89. *Ibid.*, p. 154.
90. P. Tillich, *Systematic Theology* (London, 1968), vol. 1, p. 143.
91. P. Tillich, *The New Being* (London, 1956), p. 120.
92. *Ibid.*, pp. 72–73.
93. Tillich, *Systematic Theology*, vol. 2, p. 15.
94. *Ibid.*, vol. 1, p. 69.
95. *Ibid.*, vol. 1, p. 71.
96. P. Tillich, *Ultimate Concern* (London, 1965), p. 143.
97. P. Tillich, 'Knowledge through Love,' *The Shaking of the Foundations* (London, 1949), pp. 109–111.
98. Tillich, *Perspectives on Protestant Theology*, p. 228.
99. Tillich, *Systematic Theology*, vol. 2, pp. 9–10.
100. *Ibid.*, vol. 1, pp. 264–265.
101. *Ibid.*, vol. 2, p. 10.
102. Tillich, *Dynamics of Faith*, p. 46; cf. S. Hook, ed., *Religious Experience and Truth* (New York, 1961), p. 315.
103. Tillich, *Dynamics of Faith*, pp. 47–48.
104. *Ibid.*, p. 54.
105. Tillich, *Utimate Concern*, p. 143.
106. *Ibid.*, p. 139.
107. *Ibid.*, p. 144.
108. *Ibid.*, p. 147.
109. R. B. Braithwaite, *An Empiricist's View of the Nature of Religious Belief* (Cambridge, Eng., 1955), p. 16.
110. *Ibid.*, p. 19.
111. *Ibid.*, p. 32.
112. T. R. Miles, *Religion and the Scientific Outlook* (London, 1959), p. 165.
113. A. Flew and A. MacIntyre, eds., *New Essays in Philosophical Theology* (London, 1955).
114. I. T. Ramsey, *Religious Language* (London, 1957), p. 14.
115. I. T. Ramsey, *Christian Discourse* (London, 1965), p. 82.
116. Ramsey, *Religious Language*, p. 37.
117. *Ibid.*, p. 38.
118. Ramsey, *Christian Discourse*, p. 55.
119. Ramsey, *Religious Language*, p. 47.
120. *Clarity is Not Enough*, ed. H. D. Lewis (London, 1963), p. 440.
121. *Ibid.*, p. 260.

122. *Ibid.*, p. 416.
123. *Ibid.*, p. 86.
124. K. Bolle, *The Freedom of Man in Myth* (Nashville, 1968), p. xiii.

NOTES TO CHAPTER NINE

1. S. T. Coleridge, *Biographia Literaria* (London, 1917), p. 18.
2. F. Schlegel, 'Philosophie der Sprache und des Wortes,' *Kritische Friedrich-Schlegel Ausgabe*, ed. E. Behler et al. (Munich, Paderborn, and Vienna, 1969), vol. 10, p. 488.
3. *Ibid.*, vol. 10, p. 490.
4. J. S. Drey, 'Ideen zur Geschichte des katholischen Dogmensystems,' *Geist des Christentums und Katholizismus. Ausgewählte Schriften katholischer Theologie im Zeitalter des Deutschen Idealismus und der Romantik*, ed. J. R. Geiselmann (Mainz, 1940), p. 246.
5. J. A. Möhler, *Die Einheit der Kirche*, ed. J. R. Geiselmann (Cologne and Olten, 1957), p. 11.
6. *Ibid.*, p. 64.
7. *Ibid.*, p. 125.
8. *Ibid.*, p. 43.
9. J. A. Möhler, 'Neue Untersuchungen der Lehrgegensätze zwischen den Katholiken und Protestanten,' quoted by H. Hammans, *Die neuern katholischen Erklärungen der Dogmentwicklung* (Essen, 1965), p. 33.
10. See J. R. Geiselmann, *Die lebendige Ueberlieferung als Norm des christlichen Glaubens—das Formalprinzip des Katholizismus dargestellt im Geiste der Traditionslehre von J. E. Kuhn* (Freiburg, 1950), p. 220.
11. *Ibid.*, p. 242.
12. *Ibid.*, p. 223.
13. *Ibid.*, p. 233.
14. H. Tristram, 'J. A. Moehler et J. H. Newman,' RevScPhilTh 27. (1938): 196.
15. J. H. Newman, *Lectures on the Present Position of Catholics in England*, 3rd ed. (Dublin, 1857), p. 266.
16. *Ibid.*, pp. 260–261.
17. J. A. Martin, *Empirical Philosophies of Religion* (New York, 1945), pp. 113–114.
18. J. Holloway, *The Victorian Sage* (London, 1953), p. 158.
19. J. H. Newman, 'Literature,' *Idea of a University* (London, 1931), pp. 273–274.
20. J. H. Newman, 'Dispositions for Faith,' *Sermons on Various Occasions* (London, 1921), p. 65.

21. J. H. Newman, 'De catholici dogmatis evolutione' (Newman-Perrone Paper), ed. T. Lynch, Greg 16 (1935): 411.

22. H. M. de Achával, ed., 'An Unpublished Paper by Cardinal Newman on the Development of Doctrine,' Greg 39 (1958): 593.

23. O. Chadwick, *From Bossuet to Newman* (Cambridge, Eng., 1957), p. 157.

24. *Ibid.*, p. 160.

25. J. H. Newman, *Oxford University Sermons* (London, 1898), p. 336.

26. H. M. de Achával, 'An Unpublished Paper by Cardinal Newman on the Development of Doctrine,' p. 596.

27. J. Ortega y Gasset, 'Las dos grandes metaforas,' *Obras Completas,* 5th ed. (Madrid, 1961), 2: 391.

28. M. Blondel, 'Raisons de ne pas croire,' L. Laberthonnière, ed. L. Canet, *Critique du laïcisme,* (Paris, 1948), p. 296.

29. *Ibid.*, p. 297.

30. J. H. Newman, *Oxford University Sermons* (London, 1898), p. 337.

31. F. von Hügel, *The Mystical Element of Religion* (London, 1923), p. 3.

32. F. von Hügel, 'Religion and Reality,' *Essays and Addresses on the Philosophy of Religion* (London, 1949), vol. 1, p. 46.

33. F. von Hügel, 'Lettre à Maurice Blondel,' *Au cœur de la crise moderniste,* ed. R. Marlé (Paris, 1960), p. 37.

34. F. von Hügel, 'Experience and Transcendence,' Dublin R 138 (1906): 363.

35. *Essays and Addresses on the Philosophy of Religion,* vol. 1, pp. 254–277.

36. H. de la Barre, *La Vie du dogme catholique* (Paris, 1898), p. 190.

37. J. Coppens, *Les Harmonies des deux testaments* (Tournai and Paris, 1949), p. 36.

38. P. Benoit, 'Le sensus plenior,' *Exégèse et théologie* (Paris, 1961), vol. 2, p. 20.

39. H. D. Köster, *Unus Mediator: Gedanken zur Marianischen Frage* (Limburg, 1950), p. 74.

40. C. Dillenschneider, *Le Sens de la foi et le progrès dogmatique du mystère marial* (Rome, 1954), p. 327.

41. E. Dhanis, 'Révélation explicite et implicite,' *Lo sviluppo del dogma secondo la Dottrina Cattolica* (Rome, 1953), p. 204.

NOTE TO CHAPTER TEN

1. G. Ebeling, 'Word of God and Hermeneutic,' *New Frontiers in Theology,* ed. J. M. Robinson, and J. B. Cobb (New York, 1964), vol. 2, p. 79, n. 2.

Bibliography

GENERAL REFERENCES

Colombo, C. 'Bibliographie über die Dogmenentwicklung.' In *Problemi e orientamenti di Teologia Dommatica*, vol. 1, pp. 381–386. Milan: C. Marzorati, 1957.

Dublanchy, E. 'Dogme III.' *Dictionnaire de théologie catholique* 4 (1911): 1603–1650.

Heinrich, J. B. 'Dogmenentwicklung.' *Kirchenlexicon*, 2nd ed., 3 (1884): 1903–1918.

Liégé, P. A. 'Dogme.' *Catholicisme* 3 (1952): 951–962.

Pinard, H. 'Dogme. Développement du dogme.' *Dictionnaire apologétique de la foi catholique* 1 (1925): 1151–1178.

Rahner, K. 'Dogmenentwicklung.' *Lexikon für Theologie und Kirche*, 2nd ed., 3 (1959): 457–463.

Schillebeeckx, E. H., and Remmens, J. 'The Development of the Apostolic Faith into the Dogma of the Church.' In *Revelation and Theology*, translated by N. Smith (Theological Soundings, vol. 1.1), pp. 57–83. New York: Sheed & Ward, 1967.

Schmaus, M. *Katholische Dogmatik*, vol. 1. 6th ed. Munich: M. Hüber, 1960.

———. *Dogma I: God in Revelation*. New York: Sheed & Ward, 1968.

Walgrave, J. H. 'Doctrine, Development of.' *New Catholic Encyclopedia* 4 (1967): 940–944.

HISTORICAL STUDIES

Adam, K. 'Die katholische Tübinger Schule.' In *Gesammelte Aufsätze zur Dogmengeschichte und Theologie der Gegenwart*, edited by F. Hofmann, pp. 389–412. Augsburg, 1936.

403

Alfaro, J. 'El progreso dogmatico en Suarez.' In *Problemi scelti de teologia contemporanea* (Analecta Gregoriana, vol. 68). pp. 95–122. Rome: Gregorian University Press, 1954.

Aquilina, S. *De progressu dogmatis secundum Melchioris Cani doctrinam.* Naples, 1963.

Barmann, L. F. 'Newman and the Theory of Doctrinal Development.' *American Ecclesiastical Review* 143 (1960): 121–129.

Baumgartner, C. 'Du Concile du Vatican au développement du dogme.' *Recherches de science religieuse* 44 (1956): 573–575.

Beumer, J. 'Theologischer und dogmatischer Fortschrift nach Duns Scotus.' *Franziskanische Studien* 35 (1953): 21–38.

———. 'Der theoretische Beitrag der Frühscholastik zum Problem des Dogmenfortschritts.' *Zeitschrift für katholische Theologie* 74 (1952): 205–206.

Bossu, L. M. 'Le Développement du dogme. Ses conditions d'après Vincent de Lérins et le concile du Vatican.' *Les Questions ecclésiastiques* 6 (1913): 115–120.

Brunner, A. 'Idee und Entwicklung bei Hegel und Newman.' *Scholastik* 32 (1957): 1–26.

Butler, C. 'The Significance of Newman today: The Theory of Development.' *Dublin Review* 233 (1959): 337–346.

Butler, W. A. *Letters on the Development of Christian Doctrine in Reply to Mr. Newman's Essay.* London, 1850.

Byrne, J. J. 'The Notion of Doctrinal Development in the Anglican Writings of J. H. Newman.' *Ephemerides theologicae lovanienses* 14 (1937): 230–286.

Cassar, C. 'The Historic and Doctrinal Development of Revelation according to Saint Thomas.' *Melita Theologica* 16 (1965): 30–47.

Cavallera, F. 'Le Document Newman-Perrone et le développement du dogme.' *Bulletin de littérature ecclésiastique* 47 (1946): 132–143, 208–225.

Chadwick, O. *From Bossuet to Newman: The idea of Doctrinal Development.* Cambridge: University Press, 1957.

Chenu, M. D. 'La Raison psychologique du développement du dogme d'apres Saint Thomas.' *Revue des sciences philosophiques et théologiques* 13 (1924): 44–51.

Chevalier, J. 'Newman et la notion de développement.' In *Trois conférences d'Oxford*, pp. 52–80. Paris, 1928.

Cross, F. L. 'Newman and the doctrine of Development.' *Church Quarterly Review* 105 (1933): 245–257.

Davis, H. F. 'Is Newman's Theory of Development Catholic?' *Blackfriars*, 39 (1958): 310–321.

———. 'Newman and the Psychology of the Development of Doctrine.' *Dublin Review* 208 (1936): 97–107.

————. 'The Theory of Development of Dogma in Newman.' Dissertation, University of Fribourg, 1930.

Finkenzeller, J. 'Offenbarung und Theologie nach der Lehre des Johannes.' In *Duns Scotus* (Beiträge zur Geschichte der Philosophie und Theologie des Mittelalters, vol. 38.5). Münster: Aschendorff, 1961.

Garcia Martinez, D. E. 'La solución de Suarez al problema de la evolución y progreso dogmatico.' *Estudios Eclesiasticos* 22 (1948): 151–165; reprinted in Garcia Martinez, D. E. , *Estudios teologicos al objeto de la fe y la evolución del dogma*, Burgos, 1953.

Geiselmann, J. R. *Die lebendige Uberlieferung als Norm des christlichen Glaubens*. Freiburg i. Br.: Herder, 1959. The best work on the position of J. E. Kuhn.

————. *Lebendiger Glaube aus geheiligter Uberlieferung: Der Grundgedanke der Theologie J. A. Möhlers und der katholischen Tübingerschule*. Mainz, 1942.

Ghellinck, J. de. 'Le Développement du dogme d'après Walafrid Strabo à propos du baptême des enfants.' *Recherches de science religieuse* 29 (1939): 481–485.

Gillis, James, Bp. *Lectures on the Essay of Development*. Edinburgh, 1846.

Guitton, J. *La Philosophie de Newman: Essai sur l'idée de développement*. Paris, 1933.

————. 'La Théorie du développement et son actualité.' *Newman-Studien*, vol. 3, pp. 77–98. Nuremberg, 1957.

Hammans, H. *Die neuern katholischen Erklärungen der Dogmenentwicklung*. Essen, 1965.

————. 'Recent Catholic Views on the Development of Dogma.' In *Man as Man and Believer*, edited by E. Schillebeeckx (Concilium, vol. 21), pp. 109–131. Glen Rock, N.J.: Paulist Press, 1967.

Heynck, V. 'Die Beurteilung der conclusio theologica bei den Franziskanertheologen des Trienter Konzils.' *Franziskanische Studien* 34 (1952): 146–205.

Hourcade, R. 'De Melchior Cano au Père Gardeil.' *Bulletin de littérature ecclésiastique* 2 (1910): 239–244.

Irons, W. J. *The Theory of Development Examined with Reference Especially to Mr. Newman's Essay*. 1846.

Joye, D. *La Théorie du Card. Newman sur le développement du dogme chrétien*. Paris, 1896.

Kasper, W. *Die Lehre von der Tradition in der Römischen Schule* (Die Uberlieferung in der neuern Theologie, vol. 5). Freiburg i Br.: Herder, 1962.

Lang, A. 'Die conclusio theologica in der Problemstellung der Spätscholastik.' *Divus Thomas* (Fribourg) 22 (1944): 256–290.

————. 'Die Gliederung und Reichweite des Glaubens nach Thomas von

Aquin und den Thomisten.' *Divus Thomas* (Fribourg) 20 (1942): 207–236, 335–346; 21 (1943): 79–97.

————. *Die loci theologici des Melchior Cano und die Methode des dogmatischen Beweises.* Munich, 1924.

Laros, M. 'Kardinal Newman und das "neue Dogma." ' *Die neue Ordnung* 5 (1951): 6–26.

Lee, J. van. *Les Idées d'Anselme d'Havelberg sur le développement des dogmes.* Tongerloo, 1938.

Lindbeck, George. 'The Problem of Doctrinal Development and Contemporary Protestant Theology.' In *Man as Man and Believer,* edited by E. Schillebeeckx (Concilium, vol. 21), pp. 133–149. Glen Rock, N.J.: Paulist Press, 1967.

Loisy, A. Firmin. 'Le Développement chrétien d'après le Cardinal Newman.' *Revue du clergé français* 17 (1899): 5–20.

Losch, S. 'J. A. Möhler und die Lehre der Entwicklung des Dogmas.' *Theologische Quartalschrift* 99 (1917–1918): 28–59; 129–152.

Madoz, J. *El concepto de la tradición en S. Vincente de Lérins* (Analecta Gregoriana, vol. 5). Rome: Gregorian University Press, 1933.

Marcotte, E. *La nature de la théologie d'après M. Cano.* Ottawa: University of Ottawa Press, 1949.

Maurice, F. D. *The Epistle to the Hebrews, With a Preface containing a Review of Mr. Newman's Theory of Development.* London, 1846.

Meuleman, G. E. *De ontwikkeling van het Dogma in de Rooms Katholieke theologie.* Kampen, 1951.

Milman, H. H. 'Newman on the Development of Christian Doctrine.' In *Savonarola, Erasme and Other Essays.* London, 1870.

Minon, A. 'L'Attitude de J. A. Moehler dans la question du développement du dogme.' *Ephemerides theologicae lovanienses* 16 (1939): 328–382.

Mounier, J. *L'Essai sur le développement de la doctrine chrétienne de Newman.* Paris, 1904.

Mozley, J. B. *The Theory of Development.* London, 1878. A critical review of Newman's essay on development.

Nédoncelle, M. 'Newman et le développement dogmatique.' *Revue des sciences religieuses* 32 (1958): 197–213.

Newman-Studien, vol. 6, edited by H. Fries and W. Becker. Nuremberg, 1964. Contributions to the Second International Newman Conference, July 24–29, 1961, on Newman's theory of development by J. H. Walgrave, E. Przywara, M. Nédoncelle, J. Stern, B. D. Deputy, H. F. Davis, C. S. Dessain, F. M. Willam, H. M. de Achaval.

Ong, W. 'Newman's Essay on Development in Its Intellectual Milieu.' *Theological Studies* 7 (1946): 3–45.

Philbin, W. J. 'The Essay on Development.' In *A Tribute to Newman,* edited by M. Tierney, pp. 116–143. Dublin, 1945.

Poulat, E. *Histoire, dogme, et critique dans la crise moderniste.* Paris: Casterman, 1962.

Pozo, C. *Contribución a la historia del problema del progreso dogmatico.* Granada, 1957.

Sala, G. B. 'L'evoluzione del Dogma nel pensiero de B. Lonergan.' *Studia Patavina* 13 (1966): 448–509.

Simonin, H. C. 'La Théologie thomiste de la foi et le développement du dogme.' *Revue thomiste* 40 (1935): 537–556.

Stephenson, A. A. 'Cardinal Newman and the Development of Doctrine.' *Journal of Ecumenical Studies* 3 (1966): 463–485.

Struman, R. 'La Perpétuité de la foi dans le controverse Bossuet-Jurieu.' *Revue d'histoire ecclésiastique* 37 (1941): 145–189.

Swisshelm, G. 'Attack of Orestes A. Brownson on Newman's Development Theory.' *St. Meinrad Essays* 12 (1959): 22–40.

Tristram, H. 'J. A. Moehler et J. H. Newman.' *Revue des sciences philosophiques et théologiques* 27 (1938): 184–204.

Veiga Coutinho, L. *Tradition et histoire dans la controverse moderniste* (Analecta Gregoriana, vol. 73). Rome: Gregorian University Press, 1954.

Voss, G. 'J. A. Möhler and the Development of Dogma.' *Theological Studies* 4 (1943): 420–444.

Walgrave, J. H. 'Newman en de idee der doctrinele ontwikkeling.' *Tidschrift voor Philosophie* 20 (1958): 510–519.

———. *Newman the Theologian,* translated by A. V. Littledale. New York: Sheed and Ward, 1960.

———. 'De ontwikkeling van de kennis volgens J. H. Newman.' *Tidschrift voor Philosophie* 5 (1943): 279–328.

———. 'Preface to J. H. Cardinal Newman.' In *Essai sur le développement due dogme,* pp. 7–48. Paris, 1964.

———. 'La Théorie newmanienne du développement dogmatique et la théologie liberale.' *Asprenas* 15 (1968): 255–279.

Walsh, J. *De Grandmaison and Gardeil on Dogmatic Development.* Rome, 1950.

William, F. M. 'J. H. Newman und P. Perrone.' *Newman-Studien,* vol. 2, pp. 120–145. Nuremberg, 1954.

Zeno, P. 'De apologetische waarde van Newman's Essay on Development.' In *Donum lustrale Catholicae Universitatis Noviomagensis oblatum,* pp. 283–302. Nijmegen, 1949.

SOURCES

Achával, H. M. de. 'An Unpublished Paper by Cardinal Newman on the Development of Doctrine.' *Gregorianum* 39 (1958): 585–596.

Adam, K. 'Das Problem des Geschichtlichen im Leben der Kirche.'

Theologisches Quartalschrift 1238 (1948): 257–300.

Allo, B. *Foi et systèmes*. Paris, 1908.

Arintero, J. G. 'El progreso dogmatico objectivo.' *Ciencia Tomista* 2 (1911): 378–393.

Bainvel, J. V. *De magisterio vivo et traditione*. Paris, 1905.

————. 'L'Église: histoire du dogme; l'évolution des idées.' *Études* 70 (1897): 5–16.

————. 'Histoire d'un dogme.' *Études* 101 (1904): 612–632.

Balić, C. 'Voraussetzungen für die Dogmatisierung einer Glaubenswahrheit.' In *Theologie in Geschichte und Gegenwart*, edited by J. Auer and H. Volk, pp. 1–20. Munich: K. Zink, 1957.

Battifol, P. 'Pour l'histoire des dogmes.' *Bulletin de littérature ecclésiastique* 6 (1905): 151–164; 7 (1906): 169–179.

Baumgartner, C. 'Tradition et magistère.' *Recherches de science religieuse* 41 (1952): 161–187.

Billot, L. *De immutabilitate traditionis contra modernam haeresim evolutionismi*. 4th ed. Rome, 1929.

Blondel, M. 'History and Dogma.' In *Letter on Apologetics and History and Dogma*, translated and edited by Alexander Dru and Illtyd Trethowan. London: Harvill, 1964; 1st French ed., 1904.

Bonifazi, D. *Immutabilità e relatività del dogma secondo la teologia contemporanea*. Rome, 1959.

Boyer, C. 'Lo sviluppo del dogma.' In *Problemi e Orientamenti di Teologia Dommatica*, vol. 1, pp. 359–386. Milan: C. Marzorati, 1957.

Cavallera, F. 'A propos de la vie du dogme.' *Bulletin de littérature ecclésiastique* 43 (1942): 69–79.

Clasen, S. 'Wachstum des Glaubens.' *Wissenchaft und Weisheit* 15 (1952): 144–149.

Congar, Y. 'Fait dogmatique et foi ecclésiastique.' *Catholicisme* 4 (1956:) 1059–1067.

De la Barre, H. *La Vie du dogme catholique, autorité, évolution*. Paris, 1898.

Delgado Varela, J. M. 'Evolución dogmatica.' *Estudios* 13 (1957): 505–571; 14 (1958): 103–161, 253–289.

Dillenschneider, C. *Le Sens de la foi et le progrès dogmatique du mystère marial* (Bibliotheca Marina Moderni Aevi, vol. 2). Rome: Academia Mariana Internationalis, 1954.

Dörholt, B. *Ueber die Entwicklung des Dogmas und der Fortschritt in der Theologie*. Münster, 1892.

Draguet, R. 'L'Évolution du dogme.' In *Apologétique*, edited by M. Brillant and M. Nédoncelle, pp. 1166–1192. Paris: Bloud et Gay, 1937.

Duhr, J. 'L'Évolution du dogme de l'Immaculée Conception.' *Nouvelle revue théologique* 83 (1951): 1013–1032.

Eloriaga, A. M. 'Es divina la autoridad de la Iglesia en sus definiciones infalibles? Se ha de eliminar la fe eclesiastica?' *Estudios Eclesiasticos* 5 (1926): 113–137, 225–243.

———. 'No cabe fe divina en ningun virtual inclusivo antes de su explicación infalible dada por la Iglesia?' *Estudios Eclesiasticos* 6 (1927): 113–133, 377–399; 7 (1928): 487–514.

———. 'Punto de partida y germen de la evolución del dogma catolico.' *Estudios Eclesiasticos* 8 (1929): 42–60.

Fernández-Jimenez, M. 'Naturaleza del conocimiento de los apóstoles acerca del depósito de la revelación.' *Revista española de teologia* 18 (1958): 3–33.

———. 'Un paso más hacia la solución del problema de la evolución del dogma. Existe el llamado virtual revelado?' *Revista española de teologia* 16 (1956): 291–339.

Flick, M., ET AL. *Lo sviluppo del dogma secondo la Dottrina Cattolica.* Rome, Gregorian University Press, 1953; first published in *Gregorianum* 3 (1952): 5–182; 34 (1953): 187–237.

Fontaine, G. *La Théologie du N.T. et l'évolution du dogme.* Paris, 1907.

García Miralles, M. E. 'Un paso más hacia la solución del problema de la evolución del dogma.' *Revista española de teologia* 17 (1957): 422–426.

Gardeil, A. 'Le Développement du dogme.' *Revue des sciences philosophiques et théologiques* 3 (1909): 447–469.

———. *Le Donné révélé et la théologie.* 2d ed. Paris, 1932.

Ginniken, J. van. *De evolutie van het dogma.* Utrecht and Nijmegen, 1926.

Grandmaison, L. de. *Le Dogme chrétien: Sa nature, ses formules, son développement.* Paris, 1928.

Guignebert, C. *L'Évolution des dogmes.* Paris, 1910.

Hemlein, J. 'Dogmenentwicklung und christliche Verkündigung.' *Trierer theologische Zeitschrift* 63 (1953): 227–232.

Joest, W. 'Endgültigkeit und Unabgeschlossenheit des Dogmas.' *Theologische Literaturzeitung* 79 (1954): 435–440.

Journet, C. *Esquisse du développement du dogme marial.* Paris, 1954. English summary by James Buckley. 'Scripture and the Immaculate Conception: A Problem in the Evolution of Dogma.' In *The Dogma of the Immaculate Conception,* edited by Edward O'Connor, pp. 3–48. Notre Dame: University of Notre Dame Press, 1958.

Köster, M. *Unus Mediator: Gedanken zur marianischen Frage.* Limburg, 1950.

———. *Volk Gottes im Wachstum des Glaubens. Himmelfahrt Mariens und Glaubenssinn.* Heidelberg, 1950.

Lenoir, V. 'L'Évolution homogène du dogme catholique.' *Revue apologétique* 41 (1925): 67–84.

Léonard, A. 'La Foi principe fondamental du développment du dogme.' *Revue des sciences philosophiques et théologiques* 42 (1948): 276–286.

Lépicier, A. *De stabilitate et progressu dogmatis*. Rome, 1908.

Lubac, H. de. 'Le Problème du développement du dogme.' *Recherches de science religieuse* 35 (1948): 130–160.

Mallet, F. 'Un nouvel entretien avec M. Blondel.' *Revue du clergé français* 38 (1904): 405–416; 513–531.

Malmberg, F. 'De Afsluiting van het depositum Fidei.' *Bijdragen. Tijdschrift voor filosofie* 13 (1952): 31–42.

Márin-Sola, F. *L'Évolution homogène du dogme catholique*. 2 vols. Fribourg, 1924. The most comprehensive work on development of doctrine in scholastic theology.

Martinez, F. G. *Estudios teologicos en torno al objecto de la fe y la evolución del dogma*. 2 vols. Oña (Spain), 1953, 1958.

Maurier, H. *Religion et développement*. Paris, 1965.

Mausbach, S. 'Die Entwicklung des katholischen Dogmas.' *Hochland* 3 (1906): 406–417.

Michel, A. 'Explicite et implicite.' *Dictionnaire de théologie catholique* 5 (1953): 1868–1877.

Möhler, J. A. *Die Einheit der Kirche oder das Prinzip des Katholizismus, dargestellt im Geiste der Kirchenväter der drei ersten Jahrhunderts*, edited by J. R. Geiselmann. Cologne and Olten, 1957; first published 1825. The main work of Möhler on the question.

Murillo, L. *Il progreso en la revelación cristiana*. Rome, 1913.

Newman, J. H. *An Essay on the Development of Christian Doctrine*, edited by C. F. Harrold. New York: Longmans, Green, 1949; first published 1845.

———. 'The Newman-Perrone Paper on Development,' edited by J. Lynch. *Gregorianum* 16 (1935): 402–444.

———. *Sermons Preached before the University of Oxford*. London, 1843.

Nicholls, D. 'Developing Doctrines and Changing Beliefs.' *Scottish Journal of Theology* 19 (1966): 280–292.

O'Doherty, E. *Doctrinal Progress and its Laws*. Dublin, 1924.

Oxenham, Henry N. 'On the Principle of Theological Developments.' In *The Catholic Doctrine of the Atonement: An Historical Review*, pp. 1–80. 4th rev. ed. London: W. H. Allen, 1895.

Palmer, W. *The Doctrine of Development and Conscience Considered in Relation to the Evidences of Christianity and of the Catholic System*. London, 1846.

Palmieri, A. *Il progresso dommatico nel concetto catholico*. Firenze, 1910.

Prunier, M. *Évolution et immutabilité de la doctrine religieuse dans l'Église*. Paris, 1904.

Rademacher, L. *Der Entwicklungsgedanke in Religion und Dogma.* Cologne, 1914.

Rahner, K. 'Considerations on the Development of Dogma.' In *Theological Investigations,* vol. 4, translated by Kevin Smyth, pp. 3–35. Baltimore: Helicon Press, 1966; 1st German ed., 1960.

———. 'The Development of Dogma.' In *Theological Investigations,* vol. 1, translated by Cornelius Ernst, pp. 39–77. Baltimore: Helicon Press, 1961.

———. *The Dynamic Element in the Church,* translated by W. J. O'Hara (Quaestiones Disputatae, vol. 12). New York: Herder and Herder, 1964.

———. *Hearers of the Word,* translated by Michael Richards. New York: Herder and Herder, 1969.

Ranft, J. 'Die lebendige Tradition, Einheit und Entwicklung.' In *Die Eine Kirche,* edited by H. Tüchle, pp. 109–134. Paderborn: 1939.

Rich, E. 'Idea of Doctrinal Development.' *Eastern Churches Quarterly* 12 (1958): 221–227.

Rondet, H. *Do Dogmas Change?,* translated by Mark Pontifex (20th Century Encyclopedia of Catholicism, volume 5). New York: Hawthorn Books, 1961; 1st French ed., 1960.

Rousselot, P. 'Notes sur le développement du dogme.' *Recherches de science religieuse* 37 (1950): 113–120.

Sanders, N. 'Openbaring, Traditie, Dogma-ontwikkeling.' *Studia catholica* 15 (1939): 1–12, 111–129.

Schillebeeckx, E. H. 'Exegesis, Dogmatics and the Development of Dogma.' In *Dogmatic vs. Biblical Theology,* pp. 147–172. Baltimore: Helicon Press, 1964.

Schlette, R. 'Dogmengeschichte und Geschichtlichkeit des Dogmas.' *Münchener theologische Zeitschrift* 14 (1963): 243–252.

Schultes, R. 'Circa dogmatum homogeneam evolutionem.' *Divus Thomas* (Piacenza) series 3:2 (1925): 83–99, 768–778.

———. 'Dogmenentwicklung oder Entwicklung oder Offenbarung.' *Theologie und Glaube* 11 (1919): 192–201.

———. 'Die fides explicita und implicita.' *Divus Thomas* (Fribourg) 2 (1915): 476–507.

———. 'Eclaircissements sur l'évolution du dogme.' *Revue des sciences philosophiques et théologiques* 14 (1925): 286–302.

———. *Fides implicita.* Regensburg, 1920.

———. *Introductio in historiam dogmatum.* Paris, 1922.

Schweitzer, W. *Schrift und Dogma in der Oekumene.* Gütersloh, 1953.

Seiterich, E. 'Das kirchliche Verständniss der Dogmenentwicklung.' *Oberrheinische pastorale Blätter* 53 (1953): 225–231, 255–263.

Semmelroth, O. 'Wesen und Werden der Dogmen.' In *Probleme der*

Gegenwart im Urteil der Kirche, edited by A. Hartmann, pp. 216–234, Frankfurt, 1952.

Simonin, H. D. ' "Implicite" et "explicite" dans le développement du dogme.' *Angelicum* 14 (1937): 126–145.

Söhngen, G. *Die Einheit in der Theologie*. Munich, 1952.

Solov'ev, V. S. *Istorija i buduščnost teokratii* ('History and Future of Theocracy'). (Sobranī Sochineniī [Collected Works], vol. 3, pp. 270–382.) St. Petersburg, 1901–1907; first published 1884. The main work of Solov'ev on the question.

Spedalieri, F. *Selectae et breviores quaestiones philosophicae et theologicae controversae*. Rome, 1950.

Stephenson, A. A. 'The Development and Immutability of Christian Doctrine.' *Theological Studies* 19 (1958): 481–532.

Taymans d'Eypernon, F. 'Le Progrès du dogme.' *Nouvelle revue théologique* 71 (1949): 687–700.

Ternun, J. 'Beiträge zur Problem der Tradition.' *Divus Thomas* (Fribourg) 16 (1938): 33–56, 197–229.

Thibaut, R. 'De ontwikkeling van het dogma.' *Het christelijk Oosten en Hereniging* 1 (1948): 100–109.

Thils, G. 'L'Évolution du dogme dans la théologie catholique.' *Ephemerides theologicae lovanienses* 28 (1952): 679–682. Considerations on Meuleman's book.

Thurian, M. 'Développement du dogme et tradition selon le catholicisme moyen et la théologie réformée.' *Verbum caro* 5 (1947): 145–167.

Tuyaerts, M. *L'Évolution du dogme*. Louvain, 1919.

van der Putte, J. C. M. *De dogmatische waarde van de theologische rederering*. Nikmegen, 1948.

Wittig, J. 'Um den Entwicklungsgedanken.' *Hochland* 22 (1924–1925): 81–102.

Index of Proper Names

413